Forensic Medicolegal Injury and Death Investigation

Forensic Medicolegal Injury and Death, second edition, provides an introduction to forensic science and coverage of injury patterns, natural disease, suicidal deaths, accidental trauma, child injury and fatalities, elder deaths, domestic violence, and mass fatality.

This revised second edition updates all sections and chapters using current references and resources, with contributions from forensic experts who bring their experiences and perspectives to the discussions and key case studies. Illustrative tables and photos have been added to the chapters, as well as the incorporation of the forensic investigator role specific to each category of injury and death covered. The chapters on specific types of injury include updated methodology, technology, current standards, and best practices in forensic investigation. The inclusion of case studies pulls together the application of information used in the investigation of actual forensic cases. Other improvements include: appendices on investigator report writing, preliminary reports of death, a death investigator supply list, information on vicarious trauma, and an appendix regarding witness testimony.

Bringing together the expertise of experienced forensic scientists, forensic pathologists, and medicolegal investigators, *Forensic Medicolegal Injury and Death Investigation*, second edition, is an invaluable reference for anyone who has direct contact with death, crime, and the medicolegal system, including nurses, physicians, attorneys, death investigators, forensic pathologists, and police detectives.

Forensic Medicolegal Injury and Death Investigation

Second Edition

Mary H. Dudley, MD
Content Editor, Lauren E. Dvorscak, MD

CRC Press
Taylor & Francis Group
Boca Raton London New York

CRC Press is an imprint of the
Taylor & Francis Group, an **informa** business

Photograph taken by the New Mexico Office of the Medical Investigator team

Second edition published 2027
by CRC Press
2385 NW Executive Center Drive, Suite 320, Boca Raton FL 33431

and by CRC Press
4 Park Square, Milton Park, Abingdon, Oxon, OX14 4RN

CRC Press is an imprint of Taylor & Francis Group, LLC

First edition published by CRC Press 2017

ISBN: 978-1-032-88596-4 (hbk)
ISBN: 978-1-032-88595-7 (pbk)
ISBN: 978-1-003-53862-2 (ebk)

DOI: 10.4324/9781003538622

Typeset in Minion
by SPi Technologies India Pvt Ltd (Straive)

Contents

Part II

INJURY RECOGNITION

Part III

NATURAL, SUICIDAL, AND ACCIDENTAL DEATHS

Preface

Forensic Medicolegal Injury and Death Investigation is designed as a reference for both students new to the field and experienced practitioners alike. *Forensic Medicolegal Injury and Death Investigation* covers the essential areas of death scene investigation, clinical forensic medicine, investigative procedures, and methodology to help determine the cause of injury and death. The second edition expands upon these topics by providing current information in this ever-changing and progressive specialty field. The comprehensive format serves as text to supplement training and didactive lectures for introduction to forensic sciences, forensic pathology, forensic nursing, and medicolegal death investigator certification review.

Effective medicolegal analysis relies on a strong investigative network. A diverse array of professional and technical specialists is necessary to make the forensic investigative system run smoothly. Even as these systems differ in size, location, and practices, the goal remains the same: to establish identity, determine the cause and type of injury, protect important forensic evidence, document and photograph the death scene, document injury, and report significant findings. The forensic team members require specialty education and training to maintain current knowledge and continuing education in their forensic specialty.

The 25 chapters and 6 appendices include various forensic topics relevant to forensic medicolegal death investigation training. This book serves to supplement didactic content for death investigators, coroners, medical examiners, forensic nurses, students, funeral directors, attorneys, organ and tissue donation personnel, and law enforcement personnel.

The second edition includes updated information to all sections and chapters using current references and resources. The contributions of forensic experts bring additional credibility to the text and explain their perspective based on their role in forensic investigation. The use of additional figures adds to the written information and readability of the text. Additional changes include chapter abstracts and incorporation of the forensic death investigator role specific to each category of injury and death. The chapters on specific types of injury include updated methodology, technology, current standards, and best practices in forensic investigation. The inclusion of scene investigation case studies and photographs from actual forensic cases reinforces the information in the text.

Mary H. Dudley, MD

About the Author

Mary H. Dudley, MD, MSN, is the former Chief Medical Examiner for Jackson County in Kansas City, Missouri. She also served as the Chief Medical Examiner, Director of Forensic Science Laboratories, and District Coroner for Sedgwick County in Wichita, Kansas, as well as Medical Examiner for Maricopa County in Phoenix, Arizona. She is board certified in anatomic and forensic pathology by the American Board of Pathology. She completed pathology residency at Penrose Hospital in Colorado Springs, Colorado, and fellowship in forensic pathology at the University of New Mexico. She founded the first Forensic Nursing Certificate Program in 1994 and originated the first Forensic Medical Investigation Course in 1996.

Dr. Dudley is a fellow member of the National Association of Medical Examiners and the American Academy of Forensic Sciences. She served as co-chair of the Medical Examiner Advisory Board for the Musculotissue Foundation, tissue Medical Director for Donor Network of Arizona, and member of the Missouri and Arizona Child Fatality Review Boards. As a member of the Disaster Mortuary Operations Response Team, she ran morgue operations during the deployment for Kirksville airplane crash in 2004, Hurricane Katrina and Hurricane Rita in 2005, Hurricane Ike in 2008, and the Joplin tornado in 2011. She also held appointment as Program Director of the Forensic Pathology Fellowship program in Jackson County Medical Examiner's Office, and Associate Professor of Clinical Pathology at the University of Missouri and University of Kansas. Dr. Dudley was the recipient of the CRC Press/Taylor Francis Group Lifetime Achievement and Author Appreciation Award presented at the 2020 American Academy of Forensic Sciences meeting.

Content Editor

Lauren E. Dvorscak, MD, has served as the Deputy Chief Medical Investigator at the Office of the Medical Investigator (OMI) for the state of New Mexico since 2020. She completed her medical education at Indiana University School of Medicine, in Indianapolis, Indiana, in 2011. She then completed a pathology residency at the University of New Mexico Hospitals, Albuquerque, New Mexico, and forensic pathology fellowship at OMI in 2016. She maintains board certifications in anatomic, clinical, and forensic pathology. Dr. Dvorscak is active in field deputy medical investigator training at OMI, contributing to and serving on the panel for project Extension for Community Healthcare Outcomes (ECHO) for medicolegal death investigators. She is also the Program Director for the Forensic Pathology Fellowship at OMI, and Autopsy Rotation Director for the pathology residents. She maintains memberships with the National Association of Medical Examiners and the American Academy of Forensic Sciences.

Contributors

James L. Caruso, MD, is the former Chief Medical Examiner and Coroner for Denver, Colorado, a position he held for 11 years. He completed 30 years in the U.S. Navy where he served as an Armed Forces Medical Examiner, Forensic Pathologist, Diving Medical Officer, and Flight Surgeon. Dr. Caruso completed a forensic pathology fellowship at the Office of the Medical Examiner for the state of Maryland and the Office of the Armed Forces Medical Examiner. He is an active member of the American Academy of Forensic Sciences (presently the Vice-President), National Association of Medical Examiners, International Association of Coroners and Medical Examiners (board member), and the American Medical Association (member of the House of Delegates). Dr. Caruso's research interests include water-related deaths and forensic toxicology. He has authored numerous book chapters, peer-reviewed publications, and scientific presentations.

Tom Hensley, F-ABMDI is currently the Chief of Operations and Investigations at the Jackson County Medical Examiner's Office (JCMEO) in Kansas City, Missouri, since 2014. He was Deputy Chief Medicolegal Death Investigator (MDI) for seven years and worked at JCMEO as an MDI since1991. Tom also worked as a medical assistant, emergency medical technician, paramedic and elected coroner. In 2017, he received the Excellence in Public Service – Distinguished Lifetime Achievement Award for Jackson County. Tom became an ABMDI-certified Diplomat and Fellow in 2002. As an affiliate member of the National Association of Medical Examiners (NAME) since 2010, Tom served on the board of directors for eight years and also served on several NAME subcommittees. In 2015, he was awarded the Mary Fran Ernst Best Affiliate Poster Presentation. Tom was a member of the Disaster Mortuary Operational Response Team (DMORT) for over 30 years and was deployed to five mass fatality incidents. In 2003, Tom was awarded the DMORT Distinguished Member of the Year Award – Region 7 at the National Medical Disaster Systems (NDMS) conference.

Cheryl L. Pozzi, RN, BSN, MS, BCFN. Cheryl Pozzi has over 45 years of varied nursing experience to include emergency, flight, workers' compensation, pediatric, forensic, and legal nursing. She has a bachelor's in Nursing

Science, master's in Industrial Safety, Postgraduate Certificate in Forensic Nursing, and Postgraduate Certificate in Animal-Assisted Therapy. She is a published author in nursing text books and journals and has been a guest speaker in national forensic conferences. Besides Cheryl's varied unique nursing experience, she is a commercial Hot-Air Balloon Pilot, has conducted Animal-Assisted Therapy for youth and adults, is an internationally recognized successful horse breeder, has participated in Bernalillo County Mounted Search and Rescue, and currently is a member of Santa Fe County Sheriff Posse Mounted Division.

LauraMae Williams, D-ABMDI, is currently a New Mexico Senior Field Deputy Medical Investigator for 32 years and plans on continuing for many more. She was the New Mexico Region II EMS Training Coordinator from 1988 to 1992. She also taught emergency medical technician students at the Community College level from 1986 to 2018. Laura Mae's primary career for 30+ years was working with students at the middle school level, a job she absolutely loved! In her spare time, she was also a volunteer firefighter and EMT-Intermediate who worked in both rural and later semi-urban areas. She became certified by the American Board of Medical Death Investigators in 2023. She currently coordinates the Office of Medical Investigator's bi-weekly project Extension for Community Healthcare Outcomes (ECHO) training for Field Medical Investigators. She is a regular presenter for ECHO sessions.

Ross E. Zumwalt, MD, is a Professor of Pathology in the Department of Pathology and Laboratory Medicine at the Mayo Clinic in Rochester, Minnesota. He is a former medical investigator and Professor of Pathology at the Office of the Medical Investigator for the state of New Mexico, as well as an Emeritus Professor of Pathology at the University of New Mexico Health Sciences Center. He received a BA from Wabash College in Crawfordsville, Indiana, and an MD from the University of Illinois College of Medicine in Chicago, Illinois. He completed an internship and residency at the Mary Imogene Bassett Hospital in Cooperstown, New York, and a pathology residency at the Southwestern Medical School in Dallas, Texas. He received forensic fellowship training at the Dallas County Medical Examiner's Office. He additionally served in the military as Director of Laboratories at the Navy Regional Medical Center in Camp Lejeune, North Carolina. He was a Deputy Coroner in Cleveland, Ohio, and a Deputy Coroner in Cincinnati, Ohio, before he came to the New Mexico Office of the Medical Investigator in 1987. Dr. Zumwalt is certified in anatomic and forensic pathology by the American Board of Pathology. He was a trustee of the American Board of Pathology from 1993 to 2004. Dr. Zumwalt served as chief medical investigator of the state of New Mexico from 1991 through 2014. Dr. Zumwalt has served as president of the National Association of Medical Examiners and is a member of the National Association of Medical Examiners, College of American Pathologists, and the American Association for the Advancement of Science. He served on a National Academy of Sciences Committee on identifying the needs of the Forensic Science Community from 2007 to 2009.

Acknowledgments

I am extremely grateful to Lauren E. Dvorscak, MD, Deputy Chief of the Office of the Medical Investigator (OMI) at the University of New Mexico for her many hours of help in updating the manuscript format, content, and photographs. I appreciate her assistance and patience with the second edition revisions and additions, including chapter abstracts, focus on the medicolegal death investigator role, case studies, and six appendices.

I thank the contributing authors for providing their expertise, current knowledge, and assistance to specific sections in my book including James L. Caruso, MD (Chapter 15: Asphyxia and Drowning Deaths), Lauren E. Dvorscak, MD (Chapter 13: Natural Deaths, Chapter 14: Suicide Deaths, Chapter 16: Environmental Deaths, Chapter 17: Fire Deaths, Chapter 24: Sudden Unexpected Infant Deaths, Appendix D: Vicarious Trauma, Case Studies for Chapter 14: Suicide Deaths, Chapter 16: Environmental Deaths, Chapter 18: Electrical Deaths, Chapter 19: Drug and Alcohol Deaths, Chapter 20: Workplace Deaths), Tom Hensley (Chapter 6: Section on Role of Medicolegal Death Investigator in Mass Fatality), Cheryl L. Pozzi, RN, BSN, MS, BCFN (Chapter 1: First Responder System, Chapter 20: Workplace Deaths), LauraMae Williams, F-ABMDI (Appendix A: Report Writing and Appendix B: Preliminary Report of Death), and Ross E. Zumwalt, MD (Chapter 25: Elder Deaths).

I especially thank Heather Jarrell, MD, Chief of the Office of the Medical Investigator (OMI) at the University of New Mexico in Albuquerque, New Mexico, for permission to use current digital photos, images, and forms to support the narrative in the manuscript.

Introduction to Forensic Investigation

I

Forensic Investigative Systems

1

MARY H. DUDLEY

OBJECTIVES

Upon completion of this chapter and the corresponding reference material, the reader will be able to:

- Describe roles and responsibilities of specialists within forensic investigative systems
- Identify the current changes in the forensic science field, as well as the need for board certification and accreditation in medical examiner offices/forensic laboratories
- Explain how the role of a death investigator interacts with that of other specialists
- Discuss how jurisdiction and local resources can differ from state to state, from county to county, and from urban areas to rural areas
- Describe how first responders to a death scene can interact with forensic investigators

Introduction

Forensic investigative systems are a broad group of professional entities that contribute to death investigation, and they provide important contributions to medicolegal analysis in the criminal justice system. Each entity has specific roles but intertwines with other agencies and professionals. Many professional and technical specialists are necessary to make the forensic investigative system operate smoothly. Depending on statutes and ordinances, differences exist in reporting deaths. Medicolegal analysis can also vary by county, state, or city jurisdictions. Understanding what constitutes a medical examiner case within the jurisdiction and how systems work together is paramount. Advances in communication, photography, documentation, community awareness, and agency standards have improved death investigations. Familiarity with the local, state, and national agencies, forensic professionals, and the systems available, as well as guidelines from the National Institute of Justice (NIJ), is key to ensuring best outcomes for death and criminal investigations. This

DOI: 10.4324/9781003538622-2

chapter describes the roles and responsibilities of professional and technical specialists as members of a multidisciplinary forensic team.

Jurisdiction

Guidelines as to what constitutes a case for the medical examiner or coroner (ME/C) are based on the types of death, reporting procedures, and state statutes. Some states have a "24-hour rule" that requires a report of death be made to the ME/C in the case of a presumed natural death that occurs during the first day of a hospital admission. Other states do not have this rule, unless the circumstances are covered under state statute. Most states require report of certain deaths to a law enforcement officer and the ME/C by any person having knowledge of the death of a human being. Generally, failure to report such death is classified as a misdemeanor, punishable by a fine or imprisonment.

By general standards, the medicolegal death investigator (MDI) is notified of a death scene by local law enforcement, which has jurisdiction over the death scene but not the body. The coroner or medical examiner has jurisdiction of the body and what is on the immediate person. Law enforcement is present to secure the scene at the time of death investigation and will typically provide preliminary information regarding the circumstances of death.

Categories of death that typically require a law enforcement or ME/C report include

- Death that occurs when not under the care of a physician (unattended)
- Death that occurs when an attending physician is not available to sign the death certificate
- Death from violence
- Sudden death in an otherwise healthy individual
- Death in prison, of a prisoner, or while in custody
- Death that occurs in a suspicious, unusual, or unnatural manner
- Death related to an accident or a disease associated with the decedent's occupation
- Death that is believed to have presented a public health hazard
- Death that occurs during surgery or while under anesthesia

Examples of Reportable Deaths

- Falls
- Blunt force or crushing injuries
- Stabbing or sharp force injuries

- Fatal gunshot wounds
- Fatal electric shocks or lightning strikes
- Fatal explosions
- Strangulations or asphyxial deaths
- Fatal motor vehicle accidents
- Drug overdoses or poisonings
- Fatal burns or fires
- Stillborn or newborn deaths, if associated with trauma or illicit drug abuse
- Rapid fatal illnesses
- Occupational deaths
- Persons found dead under unknown or suspicious circumstances
- Clustering of undiagnosed infectious disease

Transplantation (Organ and Tissue Donation)

Permission to transplant organs or tissue is requested of and granted by the next of kin of the decedent. The ME/C must also grant permission for donation in a medicolegal case prior to donation. The ME/coroner's office works closely with the organ procurement organization to coordinate organ/tissue recovery prior to autopsy within time constraints. If permission for procurement occurs prior to autopsy, the MDI's role is often to liaison between the donation agency and the coroner/ME's office to ensure appropriate medical records of donation are received and samples for ancillary testing are procured. Tissue donation may also occur after autopsy examination in some circumstances, also within time constraints. In these situations, the MDI is often responsible for clearly communicating to the autopsy team any restrictions or requests for sample collections during autopsy that may be requested from the donation agency.

Specialties in Forensic Medical Investigation

Forensic Pathology

Pathology is the study of injury or natural disease; forensic pathology is the interface between pathology and the law. Forensic pathology became a recognized medical specialty in 1959.

The forensic pathologist is a medical doctor with 4 or 5 years of residency training in anatomic and clinical pathology and an additional year of fellowship training in forensic pathology. The forensic pathologist is generally appointed as an ME or may be elected to the ME/coroner's office. Forensic pathologists may also contract with the ME/coroner's office to provide forensic autopsy services. Forensic pathologists determine the cause and manner of death for cases that are under the office's jurisdiction.

The forensic pathologist may be called to the scene of death and interact with death scene investigators, as well as investigators from other systems. Rarely, the forensic pathologist may be the one who pronounces the victim dead. The forensic pathologist performs the forensic autopsy, issues an autopsy report, preserves tissue samples as required by state law, and creates a death certificate. As ME/C, the forensic pathologist also will grant permission for cremation and will provide court testimony as an expert witness. The forensic pathologist generally coordinates the involvement of forensic specialist consultants. Forensic pathologists are board certified by the American Board of Pathology. Board certification ensures public trust in a physician's ability to have mastered their chosen subspecialty. Obtaining board certification in forensic pathology demonstrates commitment to continuous learning and indicates that professionals uphold standards for professionalism and ethics as determined by their peers. Ultimately, board certification standardizes a basis of knowledge that the physician must obtain and maintain to be considered competent to practice a chosen specialty of medicine.

Medicolegal Death Investigators

The forensic medicolegal investigator has a basic knowledge of medicolegal death investigation and clinical forensic investigation (the "living" forensic cases). MDIs are nationally certified by the American Board of Medicolegal Death Investigators. MDIs are generally full-time employees of the ME/coroner's office and function under the direction and supervision of the ME.

Scene investigation is of paramount importance in any medicolegal inquiry of a death. As in clinical medicine where a comprehensive medical history provides 50%–75% of the information necessary for a diagnosis, a properly conducted scene investigation can provide the majority of information significant to a particular case for the forensic pathologist. The MDI functions as the "eyes and ears" of the forensic pathologist and relays pertinent information to the forensic pathologist prior to autopsy. Authority and primary responsibility of crime scene investigation remain with the law enforcement agency, whereas the forensic pathologist/ME/C has state statutory authority and responsibility to conduct a medicolegal investigation and has jurisdiction of the body at the scene.

Duties of the MDI are not only to investigate death scenes but also to aid in the identification of legal next of kin, obtain basic information pertinent to identification of remains, and ensure information is accurately updated in databases such as the National Missing and Unidentified Persons System (NamUs). NamUs is a centralized system that serves as a repository of information on missing, unidentified, and unclaimed persons across the United States. This system helps match unidentified remains with those individuals who have been reported missing.

Forensic Odontology

Forensically trained, licensed dentists who work for the ME/C system are known as forensic odontologists. Depending on the size and structure of the ME/C department, the forensic odontologist may be employed in forensics on a full-time basis or as a consultant on a contractual basis.

The scope of the forensic odontologist's responsibilities generally involves the identification of victims based on dental comparison in individual situations such as fire deaths and decomposition or in mass disasters such as explosions, building collapses, or aircraft accidents. One major aspect of forensic odontology is the comparison of antemortem and postmortem dental X-rays to make confirmed identities. Forensic odontologists are also called upon to identify and match characteristics of bite marks or other patterned injuries that may be related to a death. Forensic odontologists can also identify evidence of child abuse from oral soft tissue or dental injuries such as a torn frenulum or avulsed tooth sustained from blunt or asphyxial injury to the mouth of a child. Additionally, as with forensic pathologists, the forensic odontologist may be called upon to testify about his or her findings in a court of law. Forensic odontologists are board certified by the American Board of Forensic Odontology.

Forensic Anthropology

Forensic anthropology involves the study of skeletal remains associated with forensic issues, including human identification and trauma. Forensic anthropologists can distinguish between human and nonhuman bones and can determine the age, sex, race, and stature from human skeletal analysis. The forensic anthropologist assists the medical examiner in scene recovery of buried or burnt remains. Forensic anthropologists are board certified by the American Board of Forensic Anthropology.

Forensic Psychology

Forensic psychologists who work with the ME/coroner's office to investigate deaths generally focus on the psychological autopsy of the deceased. The psychological autopsy is a document obtained by interviewing next of kin and friends of the deceased and by reviewing psychiatric history to determine the mental state of the individual at the time of death to help in determination of the manner of death, for example, suicide vs. accident. Within the realm of criminalistics and law enforcement, the forensic psychologist consults on the mental health history of the decedent as well as that of the assailant. Psychological profiles of the perpetrators offer valuable clues regarding mental state at the time of the crime and/or competency to testify. The forensic psychologist may also be called upon to offer testimony for the defense and/or prosecution in a court of law.

Forensic psychologists have an advanced university degree. Licensure for this specialty is required by some states but not all. The roles of a psychologist and psychiatrist (medical doctor) may overlap in the field of forensic investigation. The psychologist generally reports the results of psychological tests and measurements, which may be valuable in victim or assailant records, whereas the psychiatrist generally deals with modalities of therapy for mental illness in the historical records of the victim and those of the suspect, including medication, electric shock, and hospitalization. Forensic psychologists are board certified by the American Board of Professional Psychology.

Forensic Toxicology

Forensic toxicologists are PhD chemists and/or toxicologists who specialize in the investigation of drugs and other substances found in the body of the deceased. Like other highly specialized individuals on the forensic investigation team, forensic toxicologists may be employed on a full-time or part-time basis by the ME/coroner's office. They are experts in examining tissue, blood, urine, gastric contents, bile, vitreous humor, and other bodily fluids for the presence of toxic substances in the body that may result in or contribute to death.

Forensic toxicologists also test for blood alcohol levels; levels of illicit drugs such as cocaine, heroin, "designer" drugs, and household chemicals that have become lethal due to high doses; and levels of prescription medications. The forensic toxicologist's role also includes maintaining the chain of custody of specimens, preserving samples for a required period of time, and supervising a technical staff to support his or her overall role. As with other specialists on the forensic investigation team, the toxicologist may be called upon to report laboratory findings in court and to testify to the significance of such findings. Forensic toxicologists are board certified by the Society of Forensic Toxicologists.

Forensic Radiology

Radiographs of the deceased are frequently necessary to determine identity and the cause, mechanism, and manner of death. In addition to the verification of bone fractures, X-ray studies can detect the presence of metal such as shrapnel, knife blade parts, bullets, or other artifacts in the body. X-rays are routinely obtained in all unidentified bodies, skeletal remains, fire deaths, airplane crashes, pipe bomb victims, decomposed bodies, child abuse deaths, and homicides.

Forensic Nursing

Forensic nurses are nurses with specialized training in forensic medical science, criminalistics, and legal issues. Completion of special courses in forensic science, forensic medical investigation, and death investigation is required to prepare forensic nurses for extended forensic nursing roles. In addition to obtaining a state license to practice as a registered nurse, a forensic nurse may be required to obtain certification in this specialty.

The American Nurses Association has recognized forensic nursing as the newest subspecialty in nursing since critical care nursing. Nurse death investigator, sexual assault nurse examiner, correctional nurse, and trauma nursing are some of the growing subspecialties available to forensic nurses. Several forensic nursing certificate programs are available in the United States and Canada.

Forensic Entomology

Forensic entomology involves the study of insect species associated with postmortem decomposition. These studies assist the ME/C in determining time of death of the decedent. The forensic entomologist studies insects present on a dead body and can estimate the time of death based on knowledge of that species' growth cycle. Some insects are collected alive, and some are preserved in alcohol at the crime scene before being sent to the entomologist's laboratory for evaluation.

Determination of the life stage of an insect is helpful in determining the postmortem time interval. For example, flies are the most common insect associated with decomposing bodies. They tend to lay their eggs in moist orifices of bodies and in areas of open injury or tissue destruction. When only fly eggs are present on a body, the forensic entomologist can generally assume that the time of death was within 1–2 days. However, this can be quite variable depending on temperature, humidity, and specific species. After eggs hatch, maggots grow until they reach the pupal stage—approximately 6–10 days under ordinary conditions. Adult flies emerge in 12–18 days. If cocaine is present in a body, the growth cycle of flies is expedited.

Forensic entomologists are also able to detect the presence of drugs in a body through their studies of insects. Maggots collected from a body can be subjected to toxicological analysis. Because maggots feed upon the tissues of a decomposed body, they can reveal the presence of various drugs in a body. By liquefying the maggots in a blender, an adequate sample can be produced for toxicological testing.

Clinical Forensic Medicine ("Living Forensic Cases")

Clinical forensic medicine is a relatively new specialty field in the United States. This specialty is defined as the application of medical and scientific knowledge of questions of the law and the civil and criminal investigations of trauma. Clinical forensic medicine residency training requires both emergency medicine and forensic medicine training. In England, clinical forensic medicine is an old specialty; the "police surgeon" has existed in England for over 100 years.

Trauma ranks higher than cancer or heart disease as the reason for hospital admission. Clinical "living" forensic medical cases encompass all violence cases, including abuse of children and the elderly, sexual assault, drug and alcohol addiction, suicide attempts, gunshot wounds, stab wounds, traffic accidents, occupational injuries, medical malpractice, therapeutic misadventures, and environmental hazards.

Most emergency department visits have potential medicolegal aspects. It is crucial that injuries are properly recognized, documented, and photographed prior to medical intervention or surgical alteration wounds. Proper collection of evidence and clothing as well as maintenance of the chain of custody and transfer of responsibility to law enforcement requires special knowledge by physicians, nurses, and emergency medical technicians (EMT).

Mortuary Science

The roles of morticians, undertakers, and funeral directors are often overlooked in the forensic investigative system but are vital in interfacing with families regarding death certificate information. Cooperation between individuals in the mortuary sciences, ME/coroner's office, and law enforcement agencies increases when each recognizes the other's role in the investigative process.

Mortuary science is a university major. Other workers in the funeral industry, such as cosmetologists who prepare the body for viewing, may attend to many of the technical aspects. Recognition of unusual circumstances during preparation of a body for funeral services can trigger an investigation from the ME/coroner's office.

Coroner System

History

The word *coroner* originates from Ferndale, England (circa 1194), when the coroner was actually appointed by the king and had various responsibilities. Coroner also means crowner; the coroner was keeper of the crown.

The coroner would also appraise and safeguard lands and goods for the king. The coroner would go to the scene when a person dies, collect what was left behind, and take it to the king. In death investigations, the coroner inspected wounds and reported accusations. The coroner could arrest suspects—he could even arrest a sheriff. As a representative of the crown, he had immense power to investigate deaths.

Coroner Systems

The coroner system was eventually adopted in the United States. Initially, every state had a coroner system and process for an elected coroner to hold a 4-year term. In some states, the coroner had to be 18 years of age and live in the state for 1 or 2 years; otherwise, there were few requirements for the office. In some locales, a mortician or local grocer may be elected coroner. If an autopsy is requested or required, the coroner contacts a pathologist to perform the autopsy. The coroner may or may not be knowledgeable about forensic science or forensic processes.

A coroner may be a medical doctor and is usually a county-elected or appointed individual. However, in most coroner states, the coroner is not required to have medical knowledge, and in some states, the individual may not be required to have a high school education. The coroner determines the cause and manner of death and signs the death certificate.

Medical Examiner Systems

Several states have instituted state-wide medical examiner systems (Figure 1.1). Some of the ME states appoint a forensic pathologist as ME. A pathologist trained in forensics is a graduate from medical school with 2 years of anatomic and 2 years of clinical pathology as well as 1 year of forensic pathology fellowship. In states with a state-wide ME system, state laws dictate specific types of death that must be referred to an ME. For example, any death that is considered to be violent, unwitnessed, unnatural, or under questionable circumstances automatically comes under the ME's jurisdiction. In such circumstances, bodies from anywhere in the state are transported to a central or regional office for autopsy. Field investigators throughout the state are trained to make decisions and notify the central office as to whether or not an autopsy should be performed. The central office has a staff of full-time board-certified forensic pathologists, forensic investigators, forensic assistants, and office staff.

The state-wide medical examiner system is an ideal system because of the availability of specialty resources at a central location. These specialties can include criminalistics, toxicology, forensic anthropology, and forensic odontology.

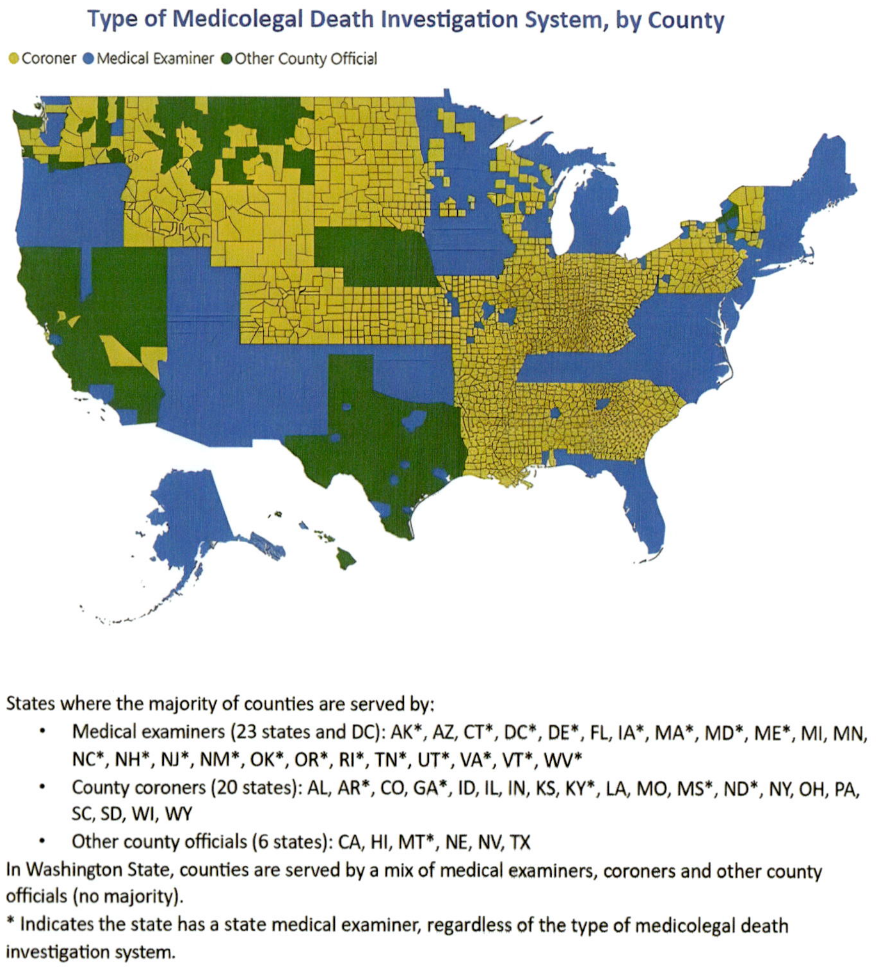

Figure 1.1 Medical examiner and coroner systems by state in the United States.

In 2009, the National Research Council published a report of the state of forensic science in the United States and included recommendations to strengthen the field, including development of uniform standards and best practices to improve overall consistency in forensic sciences. Recommendations including board certification for pathologists, certifications for MDIs, and accreditation of forensic science laboratories are some examples aimed to set minimum requirements and ensure appropriate death investigation across the nation.

Further, in 2024, the NIJ published an updated guide for death scene investigation, also highlighting the importance of standardization in death scene investigation, further contributing to standards in improving the Forensic Investigative System in the United States.

Mixed Medical Examiner/Coroner System

The ME/C is required to determine the cause and manner of death under many situations. These situations include deaths that have occurred as a result of occupation or violence, in-custody deaths, unexplained deaths, deaths under suspicious circumstances, sudden deaths while apparently in good health, deaths where there was no physician in attendance, and deaths where the attending physician was unable to certify the cause of death. As an example, if an elderly person with a 40-year history of heart disease was seen by his doctor a week prior to dying at home, then the physician who managed the heart problem authorizes and signs the death certificate. However, if a 40-year-old person with no medical history was only seen, for example, once or twice by an ophthalmologist for an isolated problem, then that ophthalmologist cannot sign the cause of death if the patient suddenly dies.

National Information Systems

The need for data collection extends beyond the state or local level. The numbers and causes of death provide the basis for "vital statistics" of the ongoing registration and coding of deaths that track trends in disease and injury in the United States.

In the United States, death certificates are filed locally, although each state and some major cities hold legal responsibility for registration and reporting of "vital" events. The Centers for Disease Control and Prevention collects epidemiological data from state health departments. Mortality data and morbidity data provide the frequency of health events. Mortality statistics are generally based on the number of deaths and causes listed on death certificates. Registration of deaths is required by law in most parts of the world. Consequently, this data provides a fairly complete record of the number of deaths, although accuracy of reported causes of deaths varies from place to place. However, the reported causes of deaths are probably an adequate indicator of the mortality count for major causes of death. A standard format for death certificates is recommended by the National Center for Health Statistics in conjunction with the Cooperative Health Statistics System. Most states have adopted the standard forms, but the amount of available information varies since each state determines the format and content of its own certificate. International comparisons of mortality are facilitated through the use of the International Statistical Classifications of Diseases, Injuries, and Causes of Death.

Mortality rates serve as an index of community health and are reported per 100,000 population. Crude death rates, cause-specific death rates, age-specific death rates, infant mortality rates, and fetal death rates are often cited by organizations and public policy planners.

As discussed previously, the NIJ also maintains a centralized repository and resource center for missing persons and unidentified decedent records called the NamUs.

First Responder System (Contributed by Cheryl L. Pozzi)

Emergency Medical Systems

Emergency medical systems (EMS) involve all those who respond to any medical problem outside of an established hospital or clinic setting. These include the following:

- EMTs
- Paramedics
- Fire service personnel
- Physicians
- Physician assistants (PA)
- Registered nurses
- Nurse practitioners
- Home health care aides
- Social workers (occasionally)

During an emergency or medical need, the primary goal is to render care to the person(s) in need of medical attention. The information presented in this section is not to take precedence over that goal. However, the goal of forensic investigation is to raise the level of awareness such that in the treatment delivery process, forensic evidence is less likely to be destroyed.

In the case of an accident or death, there is almost always a first responder. The first responder may plan to be at the scene or may simply happen to be there at the time of the incident. First responders are trained either formally or on the job to assist victims of accident or injury. An organized EMS is expected to be first on the scene, but untrained citizens often appear first and notify the EMS. Regardless of the level of training of the first responder, the goal is to maintain life and prevent further injury to the victim(s). All other goals are secondary to this.

Every city and county has some type of identified first responder. Care may be given by a person with Red Cross training in first aid or rescue breathing and cardiopulmonary resuscitation (CPR). Other areas may have fire departments or an EMS with PAs, EMTs, or nurses competent in trauma care, experienced with highly technical equipment, and in constant contact with trauma physicians. Regardless of the sophistication of EMS responders, a few are trained to preserve or collect specific types of evidence that may be valuable in determining the cause of death.

First responders have received varying levels of training. A first responder may include anyone from a volunteer who attends an 8-hour basic Red Cross course to a paid paramedic with a degree in a science area. Paramedics have completed a course of approximately 1000 hours with an internship; this can be extended to 2000 hours in training or the equivalent of a full-time job for 1 year. An EMT course is at least 80 clock hours, with an internship commonly served in an emergency department; it is essentially the basic preparation for a paid (professional) position in an ambulance crew or fire department.

Chain of command at an accident scene usually follows level of training and whoever is first on the scene. It is customary that the first responder at a scene starts appropriate care and continues that care. The exception is when someone with greater training arrives after care has begun or the victim is transferred to a transport team.

Many systems use a military ranking system, which may correspond to training and additional levels of experience in emergency care. At the scene of an accident, however, there is usually too little time to identify roles and what level of training is held by whom. Within a city or county, people often know one another from experience and exposure. Ultimately, with many responders on a scene, a medical director coordinates all activities.

Types of Systems

Most cities or fire districts have a paid fire department that employs EMTs and paramedics. This is where a 911 call is usually answered. However, some counties use a different telephone number that is routed through the sheriff's office. The system may be governmental, private, or a combination of both, with some services contracted by the government.

A two-tier regional system is one in which the fire department responds to 911 calls with a truck or rescue squad but does not transport the victim. A private ambulance company is called to transport the patient to the nearest emergency medical care facility. Private ambulance companies monitor police calls and often appear on the scene quickly, reducing response time. In a two-tier system, all firefighters are usually trained as both EMTs and firefighters.

A one-tier system has specialty units within the fire department which respond and subsequently transport victims to hospitals. These departments are large and staffed by personnel who respond to medical emergencies; they are not required to respond to other types of emergencies such as fires unless it is reported that people have been injured.

Counties that overlap major cities often have their own fire-rescue system. In areas where the boundaries are uncertain (such as a field or park rather than a street or fence), service may overlap. County systems might have a professional or volunteer available at all times at the fire department. In small communities, volunteers respond to calls from their homes. From home, they may go immediately to the emergency or to a central fire station to pick up a rescue vehicle.

Collaboration Between EMS and Investigators

There are a few mechanisms, if any, for feedback to EMS about investigations related to an accident or injury. First responders are generally not trained in evidence collection. However, evidence destruction or preservation affects many people and agencies that respond to the scene. Once the "rescue" is complete, the EMS is no longer involved unless the investigation also involves its efforts.

EMS Specialists

The following types of investigators may follow the first responder.

Medical Examiner

The ME develops an understanding of the cause, mechanism, and manner of death based on available facts. Some may believe that the ME needs only a body to complete his or her work. However, MEs also collect evidence as necessary from clothing or the scene to identify potential causes of death and to determine the manner of death.

Police

Police investigators need items such as clothing, materials from the scene, photographs, and exact positions of people and objects at the scene in order to conduct their investigation. Their training provides for proper collection and preservation of evidence. Evidence that is missing or altered may cause confusion and jeopardize a criminal case.

Insurance Representative or Investigator

Life insurance companies only need to establish that a person has died, the time of death, and the cause and manner of death (for example, accident, suicide, or natural). Other insurance companies need to make decisions regarding the cause of injury or death and potential liability involved. Altered evidence may provide a false implication, and the company may ultimately adjust the insurance rates based on cumulative information. Part of the information used in the investigation is obtained from the medical record that begins with EMS documentation.

Private Investigator

Private investigators look at evidence long after the accident has occurred. Either a government agency, such as the police or fire department, or a private citizen may hire a private investigator to study the findings in a death or disability. Motorcycle helmets, clothing, contents left inside an accident vehicle, broken roadway signs, and broken automotive parts from the scene can provide a multitude of information at later dates.

Accident Reconstructionists

Accident reconstructionists reconstruct accident scenes and events preceding and following injury or death. Preservation of evidence and good charting frequently play a role in cases long after the fact. The availability of accurate information assists these professionals in recreating an accurate scenario of the occurrence. Their work, in turn, may assist insurance companies, police departments, or attorneys in civil litigation cases.

Biomechanical Engineers

Biomechanical engineers use information in the same manner as accident reconstructionists; however, more emphasis is placed on the mechanism of how injuries occur. They use evidence found on the body, objects involved in the death, and injuries identified by physicians or MEs. They also use automotive pieces, paint smears on solid highway poles, vehicle interiors, helmets, brakes, and other equipment to duplicate the types of injuries that were caused and to help understand the biomechanics involved in the accident.

Safety Investigators

Major companies need information from the scene to determine the causes of work-related accidents. Occupational injuries are not always paid for by worker's compensation insurance. If the employee did not follow company procedure, was behaving in a negligent manner, or did not act "like a reasonable and prudent" person, then the individual may be at fault. On the other hand, if faulty equipment was involved or company representatives did not follow procedures, then the company may be liable. In any case, prevention of further accidents relies on the investigation of the safety investigator. New procedures or safety devices can emerge from in-depth inquiry and assist in the prevention of work-related deaths.

Documentation

Each agency has its own report form. Forms use "fill in the blank" and "circle the most appropriate" formats for quick and easy use. A section on the back of the form is also available for a narrative response. However, narrative notes tend to be hastily written and usually offer little detail.

Any EMS must ensure quality documentation—a narrative, diagram, photograph, taped voice recording, checklist, or any combination thereof that provides quick and accurate recording during a response. An audit of flight responses showed a great diversity and inconsistency in record-keeping. Many medical personnel have stated they are afraid to say too much about a death in case it would "pin them into a position at a later date" or come across as if "they know it all" or are commenting about things that are "not relevant." However, lack of information at a later date could cause more difficulty for the person who recorded the information if they are called to trial and need to recall details about the incident. Good charting can help paint an accurate picture for those who may be called upon to put everything together at a later date. Reports should be factual and objective.

One should make it part of his or her regular documentation to note all surroundings, all items on and around the person, and how the person was found on arrival. If anything at the scene is moved or changed in any manner, document it and notify investigators. Do not assume that because you notified the investigator or police, they documented the changes. The best consequence is multiple forms of documentation from different persons and professionals for future comparison.

EMS Procedures

The following are steps that EMS workers can take to facilitate an injury or death investigation. By integrating these steps into a quick response, first responders can contribute to their own "risk management" and minimize potential liability.

- Label anything that is removed from an accident scene or victim's body with the exact location as to where the article was found.
- If assistance is available at an accident scene, assign someone to take photographs. Photographs are one of the most valuable pieces of information for all concerned parties, including EMS. Digital photographs should indicate how the victim(s) and/or patient(s) was found and include all injuries from various angles, all pertinent items around the scene and/or body, all vehicles involved from various angles, etc. Photographs of bruises that EMS may not consider significant may assist a reconstructionist or biomechanical engineer in understanding which body parts struck which objects resulting in certain injuries. Photographs of various aspects of vehicles at the scene may be very useful at a later time when the vehicles are unavailable or may have been destroyed after the accident. These should include both interior and exterior shots, close-up shots, and distance shots. Photographs indicating details such as blood stains on the ground where people were found if they were thrown from the vehicle, how they were found initially, whether the seatbelt was in use, or whether

the front seat driver was found in the back seat provide very useful information and can also be used in defense of EMS if necessary.

- Leave as much as possible of the accident or injury scene intact while still providing care to the victim(s). Police and investigators follow the EMS and need to document and photograph clothing, materials, body positions, papers or letters, medical supplies, mechanisms, or other items about the person.
- Ensure that any statements obtained from the subject, bystanders, or witnesses identify the speaker such that the reader of a report can separate EMS's observations from a third-party's reporting.
- Do not alter any evidence at the scene. Pay attention to surroundings and do not disturb evidence. Whether one is in a house or at an accident scene outdoors, there may be valuable evidence all around.
- Use appropriate terminology. Review any records at the end of a shift or promptly the next day to ensure that there will be no confusion as to the meaning of any recording. The only abbreviations used in a record should be from a standard list of abbreviations. This list can contain selective codes as long as these are routinely used and widely accepted by the EMS.
- List all personal items removed from the scene such as a motorcycle helmet, clothing, or wallets. List and describe any contents left inside an accident vehicle, such as "clothing cut from victim, including brown loafer-style shoe left in back seat of automobile."
- Specialists may use EMS records as part of an accident or crime reconstruction. Be specific and note time sequences in the record; use exact time, numerals, or letters to indicate sequence.
- Avoid cutting through holes in clothing. Create a separate opening to cut clothing from the victim. If clothing falls to the side at the scene or in the transport vehicle, assign someone to bag the clothing and label it with the victim's name. Loss of clothing may equate to evidence being discarded. The clothing becomes part of the chain of evidence and should be given only to the person responsible for such evidence at the destination. Evidence that can be obtained from clothing varies and may include the sizes of holes in clothing, gunpowder residue, hair, blood, body tissue, semen, body fluid spatters, and fibers from objects that have been hit or that have been used to hit the victim.
- Save any blood from injuries to EMS personnel—to differentiate from that of the victim(s).
- Move about carefully to avoid stepping on evidence or moving objects to another location.
- Notify the police or fire person in command if the victim is moved for more convenient access. There are cases where one must move

rescue efforts from one place to another. Movement is not a problem as long as the move is documented in EMS notes.

- Communication—both written and verbal—is essential. Photographs are encouraged and provide useful information for many agencies. Communication with other agencies is also important. Different views are shared through communication. However, the intent is not for one agency to influence the perspective of another. Small pieces of information from one individual may assist another in making more sense of another small piece of information that does not seem to fit. Communication can also offer insight into the effectiveness of collaborative efforts and potential need for improvement.
- In cases where the victim is already deceased, it may be necessary to review company policies regarding requirements for performing rescue procedures. In such cases as homicide, suicide, sexual assault, abuse, sudden infant death syndrome, and automotive and airline deaths, there are situation-specific details that require special attention. The various forms of evidence that can be found on or around a person vary from case to case. If a person is already deceased, notations about the surroundings, body position, and artifacts around the body as well as calling the death investigators are important. If death must first be determined but is highly suspicious, rescue procedures can still be performed without disturbing evidence.
- Sudden unexpected infant death is a delicate area. While one's instinct may be to perform rescue procedures on the dead child, those efforts may prevent accurate death analysis. EMS training provides the rescuer with the knowledge to determine signs of death. Rigor mortis, livor mortis, and cold skin are good indications of death. Parents or those who called rescuers to the scene may be expecting "child-saving procedures." In some cases where there are obvious signs of death, it is far more prudent to be upfront and honest with the family and offer support rather than attempt to perform heroic techniques that will give them false hope. Leave the body as it is and call the investigative team to conduct a more accurate analysis if that is the policy in one's jurisdiction.

The EMS person may have to check with company policies regarding termination of CPR procedures. Some EMS systems do not allow EMTs to make the decision as to when rescue efforts should not be performed. Such policies should be discussed and reviewed.

Activities during EMS care can change the direction of any investigation. Clear and concise evidence presentation and documentation provides important information for the emergency department or other agencies trying to understand the cause, mechanism, and manner of death. A "forensic-wise" rescue worker is an asset to any community and department. EMS personnel may not be aware that forensic professionals rely on all pieces of evidence after the "rescue" itself is completed and that they play an important role as members of the forensic team and often interact with MDIs. First responders and MDIs, as the last of the first responders, must also be cognizant of their own psychological stress. Please refer to Appendix D for additional information on vicarious trauma.

Bibliography

Centers for Disease Control and Prevention, Collaborating Office for Medical Examiners and Coroners. 2023. *Medicolegal Death Investigation Systems, by County.* https://www.cdc.gov/nchs/comec/Medical-Death-Investigation-System-by-County.pdf

Clark, S., Ernst, M., Haglund, W., and Jetzen, J. 1996. *Medicolegal Death Investigator: A Systematic Training Program for the Professional Death Investigator.* Big Rapids, MI: Occupational Research and Assessment, Inc.

Committee of Identifying the Needs of the Forensic Sciences Community, National Research Council. 2009. *Strengthening Forensic Science in the United States: A Path Forward.* https://www.nap.edu/catalog/12589.html

DiMaio, V.J.M. and Molina, K. 2022. *DiMaio's Forensic Pathology*, 3rd ed. Boca Raton, FL: CRC Press.

Dolinak, D., Matshes, E., and Lew, E. 2006. *Forensic Pathology: Principles and Practice.* Burlington, MA: Elsevier.

Kumar, V., Abbas, A., Fausto, N., Robbins, S., and Cotran, R. 2005. *Robbins and Cotran Pathologic Basis of Disease.* Philadelphia, PA: Elsevier Saunders.

National Institute of Justice. (2024). Death Investigation: A Guide for the Scene Investigator. https://nij.ojp.gov/library/publications/death-investigation-guide-scene-investigator-2024

Spitz, W. and Fischer, R. 1993. *Medicolegal Investigation of Death: Guidelines for the Application of Pathology to Crime Investigation.* Springfield, IL: Charles C. Thomas Press.

Cause and Manner of Death

2

MARY H. DUDLEY

OBJECTIVES

Upon completion of this chapter and the corresponding reference material, the reader will be able to:

- Differentiate between cause, mechanism, and manner of death
- Describe the need for accurate information on a death certificate
- List information that medicolegal death investigators often obtain to aid in completion of the death certificate

Introduction

This chapter differentiates between the cause and manner of death while describing the need for accurate information on a death certificate. Cause-of-death statements are sometimes redundant or confusing as written on a death certificate, especially when mechanisms of death are erroneously listed in place of the injury, poisoning, or natural disease process that ultimately resulted in death. When information about the death is erroneously recorded, reviewers for a State Office of Vital Statistics may refer the death certificate to the medical examiner (ME)/coroner for reissue prior to burial or cremation. Precise identification of cause and manner of death is also required as it relates to liability issues and insurance claims. Attention to the definitions of cause and manner of death assists in completion and interpretation of death certificates. Further, medicolegal death investigators are instrumental in obtaining background information for proper death certification.

Definitions

The cause of death is the disease or injury responsible for initiating the lethal sequence of events that results in death. A competent cause of death should be etiologically specific. The underlying or proximate cause of death is that which, in a natural and continuous sequence unbroken by sufficient intervening cause, produces the fatality and without which the end result would

DOI: 10.4324/9781003538622-3

not have occurred; it is the cause of death and should be recorded as such on the death certificate. The immediate cause of death, on the other hand, is the event or sequence of events in the underlying cause that immediately precedes the death. There may be one or more immediate causes, and they may occur over a prolonged interval, but none absolves the underlying cause of its ultimate responsibility. For example, the underlying proximate cause of death may be a fractured femur with the immediate cause of death as pneumonia. In completing a death certification, the forensic pathologist would list under Part I of the death certificate, "pneumonia due to fractured right femur." The manner of death would be checked as "accident."

The mechanism of death is altered physiology and biochemistry whereby the cause exerts its lethal effect. Mechanisms of death lack etiological specificity and are unacceptable as substitutes for causes of death. Common mechanisms of death include congestive heart failure, cardiac arrhythmias, sepsis, exsanguination, renal failure, and hepatic failure. The term "cardiorespiratory arrest" ordinarily is meaningless for purposes of death certification; it is a description of being dead—not a cause of death.

Manner of death explains how the cause arose, whether natural or violent. A death must be only one of five classifications with regard to manner—natural, accident, homicide, suicide, or undetermined. Data from 2021 from the New Mexico Office of the Medical Investigator breaks down case types by manner of death and is represented in a pie chart (Figure 2.1). At the time of

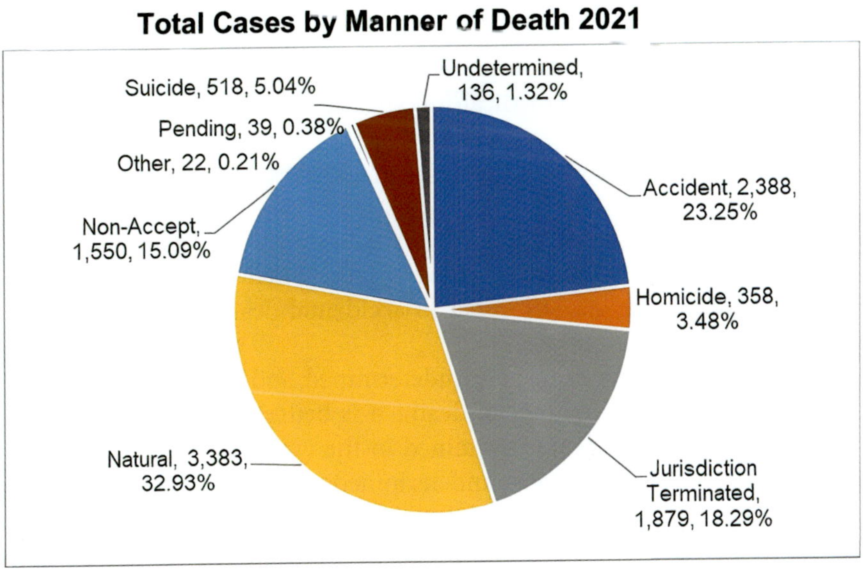

Figure 2.1 Comparison chart of manner of death in a statewide medical examiner system.

the report, a very low percentage of cases were pending or "other." This chart also lists cases that were reported to the ME but deemed to not fall under the ME's jurisdiction (non-accept and jurisdiction terminated). The largest portion of cases examined by the state-wide ME in New Mexico in 2021 were natural deaths, followed by accidental deaths, suicide, homicide, and undetermined. Any physician may sign a death certificate for a natural death. However, an ME/coroner is the only individual legally authorized to sign a death certificate if the manner of death is accident, homicide, suicide, or undetermined.

Determinations

The ME/coroner determines the cause and manner of death. Because the cause and manner of death are opinions, judgment is required to formulate both for reporting on the death certificate. The degree of certainty required to classify the manner of death depends on the circumstances of the death. Although such issues will be discussed in further detail later, a general scheme of incremental "degrees of certainty" is as follows, as outlined in the National Association of Medical Examiners Guidelines for Manner of Death Classification:

- Undetermined (less than 50% certainty)
- Reasonable medical or investigative probability (greater than a 50–50 chance; more likely than not)
- Preponderance of medical/investigative evidence (about 70% or greater certainty)
- Clear and convincing medical/investigative evidence (90% or greater certainty)
- Beyond any reasonable doubt (essentially 100% certainty)

In most ME/coroner jurisdictions, the classifications of death show that the greatest number is attributed to natural deaths where people died at home (60%); the remaining are attributed to accidental deaths (20%), homicides (10%), and suicides (10%).

All agencies have cases that are undetermined, and sometimes it is impossible to determine the manner of death. It is better for the ME/coroner to leave these cases open as undetermined in the event they are reopened for investigation in the future. Most undetermined cases involve skeletal remains or decomposed bodies. However, sometimes circumstances surrounding a death are unclear, and one must rule the manner as undetermined—even after complete scene investigation, autopsy, and review of toxicology results have been performed.

Death Certification

The death certificate is a legal document certifying the identification of the decedent, date and time of death, and the cause and manner of death (Figure 2.2). Within the portion to complete by the medical certifier, Part I is the cause of death statement, and Part II is any other significant contributory conditions in death, filled out by the pathologist or coroner. However, there are a number of ancillary questions that must be answered to fill out the death certificate completely within the medical certifier section, which rely on medicolegal death investigator (MDI)–obtained information. The mechanism of death should not be included on the death certificate. Medical treatment often attempts to modify or ameliorate mechanisms rather than causes of illness, thereby focusing clinical attention on mechanisms to the exclusion of causes. For example, digitalis is appropriate treatment for congestive heart failure but does not do anything for coronary atherosclerosis. It is appropriate for autopsies to attempt to clarify and elucidate pathophysiological mechanisms, but the underlying or proximate cause of death should not be lost in the process and thereby be omitted on the death certificate.

There may be one or more immediate causes of death, and they may occur over a prolonged interval, but none absolves the underlying cause of its ultimate responsibility. For example, a man sustains a transabdominal gunshot wound with perforation of the colon. Despite treatment over a period of 3 months, he develops peritonitis, septicemia, disseminated intravascular coagulation, hepatic and renal failure, bronchopneumonia, and adult respiratory distress syndrome. Gunshot wound of the abdomen is the underlying or proximate cause of death listed in Part I of the death certificate.

Part II of the death certificate includes "other significant conditions" and should be used only for those conditions that contribute to death but are unrelated to the cause(s) listed in Part I of the death certificate. "Other significant conditions" is not a repository for medically interesting or curious findings that do not offer a pathophysiological contribution to death.

The following types of death require a report and investigation from the ME/coroner's office, completion of the death certificate, and the ME/coroner's signature on the death certificate:

- Violent, unnatural, unattended deaths
- A result from an accident
- A result from a homicide
- A result from a suicide
- In custody
- Occupational
- Unexpected

U.S. STANDARD CERTIFICATE OF DEATH

LOCAL FILE NO. STATE FILE NO.

NAME OF DECEDENT ________ For use by physician or institution

To Be Completed/ Verified By: FUNERAL DIRECTOR:

1. DECEDENT'S LEGAL NAME (Include AKA's if any) (First, Middle, Last)
2. SEX
3. SOCIAL SECURITY NUMBER
4a. AGE-Last Birthday (Years)
4b. UNDER 1 YEAR Months Days
4c. UNDER 1 DAY Hours Minutes
5. DATE OF BIRTH (Mo/Day/Yr)
6. BIRTHPLACE (City and State or Foreign Country)
7a. RESIDENCE-STATE
7b. COUNTY
7c. CITY OR TOWN
7d. STREET AND NUMBER
7e. APT. NO.
7f. ZIP CODE
7g. INSIDE CITY LIMITS? □ Yes □ No
8. EVER IN US ARMED FORCES? □ Yes □ No
9. MARITAL STATUS AT TIME OF DEATH □ Married □ Married, but separated □ Widowed □ Divorced □ Never Married □ Unknown
10. SURVIVING SPOUSE'S NAME (If wife, give name prior to first marriage)
11. FATHER'S NAME (First, Middle, Last)
12. MOTHER'S NAME PRIOR TO FIRST MARRIAGE (First, Middle, Last)
13a. INFORMANT'S NAME
13b. RELATIONSHIP TO DECEDENT
13c. MAILING ADDRESS (Street and Number, City, State, Zip Code)
14. PLACE OF DEATH (Check only one: see instructions)
IF DEATH OCCURRED IN A HOSPITAL: □ Inpatient □ Emergency Room/Outpatient □ Dead on Arrival
IF DEATH OCCURRED SOMEWHERE OTHER THAN A HOSPITAL: □ Hospice facility □ Nursing home/Long term care facility □ Decedent's home □ Other (Specify):
15. FACILITY NAME (If not institution, give street & number)
16. CITY OR TOWN, STATE, AND ZIP CODE
17. COUNTY OF DEATH
18. METHOD OF DISPOSITION: □ Burial □ Cremation □ Donation □ Entombment □ Removal from State □ Other (Specify):
19. PLACE OF DISPOSITION (Name of cemetery, crematory, other place)
20. LOCATION-CITY, TOWN, AND STATE
21. NAME AND COMPLETE ADDRESS OF FUNERAL FACILITY
22. SIGNATURE OF FUNERAL SERVICE LICENSEE OR OTHER AGENT
23. LICENSE NUMBER (Of Licensee)

To Be Completed By: MEDICAL CERTIFIER

ITEMS 24-28 MUST BE COMPLETED BY PERSON WHO PRONOUNCES OR CERTIFIES DEATH
24. DATE PRONOUNCED DEAD (Mo/Day/Yr)
25. TIME PRONOUNCED DEAD
26. SIGNATURE OF PERSON PRONOUNCING DEATH (Only when applicable)
27. LICENSE NUMBER
28. DATE SIGNED (Mo/Day/Yr)
29. ACTUAL OR PRESUMED DATE OF DEATH (Mo/Day/Yr) (Spell Month)
30. ACTUAL OR PRESUMED TIME OF DEATH
31. WAS MEDICAL EXAMINER OR CORONER CONTACTED? □ Yes □ No

CAUSE OF DEATH (See instructions and examples)
32. **PART I.** Enter the chain of events--diseases, injuries, or complications--that directly caused the death. DO NOT enter terminal events such as cardiac arrest, respiratory arrest, or ventricular fibrillation without showing the etiology. DO NOT ABBREVIATE. Enter only one cause on a line. Add additional lines if necessary.

Approximate interval: Onset to death

IMMEDIATE CAUSE (Final disease or condition ---------> resulting in death) a. ______ Due to (or as a consequence of):
Sequentially list conditions, if any, leading to the cause listed on line a. Enter the **UNDERLYING CAUSE** (disease or injury that initiated the events resulting in death) **LAST**
b. ______ Due to (or as a consequence of):
c. ______ Due to (or as a consequence of):
d. ______

PART II. Enter other significant conditions contributing to death but not resulting in the underlying cause given in PART I
33. WAS AN AUTOPSY PERFORMED? □ Yes □ No
34. WERE AUTOPSY FINDINGS AVAILABLE TO COMPLETE THE CAUSE OF DEATH? □ Yes □ No
35. DID TOBACCO USE CONTRIBUTE TO DEATH? □ Yes □ Probably □ No □ Unknown
36. IF FEMALE: □ Not pregnant within past year □ Pregnant at time of death □ Not pregnant, but pregnant within 42 days of death □ Not pregnant, but pregnant 43 days to 1 year before death □ Unknown if pregnant within the past year
37. MANNER OF DEATH □ Natural □ Homicide □ Accident □ Pending Investigation □ Suicide □ Could not be determined
38. DATE OF INJURY (Mo/Day/Yr) (Spell Month)
39. TIME OF INJURY
40. PLACE OF INJURY (e.g., Decedent's home; construction site; restaurant; wooded area)
41. INJURY AT WORK? □ Yes □ No
42. LOCATION OF INJURY: State: City or Town: Street & Number: Apartment No.: Zip Code:
43. DESCRIBE HOW INJURY OCCURRED:
44. IF TRANSPORTATION INJURY, SPECIFY: □ Driver/Operator □ Passenger □ Pedestrian □ Other (Specify)
45. CERTIFIER (Check only one):
□ Certifying physician-To the best of my knowledge, death occurred due to the cause(s) and manner stated.
□ Pronouncing & Certifying physician-To the best of my knowledge, death occurred at the time, date, and place, and due to the cause(s) and manner stated.
□ Medical Examiner/Coroner-On the basis of examination, and/or investigation, in my opinion, death occurred at the time, date, a nd place, and due to the cause(s) and manner stated.
Signature of certifier: ______
46. NAME, ADDRESS, AND ZIP CODE OF PERSON COMPLETING CAUSE OF DEATH (Item 32)
47. TITLE OF CERTIFIER
48. LICENSE NUMBER
49. DATE CERTIFIED (Mo/Day/Yr)
50. **FOR REGISTRAR ONLY**- DATE FILED (Mo/Day/Yr)

To Be Completed By: FUNERAL DIRECTOR

51. DECEDENT'S EDUCATION-Check the box that best describes the highest degree or level of school completed at the time of death.
□ 8th grade or less
□ 9th - 12th grade; no diploma
□ High school graduate or GED completed
□ Some college credit, but no degree
□ Associate degree (e.g., AA, AS)
□ Bachelor's degree (e.g., BA, AB, BS)
□ Master's degree (e.g., MA, MS, MEng, MEd, MSW, MBA)
□ Doctorate (e.g., PhD, EdD) or Professional degree (e.g., MD, DDS, DVM, LLB, JD)

52. DECEDENT OF HISPANIC ORIGIN? Check the box that best describes whether the decedent is Spanish/Hispanic/Latino. Check the "No" box if decedent is not Spanish/Hispanic/Latino.
□ No, not Spanish/Hispanic/Latino
□ Yes, Mexican, Mexican American, Chicano
□ Yes, Puerto Rican
□ Yes, Cuban
□ Yes, other Spanish/Hispanic/Latino (Specify) ______

53. DECEDENT'S RACE (Check one or more races to indicate what the decedent considered himself or herself to be)
□ White
□ Black or African American
□ American Indian or Alaska Native (Name of the enrolled or principal tribe) ______
□ Asian Indian
□ Chinese
□ Filipino
□ Japanese
□ Korean
□ Vietnamese
□ Other Asian (Specify) ______
□ Native Hawaiian
□ Guamanian or Chamorro
□ Samoan
□ Other Pacific Islander (Specify) ______
□ Other (Specify) ______

54. DECEDENT'S USUAL OCCUPATION (Indicate type of work done during most of working life. DO NOT USE RETIRED).
55. KIND OF BUSINESS/INDUSTRY

REV. 11/2003

Figure 2.2 US standard death certificate Parts I and II.

MEDICAL CERTIFIER INSTRUCTIONS for selected items on U.S. Standard Certificate of Death
(See Physicians' Handbook or Medical Examiner/Coroner Handbook on Death Registration for instructions on all items)

ITEMS ON WHEN DEATH OCCURRED
Items 24-25 and 29-31 should always be completed. If the facility uses a separate pronouncer or other person to indicate that death has taken place with another person more familiar with the case completing the remainder of the medical portion of the death certificate, the pronouncer completes Items 24-28. If a certifier completes Items 24-25 as well as items 29-49, Items 26-28 may be left blank.

ITEMS 24-25, 29-30 – DATE AND TIME OF DEATH
Spell out the name of the month. If the exact date of death is unknown, enter the **approximate** date. If the date cannot be approximated, enter the date the body is found and identify as **date found**. Date pronounced and actual date may be the same. Enter the exact hour and minutes according to a 24-hour clock; estimates may be provided with "Approx." placed before the time.

ITEM 32 – CAUSE OF DEATH (See attached examples)
Take care to make the entry legible. Use a computer printer with high resolution, typewriter with good black ribbon and clean keys, or print legibly using permanent **black** ink in completing the CAUSE OF DEATH Section. **Do not abbreviate** conditions entered in section.

Part I (Chain of events leading directly to death)
•Only **one** cause should be entered on each line. Line (a) **MUST ALWAYS** have an entry. **DO NOT** leave blank. Additional lines may be added if necessary.
•If the condition on Line (a) resulted from an underlying condition, put the underlying condition on Line (b), and so on, until the full sequence is reported. **ALWAYS** enter the **underlying cause of death** on the lowest used line in Part I.
•For each cause indicate the best estimate of the interval between the presumed onset and the date of death. The terms "unknown" or "approximately" may be used. General terms, such as minutes, hours, or days, are acceptable, if necessary. **DO NOT** leave blank.
•The terminal event (for example, cardiac arrest or respiratory arrest) should not be used. If a mechanism of death seems most appropriate to you for line (a), then you must always list its cause(s) on the line(s) below it (for example, cardiac arrest **due to** coronary artery atherosclerosis *or* cardiac arrest **due to** blunt impact to chest).
• If an organ system failure such as congestive heart failure, hepatic failure, renal failure, or respiratory failure is listed as a cause of death, always report its etiology on the line(s) beneath it (for example, renal failure **due to** Type I diabetes mellitus).
•When indicating neoplasms as a cause of death, include the following: 1) primary site *or* that the primary site is unknown, 2) benign or malignant, 3) cell type *or* that the cell type is unknown, 4) grade of neoplasm, and 5) part or lobe of organ affected. (For example, a primary well-differentiated squamous cell carcinoma, lung, left upper lobe.)
•Always report the fatal injury (for example, stab wound of chest), the trauma (for example, transection of subclavian vein), and impairment of function (for example, air embolism).

PART II (Other significant conditions)
•Enter all diseases or conditions contributing to death that were not reported in the chain of events in Part I and that did not result in the **underlying cause of death**. See attached examples.
•If two or more possible sequences resulted in death, or if two conditions seem to have added together, report in Part I the one that, in your opinion, most directly caused death. Report in Part II the other conditions or diseases.

CHANGES TO CAUSE OF DEATH
Should additional medical information or autopsy findings become available that would change the cause of death originally reported, the original death certificate should be amended by the certifying physician by **immediately** reporting the revised cause of death to the State Vital Records Office.

ITEMS 33-34 - AUTOPSY
•33 - Enter "Yes" if either a partial or full autopsy was performed. Otherwise enter "No."
•34 - Enter "Yes" if autopsy findings were available to complete the cause of death; otherwise enter "No". Leave item blank if no autopsy was performed.

ITEM 35 - DID TOBACCO USE CONTRIBUTE TO DEATH?
Check "yes" if, in your opinion, the use of tobacco contributed to death. Tobacco use may contribute to deaths due to a wide variety of diseases; for example, tobacco use contributes to many deaths due to emphysema or lung cancer and some heart disease and cancers of the head and neck. Check "no" if, in your clinical judgment, tobacco use did not contribute to this particular death.

ITEM 36 - IF FEMALE, WAS DECEDENT PREGNANT AT TIME OF DEATH OR WITHIN PAST YEAR?
This information is important in determining pregnancy-related mortality.

ITEM 37 - MANNER OF DEATH
•Always check Manner of Death, which is important: 1) in determining accurate causes of death; 2) in processing insurance claims; and 3) in statistical studies of injuries and death.
•Indicate "Pending investigation" if the manner of death cannot be determined whether due to an accident, suicide, or homicide within the statutory time limit for filing the death certificate. This should be changed later to one of the other terms.
•Indicate "Could not be Determined" **ONLY** when it is impossible to determine the manner of death.

ITEMS 38-44 - ACCIDENT OR INJURY – to be filled out in all cases of deaths due to injury or poisoning.
•38 - Enter the exact month, day, and year of injury. Spell out the name of the month. **DO NOT** use a number for the month. (Remember, the date of injury may differ from the date of death.) Estimates may be provided with "Approx." placed before the date.
•39 - Enter the exact hour and minutes of injury or use your best estimate. Use a 24-hour clock.
•40 - Enter the general place (such as restaurant, vacant lot, or home) where the injury occurred. **DO NOT** enter firm or organization names. (For example, enter "factory", **not** "Standard Manufacturing, Inc.")
•41 - Complete if anything other than natural disease is mentioned in Part I or Part II of the medical certification, including homicides, suicides, and accidents. This includes all motor vehicle deaths. The item **must** be completed for decedents ages 14 years or over and may be completed for those less than 14 years of age if warranted. Enter "Yes" if the injury occurred at work. Otherwise enter "No". An injury may occur at work regardless of whether the injury occurred in the course of the decedent's "usual" occupation. Examples of injury at work and injury not at work follow:

Injury at work	**Injury not at work**
Injury while working or in vocational training on job premises	Injury while engaged in personal recreational activity on job premises
Injury while on break or at lunch or in parking lot on job premises	Injury while a visitor (not on official work business) to job premises
Injury while working for pay or compensation, including at home	Homemaker working at homemaking activities
Injury while working as a volunteer law enforcement official etc.	Student in school
Injury while traveling on business, including to/from business contacts	Working for self for no profit (mowing yard, repairing own roof, hobby)
	Commuting to or from work

•42 - Enter the complete address where the injury occurred including zip code.
•43 - Enter a brief but specific and clear description of how the injury occurred. Explain the circumstances or cause of the injury. Specify **type of gun** or **type of vehicle** (e.g., car, bulldozer, train, etc.) when relevant to circumstances. Indicate if more than one vehicle involved; specify type of vehicle decedent was in.
•44 -Specify role of decedent (e.g. driver, passenger). Driver/operator and passenger should be designated for modes other than motor vehicles such as bicycles. Other applies to watercraft, aircraft, animal, or people attached to outside of vehicles (e.g. surfers).

Rationale: Motor vehicle accidents are a major cause of unintentional deaths; details will help determine effectiveness of current safety features and laws.
REFERENCES
For more information on how to complete the medical certification section of the death certificate, refer to tutorial at http://www.TheNAME.org and resources including instructions and handbooks available by request from NCHS, Room 7318, 3311 Toledo Road, Hyattsville, Maryland 20782-2003 or at www.cdc.gov/nchs/about/major/dvs/handbk.htm

REV. 11/2003

Figure 2.2 (Continued)

Cause-of-death – Background, Examples, and Common Problems

Accurate cause of death information is important
•to the public health community in evaluating and improving the health of all citizens, and
•often to the family, now and in the future, and to the person settling the decedent's estate.

The cause-of-death section consists of two parts. **Part I** is for reporting a chain of events leading directly to death, with the **immediate cause** of death (the final disease, injury, or complication directly causing death) on line a and the **underlying cause** of death (the disease or injury that initiated the chain of events that led directly and inevitably to death) on the lowest used line. **Part II** is for reporting all other significant diseases, conditions, or injuries that contributed to death but which did not result in the underlying cause of death given in **Part I**. **The cause-of-death information should be YOUR best medical OPINION.** A condition can be listed as "probable" even if it has not been definitively diagnosed.

Examples of properly completed medical certifications

CAUSE OF DEATH (See instructions and examples)

Approximate interval: Onset to death

32. **PART I.** Enter the chain of events--diseases, injuries, or complications--that directly caused the death. DO NOT enter terminal events such as cardiac arrest, respiratory arrest, or ventricular fibrillation without showing the etiology. DO NOT ABBREVIATE. Enter only one cause on a line. Add additional lines if necessary.

		Approximate interval: Onset to death
IMMEDIATE CAUSE (Final disease or condition --------> resulting in death)	a. Rupture of myocardium Due to (or as a consequence of):	Minutes
Sequentially list conditions, if any, leading to the cause listed on line a. Enter the	b. Acute myocardial infarction Due to (or as a consequence of):	6 days
UNDERLYING CAUSE (disease or injury that initiated the events resulting	c. Coronary artery thrombosis Due to (or as a consequence of):	5 years
in death) **LAST**	d. Atherosclerotic coronary artery disease	7 years

PART II. Enter other significant conditions contributing to death but not resulting in the underlying cause given in PART I

Diabetes, Chronic obstructive pulmonary disease, smoking

33. WAS AN AUTOPSY PERFORMED? ■ Yes ☐ No

34. WERE AUTOPSY FINDINGS AVAILABLE TO COMPLETE THE CAUSE OF DEATH? ■ Yes ☐ No

35. DID TOBACCO USE CONTRIBUTE TO DEATH?
■ Yes ☐ Probably
☐ No ☐ Unknown

36. IF FEMALE:
■ Not pregnant within past year
☐ Pregnant at time of death
☐ Not pregnant, but pregnant within 42 days of death
☐ Not pregnant, but pregnant 43 days to 1 year before death
☐ Unknown if pregnant within the past year

37. MANNER OF DEATH
■ Natural ☐ Homicide
☐ Accident ☐ Pending Investigation
☐ Suicide ☐ Could not be determined

CAUSE OF DEATH (See instructions and examples)

32. **PART I.** Enter the chain of events--diseases, injuries, or complications--that directly caused the death. DO NOT enter terminal events such as cardiac arrest, respiratory arrest, or ventricular fibrillation without showing the etiology. DO NOT ABBREVIATE. Enter only one cause on a line. Add additional lines if necessary.

		Approximate interval: Onset to death
IMMEDIATE CAUSE (Final disease or condition --------> resulting in death)	a. Aspiration pneumonia Due to (or as a consequence of):	2 Days
Sequentially list conditions, if any, leading to the cause listed on line a. Enter the	b. Complications of coma Due to (or as a consequence of):	7 weeks
UNDERLYING CAUSE (disease or injury that initiated the events resulting	c. Blunt force injuries Due to (or as a consequence of):	7 weeks
in death) **LAST**	d. Motor vehicle accident	7 weeks

PART II. Enter other significant conditions contributing to death but not resulting in the underlying cause given in PART I

33. WAS AN AUTOPSY PERFORMED? ■ Yes ☐ No

34. WERE AUTOPSY FINDINGS AVAILABLE TO COMPLETE THE CAUSE OF DEATH? ■ Yes ☐ No

35. DID TOBACCO USE CONTRIBUTE TO DEATH?
☐ Yes ☐ Probably
■ No ☐ Unknown

36. IF FEMALE:
☐ Not pregnant within past year
☐ Pregnant at time of death
☐ Not pregnant, but pregnant within 42 days of death
☐ Not pregnant, but pregnant 43 days to 1 year before death
☐ Unknown if pregnant within the past year

37. MANNER OF DEATH
☐ Natural ☐ Homicide
■ Accident ☐ Pending Investigation
☐ Suicide ☐ Could not be determined

38. DATE OF INJURY (Mo/Day/Yr) (Spell Month)	39. TIME OF INJURY	40. PLACE OF INJURY (e.g., Decedent's home; construction site; restaurant; wooded area)	41. INJURY AT WORK?
August 15, 2003	Approx. 2320	road side near state highway	☐ Yes ■ No

42. LOCATION OF INJURY: State: Missouri City or Town: near Alexandria
Street & Number: mile marker 17 on state route 46a Apartment No.: Zip Code:

43. DESCRIBE HOW INJURY OCCURRED:
Decedent driver of van, ran off road into tree

44. IF TRANSPORTATION INJURY, SPECIFY:
■ Driver/Operator
☐ Passenger
☐ Pedestrian
☐ Other (Specify)

Common problems in death certification

The **elderly decedent** should have a clear and distinct etiological sequence for cause of death, if possible. Terms such as senescence, infirmity, old age, and advanced age have little value for public health or medical research. Age is recorded elsewhere on the certificate. When a number of conditions resulted in death, the physician should choose the single sequence that, in his or her opinion, best describes the process leading to death, and place any other pertinent conditions in Part II. If after careful consideration the physician cannot determine a sequence that ends in death, then the medical examiner or coroner should be consulted about conducting an investigation or providing assistance in completing the cause of death.

The **infant decedent** should have a clear and distinct etiological sequence for cause of death, if possible. "Prematurity" should not be entered without explaining the etiology of prematurity. Maternal conditions may have initiated or affected the sequence that resulted in infant death, and such maternal causes should be reported in addition to th e infant causes on the infant's death certificate (e.g., Hyaline membrane disease **due to** prematurity, 28 weeks **due to** placental abruption **due to** blunt trauma to mother's abdomen).

When **SIDS** is suspected, a complete investigation should be conducted, typically by a medical examiner or coroner. If the infant is under 1 year of age, no cause of death is determined after scene investigation, clinical history is reviewed, and a complete autopsy is performed, then the death can be reported as Sudden Infant Death Syndrome.

When processes such as the following are reported, additional information about the etiology should be reported:

Abscess	Carcinomatosis	Disseminated intra vascular coagulopathy	Hyponatremia	Pulmonary arrest
Abdominal hemorrhage	Cardiac arrest	Dysrhythmia	Hypotension	Pulmonary edema
Adhesions	Cardiac dysrhythmia	End-stage liver disease	Immunosuppression	Pulmonary embolism
Adult respiratory distress syndrome	Cardiomyopathy	End-stage renal disease	Increased intra cranial pressure	Pulmonary insufficiency
Acute myocardial infarction	Cardiopulmonary arrest	Epidural hematoma	Intra cranial hemorrhage	Renal failure
Altered mental status	Cellulitis	Exsanguination	Malnutrition	Respiratory arrest
Anemia	Cerebral edema	Failure to thrive	Metabolic encephalopathy	Seizures
Anoxia	Cerebrovascular accident	Fracture	Multi-organ failure	Sepsis
Anoxic encephalopathy	Cerebellar tonsillar herniation	Gangrene	Multi-system organ failure	Septic shock
Arrhythmia	Chronic bedridden state	Gastrointestinal hemorrhage	Myocardial infarction	Shock
Ascites	Cirrhosis	Heart failure	Necrotizing soft-tissue infection	Starvation
Aspiration	Coagulopathy	Hemothorax	Old age	Subdural hematoma
Atrial fibrillation	Compression fracture	Hepatic failure	Open (or closed) head injury	Subarachnoid hemorrhage
Bacteremia	Congestive heart failure	Hepatitis	Paralysis	Sudden death
Bedridden	Convulsions	Hepatorenal syndrome	Pancytopenia	Thrombocytopenia
Biliary obstruction	Decubiti	Hyperglycemia	Perforated gallbladder	Uncal herniation
Bowel obstruction	Dehydration	Hyperkalemia	Peritonitis	Urinary tract infection
Brain injury	Dementia (when not otherwise specified)	Hypovolemic shock	Pleural effusions	Ventricular fibrillation
Brain stem herniation	Diarrhea		Pneumonia	Ventricular tachycardia
Carcinogenesis				Volume depletion

If the certifier is unable to determine the etiology of a process such as those shown above, the process must be qualified as being of an unknown, undetermined, probable, presumed, or unspecified etiology so it is clear that a distinct etiology was not inadvertently or carelessly omitted.

The following conditions and types of death might seem to be specific or natural but when the medical history is examined further may be found to be complications of an injury or poisoning (possibly occurring long ago). Such cases should be reported to the medical examiner/coroner.

Asphyxia	Epidural hematoma	Hip fracture	Pulmonary emboli	Subdural hematoma
Bolus	Exsanguination	Hyperthermia	Seizure disorder	Surgery
Choking	Fall	Hypothermia	Sepsis	Thermal burns/chemical burns
Drug or alcohol overdose/drug or alcohol abuse	Fracture	Open reduction of fracture	Subarachnoid hemorrhage	

REV. 11/2003

Figure 2.2 (Continued)

FUNERAL DIRECTOR INSTRUCTIONS for selected items on U.S.

Standard Certificate of Death (For additional information concerning all items on certificate see Funeral Directors' Handbook on Death Registration)

ITEM 1. DECEDENT'S LEGAL NAME
Include any other names used by decedent, if substantially different from the legal name, after the abbreviation AKA (also known as) e.g. Samuel Langhorne Clemens AKA Mark Twain, **but not** Jonathon Doe AKA John Doe

ITEM 5. DATE OF BIRTH
Enter the full name of the month (January, February, March etc.) Do not use a number or abbreviation to designate the month.

ITEM 7A-G. RESIDENCE OF DECEDENT (information divided into seven categories)
Residence of decedent is the place where the decedent actually resided. The place of residence is not necessarily the same as "home state" or "legal residence". Never enter a temporary residence such as one used during a visit, business trip, or vacation. Place of residence during a tour of military duty or during attendance at college is considered permanent and should be entered as the place of residence. If the decedent had been living in a facility where an individual usually resides for a long period of time, such as a group home, mental institution, nursing home, penitentiary, or hospital for the chronically ill, report the location of that facility in item 7. If the decedent was an infant who never resided at home, the place of residence is that of the parent(s) or legal guardian. **Never** use an acute care hospital's location as the place of residence for any infant. If Canadian residence, please specify Province instead of State.

ITEM 10. SURVIVING SPOUSE'S NAME
If the decedent was married at the time of death, enter the full name of the surviving spouse. If the surviving spouse is the wife, enter her name prior to first marriage. This item is used in establishing proper insurance settlements and other survivor benefits.

ITEM 12. MOTHER'S NAME PRIOR TO FIRST MARRIAGE
Enter the name used prior to first marriage, commonly known as the maiden name. This name is useful because it remains constant throughout life.

ITEM 14. PLACE OF DEATH
The place where death is pronounced should be considered the place where death occurred. If the place of death is unknown but the body is found in your State, the certificate of death should be completed and filed in accordance with the laws of your State. Enter the place where the body is found as the place of death.

ITEM 51. DECEDENT'S EDUCATION *(Check appropriate box on death certificate)*
Check the box that corresponds to the highest level of education that the decedent completed. **Information in this section will not appear on the certified copy of the death certificate. This information is used to study the relationship between mortality and education (which roughly corresponds with socioeconomic status). This information is valuable in medical studies of causes of death and in programs to prevent illness and death.**

ITEM 52. WAS DECEDENT OF HISPANIC ORIGIN? *(Check "No" or appropriate "Yes" box)*
Check "No" or check the "Yes" box that best corresponds with the decedent's ethnic Spanish identity as given by the informant. Note that "Hispanic" is not a race and item 53 must also be completed. Do not leave this item blank. With respect to this item, "Hispanic" refers to people whose origins are from Spain, Mexico, or the Spanish-speaking Caribbean Islands or countries of Central or South America. Origin includes ancestry, nationality, and lineage. There is no set rule about how many generations are to be taken into account in determining Hispanic origin; it may be based on the country of origin of a parent, grandparent, or some far-removed ancestor. Although the prompts include the major Hispanic groups, other groups may be specified under "other". "Other" may also be used for decedents of multiple Hispanic origin (e.g. Mexican-Puerto Rican). **Information in this section will not appear on the certified copy of the death certificate. This information is needed to identify health problems in a large minority population in the United States. Identifying health problems will make it possible to target public health resources to this important segment of our population.**

ITEM 53. RACE *(Check appropriate box or boxes on death certificate)*
Enter the race of the decedent as stated by the informant. Hispanic is not a race; information on Hispanic ethnicity is collected separately in item 52. American Indian and Alaska Native refer only to those native to North and South America (including Central America) and does not include Asian Indian. Please specify the name of enrolled or principal tribe (e.g., Navajo, Cheyenne, etc.) for the American Indian or Alaska Native. For Asians check Asian Indian, Chinese, Filipino, Japanese, Korean, Vietnamese, or specify other Asian group; for Pacific Islanders check Guamanian or Chamorro, Samoan, or specify other Pacific Island group. If the decedent was of mixed race, enter each race (e.g., Samoan-Chinese-Filipino or White, American Indian). **Information in this section will not appear on the certified copy of the death certificate. Race is essential for identifying specific mortality patterns and leading causes of death among different racial groups. It is also used to determine if specific health programs are needed in particular areas and to make population estimates.**

ITEMS 54 AND 55. OCCUPATION AND INDUSTRY
Questions concerning occupation and industry must be completed for all decedents 14 years of age or older. This information is useful in studying deaths related to jobs and in identifying any new risks. For example, the link between lung disease and lung cancer and asbestos exposure in jobs such as shipbuilding or construction was made possible by this sort of information on death certificates. **Information in this section will not appear on the certified copy of the death certificate.**

ITEM 54. DECEDENT'S USUAL OCCUPATION
Enter the usual occupation of the decedent. This is not necessarily the last occupation of the decedent. Never enter "retired". Give kind of work decedent did during most of his or her working life, such as claim adjuster, farmhand, coal miner, janitor, store manager, college professor, or civil engineer. If the decedent was a homemaker at the time of death but had worked outside the household during his or her working life, enter that occupation. If the decedent was a homemaker during most of his or her working life, and never worked outside the household, enter "homemaker". Enter "student" if the decedent was a student at the time of death and was never regularly employed or employed full time during his or her working life. **Information in this section will not appear on the certified copy of the death certificate.**

ITEM 55. KIND OF BUSINESS/INDUSTRY
Kind of business to which occupation in item 54 is related, such as insurance, farming, coal mining, hardware store, retail clothing, university, or government. DO NOT enter firm or organization names. If decedent was a homemaker as indicated in item 54, then enter either "own home" or "someone else's home" as appropriate. If decedent was a student as indicated in item 54, then enter type of school, such as high school or college, in item 55. **Information in this section will not appear on the certified copy of the death certificate.**

NOTE: This recommended standard death certificate is the result of an extensive evaluation process. Information on the process and resulting recommendations as well as plans for future activities is available on the Internet at: http://www.cdc.gov/nchs/vital_certs_rev.htm.

REV. 11/2003

Figure 2.2 (Continued)

Role of Medicolegal Death Investigator in Obtaining Death Certificate Information

A primary role of the medicolegal death investigator is to obtain information pertinent to aid in the determination of cause and manner of death. Beyond scene investigation, medicolegal death investigators are instrumental in obtaining data that is required for completion of the final death certificate (within the portion to be completed by the medical certifier, apart from Parts I and II). The medicolegal death investigator, thus, plays a vital role in death certification. When information is missing or incomplete, the death certificate process is delayed, ultimately resulting in delays for families of decedents. The following information is important for the completion of death certificates, with areas on the standard death certificate for data entry:

- Date of death
- Location of death
- Location of injury
- Date of injury
- Pregnancy status
- Injury at work
- Transportation-related fatality
- Recent surgery information

Please refer to Chapter 3 for a complete description of MDI duties at the scene.

Legal Issues Surrounding Death

Death can result in a number of legal issues. If the individual has life insurance, the insurance company must have proof of the death in order to pay the claimant. Accident or health insurance companies require that the cause of death be known to ensure that another party is not responsible for the payment of treatment or liable expenses. Wills that are based on successive inheritance need proof of the date and time of death. In situations where many people die as a result of the decedent's actions, the time of death of all decedents may be important to establish charges.

Proper identity of the decedent is vital and of priority. Identification may require assistance from multiple forensic specialists, including forensic pathologists, police agencies for fingerprints, forensic anthropologists for skeletal examination and comparison, forensic odontologists for dental identification, DNA experts, and a host of other types of experts, depending on the case. Forensic team experts are needed especially if the individual cannot be visually identified in circumstances such as fire deaths, decomposition, aircraft accidents, or skeletal remains. Notification of the next of kin is most properly done in person rather than by telephone. It is often accomplished by law enforcement personnel, or by ME/coroner's office.

The investigation of cause and manner of death is a priority of the medical investigative team. Civil and criminal actions often depend on the results of these findings. Documentation of findings and correct information on death certificates facilitate the processing of insurance information, workers' compensation claims, and legal disputes. The manner of death is important to surviving relatives as some insurance policies pay "double" indemnity for accidental deaths and may not pay at all for suicides.

Bibliography

Clark, S., Ersnt, M., Haglund, W., and Jetzen, J. 1996. *Medicolegal Death Investigator: A Systematic Training Program for the Professional Death Investigator.* Big Rapids, MI: Occupational Research and Assessment, Inc.

Hanzlick, R., Hunsaker, J., and Davis, G. 2002. *A Guide for Manner if Death Classification*, 1st ed. Atlanta, GA: National Association of Medical Examiners.

Heron, M. 2015. *National Vital Statistics Report for 2012*, Vol. 64, p. 10. Atlanta, GA: Centers for Disease Control and Statistics.

National Institute of Justice. (2024). Death Investigation: A Guide for the Scene Investigator. https://nij.ojp.gov/library/publications/death-investigation-guide-scene-investigator-2024

United States Standard Death Certificate, Centers for Disease Control and Prevention. (2003) https://www.cdc.gov/nchs/data/dvs/death11-03final-acc.pdf

Death Scene Investigation

3

MARY H. DUDLEY

OBJECTIVES

Upon completion of this chapter and corresponding reference material, the reader will be able to

- Describe the national guidelines established by the American Board of Medicolegal Death Investigators and National Institute of Justice for death scene investigation
- Complete the duties associated with death scene investigation
- Complete photographing of the death scene and the body
- Demonstrate ability to collect biological evidence, fibers, and bullets from a crime scene
- Understand the role and function of forensic photography in death scene investigation

Introduction

Medicolegal death investigation requires specialized education, training, and skills that assist the medical examiner (ME), coroner, and forensic pathologist to determine the cause and manner of death for cases that are within their jurisdiction. The medicolegal death investigator (MDI) must be able to recognize signs of natural disease, injury, and suspicious deaths through his or her examination and assessment of the body at the death scene. The death scene reveals information and clues as to the cause and manner. The MDI is the "eyes and ears" of the forensic pathologist in order to assess the circumstances of death and to assist in determining the manner of death. It is crucial that the trained investigator be able to recognize, photograph, and document specific information relevant to the various potential causes and manners of every death. Not only is it important for the MDI to be consistent with data collection for every scene, every time, but the MDI has only one opportunity to obtain vital information to record the who, what, where, when, and why of the death scenario. This chapter details the purpose of the scene investigation and the basic duties of the MDI.

DOI: 10.4324/9781003538622-4

Duties of the MDI at the Death Scene

Duties of the forensic pathologist or MDI prior to and at the death scene include:

- Maintaining a stocked tool kit for death investigators (refer to Appendix C)
- Verifying that a death has occurred and officially pronouncing death
- Aiding in establishing identity and when last known/seen alive
- Obtaining information regarding next of kin and preferred funeral home
- Collecting information about circumstances of death and background information, including medical history of the decedent (refer to Appendix B: example worksheet for preliminary report of death)
- Interviewing witnesses for what occurred, who else may have witnessed anything, and any pertinent medical or social history of the decedent
- Assuming jurisdiction of the body, clothing, and physical evidence associated with the body
- Examining the body
- Preventing alteration, contamination, and destruction or concealment of evidence
- Preserving clothing, personal effects, and trace evidence
- Collecting evidence on body, if indicated
- Recognizing extraneous materials at the scene that might have been used for resuscitation or treatment of the decedent
- Preventing postmortem injury
- Ensuring the body is placed in a clean, unused body bag and the decedent's hands are protected by paper bags when applicable
- Securing remains with appropriate case number and labels
- Establishing and maintaining chain of custody for the body, clothing, and physical evidence associated with the body
- Documenting the scene via photographs, report, and diagrams when necessary (refer to Appendix A)

In 2024, the National Institute of Justice published a guide for the death scene investigator. Sections of the document include the following.

Death Scene

Observations at the death scene are important not only to establish cause and manner of death but also to help estimate approximate time of injury or death. Some helpful tips for observations are as follows:

- Presence or absence of milk, mail, and/or newspapers. Look at postmarks or datelines.
- Are lights on or off? Is the television on or off? Are appliances on or off?
- Clothing worn by the deceased such as street clothes, night wear, or work clothes.
- Kitchen dishes and food on the stove or table.
- With newborn deaths, note the clothes, towels, or newspapers that may provide wrapping.

Physical Evidence at the Crime Scene

Physical refers to those characteristics of or relating to tangible items or the result of natural law—as opposed to those relating to mental, moral, spiritual, or imaginary concepts. It relates to those areas dictated by natural science. *Evidence* refers to something that furnishes proof and can be legally submitted to a tribunal to ascertain the truth of a matter. It can also arise from information provided by one who bears witness or voluntarily confesses to a crime and testifies for the prosecution against his or her accomplices.

Without physical evidence, the attempt to prove a case is extremely difficult. One cannot fully depend on eyewitness reports since people have different perceptions as to what they see. For example, sociologists have found that when several witnesses are asked to report what they saw regarding an automobile collision, they report several versions of what may have actually occurred. Some may see an opportunity to gain notoriety if they are asked to serve as a witness to a crime. These situations can result in inaccurate and/or exaggerated accounts of what occurred or be disregarded as "hearsay." Identification of physical evidence can provide irrefutable information that can be used in a court of law.

Death Scene Photography

One of the most critical aspects of any death scene investigation is successful and proper photography. With regard to death scene information, it is certainly true that a picture is worth a thousand words. Photographs provide invaluable information to the investigation team. High-quality equipment facilitates the job, but there is no substitute for careful, conscientious work by the investigator. The death scene should be photographed immediately upon its discovery before anything is disturbed or moved. All angles should be considered during death scene photography. Photographs should include overall views, midrange views, and close-ups of the scene and victims. Too many photographs are always better than too few.

Purpose

The purpose of death scene photography is to visually record the scene as it was found. Those photographs will then be used by police investigators and prosecution and defense attorneys to present their cases to a judge and jury in a court of law. For that reason, it is important to ensure that police equipment (camera cases, briefcases, clipboards, etc.) and investigative personnel are not included in the photographs. The investigation team's efficiency depends, to a large extent, on professional-quality photographs of the death scene; photographs that are not taken properly render loss of important information and may jeopardize the case.

It is important to remember that, if one has never been to the death scene, it is often difficult to accurately visualize only through photographs how the scene actually appeared and where things were in relation to each other. Thus, careful attention to detail by the photographer is essential to ensure that the photographs are of value.

Three Stages of Death Scene Photography

When photographing a death scene, the photographer must keep in mind that the camera has a limited field of view. In order to compensate for this limitation, the scene must be photographed in three stages.

Stage One: Overall Photographs

The purpose of the overall photographs is to include in one photograph as much information about a death scene as possible. These photographs should be taken before anything at the scene is disturbed or moved. They should serve as a record of how the scene was found (Figure 3.1).

The goal of the photographer should be to ensure that every single item within the death scene appears in at least one photograph. This is extremely important as investigators do not always know what is important during the initial death scene search. Something initially overlooked will hopefully be preserved in an overall photograph.

Overall photographs should be taken such that the person viewing them will see the scene as a whole rather than focus on one particular aspect or detail. The overall photographs also serve as references for midrange and close-up photographs.

In taking overall death scene photographs, the photographer moves as far back as possible to encompass the entire scene. This may require a position across the street or atop an automobile or building. If a building is being

Figure 3.1 Overall photograph of death scene.

photographed, photographs should be taken of all sides of the building as well as the business sign and address. Photographs of nearby street signs, cross streets, etc., should also be taken. If the scene is in an isolated area, one should attempt to locate a recognizable landmark such as a nearby hill, unusual tree, or power line pole. If the scene is indoors, stop inside the doorway and photograph the room panoramically in overlapping segments starting at one corner of the room and moving to the opposite side. Follow the same procedure for each corner of the room and in other relevant rooms. A normal 50-mm lens can usually be used for outdoor overalls; however, a wide-angle 35-mm lens is preferable for both indoor and outdoor overall photographs.

Helpful hint: Turn the camera sideways for indoor overalls. This will allow for a ceiling-to-floor photograph that provides more information. The use of a wide-angle lens can also produce a considerable amount of distortion in an image; if so, a normal 50-mm lens should be used instead. Film is relatively cheap. Therefore, many photographs are encouraged. Remember, too many photographs are always better than too few!

Stage Two: Midrange Photographs

The purpose of a midrange photograph is to focus the attention of the viewer on a particular object. However, it should still be taken from a position far

Figure 3.2 Midrange photograph of death scene.

enough away that the overall surroundings remain important. Midrange photographs should be free of distortion. Therefore, the normal 50-mm lens is recommended (Figure 3.2).

Indicator Cards When it has been determined what evidence will be collected and the overall photographs have been taken, indicator cards or evidence markers should be placed with the evidence and photographed again. Thus, there are two sets of photographs for the scene—one to show the scene undisturbed (as it was found) and a second to show the scene with the evidence cards in place. Indicator cards serve as easy references for everyone involved.

Use of Scales When a scale is used, relationships are more clearly defined. The addition of a scale to a photograph of evidence that is not to be collected such as a bullet graze, fingerprint, bloodstain, shoe print, or tire track is essential. The placement of an L-shaped ruler or two ruled scales at 90 degrees to each other to frame an impression or stain allows for any distortion in the photograph to be detected and potentially corrected at the printing stage. The camera should be placed at a 90-degree angle to the subject matter and the scales. Pens, coins, and paper clips are not recommended as scales unless as a final resort. A clearly legible ruler or scale is best. Without an appropriate scale, many photographs are rendered worthless.

Helpful hint: The American Board of Forensic Odontology No. 2 scale has two scales set at 90 degrees to each other. In addition, circle indicators are printed on the scale and can be used to correct distortion during printing. When photographing injuries such as bruises, photograph them with and without scales and color charts.

Lighting and Flash Considerations The photographer should always be aware of the amount and source(s) of light available in order to determine when a flash is necessary. The flash should be positioned properly in order to maintain appropriate lighting in the photograph. The creation of shadows can obliterate areas of a photograph, which may be vital to the investigation. For example, the photographer should be aware of doorjambs and other objects that might create unwanted shadows. Footprints and tire tracks should be photographed with oblique lighting from all four sides of the print to create shadows that highlight the individual characteristics of the print.

Helpful hint: The photographer should check the camera settings every two or three frames (especially when using flash). One erroneous setting could ruin the remaining exposures.

Following is the checklist for using a flash:

- Is the flash turned on?
- Is the flash set to "manual" or "auto" mode?
- Is the light sensitivity, or American Standards Association/International Organization for Standardization (ASA/ISO) setting correct?
- Is the flash charging fully between flashes?

Following is the checklist for the camera:

- Is the shutter speed properly set to be synchronized with the flash?
- Is the f-stop properly set for the flash setting (auto or manual)?
- Is the thru-the-lens light meter functioning properly?

A word of caution: One should not take a picture of anything he or she does not want anybody to see. All pictures taken at a death scene are evidence and can be used in court by the defense or prosecution.

Stage Three: Close-Up Photographs

Every piece of evidence present at a death scene does not necessarily need to be photographed in close-up. Close-ups should be taken when important

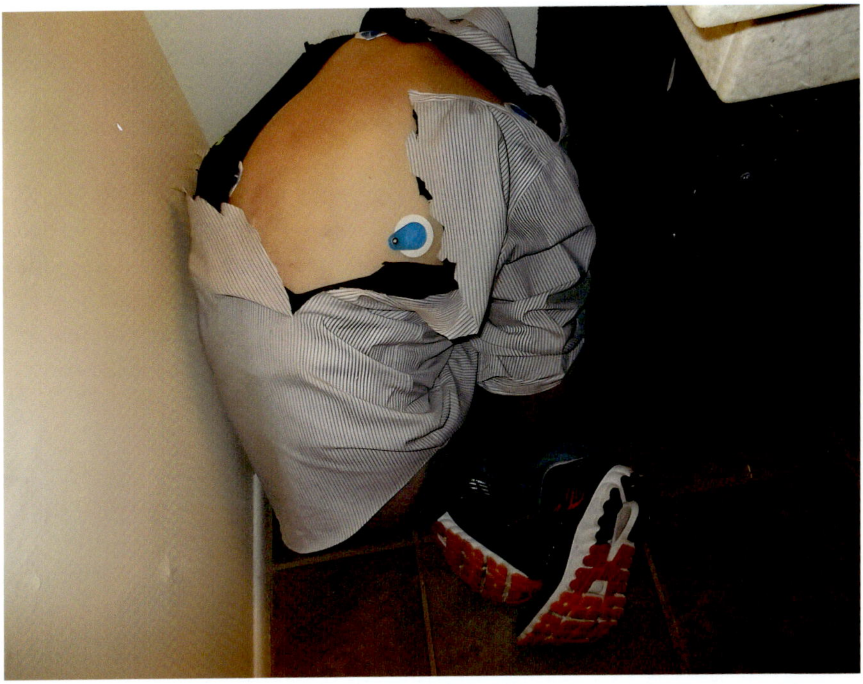

Figure 3.3 Close-up photograph of the death scene.

aspects of a piece of evidence are not depicted in the overall or midrange photographs (Figure 3.3). Good close-up photographs show direction of travel or pattern of injury. An example of when close-up photography might not be necessary is where multiple cartridge casings of the same brand are on the ground in a group; a close-up of each casing does not reveal any new information. If, on the other hand, the casings are of different brands, then close-ups would have more value. Close-ups can be taken from a distance with a telephoto lens or up close with a macro lens. In some instances, the telephoto is preferred because it is easier to light the subject with a flash positioned away from the subject.

Helpful hint: Use the smallest f-stop possible to improve the depth of field, particularly with extreme close-ups.

As a general note about death scene photography, photographs are not necessarily taken in the order of all overalls, then all midranges, then all close-ups. Usually all overalls are taken upon discovery of the death scene, and then midranges and close-ups are taken in sequence as evidence is discovered.

Video Videotape is an excellent method for recording a death scene. Video, in combination with still photographs, can provide a jury with a better sense of the death scene and the relationships between pieces of evidence. The microphone should not be used as it can record unwanted comments from others at the scene. Narration of the videotape is also not recommended; comments made at the scene may later prove incorrect. If narration is desired, it should be dubbed in later from a prepared script. When taping a scene, one should pan *very slowly* and hold the camera as steadily as possible. Do not move too fast since vital information might be overlooked (it can also make viewers motion sick). Use the zoom sparingly; overuse is distracting and can contribute to nausea.

Pearls of Photography

- Always check your equipment; carry a back-up camera, flash, and extra batteries.
- Avoid undershooting. Bracket the photographs.
- Remember that batteries are sensitive to temperature extremes.

Legal Aspects of Photography The photograph is considered one of the best methods of documentation. Photographs can prolong evidence that otherwise may deteriorate with time. They must be taken as soon as possible particularly when dealing with perishable evidence. Photographs again can depict a scene more cleverly than perhaps a witness can articulate it. They may be used to "jog" a witness's memory. A photograph may also contain elements that were initially overlooked by investigators or that may have been forgotten by witnesses. Most importantly, photographs lend credibility to testimony and help jurors actually visualize rather than imagine the variables of the death scene, lending to more objectivity.

Admissibility of Photographs Photographs cannot prejudice or mislead the jury; therefore, factual photographs are better than those that are overdramatized. Photographs must be authenticated by a witness who was present during the shoot. The photographer is responsible for identifying evidence in a photograph and testifying to the accurate portrayal of its content and to the fact that it was not subject to tampering.

Identifying the Photograph Hundreds of photographs are often taken—perhaps at different times and by different photographers. Therefore, it is recommended that a log be kept to detail the following:

- Date and time the photograph was taken
- Name of photographer and title
- Type of equipment used

- Description of the angle at which the photograph was taken in relation to subject (e.g., "bullet hole in SW wall")
- Clarifying comments (e.g., rain equipment, probes, hot or cold conditions)

Chain of Accountability Photographs are considered as important as physical evidence. Therefore, a chain of accountability is necessary—from photographers to crime laboratory (logs in time, person submitting the disc (chip), time, and date). The laboratory also logs the number of prints made, who received them (Federal Bureau of Investigation, police department, etc.), and each time a photograph is released, returned, moved, or handled. A disruption in chain of accountability could discredit the validity of the photograph.

Evidence Identification: Documentation and Collection

Evidence collection is important since it represents materials that may have to be presented in a court of law. Because of that possibility, certain procedures must be followed in the collection of evidence to ensure that it can be admitted into the court case.

The following guidelines should be considered during the process of evidence collection:

- All major investigations must first have one person to lead the investigation. That person must first decide the type of crime that exists. Once that is determined, the necessary resources must be considered, including the types of experts required from various disciplines (ME/coroner, forensic odontologist, forensic anthropologist, criminologist, hazardous materials team, Federal Aviation Association, National Transportation Safety Board, bomb technician, etc.), crime scene processing equipment, and manpower.
- To ensure an orderly process, the lead investigator must know who has been at the crime scene (first responders, rescue personnel, initial law enforcement personnel, photographers, witnesses, etc.). All traffic patterns should be ascertained in order to know potential contributions or deletions made by previous investigative personnel. After a briefing on all known facts, the lead investigator makes an assessment of the crime scene, which enables him or her to develop an organized plan as to how to approach and sequentially process the scene. A good initial step minimizes any chance of destroying evidence or overlooking valuable information. It is also critical to minimize the number of personnel permitted at the crime scene.

- The best way to approach a crime scene is to work inward toward the body from the outside scene perimeter. Avoid initial focus on the body as this may create a "tunnel vision" approach to the study of the overall situation, thereby overlooking important forensic evidence surrounding the body. The scene may hold clues as to the cause of death by thermal injury, drugs, firearms, etc.
- If blood has been shed at the scene, all investigative personnel must utilize appropriate personal protective equipment (PPE). This may include gowns, masks, gloves, goggles, or eye shields, shoe and head covers, and respirators. If at any point during the investigation any blood or biological matter is transferred to the protective wear of anyone involved, a new piece of PPE must replace the affected garment. The contaminated piece of PPE must be discarded in containers placed at appropriate locations near the crime scene.
- A complete rough diagram of the structure or area can be created during the initial overview of the scene; this provides the opportunity to note positions of significant items within the scene. A more detailed sketch of the primary scene should also note evidence items and their positions, orientations, and relationships to the body. Good methods for diagramming include

    - A general overall approach with dimensions of structures, rooms, furniture, etc.
    - A specific diagram for the death scene (bedroom, living room, kitchen, etc.)
    - A series of diagrams to document locations of evidence items or to indicate bloodstain patterns

The process of evidence collection is one of the most important steps during crime scene investigation. When evidence is properly collected, valuable information contained in or with the evidence can be preserved for presentation in court. If evidence is mishandled, that same information can be lost or ruled as inadmissible by the court.

Packaging Evidence

Prior to actual collection of the evidence, the investigator must decide what containers are needed for the various types of evidence to be seized. That decision should be based on the need to

- Provide proper evidence preservation (protection)
- Prevent evidence from being compromised, contaminated, destroyed, damaged, or altered

Among the types of protective containers are

- *Paper bags*: New paper bags are one of the most universally accepted containers for most evidence collected. Since they can be readily purchased almost anywhere in bulk and in various sizes from large "shopping bag" size to small "lunch bag" size, they remain popular among investigators. They provide an excellent container for clothing, bedding, shoes, numerous articles from a home or office, beer cans, bottles, and hats and for protecting trace evidence on the hands of the deceased. Unlike most plastic containers, paper bags are not airtight; therefore, biological evidence will not degrade.
- *Envelopes*: Like paper bags, new envelopes can be purchased almost anywhere and in various sizes from large document size to small coin envelope size. Envelopes can be used for small items.
- *Butcher paper rolls*: This type of paper is excellent for viewing, photographing, and packaging evidence. Pieces of butcher paper can also be laid between folds of clothing or other large cloth items to separate and help prevent cross-contamination of biological evidence.
- *Pharmacy fold paper*: These small 6- or 8-inch sheets of paper are useful for packaging small forensic evidence. Pharmacy fold paper can be formed into a small package. This is an ideal method for collecting fibers, hairs, paint chips, and samples of dried blood; this helps prevent damage or degradation to the sample.
- *Vials*: Plastic vials are useful for containing various types of evidence that are not biological in nature. This may include bullet casings, matches, cigarette butts, soil samples, paint chips, and debris. Glass vials are useful for containing various types of liquids that could potentially react chemically to plastic (such as through melting or dissolution). Unlike plastic vials, glass vials have screw-on lids that prevent leakage. Glass vials can be used for corrosive chemicals, loose pills, alcohol samples, liquid samples found in drinking glasses, etc. (Note: The main drawback of using glass evidence containers is their potential for breakage; glass vials must be packaged carefully to avoid damage.)
- *New metal paint cans*: Cans can also be purchased in various sizes (from one gallon to one pint). Most fire stations maintain a ready supply of these for their use in collecting evidence in arson cases. These are excellent for collecting flammable liquids, accelerants, and volatiles. These containers are excellent for collecting samples of glass, fine clay, soil, and sharp items.
- *Syringe holders*: These are required for packaging hypodermic needles. Use of syringe holders also ensures that syringes remain in the same condition as when they are found. Investigators at a crime scene

as well as those who have to handle evidence at a later date (evidence custodian, criminalist, officers of the court, etc.) must be protected from accidental punctures when they handle evidence.

- *Cardboard boxes*: These can be used to secure knives, guns, and other sharp instruments. Various sizes are easily obtained. Suspected weapons should be tied/secured to the bottom of the box to avoid slippage of the item.
- *Indelible ink marking pens*: These are essential for investigators. All containers that hold evidence items must be labeled with permanent marker identification. Containers must be sealed with evidence tape, and proper chain-of-custody information must be documented.

Fingerprints

Fingerprints (when available) are the best evidence for identification because the individual characteristics of fingerprints remain constant throughout a person's life. Individual characteristics make each print unique and allow for specific identification of individuals. Fingerprints can be entered into a national database Automated Fingerprint Identification System for comparison. In general, the most latent fingerprint processing is done at the scene. Exceptions are items such as tape or paper prints that require chemical processing. Some items require a laboratory environment in order for experts to utilize controlled testing techniques to obtain optimum results. Some items may require enhancement through specialized lighting to capture additional ridge detail. Circumstances such as these also require photography of the latent print. Consideration should be given to careful transport of small items, items with difficult surfaces from which to obtain prints, or any items requested by the latent print examiner.

Biological Evidence

Collection of biological samples is important for forensic investigation. Information that can be obtained from biological samples includes

- Blood spatter pattern
- Blood stain patterns
- Semen or saliva stains
- DNA information

Before collecting any biological samples, one must determine whether the samples offer any value to the investigation. A photograph of the sample in situ can help the investigator determine the importance of the sample. Exercise caution when collecting samples; latex gloves should be worn. After the sample is collected, it must be protected through drying and refrigeration as soon as possible.

Clothing

It is important to collect clothing in nearly every homicide, assault, fire death, firearms death, electrical death, or motor vehicle accident. Evidence from clothing of those involved can provide important information.

The victim's clothing can provide

- Bloodstains, burns, or tire-mark patterns that help with reconstruction of the situation that led to the death
- Type and size of weapon used such as width of a knife blade and range of fire of a firearm
- Trace evidence including samples of
    - The suspect's blood, body fluids, hair, and clothing fibers
    - Paint chips from a hit-and-run vehicle or accelerants on clothing from arson

The suspect's clothing can provide

- Trace evidence including samples of the victim's blood, body fluids, hair, and clothing fibers
- Bloodstain patterns that help with reconstruction of the situation, which led to the death

Prior to packaging bloodstained clothing, one must ensure that the stains are dry and patterns are not destroyed during the packaging process. In situations where proximity testing of gunshot residue is required, extremely careful handling of the clothing must be ensured since residues can be easily dislodged. The ideal method of packaging bloodstained clothing is to place a paper towel over the gunshot area and fold the clothing carefully over it. Again, the value of good photographs cannot be overstated.

Fibers and Hairs

When fibers or hairs are found at a crime scene, they should be collected as they are found since they can easily be lost. An examination of hair can indicate

- Whether it is human or animal
- Body region from which it originated (head, chest, or pubis)

- Whether it was forcibly removed or fell out
- Whether it was burned, cut, crushed, dried, or bleached
- Blood groups if the root is attached
- Racial groups
- Information provided through DNA analysis

DNA Analysis

DNA contains the genetic blueprint. DNA strands in the shape of a "twisted ladder" or double helix can be mapped by genetic patterns. Since each person's DNA differs, DNA mapping provides a unique identity marker.

Extraction

Police and scientists use any available cell tissue found at a crime scene—blood, semen, tissue, bone marrow, hair, urine, saliva, wood pulp, cheek scrapings, fingernails—for DNA typing to compare with a suspect's genetic coding.

Fragmentation

A DNA strand from a sample is dissolved in a "restriction enzyme" that breaks the DNA molecule, or double helix, into thousands of pieces. Laboratory scientists know which fragments have specific DNA coding signifying unique traits for comparison.

Lining Up the Fragments

The chosen DNA fragments are placed in an electrically charged gel. The negatively charged DNA drifts toward the positive pole on the gel slab, with smaller fragments moving faster. This process of electrophoresis leaves DNA fragments arranged according to length.

Radioactive Probe

These bands are transferred to a nylon membrane. Radioactive DNA fragments containing specific coding that varies greatly from person to person are applied as "probes." These special radioactive probes bind with complementary DNA fragment landmarks on the fragments.

Comparative Analysis

An x-ray film is laid over the nylon membranes and reveals the size of each piece upon which each landmark falls; the process may take 1 or 2 days or much longer due to a backlog of cases. The DNA bands (DNA fingerprint), which by now resemble a Universal Product Code symbol, are transferred onto the file as a result of the radioactivity. The bars are lined up. If those from the crime scene evidence line up with those from the suspect, prosecutors use the band patterns in court to claim that a coincidental match would be extremely rare—the probability of a match is 1 in 100 million.

DNA Evidence in Forensic Cases

Since first introduced in U.S. courts in 1987, DNA evidence is now generally accepted in most courts. DNA evidence is used in current and cold cases to include or exclude suspects. Proper collection and preservation of biological evidence at the scene is extremely important for future investigation. DNA can be entered into the national DNA database, Combined DNA Index System, for comparison.

The power of DNA prints comes from its precision, which is immensely greater than standard analysis of blood, semen, or hair. Although DNA fingerprinting has attained mythic status in the public mind—one critic calls it "a fist on the scales of justice"—outweighing all other evidence, it is not an infallible crime solver. It is problematic enough that the very term "DNA fingerprinting" is not allowed in some courts and is replaced by DNA typing or DNA profiling in order to not dazzle jurors into thinking that DNA evidence is as unambiguous as an ordinary fingerprint. That is because DNA tests do not compare each of the 3 billion chemical units of a person's heredity. (If they did, there would be no dispute that a match is a match; DNA is unique to every individual except identical twins.) Instead, the tests compare only three to six regions of DNA—up to 13 core loci.

Firearms

Before a weapon is touched or moved at the scene of a crime, notes should be made regarding its position and placement, hammer position, safety position, visible blood, hairs, dust, etc. The weapon should be handled on its knurled or serrated surfaces. Common sense can help ensure that personal safety is addressed and that fingerprints are not added or removed.

Ammunition

When cartridges, fired cases, and projectiles are found at a crime scene, special attention is required to document their locations. Occasionally, the shooter's and/or victim's positions can be determined. Bullets and casings need to be handled with a gloved hand (not metal forceps), packaged separately, and preferably wrapped in tissue to prevent the possibility of scratching or otherwise damaging the items. Care must be taken to avoid any introduced marks or imprints to ensure the evidence remains in the exact condition in which it was found. Once packaged, the container should be sealed and marked.

Casings and projectiles can reveal the type and brand of ammunition, and comparisons can be made to determine whether a bullet or casing was fired from a specific weapon by the firearms examiner. A national database National Integrated Ballistics Information Network can link projectiles and casings to those used in other crimes.

Toolmarks

Toolmarks are often left behind when a forced entry is made into a building. If tools are recovered from the scene, they can be subjected to tests and comparisons similar to those applied to bullet analyses. Recovery of toolmarks may require the entire piece to be removed and sent to the laboratory for analysis. If that is not possible, silicone casts can be made. Beyond that, scale graphs should be obtained.

Shoe and Tire Prints

Nearly every shoe and tire print has individual characteristics that could make it unique and identifiable. Photographs of these items are generally taken upon arrival at the crime scene as these types of evidence are easily destroyed.

Documents

Documents are collected primarily for

- Content
- Possibility of latent fingerprints

These items should be handled with tweezers or forceps or by the edges to avoid destroying or leaving latent fingerprints. Authorship can often be determined through handwriting analysis.

Organizing Evidence

The lead investigator should establish a central collection point at the scene of crime where all evidence is initially marked, numbered, and inventoried. As evidence is collected, a written inventory should include the item, indicator number, and location it is found. This master list of all items is retained for later cross-reference. It also serves as a double check of the collection to ensure that all evidence has been collected. Upon finalization of this list and packaging of items to be removed, the investigator should make a final walk-through of the crime scene to ensure that no evidence has been overlooked and that all investigative equipment has been returned to its proper place and secured.

Debriefing

The lead investigator should finalize the crime scene investigation process with a debriefing of all personnel involved. At this time, he or she must ensure that the process has been explored to the fullest extent possible. The lead investigator may also obtain further input from members of the team before concluding the process and thanking team members. The chain of communication should be clearly established prior to commencement of the next stage of investigation. The value of this communication contributes to improved procedures when the team reconvenes.

Team Approach

Team approach to crime scene work is essential and works efficiently when every member of the team knows his or her role and carries out individual responsibilities. Most members of such a team are experts in their own realms; the lead investigator should be able to meld the offerings of each expert into the overall process.

Psychological Stress and Vicarious Trauma in MDIs

As the last of the first responders, MDIs are exposed to a variety of traumatic situations that have an impact on individual resilience. Definitions of vicarious trauma and tools to maintain resilience are outlined in Appendix D. Refer to Appendix D for additional resources.

Bibliography

Clark, S., Ernst, M., Haglund, W., and Jetzen, J. 1996. *Medicolegal Death Investigator: A Systematic Training Program for the Professional Death Investigator.* Big Rapids, MI: Occupational Research and Assessment, Inc.

DiMaio, V.J.M., & Molina, D.K. (2022). *DiMaio's Forensic Pathology* (3rd ed.). Boca Raton, FL: CRC Press, Inc.

Fisher, B.A.J. 1993. *Techniques of Crime Scene Investigation* (4th ed.). Boca Raton, FL: CRC Press, Inc.

National Institute of Justice. (2024). Death Investigation: A Guide for the Scene Investigator. https://nij.ojp.gov/library/publications/death-investigation-guide-scene-investigator-2024

Redsicker, D.R. 2000. *The Practical Methodology of Forensic Photography* (2nd ed.). Boca Raton, FL: Taylor & Francis Group.

Postmortem Changes

4

MARY H. DUDLEY

OBJECTIVES

Upon completion of this chapter and corresponding reference material, the reader will be able to

- Describe three methods for determining time of death or injury
- List situations where body position and postmortem findings may indicate that the body was moved after death
- Discuss the significance of establishing time of death
- Define a list of terms that describe signs of death
- Describe actions of insects on a body

Introduction

The medical examiner (ME)/coroner is responsible for establishing the time of death or injury. Changes in body temperature, stiffness of the body, or color changes at the time of scene investigation can help establish the time a person died. Terminology frequently used to describe signs of death tends to range greatly. The use of standardized descriptive terms will help to clarify observations about the appearance of the body. This chapter discusses frequently used terms that describe postmortem changes and factors that help establish time of death or injury.

Rigor Mortis

Rigor mortis means rigidity of the body. Rigidity of the muscles is triggered by a chemical reaction due to the depletion of adenosine triphosphate (ATP). Rigor mortis begins almost immediately after death starting in the small muscles—mainly those around the eyes, face, and fingers—and extending to the larger muscle groups as time passes. Rigor mortis peaks in about 12 hours and then begins to disappear at 24 hours. Temperature affects muscle tension; if the area is warm, rigor speeds up and then begins to disappear earlier or in

DOI: 10.4324/9781003538622-5

approximately 8 hours. The rigor response can be interrupted when muscles are manipulated. For example, rigor can be broken when clothing is removed. Consequently, progression of rigor mortis should be evaluated prior to moving a body's position or clothing and prior to long bone donation.

The following conditions imitate or mimic rigor mortis:

- Cadaveric spasm or instant rigidity, which occurs at the moment of death. This can occur during violent deaths or exercise. The mechanism relates to rapid depletion of ATP.
- Freezing. Frozen muscles may mimic rigor.
- Heat stiffening. Heat coagulates muscle and causes shortening of the muscle and flexion at the joint.
- Fusion of bones. Abnormalities of the skeleton may cause deformity of the bones at the joints that mimics rigor mortis.

Livor Mortis

Livor mortis is a red-purple discoloration of the body that occurs in dependent parts of the body—those parts closest to the floor—by gravitational pooling of blood, except in areas exposed to pressure. Livor mortis begins when blood circulation ceases. For example, a person who dies in a supine (face up) position should show lividity in the backs of the arms, legs, and trunk. If the person is sitting at the time of death, lividity appears along the buttocks, lower legs, feet, and possibly hands. It becomes noticeable in 30–40 minutes in dependent areas but not in pressure areas where the blood is pushed to the side (Figure 4.1).

Accentuated livor mortis may mimic bruising. Tardieu spots, red or purple patches on the body, refer to actual bleeding into areas of intense livor mortis. Tardieu spots are sometimes seen in asphyxial deaths and hangings. Other bleeding such as mucosal bleeding may occur from the nose because of intense livor mortis.

Cherry-red lividity is seen instead of purple blotchy discoloration in three situations:

1. Carbon monoxide poisoning
2. Cold (as when the body is refrigerated)
3. Cyanide poisoning

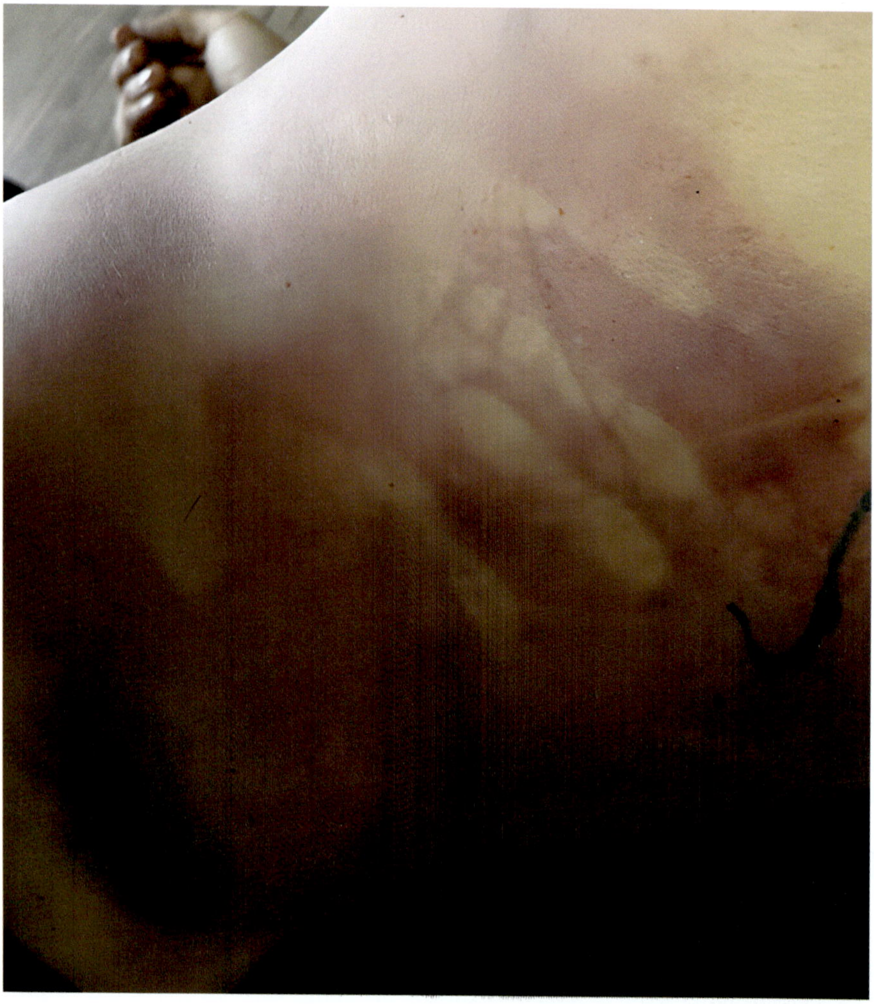

Figure 4.1 Photograph of livor mortis with blanching.

Algor Mortis

Algor mortis is the cooling of the body as temperature is lost from the body. There is no decrease in temperature during the first hour after death; after the first hour, temperature decreases at a rate of 1.5°F per hour. Early rectal or core temperature taken at the scene may be helpful in establishing the time of death as the body eventually equalizes with the room or environmental temperature. However, this is not standard practice in most MEs' offices.

One equation used to calculate postmortem interval in hours is the Glaister equation, which is as follows:

$$\text{Postmortem interval}\left(\text{hours}\right) = \left(98.7^{\circ}\text{F} - \text{body temperature F}\right)/1.5$$

This equation assumes that a body cools at a constant rate of 1.5°F per hour from a normal temperature of 98.7°F.

Postmortem Drying Artifacts

The body begins to dehydrate after death, but the extent and rate of drying depend on climate and humidity. For example, dry, arid climates can cause mummification. In these climates, the fingers and hands are the first to become extremely dehydrated.

Some signs of postmortem drying may be misinterpreted as signs of injury. For example, mucous membranes around the lips dry to a dark-red or purple color; these may appear to be bruises or abrasions. "Tache noire" refers to drying of the conjunctiva when the eyelids are left open after death. These markings are red to brown, horizontally situated, and sharply circumscribed and show midbulbar discoloration; tache noire may be mistaken as a trauma injury (Figure 4.2). The dark-red color of a dry scrotum or dried diaper rash may appear to be abrasions.

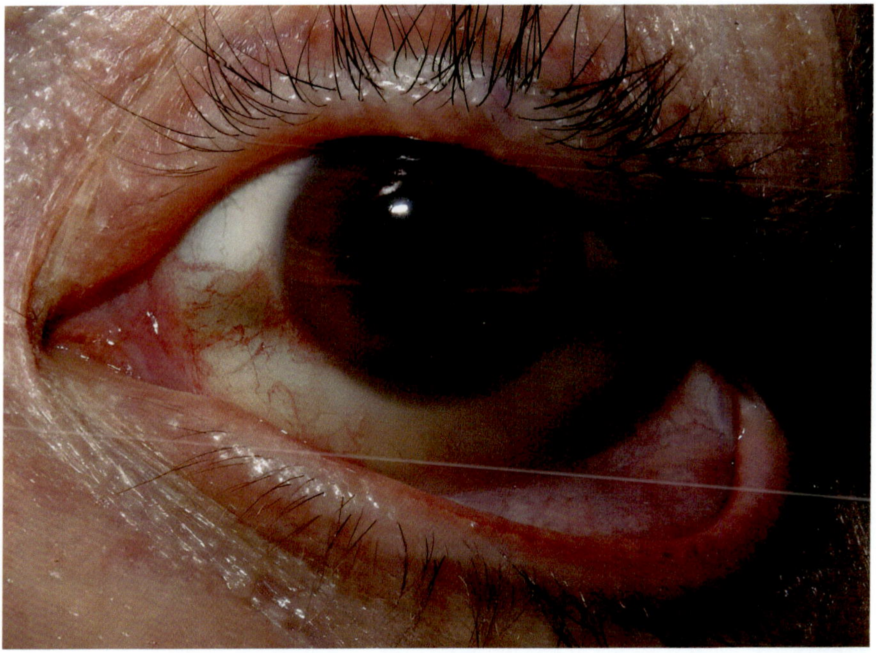

Figure 4.2 Postmortem drying of conjunctivae (tache noire).

Putrefaction

Putrefaction changes are due to bacterial activity after death. Putrefaction changes are temperature dependent. With decomposition changes, there may be a purple to green discoloration of the skin and marbling of the blood vessels. Over time, the internal organs become soft and decompose. The earliest area of green discoloration is often the lower-right abdomen. Purge is a browned decomposition fluid that may drain from the nose and mouth and be misinterpreted as hemorrhage.

Skin slippage, where the skin slides from its attachment, may be misinterpreted as an injury, burn, or blister. The outer layer slips away and the undersurface becomes red with drying and may appear similar to an abrasion (Figure 4.3). In such cases, it is extremely important to bag the hands to preserve fingerprint integrity in transport.

Bloating results from gas produced by microorganisms in the gut. The abdomen, face, scrotum, and eventually the entire body become distended. Bloating gives the false appearance of obesity in an otherwise thin or average-weight person. Bloating also occurs if the body is in water or a damp climate.

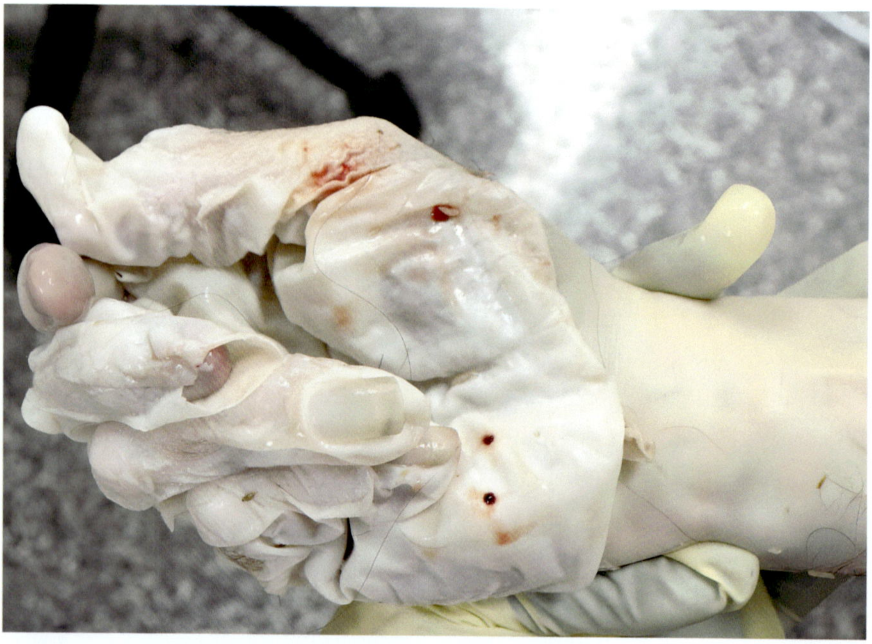

Figure 4.3 Skin slippage of the hands.

Insect and Animal Activity

The age of insect larvae on a body can be used to estimate time of death. Forensic entomologists say that "critters" are the first to arrive at the scene because they seek damp, moist areas such as the nose, mouth, eyes, or areas of injury in which to lay their eggs. An entomologist can judge the time interval based on the stage of insect development from egg to pupa, to larvae, to "critter," or to adult flies. Other insects such as beetles or other animals are often next to arrive at the scene depending on geographic region.

During the immediate postmortem period, ants and roaches may cause damage to the body that mimics injury. Maggot activity may also alter preexisting injuries or create defects in the soft tissue that can be confused as injuries.

Worms, bugs, and insects are collected from around the body and kept alive as well as preserved in alcohol. Later, they are examined by a forensic entomologist. Studies on cocaine overdoses have found that larvae and maggots can be used to register cocaine levels when very little tissue remains.

Animals can affect postmortem conditions both indoors and outdoors. For example, rats may chew on exposed features of a body indoors. Domestic cats and dogs may also feed on a body if there is no other food available (Figure 4.4). In the outdoors, wild animals may skeletonize body remains within 1 week.

Postmortem Injuries

Contusions, lacerations, abrasions, fractures, and burns may be incurred after death. Injuries after death are indistinguishable from those formed shortly before death or at the time of death. With lacerations, tears of the skin caused by blunt force can "bleed" if they are made after death when blood is still in a liquid state in the vessels. Scratches or abrasions, on the other hand, may appear yellow or orange in areas where livor mortis has not developed. Postmortem burns are also indistinguishable from antemortem thermal injuries.

Postmortem Medical, Surgical, and Embalming Artifacts

Cardiopulmonary resuscitation can cause broken ribs and bruises to the chest. Patterned burns on the chest may result from defibrillator paddles. Bruises and abrasions of the face and mouth may result from mouth-to-mouth

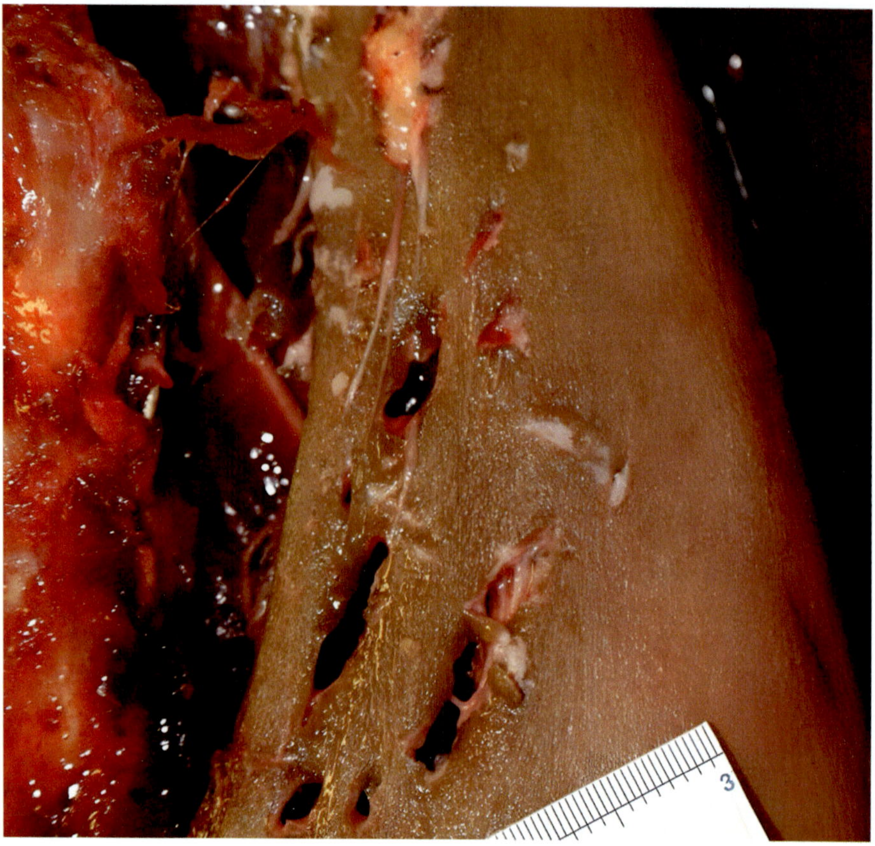

Figure 4.4 Example of animal predation.

resuscitation. Surgical incisions from advanced efforts at resuscitation may mimic stab wounds or other antemortem injuries.

Body preparations for transport or embalming can also result in artifacts. For example, bindings or wrappings used to prepare a body for transport after pronouncement of death may create artifacts that suggest premortem injury. Embalming artifacts left from arterial and trocar embalming can create defects that may be confused with antemortem injuries (Figure 4.5). In addition, cosmetic preparations for funeral viewing mask premortem bruises.

Other Factors Useful in Establishing Time of Death

Time of death is based on many observations before the ME/coroner performs an autopsy. The first people to arrive at the scene must document the condition of the body. As others arrive, documentation may change as the

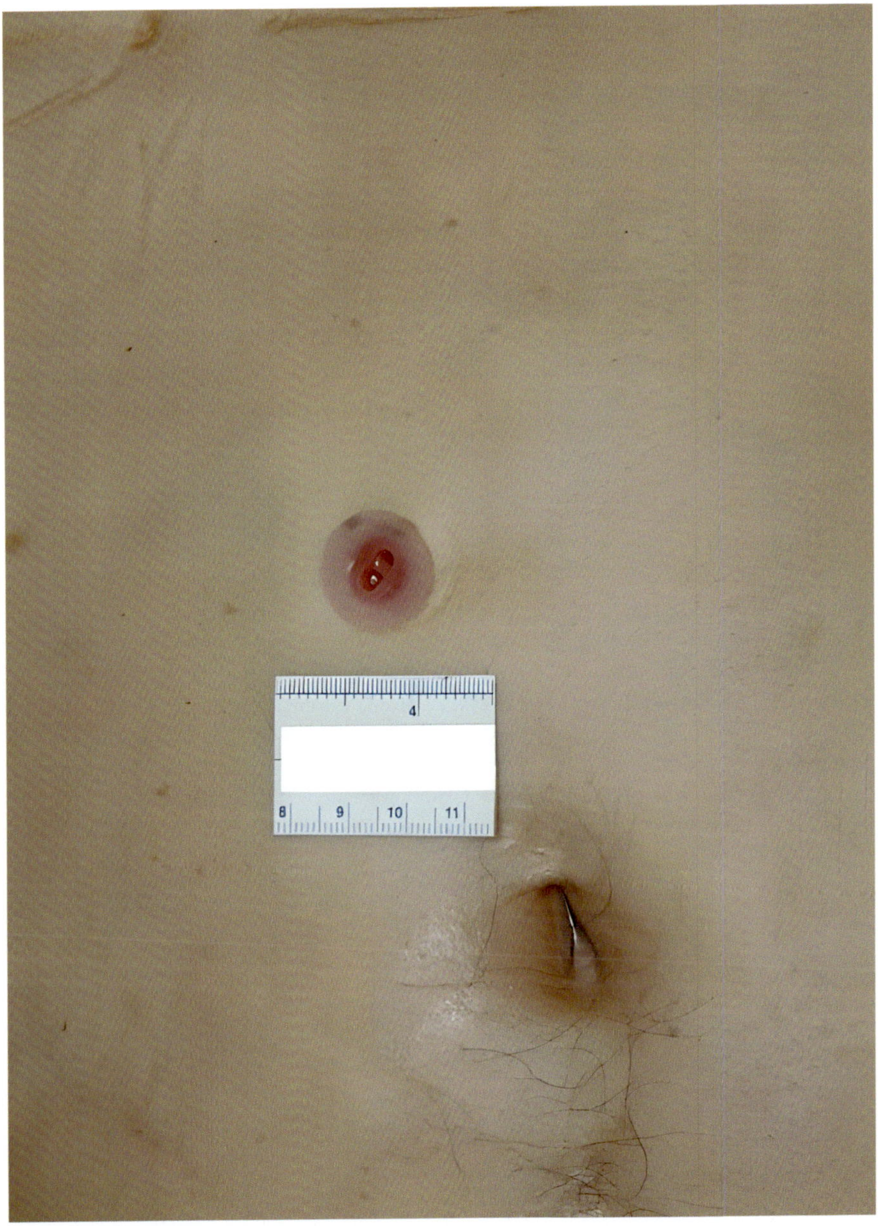

Figure 4.5 Postmortem embalming trocar.

appearance of the body changes over time. Scene investigation and interviews are also useful in establishing time of death. Presence of mold on the body, state of vegetation beneath a body, and chemical changes in body fat can all be used to establish time of death. Occasionally, weather affects the stages of decomposition. For instance, if someone dies outside in October and a snowfall occurs, the body may be well preserved by the cold weather if not found until spring. Patterned animal artifacts are generally localized and show little hemorrhagic reaction to underlying tissue. It is the medicolegal death investigator's role at the scene to document any findings that may help establish an overall timeline of death but not to make presumptive estimates or assumptions based on the findings at the scene or by examination.

Changes in body fluids may be useful in establishing time of death. For example, vitreous electrolytes may be useful to establish time of death during the first 24 hours. Vitreous potassium levels increase linearly, although time of death may vary up to 4 hours. Stomach contents reflect the character of the last meal; food remains undigested for up to 2 hours after eating and may provide useful clues to the time of death and whereabouts of the decedent prior to death.

Bibliography

Clark, S., Ernst, M., Haglund, W., and Jetzen, J. 1996. *Medicolegal Death Investigator: A Systematic Training Program for the Professional Death Investigator*. Big Rapids, MI: Occupational Research and Assessment, Inc.

DiMaio, V.J.M. and Molina, D.K. (2021). *DiMaio's Forensic Pathology* (3rd ed.). Boca Raton, FL: CRC Press, Inc.

Spitz, W. and Fischer, R. 1993. *Medicolegal Investigation of Death: Guidelines for the Application of Pathology to Crime Investigation*. Springfield, IL: Charles C. Thomas Press.

Forensic Pathology

5

MARY H. DUDLEY

OBJECTIVES

Upon completion of this chapter and corresponding reference material, the reader will be able to

- Discuss the role and function of the forensic pathologist in forensic medical investigation
- Describe the forensic pathologist's role in medical quality control
- Describe the purpose of a forensic autopsy
- Explain the general procedure of a forensic autopsy
- Discuss types of information available following an autopsy
- Discuss the role of the forensic pathologist as an expert witness

Introduction

Forensic pathology applies the principles and knowledge of pathology to legal matters. Medical examiners/forensic pathologists have legal jurisdiction to determine the cause and manner of death. Forensic autopsy may be needed to determine the cause of death and extent of internal injuries, and recover evidence. Scene investigation is of paramount importance in any medicolegal inquiry of death to understand the circumstances surrounding death and to help determine the manner of death. As in clinical medicine where a comprehensive medical history provides 50%–75% of the information necessary for a diagnosis, scene investigation provides the forensic pathologist with the majority of information about a particular case. Autopsy and ancillary testing provide the remainder of information to determine the cause and manner of death. The sequence of forensic autopsy includes external examination, internal examination, tissue samples for microscopic examination, and fluid recovery for toxicology. This chapter outlines the role of the forensic pathologist and discusses forensic autopsy as a part of the medicolegal death investigation process.

DOI: 10.4324/9781003538622-6

The Death Scene

Authority and primary responsibility for crime scene investigation remain with law enforcement agencies. However, the medical examiner/coroner has legal authority and responsibility to conduct a medicolegal investigation and to secure the remains of any decedents.

The forensic pathologist and/or designee (medicolegal death investigator) attends the death scene for various purposes. For example, information and evidence from the scene are necessary to

- Estimate the time of death
- Assess and interpret wounds
- Determine the extent of injuries and estimated amount of bleeding at the scene
- Determine the cause and manner of death
- Correlate scene findings with circumstances of death, medical history, and autopsy findings
- Provide clues to distinguish between antemortem and postmortem artifacts
- Reconstruct events thereby assisting law enforcement agencies in formulating questions related to death

Medical Quality Control

The issue of quality assurance/quality control (QA/QC) is a popular management concept of the past two decades. QA/QC is primarily directed toward self-monitoring and self-correcting activities. Risk management of professional activities is important for individuals or agencies to reduce liability and cost. QA/QC committees review standards of care to assess preventability of morbidity and mortality and to improve patient care.

The forensic pathologist plays an active role in medicolegal problems related to expected and unexpected deaths in hospitals and nursing care facilities. The forensic pathologist often collaborates with medical or trauma review teams or acts as a consultant to "in-house" investigators. Injuries sustained while under medical care, such as a fall within a hospital or nursing home or asphyxial injuries from restraints or hospital treatment, are examples of need for a forensic investigation. Assaults on patients or professional staff by other patients or professional staff occur and require confirmation as to cause of death or injury.

Institutional investigations may be conducted when a number of deaths occur by the same methods in the same or similar surroundings. Disconnection of life-support machinery and mass murders by nursing staff are examples of such circumstances.

Other QA/QC settings within the institution may relate to diagnostic or therapeutic procedures and drug-related injuries and/or deaths. Examples include surgical complications, complications from indwelling or temporary catheters, use of medical equipment, blood transfusions, radiation therapy, and anesthesia. Drug side effects, hypersensitivity reactions, over- or under-dosage, and wrongly administered drugs may be the causes for review of circumstances and deaths.

Individual and group practices are common subjects for QA/QC reviews. Malpractice can apply to any professional health-care providers within an agency, but the physician is the most common legal target. Neglect, misdiagnosis, uninformed consent, refusal of treatment, and incorrect, inadequate, or outdated treatment are all types of malpractice.

Medicolegal problems that may involve the forensic pathologist also encompass chronic industrial or agricultural exposure that leads to carcinogenesis and disability. The effects of remote trauma that contribute or do not contribute to death are within the realm of the medicolegal problems that may relate to QA/QC.

Forensic Autopsy

Purpose of Forensic Autopsy

Forensic autopsy is conducted to answer medicolegal questions regarding the cause and manner of death. The primary difference between a forensic autopsy and a hospital autopsy is that a forensic autopsy is more oriented toward the external examination than toward the internal examination and organ systems. Findings are reported to families, juries, and law enforcement personnel in layman terms rather than to physicians in medical terms.

Objectives for Medicolegal Autopsy

The purpose of a forensic autopsy differs from that of a hospital autopsy. The forensic autopsy attempts to accomplish the following:

- Determines the cause, manner, and time of death and recovers, identifies, and preserves evidentiary material
- Provides interpretation and correlation of facts and circumstances related to death
- Provides a factual, objective medical report for law enforcement, prosecution, and defense agencies

- Separates death due to disease from death due to external causes for protection of the innocent
- Identifies unknown remains

External Examination

External examination begins with a head-to-toe examination. This includes notations about eye color, height, weight, hair color, gender, and presence or absence of rigor mortis. Abrasions, contusions, scars, or puncture wounds are carefully documented. Injection marks from drug use can be found almost anywhere on the body, including between the toes. With cocaine overdoses, a purple contusion (bruise) with a whitish center might be found.

The insides of the wrists are examined for the possibility of prior suicide attempts; these are usually seen as linear scars (hesitation marks). Surgical incisions help document prior medical conditions or surgical history. This is particularly helpful if no medical records are available. Photographs can be taken to document any significant findings related to the cause or manner of death. X-rays are taken on all homicides, decomposed bodies, gunshot wound cases, and unidentified bodies. Stab wounds may also require an x-ray to determine if the tip of the blade remains embedded in the body. X-rays are recommended for all child fatalities to identify injury or to detect signs of child abuse such as previous trauma or healing fractures.

Internal Examination

After the initial Y-shaped tissue incision (Figure 5.1) over the chest, the rib cage is removed first (Figures 5.2 and 5.3). Samples for toxicological analysis are collected from heart blood, peripheral blood, body fluids, solid organs, and vitreous fluid as standard procedure. Vitreous fluid is clear and may be used to detect ethyl alcohol or may be used in other biochemistry tests. Samples taken for toxicology also include brain and liver tissue, urine, stomach contents, and bile. Other samples required depend on suspected cause and/or manner of death. Samples are analyzed in the toxicology laboratory.

All internal organs are eviscerated in one block or through organ-by-organ dissection. Block removal, in which the chest and abdominal contents form one continuous block, allows for close examination of the relationships between organs. The proximity of organs is helpful in some instances to follow the path of penetrating injuries. All organs are examined grossly for injury and/or natural disease. Upon removal, all organs are weighed and the weight is recorded.

The small bowel is tied off at the second part of the duodenum. A ligature around the sigmoid colon prevents spillage of contents when the bowel is cut. The large and small intestines are cut away from the major blood vessels and

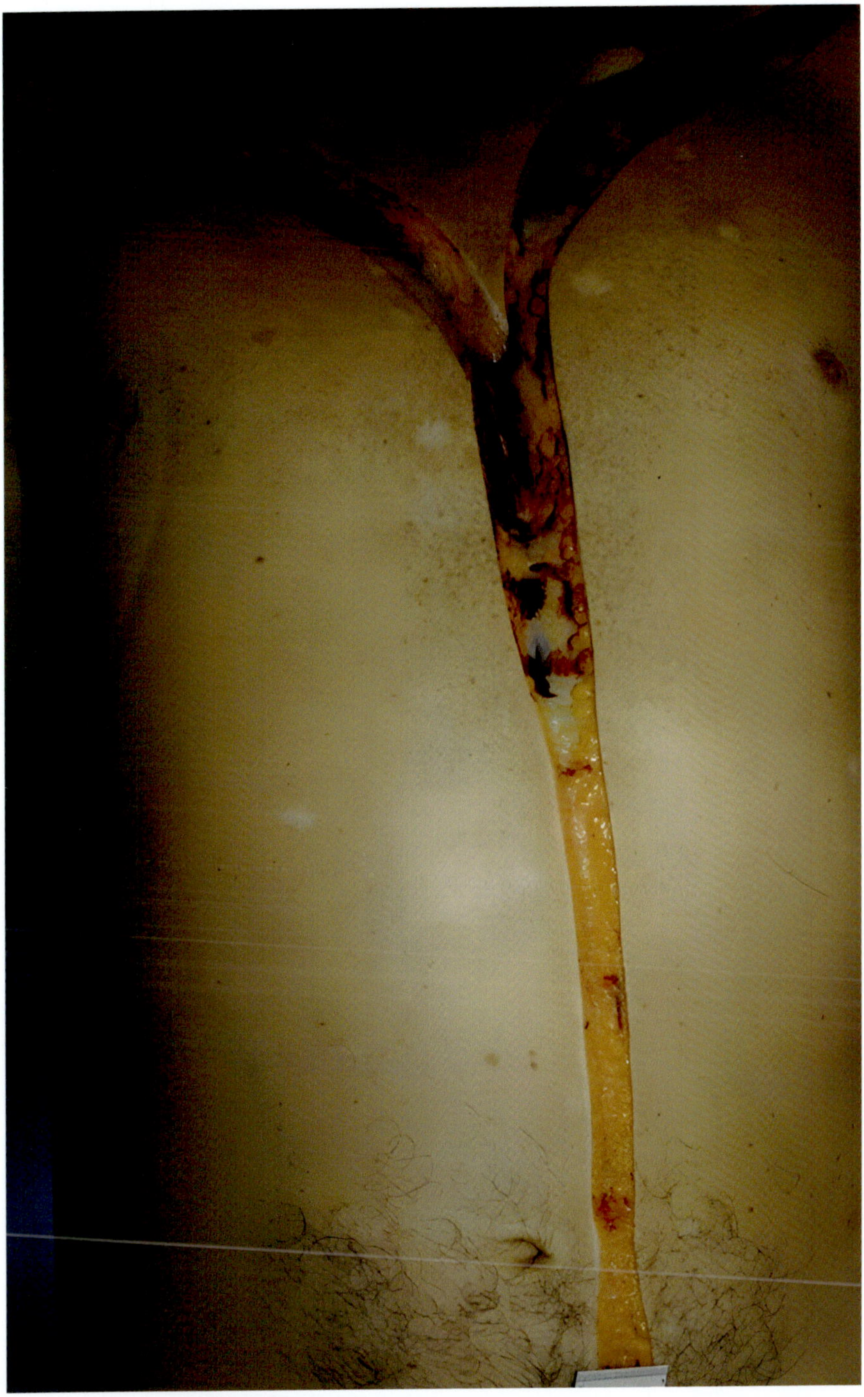

Figure 5.1 Y-shaped incision.

Figure 5.2 Autopsy photograph with chest plate intact.

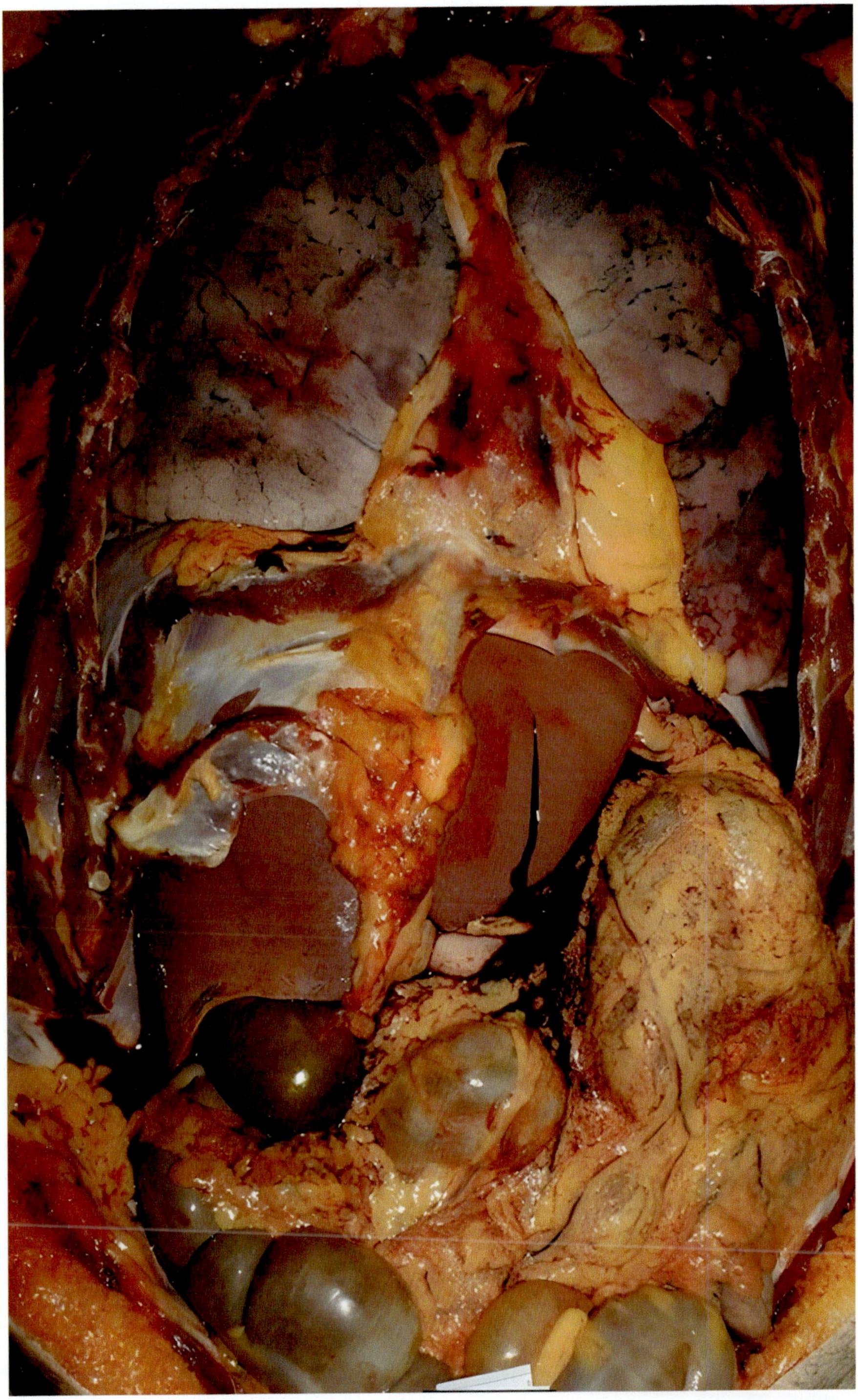

Figure 5.3 Autopsy photograph with chest plate removed, organs in situ.

their attachments at the back of the abdomen. The femoral and carotid arteries may be tied off to assist the funeral directors for embalming purposes.

The rib cage and spinal column can be seen from the base of the brain down through the pelvis after the internal organs are removed. The ribs and vertebrae are examined for fractures, hemorrhage, or hidden injuries.

The heart is examined for natural disease or injury by external and internal inspection. The coronary arteries are serially horizontally sectioned at 5-mm intervals to check for narrowing by atherosclerotic plaque prior to cross-sectioning the heart starting at the apex and ending at the papillary muscles at 1-cm sections. The heart is then opened along the right posterior and anterior septum, left lateral wall, and left anterior septum to inspect the heart chambers and valves. The aorta, vena cava, and branches of the aorta to the kidneys, stomach, and intestines are examined.

The lungs, pulmonary arteries, and bronchi are examined. Black carbon pigment that often marks the surfaces of both lungs in adults is due to smoking, second-hand smoke, or environmental or industrial pollution. The bronchial tree is examined for foreign material such as aspirated food, soot from smoke inhalation, tumors, or pus from pneumonia. The pulmonary arteries may be occluded by emboli (blood clots from leg veins). The lungs normally have a spongy character due to the mixture of air and fluids that is usually present. After death, the back of the lungs becomes darker and heavier as a result of blood pooling if the body had been lying supine.

The adrenal glands lie within fat on either side of the aorta directly above the kidneys. The central medulla of the adrenals produces adrenaline and noradrenaline (epinephrine and norepinephrine), while the outer cortex produces steroids such as cortisone. The kidney filters blood and produces urine that is carried to the bladder through a small tube called the ureter. The kidneys are also padded in fat and encased within a thin capsule; the fat and capsule can be peeled away from a normal kidney surface for further examination.

Just beneath the left hemidiaphragm lies the spleen. The spleen functions as a filter of old red and white blood cells and platelets.

The stomach lies roughly in front of and to the right side of the spleen and drains into the small bowel or duodenum. The stomach contents are collected and saved for analysis. Gastric contents can show partially digested food, drugs, or liquids and are analyzed for toxicology. Sometimes odors such as alcohol can be detected during dissection.

The biliary tract begins with the gallbladder that looks like a green sack attached to the liver. It has a duct that drains into the duodenum through the head of the pancreas. The same duct is shared with the pancreas that lies behind the stomach and produces insulin and digestive enzymes.

The liver appears spongy and dark purple and is one of the largest body organs. The liver functions to help break down fat, carbohydrates, and protein into usable forms. The liver also produces bile to aid digestion. Fatty changes in the liver are most commonly due to alcohol abuse. Liver samples are saved for toxicology.

The pelvic organs include the uterus, ovaries, and fallopian tubes in the female and the prostate gland, testicles, and spermatic cord in the male. Both genders have a bladder and urethra. In the male, the prostate appears as a firm rubbery gland at the base of the bladder.

The head is examined following removal of the thoracic and abdominal organs. A coronal incision is made over the top of the head behind the ears. When the scalp is reflected forward and backward from this central incision, the pathologist examines the internal surfaces of the scalp and surfaces of the skull (Figure 5.4). Examination for subscalpular or subgaleal hemorrhages is completed. The skullcap is removed with a bone saw to reveal the brain. Further examination of the brain includes a view of the brain surface to examine the cerebral hemispheres, including the frontal, temporal, parietal, and occipital lobes. At the posterior and base of the brain, the cerebellum surrounds the brainstem that includes the midbrain, pons, and medulla. The brain receives its blood supply from the vertebral arteries and carotid arteries. The cerebellum and brainstem are dissected from the internal cerebral hemispheres at the midbrain and are serially sectioned and examined.

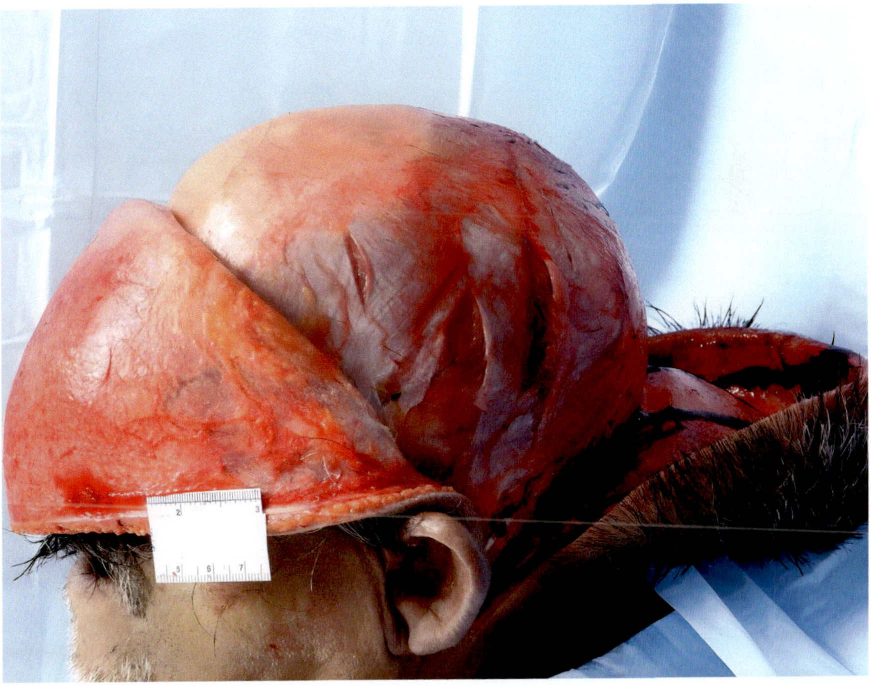

Figure 5.4 Reflection of the scalp to view the periosteum.

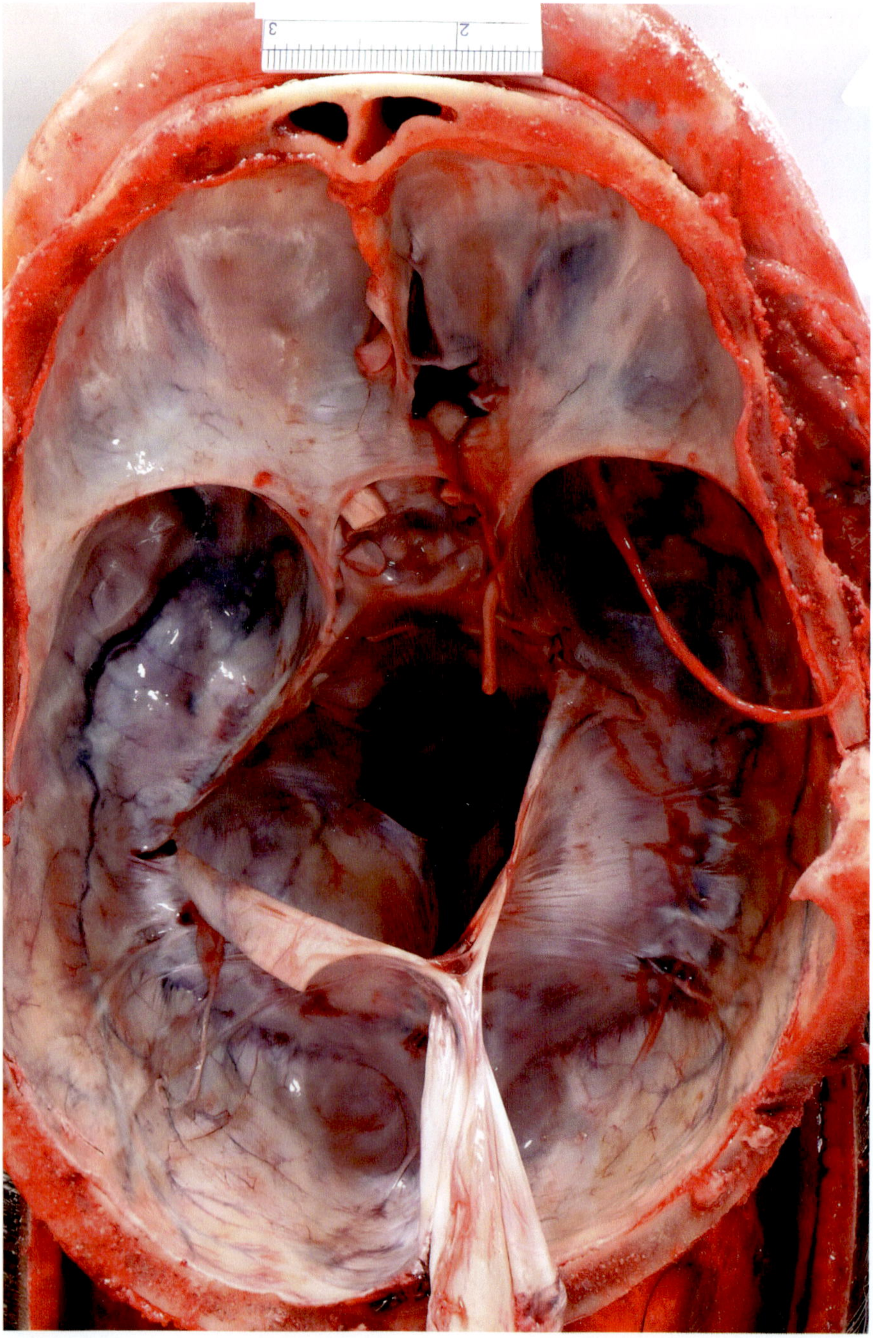

Figure 5.5 Base of skull prior to the removal of the dura.

After examination for epidural or subdural hemorrhages, the dura (skull covering) is removed from the skull (Figure 5.5), and the skull is examined for fractures. The cerebral hemispheres consist of gray matter and white matter that are responsible for higher mental functions. The brain is serially sectioned and examined for tumors, trauma, or other abnormalities. Within the deeper structures of the brain are the lateral ventricles that become narrowed with cerebral edema or brain swelling.

The neck block, including the tongue, trachea, larynx, thyroid gland, hyoid bone, epiglottis, and esophagus, is removed last. Careful layered dissection of the neck strap muscles will demonstrate any possible bruises or fractures that might relate to such actions as strangulation or hanging. The hyoid bone is removed from the thyroid cartilage. The hyoid bone is horseshoe shaped and is examined for fractures. Beneath the hyoid is the epiglottis that closes down over the opening to the airway in the larynx. Beneath the epiglottis are the vocal cords, and posterior to the larynx is the opening to the esophagus. The larynx is opened posteriorly to inspect for a lodged food bolus or any other abnormalities.

With a suspected seizure, the tongue should be examined for injury. The tongue is sectioned to ensure that there are no contusions or lacerations.

Tissue Processing

When dissection is complete, organs are separated and weighed individually. Each organ's weight is recorded. The organs are dissected, and a small tissue sample is put into formaldehyde. These tissue samples are used to make histology slides for examination under a microscope. Sections are also saved for future use. State statutes determine the length of time tissue samples must be saved.

Autopsy Report

The forensic pathologist summarizes the autopsy findings in a report along with body diagrams, which becomes part of the permanent file, along with the scene investigation report and scene photographs. The final report is issued when the toxicology results, microscopic exam, and other studies are completed and a final diagnosis has been reached. The ME/coroner issues a death certificate that states the cause and manner of death. A copy of the autopsy report is part of the permanent case file and may be sent to the investigating office and family upon request. This report, along with contents of the permanent file, can be used in a court of law and lays the foundation for the pathologist as an expert witness (see Appendix E). The death certificate is filed with the State Bureau of Vital Statistics.

Bibliography

Connolly, A., Finkbeiner, W., Ursell, P., and Davis, R. 2015. *Autopsy Pathology: A Manual and Atlas* (3rd ed.). Philadelphia, PA: Elsevier Saunders.

DiMaio, V.J.M. and Molina, D.K. (2021). *DiMaio's Forensic Pathology* (3rd ed.). Boca Raton, FL: CRC Press, Inc.

Kumar, V., Abbas, A., Fausto, N., Robbins, S., and Cotran, R. 2005. *Robbins and Cotran Pathologic Basis of Disease*. Philadelphia, PA: Elsevier Saunders.

Mass Fatality Management 6

MARY H. DUDLEY AND
TOM HENSLEY

OBJECTIVES

Upon completion of this chapter and corresponding reference material, the reader will be able to

- Define three areas of operation for a mass fatality management
- Describe the role of the incident scene investigators
- List the stations of the temporary morgue
- Identify the functions of the team leaders of the morgue stations in collecting information for victim identification
- Discuss the role of personnel at the family assistance center

Introduction

This chapter describes three main areas of operation of mass fatality management, including the incident site/body recovery, morgue operations, and the family assistance center. The forensic pathologist generally oversees morgue operations, and the medicolegal death investigator (MDI) can function at the incident site, the mobile morgue, or the family assistance center as needed. The main points of focus for this chapter include defining a mass fatality incident, the role of the MDI, historical perspectives, and the importance of the federal disaster mortuary recovery team (DMORT).

Mass Fatality Incident

A mass fatality incident is defined as an occurrence of multiple deaths that overwhelms the usual routine capability of an agency. Preplanning and training with community partners are essential goals to prepare for a mass fatality event. It is important to know the resources available at the local, state, and national levels for the three basic activities that follow a disaster, including rescue and treatment of survivors, repair and maintenance of basic services, and the recovery and management of bodies. Many communities have annual

DOI: 10.4324/9781003538622-7

mass casualty exercises involving multiple medical, law enforcement, and fire disciplines.

It is important to plan for the various possible types of disasters that may occur in your area of the country, for example, hurricanes along the coast or tornadoes in the Midwest. However, many different types of disasters may occur in any jurisdiction, including natural, terrorist, accident, biological, man-made, or radiation disasters. It is important not only to have a plan but also to remember that all disasters are unique and, even with preplanning, there will be unexpected events that occur. It is important to have a flexible and adaptable plan in place.

Mass fatality disasters occur every year in some part of the world. The location of the event belongs to that particular local jurisdiction and government. The outcome of how well the disaster was managed is directly related to how well the local jurisdiction has planned and exercised their predeveloped disaster plan. Most jurisdictions do not have funds earmarked for this purpose and therefore rely on state and federal agencies to augment the local jurisdiction's response with personnel, supplies, and equipment.

Role of the MDI in Mass Fatality

The medicolegal death investigator (MDI) plays a vital role in mass fatality preparedness and management. The MDI may be called upon at the local, state, and federal levels to assist with mass fatality management, training exercises, and deployment. The components of a daily death investigation the MDI conducts are the same when a mass fatality incident occurs. The common components include responding to death scenes, gathering information about the body condition, position and type of environment, photographing/documenting the scene and body, looking for information at the scene that will assist in making positive identifications, finding next of kin and developing medical history, identifying, documenting, and packaging evidence, and taking custody of the body. The MDI may be utilized in all areas of the mass fatality incident due to their versatility. They may function as the recovery director and/or team leaders to direct the activities of others or function as support staff for any part of the mission.

Historical Perspective

In the past 32 years, there have many mass fatality disasters due to floods, airline crashes, terrorist attacks, hurricanes, and tornados. On July 12, 1993, the Missouri River flooded and disinterred 793 caskets at the Hardin Cemetery in Hardin, Missouri. On August 6, 1997, Korean Airline Flight 801 crashed into Nimitz Hill in Guam, claiming the lives of 228 passengers. On September 11, 2001, the United States experienced a terrorist attack in New York, the Pentagon in Arlington County, Virginia, and Shanksville, Pennsylvania. Terrorists hijacked four commercial airplanes with people on board. All four airplanes crashed, claiming the lives of 2,996 people on the planes and on the ground. On November 12, 2001, during the mass fatality operation of the terrorist attack, American Airline flight 587 crashed in Queens, New York City, New York. The crash claimed the lives of 260 people on board. On August 26, 2005, Hurricane Katrina and later Hurricane Rita came to shore on the Gulf coast of the United States affecting New Orleans, Louisiana, Gulfport, Mississippi, and surrounding parishes and counties. The hurricanes caused widespread destruction and numerous fatalities along the Gulf coast as well as disinterring numerous caskets and crypts. There were a total of 1,833 fatalities and 614 disinterred caskets and crypts. On May 22, 2011, a tornado struck the southwest city of Joplin, Missouri, claiming the lives of 158 people. These types of large-scale disasters can easily overwhelm a local jurisdiction's ability to process fatalities in a timely manner, often requiring a need for federal assistance (Figure 6.1).

HISTORICAL PERSPECTIVE

DATE	LOCATION	FATALITIES
July 12, 1993	Hardin Cemetery Disaster	793 Caskets *2
August 6, 1997	Korean Airline KAL #801	228 Fatalities *3
September 11, 2001	Terrorist Attack- New York City Pentagon-Arlington County, VA. Shanksville, PA	2996 Fatalities *4
November 12, 2001	American Airlines Flight 587 Crash	260 on board Fatalities *5
August 26, 2005	Hurricane Katrina/Rita Louisiana, Mississippi	1833 Fatalities *6 614 Caskets (NDMS 9-19-06)
May 22, 2011	Joplin, Missouri Tornado	158 Fatalities *7

Figure 6.1 Historical perspective.

DMORT Federal Response Team

The Disaster Mortuary Operational Response Team (DMORT) is a volunteer team of medical, forensic personnel and equipment operators, usually from the same geographic region. The United States is divided into 10 regional teams. The teams were formed under the guidance of the federal National Disaster Medical System (NDMS). All the volunteers have specific training/skills in victim identification, mortuary services, forensic pathology, anthropology methods, and light and heavy equipment operations. The DMORT members are activated through the federal government when requested by local and state officials. The team works under the guidance of local authorities by providing technical assistance and personnel to recover and identify the remains of disaster victims. DMORT teams 1, 2, and 3 are located on the northeast portion of the United States. DMORT team 4 is located in the southeast portion of the US. DMORT team 5 is located in the far north Great Lakes area. DMORT team 6 is in the southern Midwest, while DMORT team 7 is in the Midwest. DMORT team 8 is in the upper Midwest plains area, while DMORT teams 9 and 10 are close to or along the West Coast (Figure 6.2).

Initial Evaluation

The initial efforts immediately after the event are focused on stabilizing the event; preventing further destruction and injury; restoring law and order; locating, triaging, and treating survivors; establishing basic utilities, and taking care of survivors' needs. After the "rescue" phase of the injured and trapped survivors, attention to "recovery" of mass fatalities will be implemented. Until then, the main focus is the rescue and treatment of the live victims by the disaster medical assistance team (DMAT).

The rescue portion of the mass fatality event usually takes less time when compared to the recovery of dead bodies. The length of time it takes to rescue the casualties and recover the bodies is dependent on numerous factors. Some of the factors include the number of casualties and fatalities, the type of scene, the challenges and obstacles for the first responders and recovery teams that also include the weather and environmental conditions, the availability of equipment, and supplies needed to accomplish the mission.

Rescuing, delivering the injured to the established medical system, and treating the injuries may last from a few hours to a few days. On the other hand, recovering and positively identifying the bodies may take from a few days to many months. To take care of the injured, the medical system already has in place facilities (hospitals) and staff to treat the injured. In contrast, the management of large number of fatalities requires locating specific areas appropriate for the operation.

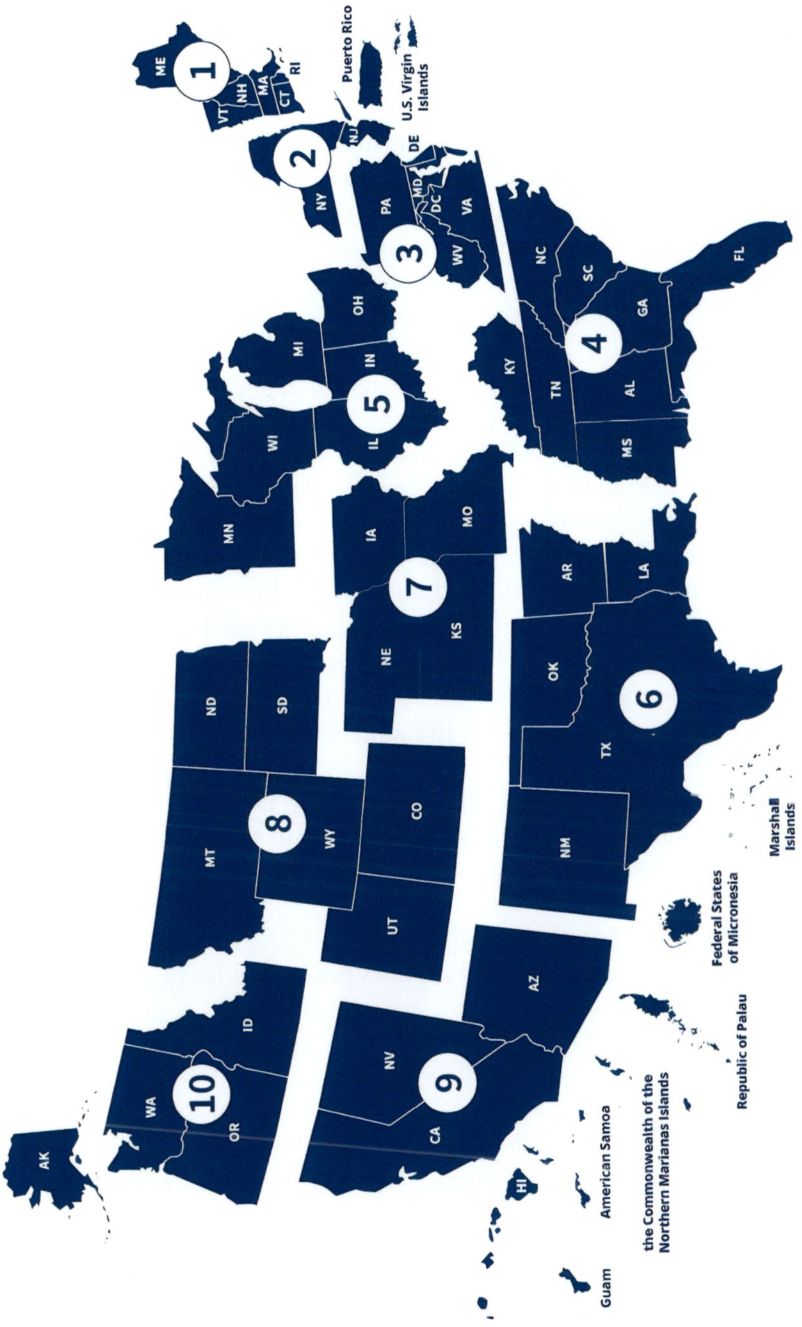

Figure 6.2 Administration for Strategic Preparedness and Response (ASPR) map of preparedness divisions.

Key points in the initial evaluation include the following:

1. An evaluation team consisting of the medical examiner, the chief investigator, and one on-duty investigator will be equipped with cellphones. The following will be evaluated:
   a. Number of fatalities involved
   b. Condition of the bodies (e.g., burned, dismembered)
   c. Difficulty anticipated in the recovery of the bodies
   d. The personnel and equipment required for the operation (e.g., fire search and rescue, heavy equipment)
   e. The accessibility of the scene to transport vehicles and the difficulties that may be encountered in transporting bodies from the scene
   f. The presence of chemical, radiological, biological, or other environmental hazards
2. Identify the personnel possibly needed to staff the morgue for identification, body examination, evidence collection, and other procedures.
3. Anticipate the type of facility that would be most useful for a family assistance center (FAC). If the victims live in the local area, their families may also be local, and housing would not be a critical issue. If the victims are predominately not local, the need for housing the families of victims would have to be anticipated.
4. If the incident is a mass fatality, contact the DMORT regional coordinator or the national DMORT organization at 800-USA-NMDS (800-872-6367):
   a. The disaster mortuary unit provided by DMORT will send an evaluation team to the location and aid in the assessment. They can activate the evaluation team and have experienced, reliable individuals on site within 8–12 hours.
   b. The disaster portable morgue units (DPMUs) are caches of highly specialized equipment and supplies pre-staged for deployment to a disaster site.

Recovery Site

No two recovery sites will be the same. Just as each disaster is unique to itself, the recovery site is also unique to itself. Depending on the incident, there may be one recovery site such as an airline crash or numerous recovery sites such as Hurricane Katrina/Rita. If the disaster is isolated to one location, there is usually one recovery site. If the disaster is widespread like the United States experienced with Hurricane Katrina/Rita, there are more than one recovery site.

There may be numerous recovery sites where as few as one decedent is located to recover or numerous recovery site/s where two or more bodies are found. As examples, due to the widespread destruction that Hurricane Katrina/Rita caused, there were numerous recovery sites where one body was recovered. There were other recovery sites such as hospitals and nursing homes in Louisiana where numerous bodies were recovered. During the 9-11 terrorist attack (the Twin Towers at the World Trade Center in New York, Shanksville, PA, farm field and The Pentagon in Arlington County, Virginia); there were three mass fatality sites and three different recovery sites. Because each incident was in a confined area where all the bodies were located, the search and rescue was confined to those areas. Numerous bodies were recovered from each of those locations. Although each site is different, there are tasks at the recovery site that need to be performed each time in order to recover the bodies in an orderly, professional manner. Each recovery site should be managed as a crime scene due to the uncertainty of the circumstances of the event at the initial onset of the disaster. Management of the recovery site as a crime scene will ensure appropriate steps have been taken to document the scene, the body, and the items on, in, or near the body as it may later be learned that evidence was discovered at the scene. The evidence appropriately collected will prove to be valuable, if the event is determined to be a crime. Locating, photographing, collecting evidence, personal effects, and other items will be important and will aid in identifying the decedent. During the planning of the mass fatality response plan, the planning must not be so restrictive that the recovery response is limited to one particular incident. The plan must address the recovery of bodies for all types of recovery sites for mass fatalities. Each recovery site will present its own challenges and unique circumstances.

Initially, at the recovery site, a walk-through assessment is conducted by the local coroner/medical examiner, MDIs, and other officials to estimate the number of total fatalities and any special equipment needed to manage the recovery of the bodies. The MDI will be useful for the walk-through assessment in order to help identify challenges and special equipment needed in order to recover the fatalities. A second walk-through may occur if outside mass fatality staff responds to and assess the scene to provide guidance, recommendations, and assistance.

A recovery director (RD) will be chosen by the coroner/medical examiner (ME) or command staff before mass fatality workers are dispatched to the recovery site. After arriving at the recovery site, the RD will meet with and organize the recovery staff. The RD duties include the following:

1. Locate a staging/evacuation area.
2. Walk through the recovery site with others to estimate the number of dead, special equipment needed, and how many refrigerated trailers will be needed.
3. Evaluate the extent of the recovery site.

4. Develop a map grid based on initial walk-through in order to perform a search for remains.
5. Order more supplies if the amount that was initially brought to the recovery site is inadequate.
6. Assign teams and responsibilities.
7. Coordinate and direct recovery team and other personnel.

The organization of the recovery site by the RD includes assigning members to recover teams such as a team leader, scribe, team members, transport personnel, and additional staff as needed.

The number of recovery teams assigned will depend upon the available personnel, the number of estimated dead, and the extent of the recovery site. Recovery teams are further assigned roles within each team. After the RD has performed his/her walk-through assessment and selected staging/evacuation area, individual recovery teams will be assigned by the RD. Each team will have an assigned grid area to recover and assigned roles. The MDI is versatile enough to fulfill any position needed at the recovery site. He/she may function as an RD, team leader, or team member.

Each mass fatality incident brings its own set of unique challenges that may require supplies and numerous pieces of special equipment and operators to run the equipment. The difficulty of the recovery may involve the use of heavy equipment, water vehicles, extrication tools, tow trucks, forklifts, pneumatic lifting devices, breathing apparatus, and other equipment.

When managing a recovery site, it must be an organized effort. The mismanagement of the recovery operation will lead to confusion and the potential for errors as the decedent is processed through the system. During the recovery site operation, the concept of the operation is appointing recovery teams and designating a staging area for collection, loading, and transporting.

The RD will maintain communications with the command staff, issues team packets with recovery forms used, collect recovery site team forms at the completion of recovery team's work, and maintain logs of assigned recovery site team members. The RD maintains transport logs, maintains trailer manifests if refrigerated trailers are used, and provides direction to transport personnel. The team leader will direct the activities of team members and activities including documenting and photographing fatalities at the scene, collecting evidence and personal effects, and transporting bodies to the temporary morgue site.

Key points in body recovery are as follows:

1. Select personnel and equipment for scene investigation and body removal:
    a. Communications—Telephones (hard line and cellular), fax machines, etc.

   b. Body bags— Resources include DMORT, airport, state funeral director's association
   c. Refrigerated trucks—Trucks at the scene and morgue
   d. Transportation—For personnel (e.g., cars and vans)
   e. Security—For scene, examination center, and FAC
   f. Identification—ID badges for all personnel
2. Select a temporary morgue site: In the event that a disaster occurs, the local county medical examiner facility may not be suitable for disaster operations. This facility will conduct day-to-day business as usual without interruption. Alternate sites for disaster operations for the temporary morgue may be identified at the time of a disaster.
3. Select a location for a FAC: The location of the FAC will depend upon the location of the incident. The center will be selected at the time of the disaster.
4. Scene investigation and body recovery
   a. Equipment and supplies—Someone in charge of equipment and supplies
   b. Protective clothing—Gloves, boots, coats, hard hats, rain suits, etc.
   c. Body bags—A good, heavy bag with six handles and c-zipper
   d. Refrigerated trucks—Metal walls and floor
   e. Transportation—For personnel
   f. Transportation for bodies—Funeral homes, contract service, etc.
   g. Tents and trucks—For storage of supplies and equipment
   h. Paint—Contrasting color for numbering body bags
   i. Flags—Stakes for marking location of body, body parts, etc.
   j. Plastic toe tags/bands—Tags with Sharpie permanent ink pens to number them
   k. Biohazard bags and boxes—For safe disposal of biohazard debris
   l. Documentation—Document body location, body parts, and personal effects
   m. Food—Have someone in charge of food services for workers
   n. Numbering—All numbers will be assigned at the scene. Use simple numbers (i.e., 1, 2, 3, …). Body numbers should be 1, 2, 3, …. Body part numbers should be P1, P2, P3, …. Personal effect numbers should be E1, E2, E3, … *Note*: Write the number on the body bag 12 inches high with white paint (if using black body bags). Place plastic toe tag on bag and body.
   o. Worker safety—Ensure that provisions are in place for the health and safety of the scene workers.
5. Scene body recovery teams and other personnel include:
   a. RD to coordinate and direct recovery teams
   b. Team leader—Preferably someone knowledgeable about human remains (e.g., pathologist, anthropologist, medical examiner)

   c. Assistant to team leader—Will assist the team leader and photographer as needed
   d. Scribe—Documentation
   e. Runner
   f. Other personnel—Sufficient number of personnel to move bodies out of the scene to the body staging area
6. Evacuation area: Transfer of the bodies/remains from the disaster site to the temporary morgue site. In natural disasters such as tornadoes, floods, etc., recovery teams and evacuation teams may have to be the same. Team members include
   a. One evacuation director
   b. Two transport personnel
   c. One scribe
   d. Staging area assistants (as needed)
   e. Clerks (as needed)

Morgue Operations

The temporary morgue will be used to process the fatalities in order to establish positive identifications. Ideally, this response location should be 12,000–15,000 square feet and have access to utilities. The objective of the morgue operation is to process bodies or sets of remains through a series of designated stations in order to identify the victims, collect postmortem data, and preserve and secure the bodies and personal effects until released for final disposition. The temporary morgue includes 10 stations of operation.

Delivering a disaster portable morgue unit (DPMU) to the site, (as provided by the federal government as part of DMORT), unloading and setting up the temporary morgue to be operational may take up to 1–3 days. Organizing the temporary morgue site also requires planning space for the refrigerated trailers that will be utilized to store the recovered fatalities.

The following outlines important points in consideration of the setup of the temporary morgue:

1. Logistics:
   a. Assemble personnel and equipment, assemble leaders in charge of supplies, equipment, and tracking personnel including the hours worked each day.
      i. Security—ID badges
      ii. Refrigerated trucks—Ramps into trucks
      iii. Protective clothing—Gloves, scrubs, shoe covers, masks, coveralls, hats, etc.
      iv. Communications—Telephones, cellphones, fax machines, P.A. systems

   v. Computers—Programs, leader and team for data processing
   vi. Records— Leader and team to coordinate postmortem and antemortem data
   vii. Office equipment—Copiers, typewriters, fax machine, computers, etc.
   viii. Receiving—The person in charge will document a log-in book, by date and time received, the person receiving the body, and the person delivering the body. The person in charge of the bodies must know the location and final disposition of bodies at all times.
   ix. Workers—To move bodies, perform lifting, and other tasks
   x. Numbering of bodies—The same numbers are used as marked on the body bag and used on the scene; this number should be used throughout the entire process.
   xi. Log books—Three: one for bodies, one for parts, one for effects
   xii. Case file—Initiated with body number. File must stay with body during entire processing. All forms and paperwork used should be available at each station. The case number should be placed on each form as it is used.
   xiii. Body trackers—Personnel to escort body and all paperwork from station to station.
   xiv. Station processing system—The stations and their order may change with the type of incident
   xv. Worker safety—Ensure that provisions are in place for the health of the team members
   xvi. Critical incident stress debriefing personnel—Will monitor workers' mental health at the morgue site and other locations as needed. Individuals skilled in massage therapy may also be useful

2. Overview: The temporary morgue facility will process all body bags delivered from the disaster site in station-by-station fashion. Data gathered from the examinations will be compiled and entered into a network computer system by clerical staff at the temporary morgue. The remains and other items will be examined in an organized approach by qualified professionals in an attempt to identify remains and to document findings for the purposes of the disaster investigation.
3. Mobile morgue floor plan (Figure 6.3):
   a. Admitting: This is the first station located inside the temporary morgue. At this station, morgue personnel will assign a body tracker to the decedent. The admitting station leader can be MDI or assign MDI trackers to each body and will issue a packet of forms to be completed as the body moves through each morgue

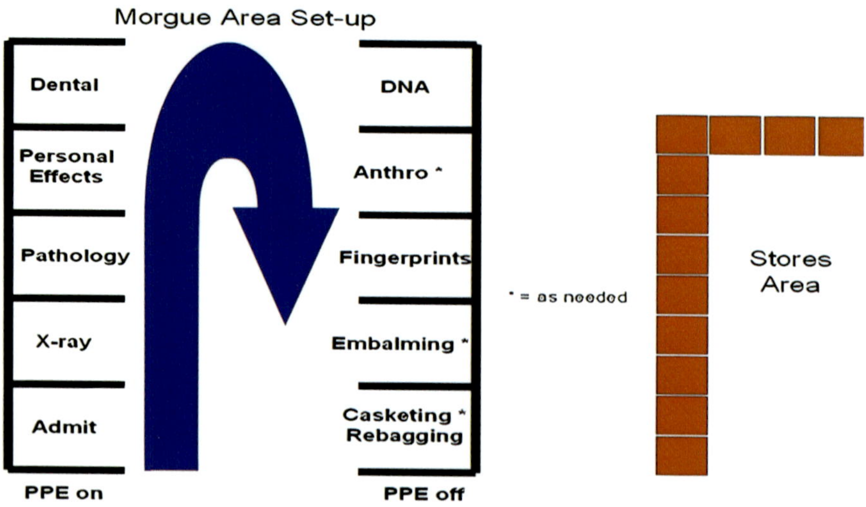

Figure 6.3 Flow of bodies through morgue for processing postmortem examination.

station. The body tracker's responsibility is to accompany the decedent to all the stations at the morgue. The body tracker will stay with the body until each station has completed its examination. The body tracker will collect all paperwork completed at each station concerning the decedent, and after the decedent has been through all stations, the decedent will be taken to the exit and placed into a clean body bag. The paperwork for that decedent will be given back to the admitting station and ultimately taken to the resource center of operations.

b. Radiography: The second station of the morgue will be radiography. The purpose of this station is to X-ray the bodies/remains to assist in identification of the victim through comparison between antemortem and postmortem X-ray, for example, dental restoration, medical prosthesis, or skeletal variances, and to identify foreign objects or evidence. After admitting, the body tracker will take the decedent to the X-ray station at which time a full body X-ray will be done. The body bag will remain closed during this time to ensure that everything in the body bag has been X-rayed prior to being examined. If, after examination, additional X-rays are requested, the body tracker will accompany the decedent back to the X-ray station for additional X-rays.
c. Assessment/pathology/photography: The third station will be assessment. At this station, the decedent will be photographed and undressed, and a complete body examination will be completed.

All scars, marks, tattoos, and distinguishing features will be noted. If any implants are located, such as pacemakers, surgical pins, bone replacements, or breast implants, they can be removed by the pathologist and used for identification. The MDI can assist the pathologist by undressing the body, photographing the body, and helping to identify features and significant injuries.

d. Personal effects: The fourth station will be personal effects. This station will be given all personal effects taken from the decedent during assessment. The MDI can assist by cleaning, photographing, documenting, and packaging personal effects. All effects will be photographed, logged, and packaged. Jewelry, watches, photo identification, billfold, paperwork, U.S. currency, and clothing will be photographed with the number that has been assigned to the decedent. A handwritten log will be completed indicating what was taken off the decedent. The effects will then be packaged and placed with the decedent prior to being taken to the next station for examination. The body tracker will be responsible for keeping the effects with the decedent. If U.S. currency is located on the decedent, the morgue supervisor will be notified, and it will be up to the supervisor whether the currency will be secured in a location other than with the decedent.
e. Odontology: The fifth station will be forensic dentistry. A complete dental workup examination will be completed by the forensic dentist. After the workup examination has been completed, the forensic dentist will compare antemortem and postmortem x-rays and records for possible identification. The MDI assists the dentist with positioning the body for dental exam, X-rays, and other tasks as requested.
f. Fingerprinting: The sixth station will be fingerprinting. At this station, personnel will make every effort to recover fingerprints from the decedent. The MDI routinely collects fingerprints and/or impressions to establish positive ID. Once fingerprints have been obtained, they will be assigned the decedent's case number and will be given to the appropriate agency for comparison and possible identification of the decedent.
g. DNA: The seventh station will be for the recovery of DNA from the decedent. DNA personnel will recover a sample of buccal swabs, blood, bone, or muscle from the decedent. The sample will be identified by the decedent's case number and stored. The chief medical examiner will determine where the samples will be sent and analyzed for identification.
h. Anthropology: The eighth station will be for anthropology examination. If needed, a forensic anthropologist will complete a forensic

examination of the decedent to determine the race, stature, sex, and age of the decedent.

i. Exit/Re-bagging: The ninth station will be for re-bagging and exiting of the decedent. When the decedent has been through all identification stations of the morgue, the decedent will be placed in a clean body bag. The body tracker will make sure that a tag is placed on the decedent and the body bag indicating the decedent's case number. The body tracker will then return all paperwork gathered from the examinations from the other stations and give the paperwork back to the personnel in admitting. The decedent will then be placed into a refrigerated truck until released to the family for final disposition. All paperwork for the decedent will be taken to the resource center and used for identification.
j. Embalming/casketing: An additional station may be required for embalming or casketing depending on the conditions of the decedent or other extenuating circumstances. If needed, mortuary staff may be required for this process, including any transportation off-site.

Family Assistance Center

FAC will be used to house and interview the next of kin to collect antemortem information about the deceased (Figure 6.4). A representative of the

Figure 6.4 Example family assistance center setup.

medical examiner's office needs to be in charge during the initial setup of the FAC. Personnel from the National Transportation and Safety Board (NTSB) organizes the center and coordinates workers as needed in the event of a transportation disaster. Other personnel may be recruited from the local funeral director's association. The FAC is a multiagency organization and cannot be handled by the medical examiner alone:

1. Site selection—It is extremely important that the site selected be functional for the incident that you are taking care of (e.g., if the families are coming from out of town, the site may be a hotel or motel). If it is a local incident and the families are local, then housing would not be a consideration and churches, business offices, and such should be considered. The location should not be too close to the actual scene and it should be easily accessible by families. Parking should be a consideration, depending on the number of families expected. Security for the parking lot and the outside, as well as the inside, of the FAC is the number one priority.
2. ME/coroner-general administration including antemortem records, postmortem records, family information, and death notification/certification.
3. American Red Cross/Salvation Army—Family support, transportation, housing, supplies, equipment, volunteer coordination.
4. Security—Parking, checkpoints, family escorts.
5. Food services—For families and staff.
6. Communications—Telephones and cellphones for workers.
7. Mental health—Family support, staff support, assisting with death notification.
8. Medical—Family care, staff care, assisting with death notification.
9. Religious support—Family support, staff support, assisting with death notification.
10. Site support—Custodial, site maintenance.

By law, the coroner/medical examiner has jurisdiction over fatalities in a mass disaster. The MDI daily tasks require the same skills and knowledge needed in managing a mass fatality event. This makes the MDI a valuable asset in any situation to accomplish or direct the activities of others to accomplish the mission. Everything from assessment of the scene to working in the morgue are all normal MDI daily activities. When managing the deaths from a mass fatality event, the responsibility is on the local ME/coroner who may need support from outside agencies to assist in managing the event.

The ME/C is responsible for several different areas during a mass fatality event, including the initial site or sites of the disaster, the temporary morgue, the Emergency Operations Center (EOC), the FAC, stress management of team members (refer to Appendix D), and the day-to-day operation of the ME/C's office. In a mass fatality incident, the ME/C is faced with a host of complex and time-sensitive responsibilities. These include identifying victims, collecting property and evidence, determining cause and manner of death, issuing death certificates, and returning bodies to their families. Both the National Association of Medical Examiners (NAME) accreditation standards and the Federal Emergency Support Function (ESF-8) require a written mass fatality plan. Preplanning and training with community partners are essential goals to adequately prepare for a mass fatality event.

Bibliography

Administration for Strategic Preparedness and Response- DMORT. Accessed November 2025. https://aspr.hhs.gov/NDMS/Pages/dmort.aspx

Administration for Strategic Preparedness and Response- Reginal Emergency Coordinators. Accessed November 2025. https://aspr.hhs.gov/REC/Pages/default.aspx

Dudley, M.H. 2013. *Mass Fatality Management Concise Field Guide*. Boca Raton, FL: CRC Press.

Hensley, T. and Dudley M.H. 2015. The role of the Medicolegal Death Investigator in a Mass Fatality. *National Association of Medical Examiners (NAME) Annual Meeting*, Charlotte, NC.

Injury Recognition II

Forensic Radiology

7

MARY H. DUDLEY

OBJECTIVES

Upon completion of this chapter and corresponding reference material, the reader will be able to

- Describe the role of the medicolegal death investigator in obtaining medical records, dental X-rays, and antemortem imaging to assist in the identification of decedents
- List five applications for forensic radiology to assist the forensic pathologist prior to the autopsy
- Describe the process of comparing antemortem to postmortem X-rays
- Discuss the uses for forensic radiology in blunt and sharp force injury and gunshot wound cases
- Describe how forensic radiology can assist in identifying injuries in child abuse and elder abuse cases
- Understand the importance of employee safety during in-house radiology

Introduction

Forensic radiology is essential to the practice of forensic pathology and is used as a diagnostic tool to accompany the forensic autopsy to recognize fractures, locate projectiles and natural disease. The medicolegal death investigator (MDI) plays a valuable role in obtaining medical records, dental records, and antemortem imaging to aid or assist in identification. This chapter details the value of forensic radiology for blunt and sharp force injuries, gunshot wounds, child and elder abuse cases, and identification.

Purpose of Forensic Radiology

Historically, radiology was provided on plain film by contracting hospital radiology services, whereas in today's modern medical examiner's offices, the autopsy suite contains in-house digital radiology equipment for plain film

DOI: 10.4324/9781003538622-9

and dental X-rays performed by trained forensic technician staff. Recently, larger jurisdictions also provide in-house postmortem computed tomography services, which have advanced the capabilities of identification and injury detection. Forensic radiology is used for identification in cases where the decedent cannot be visually identified due to facial trauma, decomposition changes, skeletal remains, fire, or in mass fatalities. Postmortem X-ray comparison can match available antemortem X-rays to postmortem autopsy X-rays to make a positive identification of an unidentified body. Other applications for forensic radiology include blunt trauma, stab wounds, gunshot wounds (GSW), child abuse, elder abuse, airplane crashes, and explosions. X-ray studies of the decedent are frequently necessary to determine the cause, manner, and mechanism of death.

Identification

Identification is possibly the most important forensic use of radiography. Scientific positive identification is needed for criminal cases, visually unidentified bodies, and to identify victims of a mass disaster, such as an airplane crash. General skeletal classification can be made into species, sex, age, race, and stature. Much of this is determined anatomically and dentally, but age determination is especially aided by radiology. In fetuses, infants, and young adults, age can be determined with great accuracy from knowledge of the appearance of ossification centers and epiphyseal fusion, as well as the development of two sets of dentition. Later in life, aging is more difficult, but work on tooth root rarefaction and remodeling for cancellous bone in the humerus, ribs, and pelvis has proven useful. Specific positive identification is made possible through a comparison of a variety of anatomical and artifactual structures by a study of antemortem and postmortem films. Rib patterns, teeth, frontal sinuses, skull parameters, injury, surgical metal appliances, and a range of congenital and acquired abnormalities are of great value but depend on a short list of potential subjects and also on the availability of antemortem films, usually from clinical medical records.

One means of positive identification is through dental X-ray comparison based on teeth characteristics, root structure, and restorations (Figure 7.1). Standard X-ray comparison can also match characteristic features, such as frontal sinus detail, as no two people, not even identical twins, have the same sinus configuration. As the sinuses are usually preserved, even in fire deaths and plane crashes, skull films can prove an absolute identification. X-ray comparison of spinal osteophytes or old healed fractures may also show positive identification. X-rays are helpful for comparison of surgical intervention, such as metal suture similarities, metal prosthesis, and devices, such as hip replacement (Figure 7.2), metal rods, or pacemakers (Figures 7.3 and 7.4).

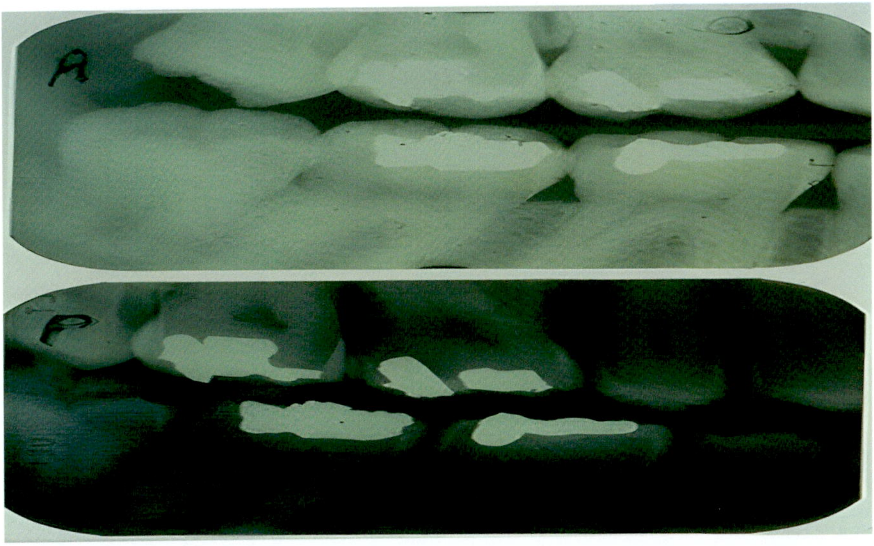

Figure 7.1 Comparison between dental X-ray postmortem to antemortem.

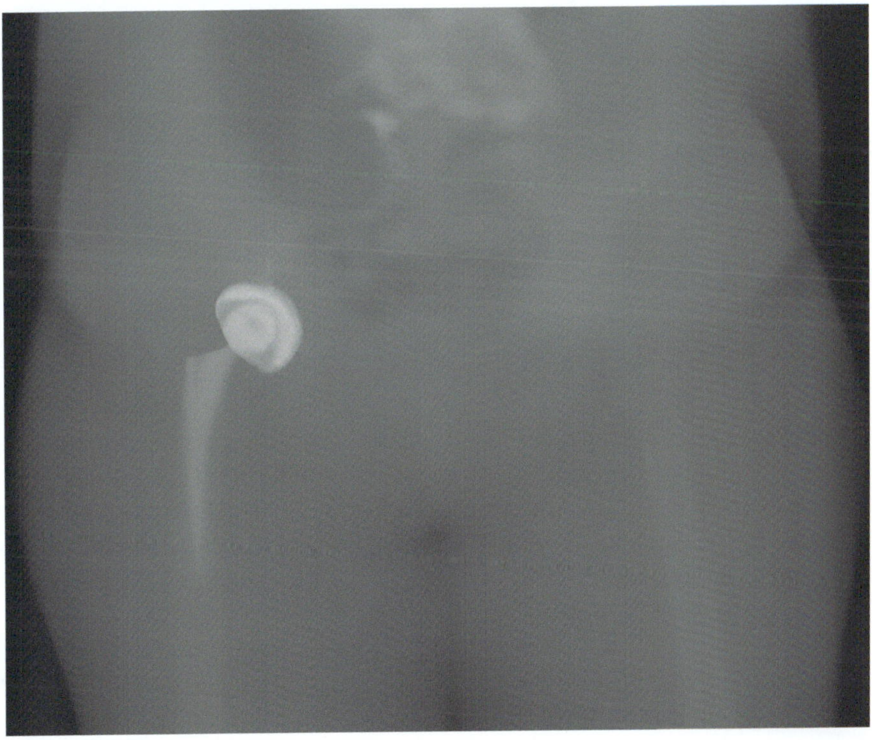

Figure 7.2 Hip replacement on X-ray.

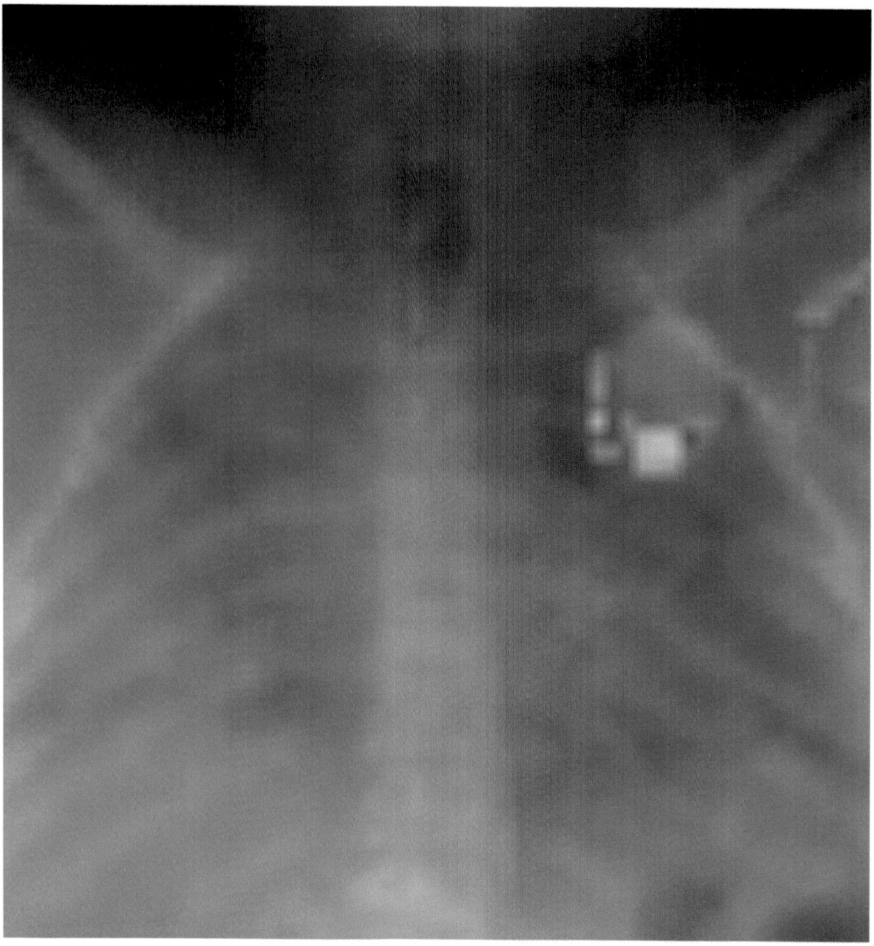

Figure 7.3 Pacemaker on X-ray.

Once these metal implants are identified on X-ray, they may be removed at autopsy to obtain the specific identification as to make model and serial numbers to identify the individual. Pacemakers and defibrillators can further be analyzed by the company for final tracings of heart activity and may be able to indicate the exact date and time of death.

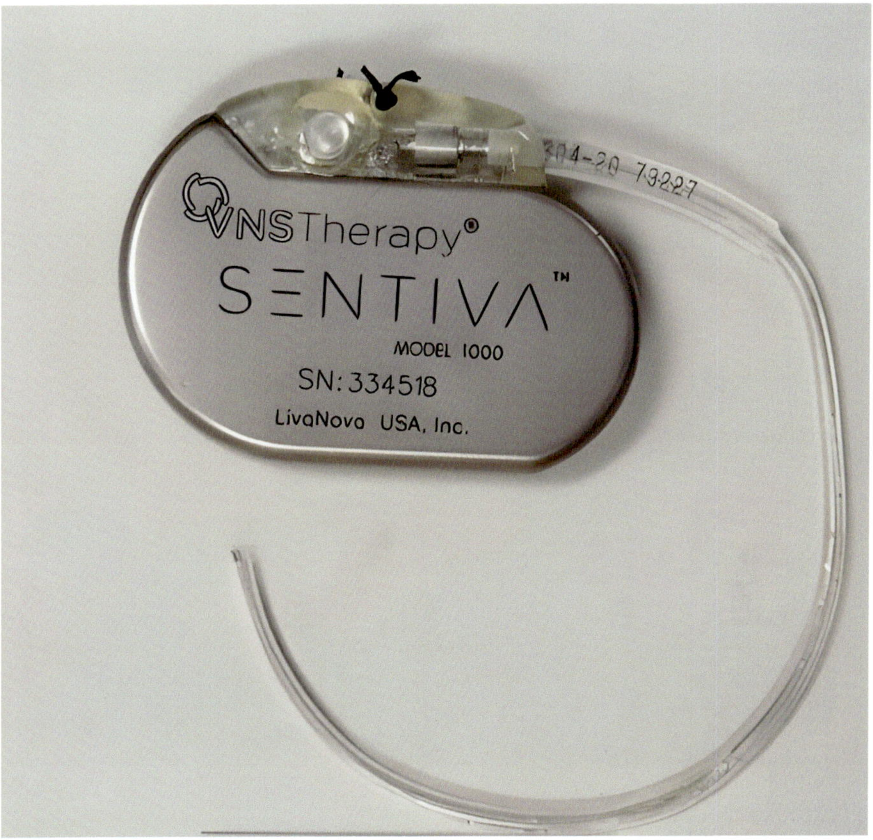

Figure 7.4 Pacemaker after removal at autopsy.

Blunt Trauma

Forensic radiology can identify the types and numbers of fractures including those not seen at autopsy including long bones and facial fractures from falls, motor vehicle accidents, and assaults. X-rays can show unique fracture characteristics and distinguish fractures of different ages of injury (Figure 7.5).

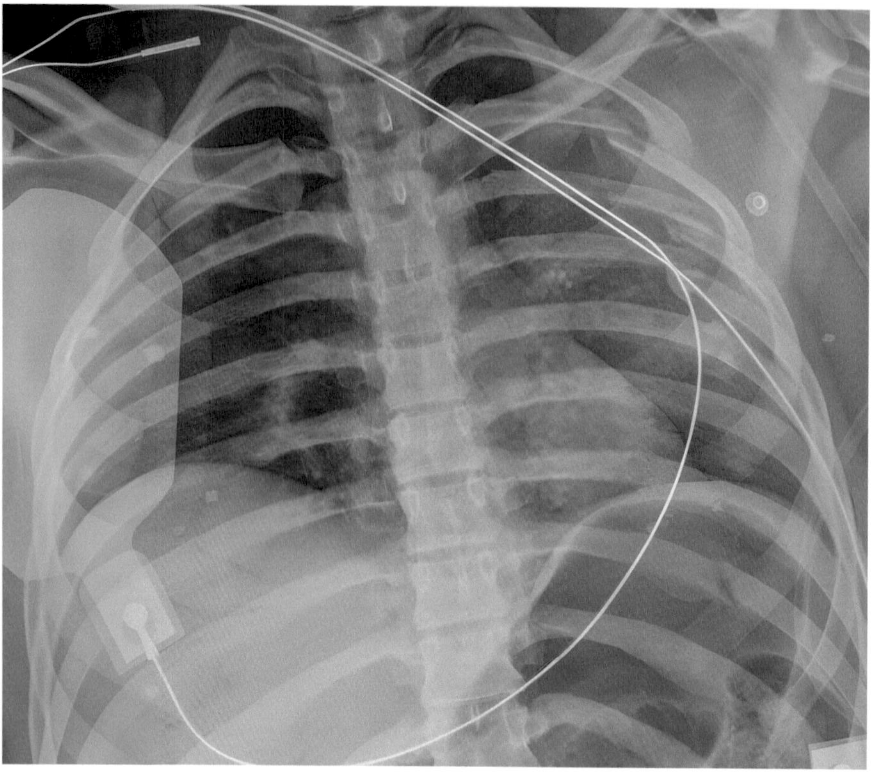

Figure 7.5 Fracture in blunt trauma.

Stab Wounds

Obviously, plain film X-rays cannot show soft tissue injury from a stab wound that may be seen with CT or MRI. However, with a penetrating stab wound injury, the object depth and location can be seen on X-ray prior to autopsy if the knife was retained (Figure 7.6) or knife tip was broken and retained in the body. In that case, it is important from safety reasons to identify the location of the sharp object prior to autopsy and to safely remove it for evidence preservation.

Gunshot Wounds

In a GSW case, it is essential to know where the projectiles are located and to help to identify the type of projectile and evaluate the track of the projectile and fragments. In wounds from rifled weapons, such as revolvers or rifles, the jacket and core or jacketed bullet must be recovered without damage for

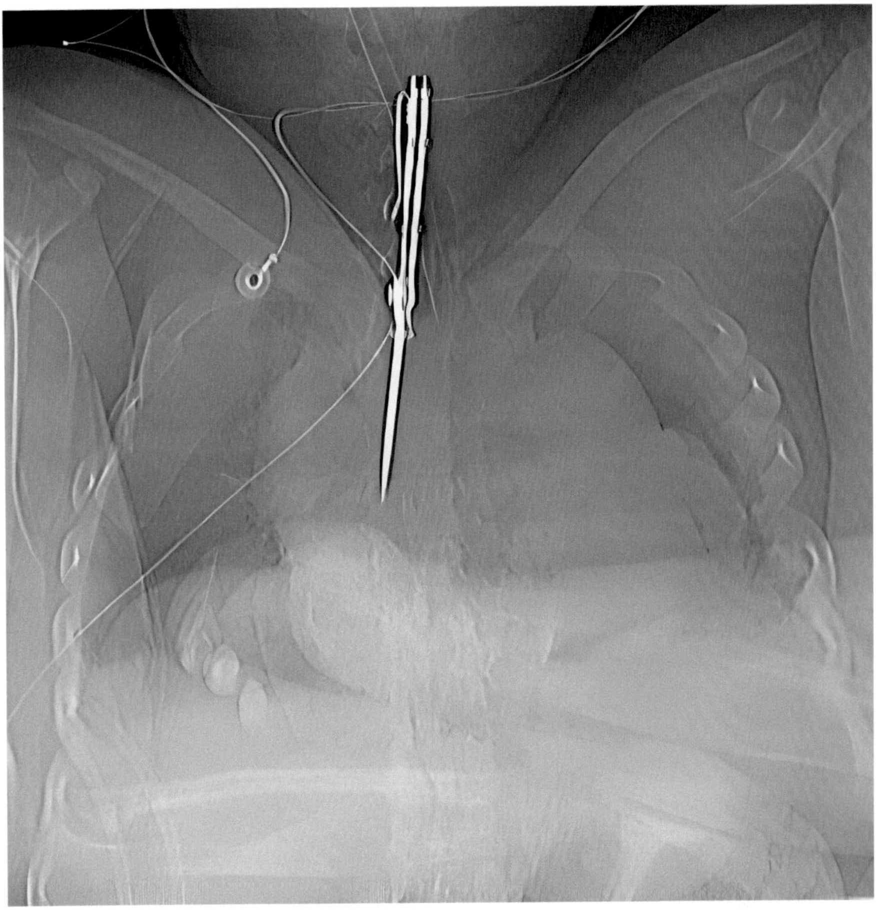

Figure 7.6 Knife injury on postmortem imaging.

evaluation by the firearms examiner to match the rifling marks with a test bullet fired from the suspect gun.

All GSW homicide cases must be X-rayed prior to autopsy through the sealed body bag to include the head, chest, and abdomen to identify the presence or absence of projectiles. After the body is undressed and cleaned, more X-rays may be needed including anterior/posterior (A/P) and lateral views and X-rays of the extremities, if GSWs are seen on the external body examination. Projectiles can take extraordinary paths inside the body and may be far away from the entrance wound. X-rays are helpful in identifying the location of the projectile that may be in soft tissue and difficult to locate at autopsy alone for removal (Figure 7.7). GSW suicides may only need X-rays of the area shot for projectile removal.

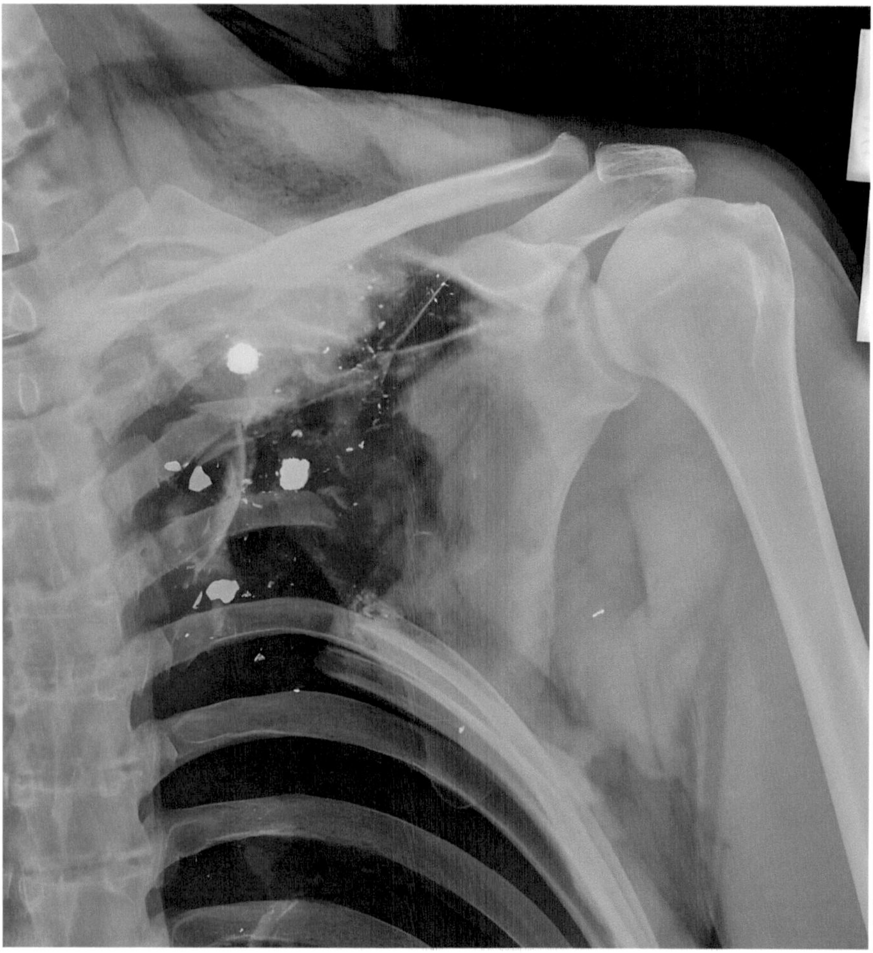

Figure 7.7 Appearance of projectiles on postmortem X-ray.

Child Abuse

Forensic radiology is important prior to autopsy in cases of sudden unexpected infant death and in suspected or known cases of nonaccidental trauma to ensure that a whole-body skeletal survey is obtained before the autopsy. Because of the disturbance of the thoracic cavity and skull during autopsy, X-ray studies must be completed before the autopsy procedure starts to rule out autopsy artifact from actual injury. Ideally, infant and child radiographs should include a suspected nonaccidental trauma series of X-rays using highly sensitive film and read by a pediatric radiologist to rule out any injury or fractures. Other modalities, such a CT or MRI, are helpful to identify abusive head injuries and timing of injuries, such as fractures or subdural or epidural hemorrhages of different ages.

Head and neck injuries in infants and children are the most common types of fatal child abuse injuries including skull fractures, vertebral fractures, cerebral edema, and subdural, epidural and subarachnoid hemorrhages. CT and/or MRI findings are helpful in the evaluation of head injury, especially in dating hemorrhages and contusions.

Other common inflicted injuries include multiple rib fractures, long bone fractures, metaphyseal (corner) fractures at the elbow, knee, and ankle joints. Corner fractures may be difficult to recognize if they are not a complete fracture and very small or have only a ragged appearance on the surface of the periosteum. One of the main characteristics of child abuse is multiple bony injury, often over a period of time, so that both recent fractures and healing lesions with callus may be seen (Figure 7.8). Previous films must be used to assess old and new fractures. Shearing of the periosteum with subperiosteal calcification on long bones and chipping of the metaphyses around knees and elbows is a characteristic finding. In small babies, multiple fractures of the ribs in the paravertebral gutter due to lateral squeezing by adult hands may leave rows of callus visible radiographically as "strings of pearls." All fractures need to be located, bones removed and decalcified, and injuries dated histologically.

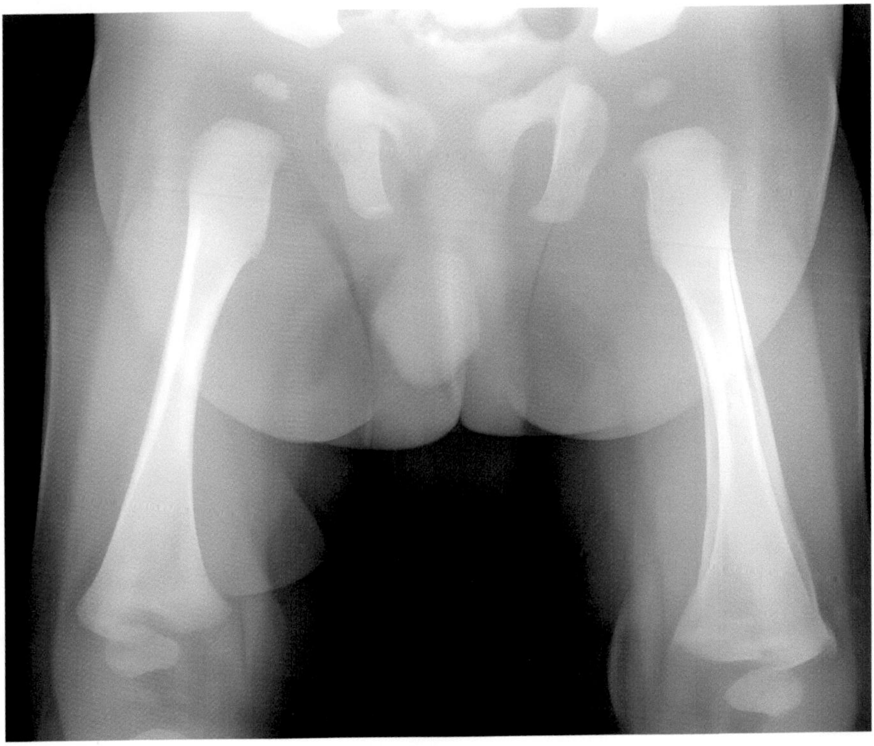

Figure 7.8 Remote fracture in child abuse.

Elder Deaths

Similar to child abuse, fractures are seen in elder abuse and may include injuries of different ages including rib fractures, long bone fractures, or hip fractures (Figures 7.9 and 7.10). History obtained by the MDI is essential for determining whether fractures are of accidental or non-accidental nature.

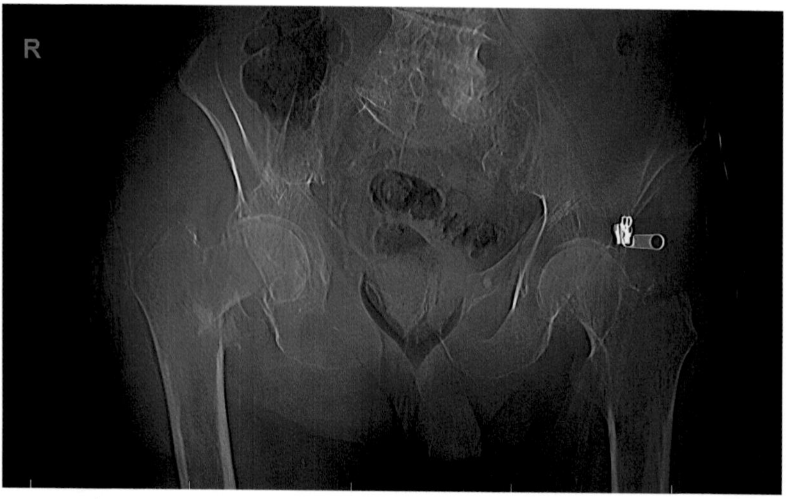

Figure 7.9 Hip fracture by X-ray.

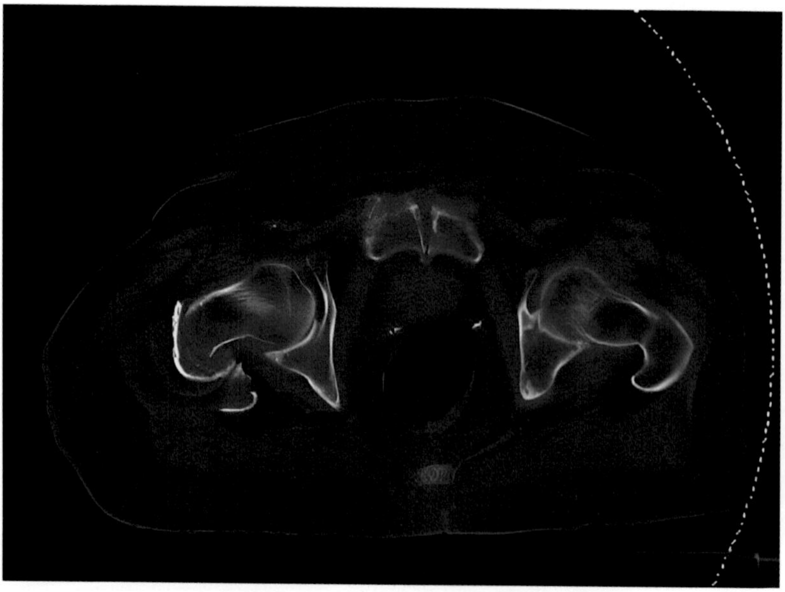

Figure 7.10 Hip fracture by postmortem computed tomography.

Bibliography

Connolly, A.J., Finkbeiner, W.E., and Ursell, P.C., Davis, R.L. 2016. Chapter 7: Autopsy photography and radiology. In Connolly, A.J., Finkbeiner, W.E., Ursell, P.C., Davis, R.L., eds., *Autopsy Pathology: A Manual and Atlas* (3rd ed.), Philadelphia, PA: Elsevier, pp. 80–89.

Grabherr, S., Egger, C., Vilarino, R., Campana, L., Jotterand, M., and Dedouit, F. 2017, June 7. Modern post-mortem imaging: An update on recent developments. *Forensic Sciences Research*, 2(2):52–64.

Thali, M.J., Viner, M.D., and Brogdon, B.G. 2010. *Brogdon's Forensic Radiology*, 2nd ed. Boca Raton, FL: CRC Press.

Blunt and Sharp Force Injuries

8

MARY H. DUDLEY

OBJECTIVES

Upon completion of this chapter and corresponding reference material, the reader will be able to

- Define the role of the medicolegal death investigator in recognizing blunt and sharp force injuries at the scene
- Differentiate between findings of blunt and sharp force injury during examination
- Describe two types of sharp force injury
- Differentiate between antemortem and postmortem injuries
- Describe three types of blunt force injuries and describe differences between hesitation marks and defense-type injuries
- Define patterned injuries and give three examples

Introduction

This chapters describes the specific forensic terminology related to blunt and sharp force injuries. The scene investigation by the medicolegal death investigator (MDI) reveals important information regarding blunt and sharp force injuries and clues regarding the nature of the injury. Wounds to the body can be intentional or accidental. Intentional wounds can be inflicted by self or others. The significance of such wounds relates to the angle, force, and instrument used to cause the wound and to the appearance of the tissue surrounding the wound. The importance of a precise wound classification is twofold—it allows clarity of communication among forensic investigators and aids in the reconstruction of events causing injury.

Blunt Force Injuries

Blunt force injuries are caused by forceful contact (blunt impact) from a broad or dull-surfaced area or object that disrupts the integrity of tissues. In general, the more the force of the impact is spread over a larger body surface, the less

DOI: 10.4324/9781003538622-10

severe is the injury. This is because the force of the blow is dissipated over a wider area. Falls, blows from non-sharp instruments, and motor vehicle accidents are often associated with this kind of injury. Blunt force injuries usually occur during accidents or homicides but may also occur with suicides involving falls from great heights.

There are three basic categories of blunt force injury:

1. Abrasions
2. Contusions
3. Lacerations

These may appear alone or in combination such as laceration or tearing of the tissue with one or more abraded margins. Fractures may also result from blunt forces.

Abrasions

Abrasions are superficial injuries that involve only the outer layers of skin or mucosal surfaces (Figure 8.1). They are the traumatic removal of skin layers by forces tangential to the skin surface. The direction of the abrasion may be shown by parallel lines. "Flaps" of skin may be torn from intact tissue when the force is sufficient or the surface of the impact is not smooth. Synonyms frequently used are scratches, scrapes, and friction marks. Scratches are linear abrasions whereas grazes describe wider abrasions. Impact abrasions are also called impressions, patterned abrasions, or imprints. Friction abrasions or brush burns are due to frictional forces. With an abrasion, there is minimal bleeding, rarely scar formation with healing, or disability. Thus, from a medical point of view, abrasions have little, if any, significance.

However, in medicolegal investigations, abrasions are never too small or insignificant. Abrasions may be the only indication of foul play or severe internal injury. For example, abrasions on the abdomen may indicate ruptured visceral organs (such as the liver or pancreas), whereas crescent abrasions on the neck may indicate fingernail marks from manual strangulation. Fingernail marks on the inner aspects of the thighs (particularly on a female) may indicate forcible rape. Abrasions on the nose or mouth of an infant or incapacitated adult direct the examiner to look for other signs of smothering (asphyxiation). Drying effects along the edges of the scrape provide some indication as to when the injury occurred. In addition, abrasions may indicate the direction in which force was applied, especially if flaps of rolled-up epidermis are attached to the terminal end of the wound. These indicate the direction in which scraping occurred. Subtypes and patterns further define and describe abrasions. The abrasion may reflect a "patterned-type injury" (Figure 8.2) of the instrument used to inflict the wound.

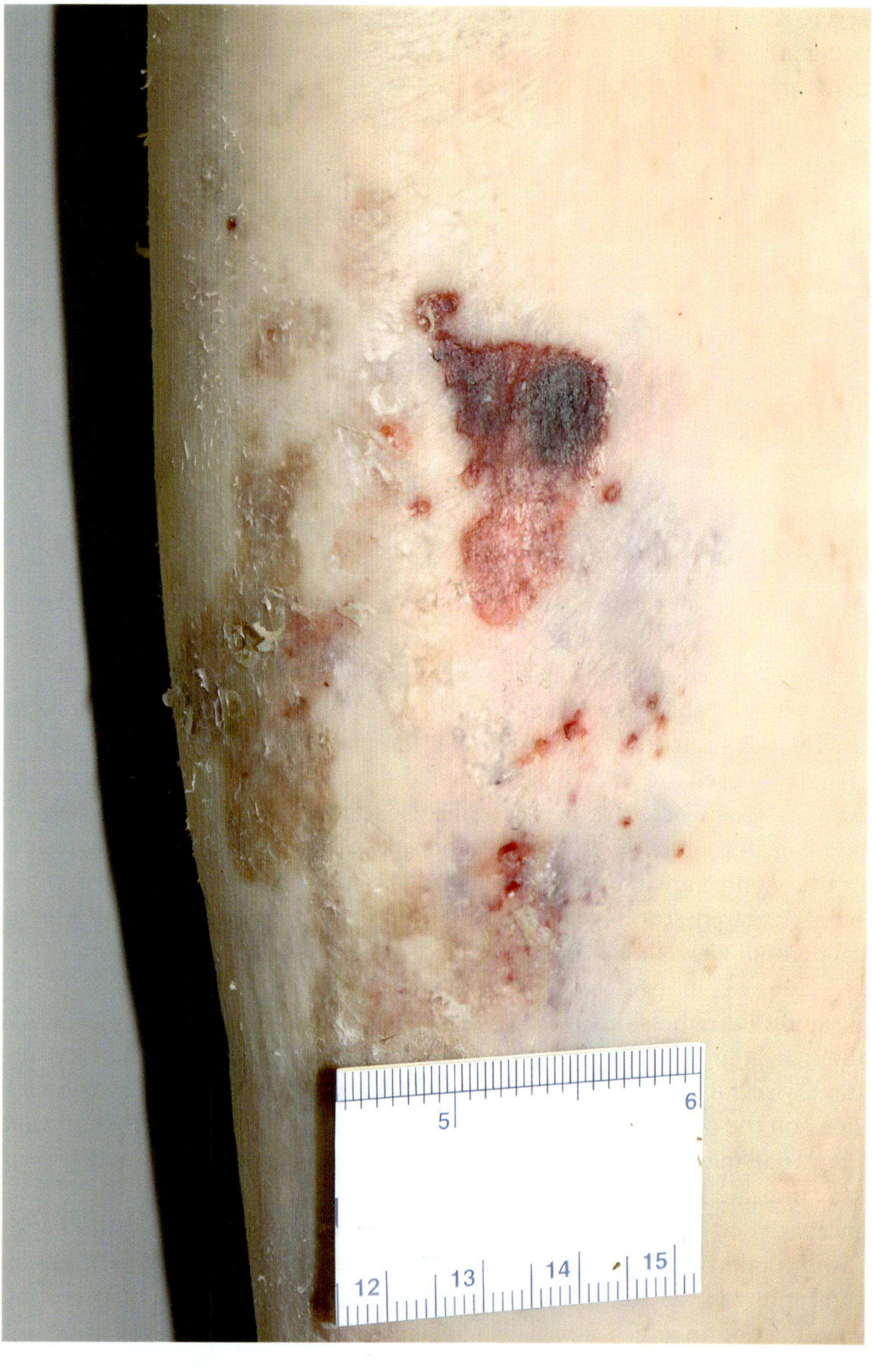

Figure 8.1 Abrasion.

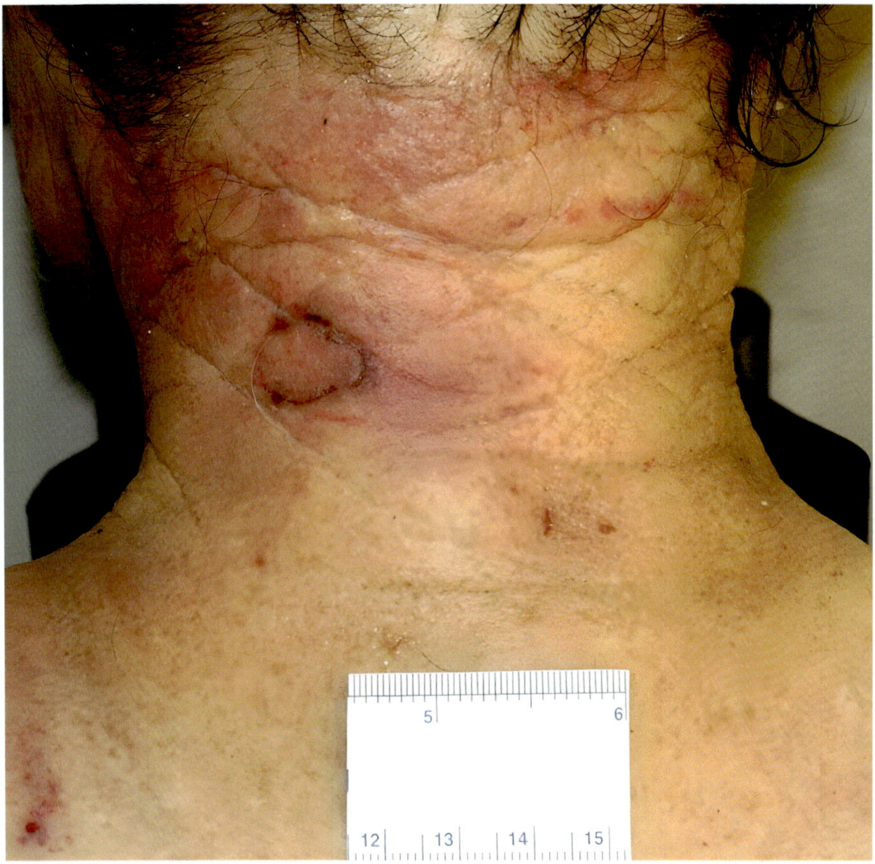

Figure 8.2 Patterned injury.

Contusions

Contusions (or bruises) are deep injuries of soft tissue with tearing and rupture of capillaries and hemorrhage beneath an intact epithelium (Figure 8.3). Both the skin and internal organs are subject to contusions. Contusions leave the skin intact, and the object that causes the contusion may leave a patterned shape on the affected skin. Unlike abrasions, contusions do not necessarily lie at the point of impact. A delay often exists between the time of injury and appearance of bruises, and contusions may remain deep-seated without an overlying external bruise. The effects of gravity exaggerate the bruising process and, postmortem, can be mimicked by lividity. The extent and severity of contusions are also influenced by the vascularity, location, and structure of the tissues bruised. Some individuals such as the elderly, alcoholics, or those with blood disorders may be "easy bruisers." "Easy bruising" can mislead the investigator regarding the force and extent of the injury. If bruising

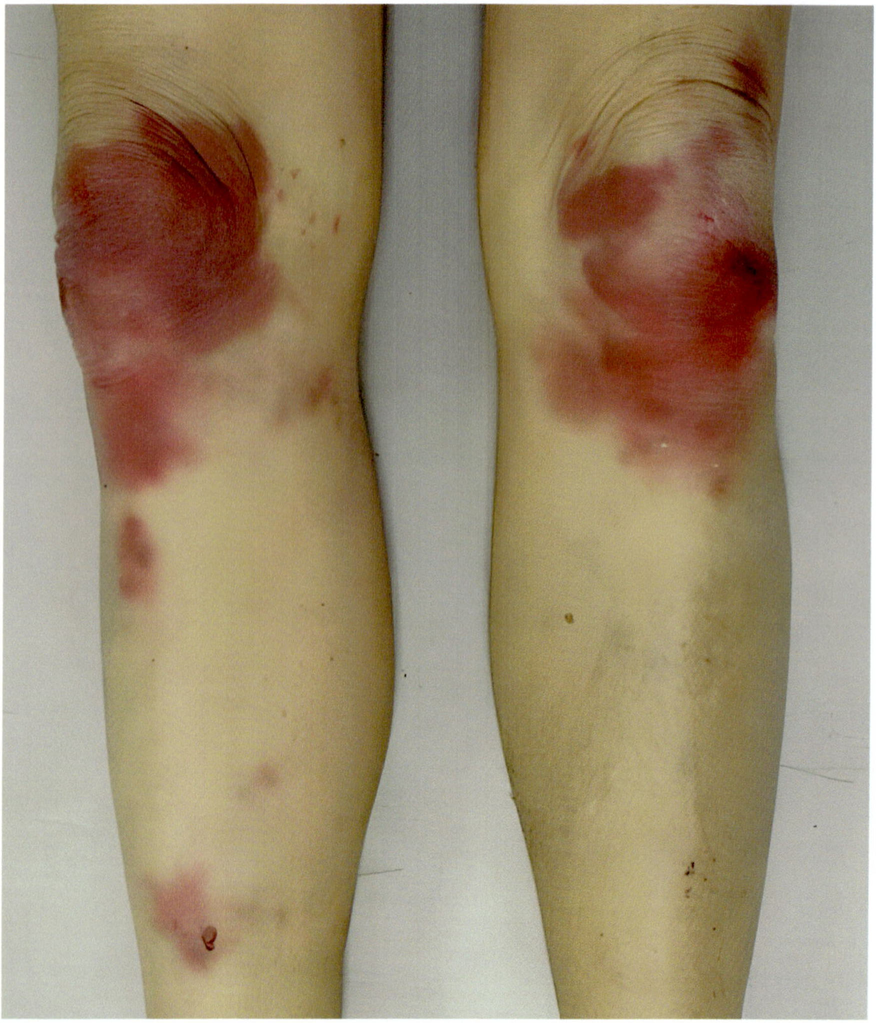

Figure 8.3 Contusions.

is present on the neck, careful layer by layer dissection and examination of underlying soft tissues of the neck provide evidence of potential force with manual strangulation. Contusions may be "dated" microscopically with the use of an iron stain—positive iron staining indicates a bruise over 3 days in age. Contusions and/or abrasions of the scapulae or spinous processes may indicate firm pressure on the body against the ground or a similar resistant surface. Such an injury may be caused by an assailant kneeling on the subject. Contusions to the thighs, particularly the inner aspects and genitalia, often result from forcible rape.

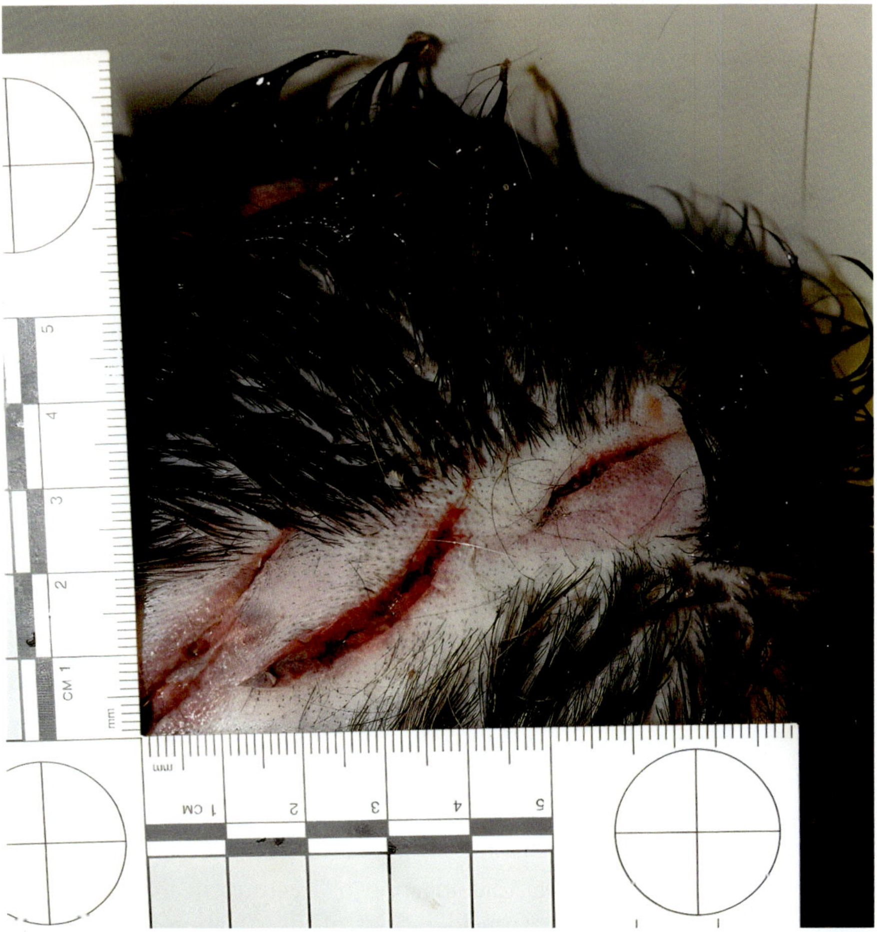

Figure 8.4 Lacerations.

Lacerations

Lacerations are tearing of the skin and underlying tissue and indicate blunt force injury (Figure 8.4). Features of lacerations include abraded edges; "undercutting" in the direction of the force; and "tissue bridging" of underlying connective tissue fibers, blood vessels, and nerves connecting the sides of the tear. Blunt trauma injury over bony prominences is particularly subject to splitting or laceration. There may also be dirt or trace evidence inside the wound. The laceration may show a distinct pattern of the blunt object used.

Combined injuries are frequent findings and can occur both externally and internally. It is important to identify and describe each injury impact site in sufficient detail to determine if the injury is a combined type. Old accidental injuries and recent traumatic injuries can occur on the same site. Internal findings may not be evident until discovered by medical treatment or by the medical examiner/coroner. These are often more extensive than is evident on external examination.

Antemortem vs. Postmortem Injury

Initial examination of the body requires differentiation between injuries caused to the victim before death and those that occur postmortem. Abrasions that occur postmortem generally have a tan, brown, dried parchment-like appearance with no vital tissue reactions noted (Figure 8.5). Antemortem bruises change in color and prominence with time; consequently, recent contusions are usually red or purple and gradually change to blue, green, brown, yellow before fading completely. However, this sequence may vary depending on the location of the bruises, vascularity, etc., and cannot be dated with exact precision. Postmortem bruises are usually small or disproportionate to the degree of force used. Application of considerable force is required to cause a postmortem bruise and must occur near the time of death while the blood is still in fluid state. Postmortem bruises and other deep bruises can be slow to appear postmortem due to gravity and diffusion of blood. Incisions of bruised areas provide evidence of hemorrhages.

Fractures

Fractures are breaks in bone. Classification of fractures in forensics is the same as in medical practice. Considerations of investigation into fractures include the following:

- Was the fracture a result of a chop injury or blunt force trauma?
- Did the fracture occur before or after other injuries?
- Was the fracture the cause of other trauma?
- Did the fracture occur before or after death?
- Are the fractures of different ages?

Sharp Force Injuries

Wounds from sharp forces can be made by sharp, pointed, or edged instruments or objects. Sharp force injuries include

- Incised wounds
- Slashes

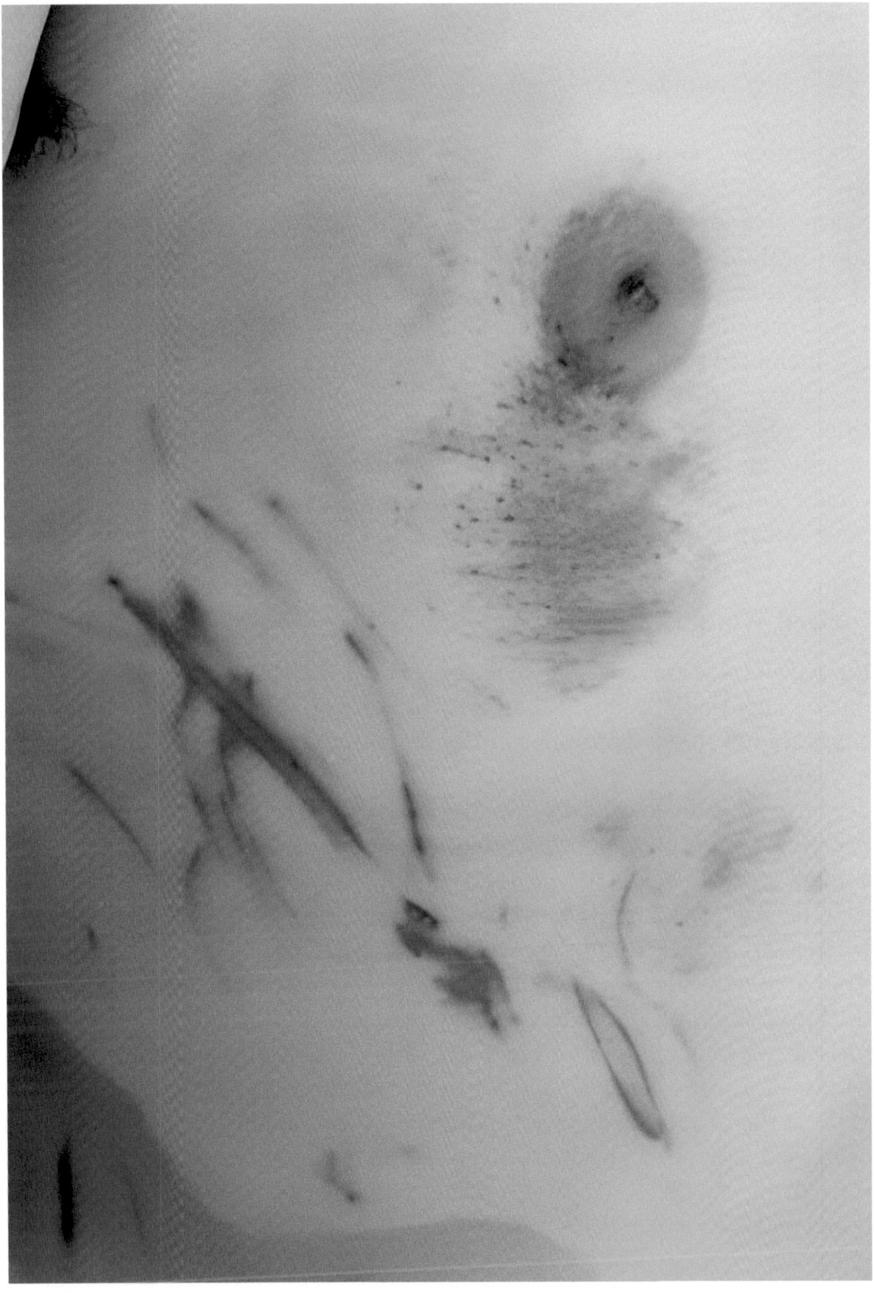

Figure 8.5 Postmortem abrasion.

- Stab wounds
- Cuts
- Chop wounds
- Surgical wounds
- Puncture wounds

Sharp force injuries include defense-type injuries that are seen on the extensor (outside) surfaces of the arms or legs or palms of the hands where the victim attempted to ward off an assailant during a homicide (Figure 8.6). Hesitation marks are self-inflicted incised wounds on the wrist or neck during attempted suicide.

Characteristic weapons demonstrable from sharp force injuries include single-edged or double-edged knives such as kitchen, craft, woodworking, hunting, and sport knives. A wound created by a pair of opened scissors indicates a patterned injury of paired puncture wounds. Injuries to cartilage and bone can also occur from sharp, pointed, or edged instruments.

Incised Wounds

Incised wounds are caused by sharp edges drawn across the body surface producing cuts that are longer than they are deep (Figure 8.7). In an incision, edges are not abraded or undermined, there is no bridging, and the edges can be realigned easily. Incised wounds usually begin rather superficially, then get deeper, and end superficially. The wound margins may be straight or jagged depending on the weapon, nature of the target tissue, and amount of force applied.

Therapeutic incised wounds are surgical incisions created by a scalpel whereas accidental wounds are knife, razor, or equipment injuries. The majority of incised wounds seen at autopsy are defensive wounds. Cuts or slashes on the lower extremities of a female suggest sexual assault. On the other hand, incised wounds on the upper extremities—especially the forearms and hands—are probably sustained when the victim raises his or her arms or grabs at the weapon in an effort to ward off the assailant's attack. These types of incised wounds may result in severed ligaments or cut bone. Remember this during the investigation of skeletal remains as cuts may be seen on the bones and offer a clue as to cause of death even in a skeletonized body.

Stab Wounds

Characteristically, stab wounds are deeper than they are wide or long (Figure 8.8). As with cuts, tissue "bridges" and undermining are absent. Margins of stab wounds are usually devoid of abrasions or bruises.

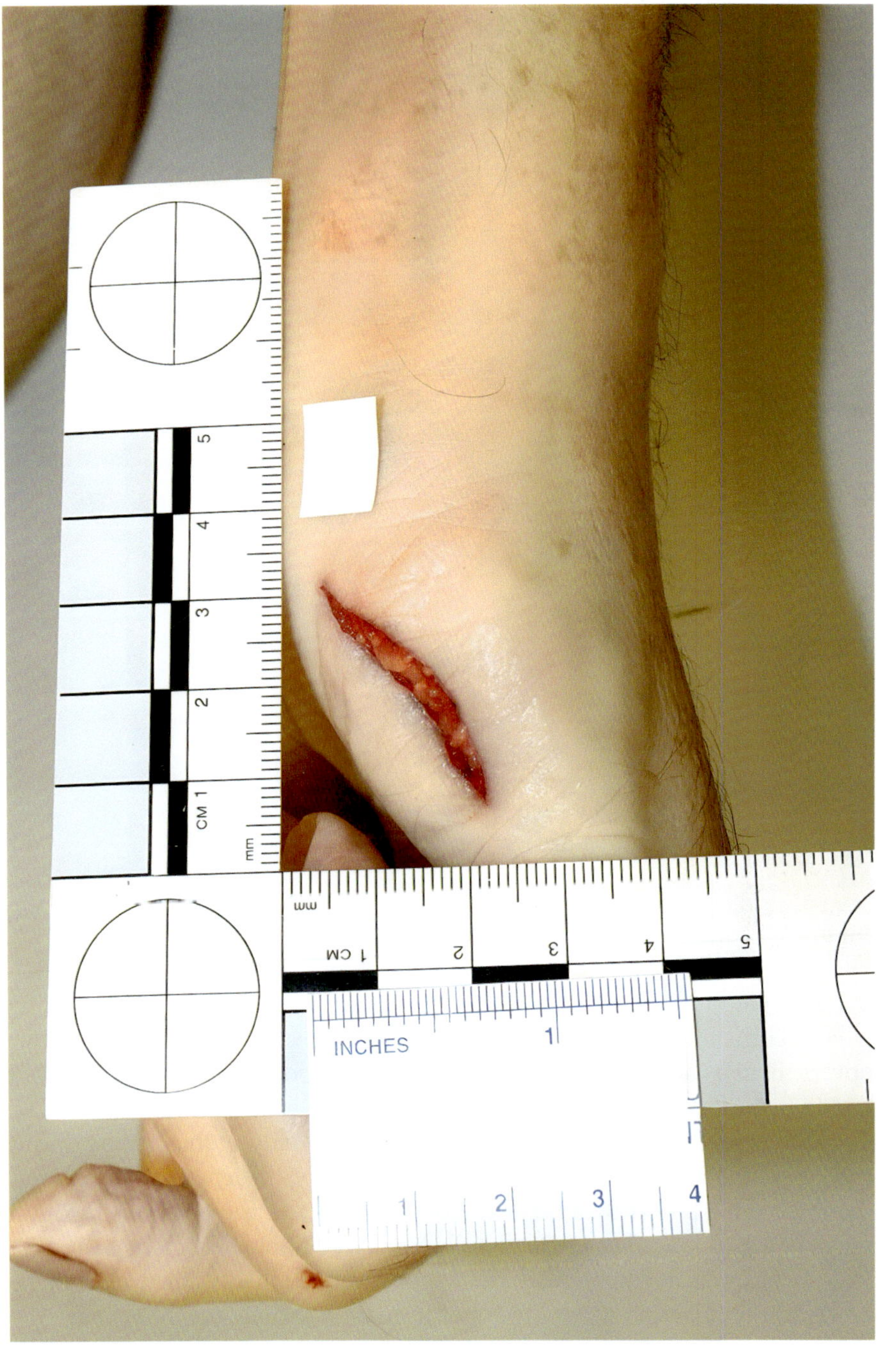

Figure 8.6 Defensive injury.

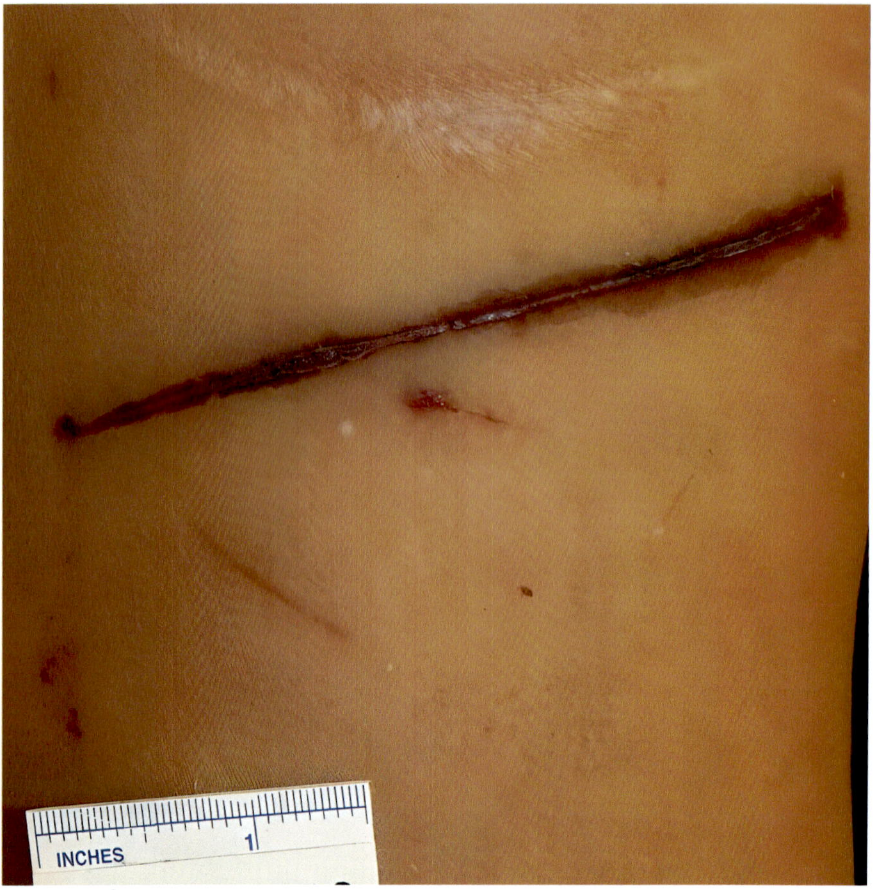

Figure 8.7 Incised wound.

Stab wounds are evident on antemortem and postmortem bodies. Entry sites documented at the scene of death may be obscured by clothing or other covers. Bruises adjacent to stab wounds may be produced by the impact of a closed fist inflicting the wound.

Stab wounds are rarely inflicted without some cutting that occurs during the thrust and withdrawal of the weapon. Therefore, the length of the external wound is often longer than the width of the blade. Abrasion or bruising of the edges of a stab wound suggests that the blade was completely inserted and the skin surface was in contact with the weapon handle; this is called a hilt mark.

Additional observations during examination include the following:

- Stab wounds of bone, cartilage, and pericardium tend to reflect the dimensions of the inflicting instrument and permit the identification of the weapon more precisely than soft tissue wounds.

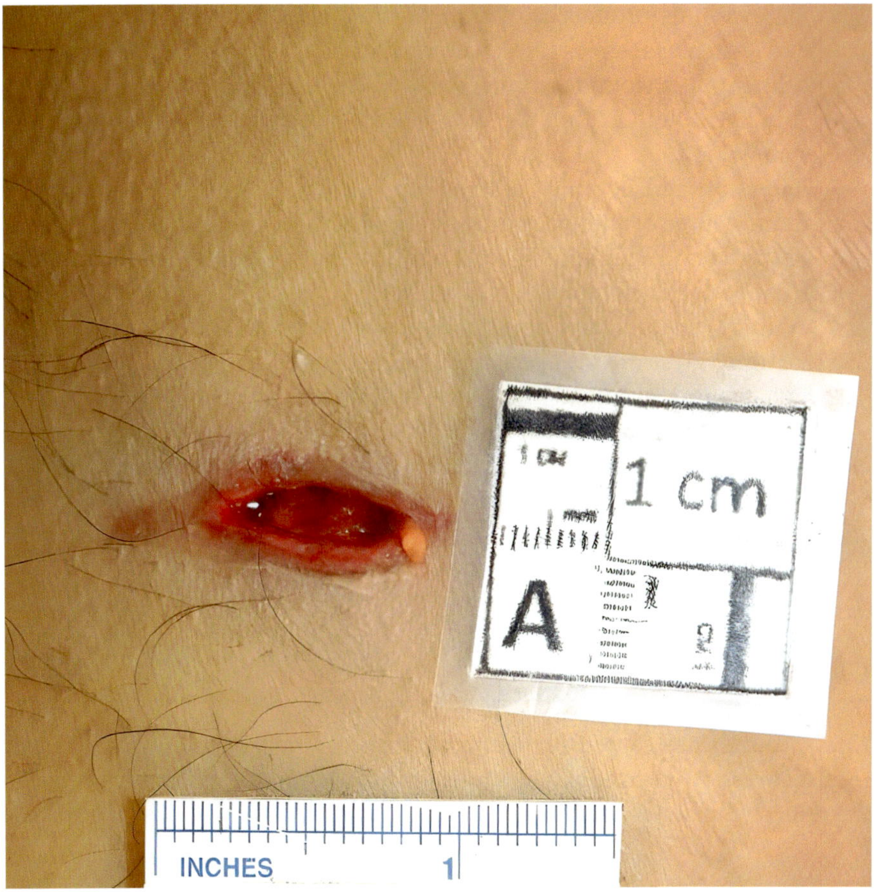

Figure 8.8 Stab wound.

- Stab wounds may represent the cross section of a weapon—for example, a single-edged knife often produces a stab wound with one sharp extremity and one blunt-edged or squared-off extremity.
- A stab wound that severs the cleavage line of Langer will gape open and distort the wound—for example, a single-edged knife wound may appear as a double-edged knife wound.
- Depth of a stab wound does not depend on length of the blade alone. Due to compression of the body, depth of a knife wound frequently exceeds length of the blade (frequently seen in stab wounds of the abdomen).
- Thickness of the blade can be rather accurately estimated by re-approximating and realigning the wound edges to reconstruct the wound and then measuring the blunt edge width.

- Stab wounds produced by a cylindrical instrument with a pointed end—such as ice picks, screwdrivers, or awls—may resemble small-caliber bullet wounds with an abraded edge.
- A bullet wound exiting the skin in a slit-like pattern may resemble a stab wound.
- Direction and depth of a stab wound can be determined only by examination of the wound track. Notation regarding the trajectory of the wound should indicate the course of the wound—for example, front to back, left to right, or downward.
- Wrinkle wounds are most commonly found in elderly or obese victims. These are inflicted in folded skin, and the defects show multiple wounds arranged linearly with skip areas of uninvolved skin.
- Penetration wounds enter organs or soft tissues.
- Perforation wounds enter and exit organs or soft tissues.
- Serrated knives may also show a patterned abrasion mark if scraped on the skin surface.

Chop Wounds

Chop wounds are caused by heavy instruments such as axes, machetes, or meat cleavers. An incised skin wound with abraded edges and a deep groove in the underlying bone is a common characteristic of chop wounds (Figure 8.9)

Photography

A blunt force injury should be photographed in both its original and cleaned states, with a label, and with and without a scale/color chart (Figure 8.10). Stab wounds should be photographed with a label, with and without a scale. Stab wounds may be held closed with a piece of clear tape if necessary to pull together the skin edges in a gaping wound. The wound should be photographed with a trajectory probe in place on the sagittal and horizontal planes of the body following the autopsy. Written documentation must include the location of the wound measured from up the heels or gluteal folds, size, shape, color, characteristics, course, trajectory, and correlation to defects in the clothing.

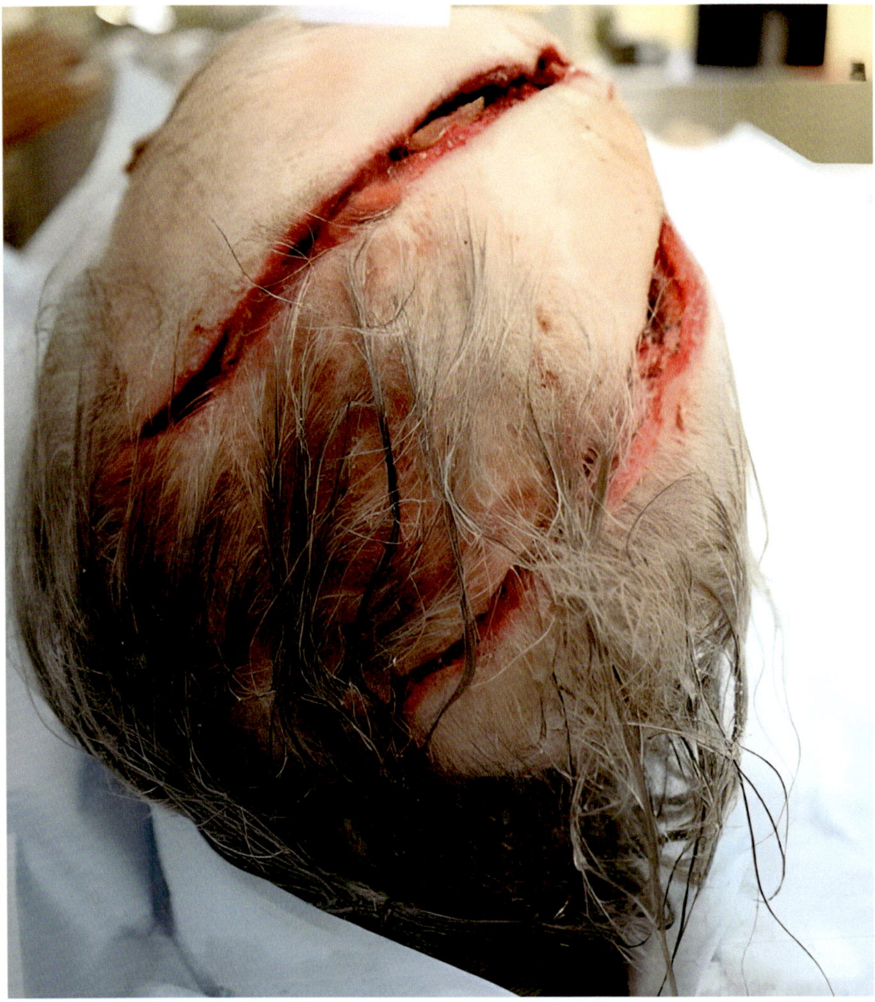

Figure 8.9 Chop wounds.

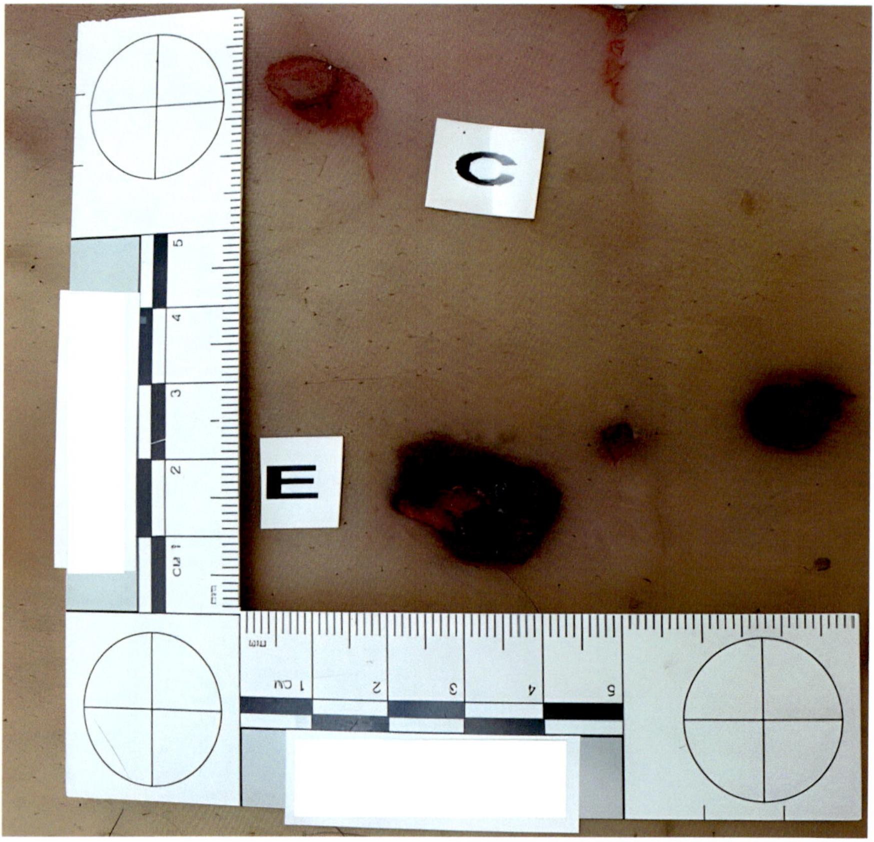

Figure 8.10 Photo of wounds with L ruler.

Bibliography

DiMaio, V.J.M. and Molina, D.K. (2021). *DiMaio's Forensic Pathology* (3rd ed.). Boca Raton, FL: CRC Press.

Dolinak, D., Matshes, E., and Lew, E. 2006. *Forensic Pathology: Principles and Practice*. Burlington, MA: Elsevier.

Spitz, W. and Fischer, R. 1993. *Medicolegal Investigation of Death: Guidelines for the Application of Pathology to Crime Investigation*. Springfield, IL: Charles C. Thomas Press.

Craniocerebral Injury

9

MARY H. DUDLEY

OBJECTIVES

Upon completion of this chapter and corresponding reference material, the reader will be able to

- Discuss the medicolegal death investigator's role at the scene in cases of craniocerebral injuries to assist in determination of how injury occurred
- Identify the physical findings, mechanisms, and complications involved in craniocerebral injuries
- Describe the characteristics of subdural, subscalpular, subgaleal, epidural, and subarachnoid hemorrhages
- Distinguish by history and examination the different types of craniocerebral injuries
- Discuss the pathological findings related to craniocerebral injuries
- Describe characteristic findings of diffuse axonal injuries, cortical contusions, and cerebral edema

Introduction

Craniocerebral injuries caused by traumatic forces to the head result in external and internal injuries with superficial or severe results. Scene investigation, including medicolegal death investigator documentation, medical history, and photographs, assists in determining the circumstances surrounding death. Accidental or homicidal circumstances are more common with head injuries as a manner of death than suicide. However, an intentional fall from great height, an intentional motor vehicle accident, or a self-inflicted gunshot wound may result in craniocerebral injuries with a suicidal manner of death. This chapter details autopsy findings related to craniocerebral injuries of the skeletal, circulatory, and nervous systems.

DOI: 10.4324/9781003538622-11

External Head Injuries

Abrasions, lacerations, and contusions are relatively common external head injuries. However, these blunt force injuries of the head are often associated with fatal internal craniocerebral injuries.

Hemorrhage and infection are the primary complications that occur with external injuries. As the face and scalp are quite vascular with blood vessels close to the surface of the skin, they are easily injured. The potential for exsanguination exists if superficial bleeding is not controlled. Infection as a result of exposure to bacteria can bridge the communication between extracranial and intracranial veins. Areas at risk are the ophthalmic and diploic veins. Suppurative phlebitis can progress to leptomeningitis and cavernous sinus thrombosis; both conditions can be fatal.

Internal Head Injuries

Head injuries can involve one or more than one layer of the scalp, skull, and/or brain, including the subscalpular, subgaleal, epidural, subdural, and subarachnoid layers. A complete forensic autopsy includes opening the head, with careful removal of the brain. The brain may be preserved in formalin for later examination by the forensic pathologist or a specialized neuropathology consultation, as necessary.

Subscalpular/Subgaleal Hemorrhage

Subscalpular hemorrhage is bruising underneath the scalp seen at autopsy when the scalp is reflected away from the skull. Subgaleal hemorrhage is bleeding of the periosteum (covering over the outer surface of the skull) (Figure 9.1).

Skull Fractures

A skull fracture indicates that there was sufficient force to break bone. However, the complications of a skull fracture can be deadly.

Significant complications include laceration of the meningeal artery resulting in an epidural hemorrhage, damage to nerves or arteries that transverse the base of the skull, laceration or contusion of the brain, and creation of a cerebral–environmental fistula.

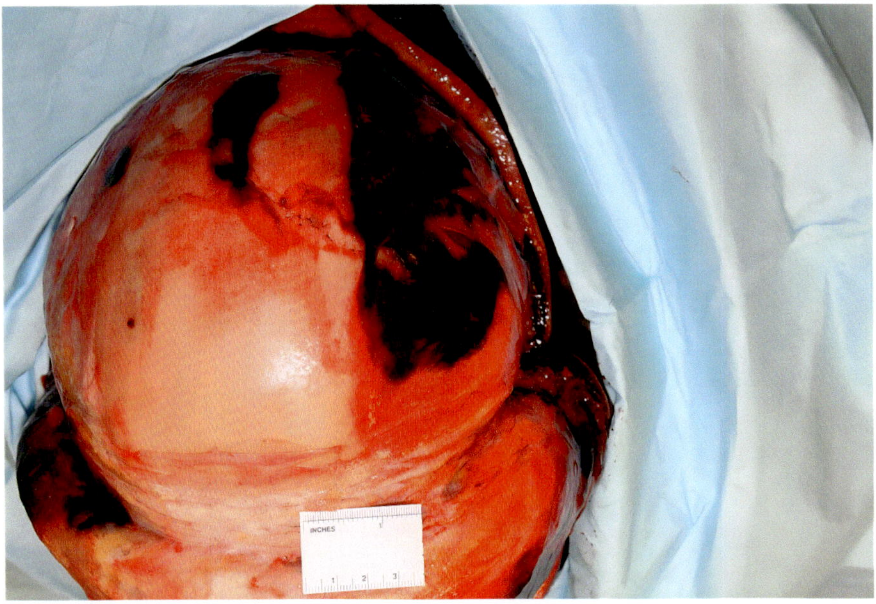

Figure 9.1 Subgaleal hemorrhage.

Generally, eight types of fractures can be described:

- Open vs. closed
- Complete vs. incomplete
- Linear vs. complex (comminuted)
- Depressed vs. nondepressed

Local deformation of the skull tends to indicate a depressed, comminuted fracture at the site of impact. Fracture lines extend radially from a central impact area and circularly at the periphery of an impact site. Fatal skull fractures are associated with complex fractures and underlying cerebral injury, as seen in motor vehicle accidents and child abuse (see Chapters 10 and 23).

General deformation is usually the result of a linear fracture. However, fractures may occur in areas distant from the impact site. Due to the architecture of the skull, broad-based impact forces tend to be diverted to the middle cranial fossae of the central basilar skull. This can be seen externally with a hinge-type fracture by observing Battle's sign (bruising behind the ears) (Figure 9.2). Orbital plate fractures over the eyes also show general deformation and cause periorbital bruising (Figure 9.3). Ring-type fractures surrounding the foramen magnum (opening to the spinal cord) have both a

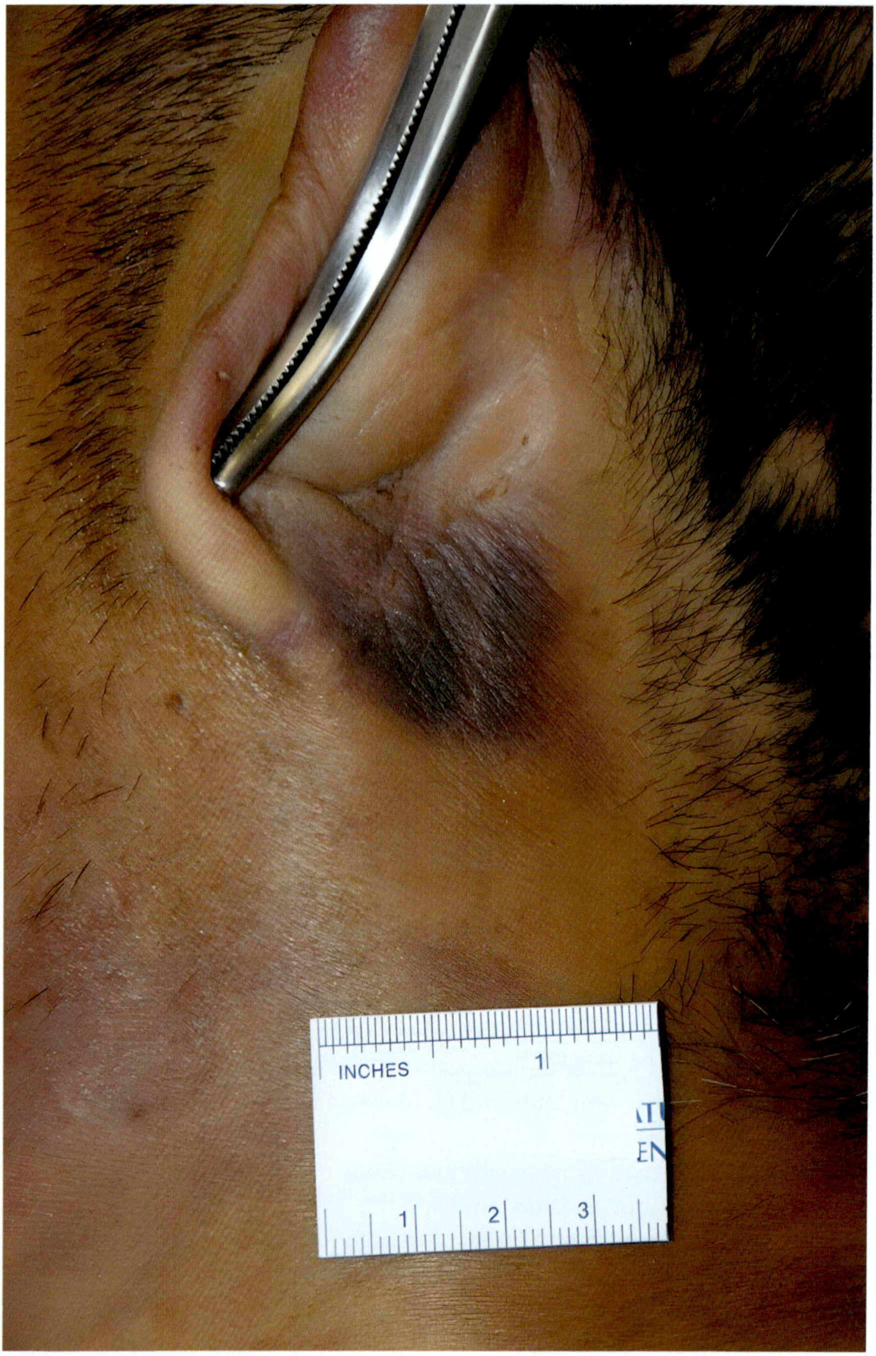

Figure 9.2 Battle's sign.

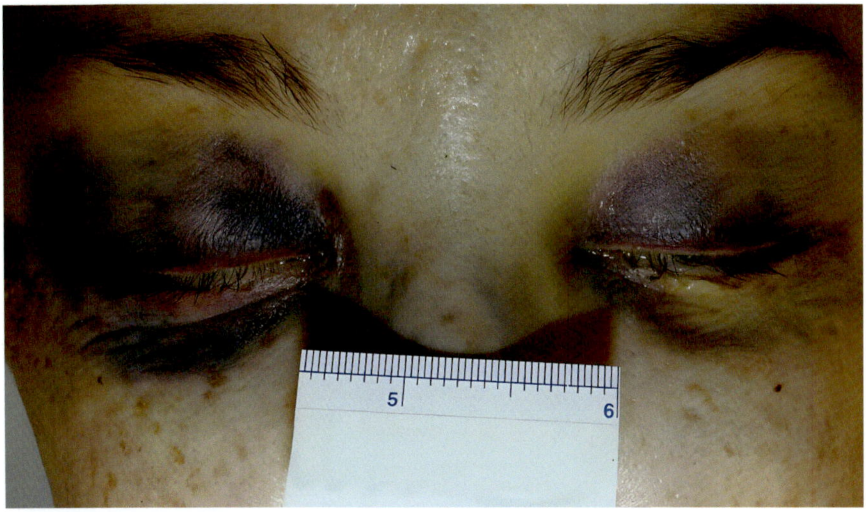

Figure 9.3 Raccoon eyes.

downward force at the vertex and an upward force via the spinal column. This type of basilar fracture is observed in fatalities involving subjects that jump from great heights.

Intracranial Extracerebral Hemorrhage

Intracranial extracerebral hemorrhage often requires differentiation between an epidural and a subdural bleed, which may be fresh hemorrhage or an older organizing hematoma. Epidural hemorrhage originates in the space between the skull and dura (Figure 9.4). This is an arterial bleed that is almost always due to disruption of a meningeal artery secondary to a skull fracture. The hemorrhage presses the dura against the brain. This causes a linear or dish-like flattening and nonuniform displacement of the brain. An epidural hemorrhage is usually fatal unless evacuated.

Subdural hemorrhage is a venous hemorrhage between the dura and leptomeninges (Figure 9.5). Subdural hemorrhage is almost always associated with trauma. Subdural hemorrhage may be associated with skull fracture but is not a direct result of the fracture. The source of subdural hemorrhage is torn bridging veins or cortical vessels. In an acute subdural hemorrhage, blood tends to have a widespread, uniform distribution over the cerebral hemisphere. There is relatively uniform displacement of the brain (Figure 9.6). The collection of blood in the subdural space is usually confined to one side, causing pressure on the brain. Acute subdural hemorrhages can occur in a fall of an elderly person taking blood thinners or in individuals with alcohol

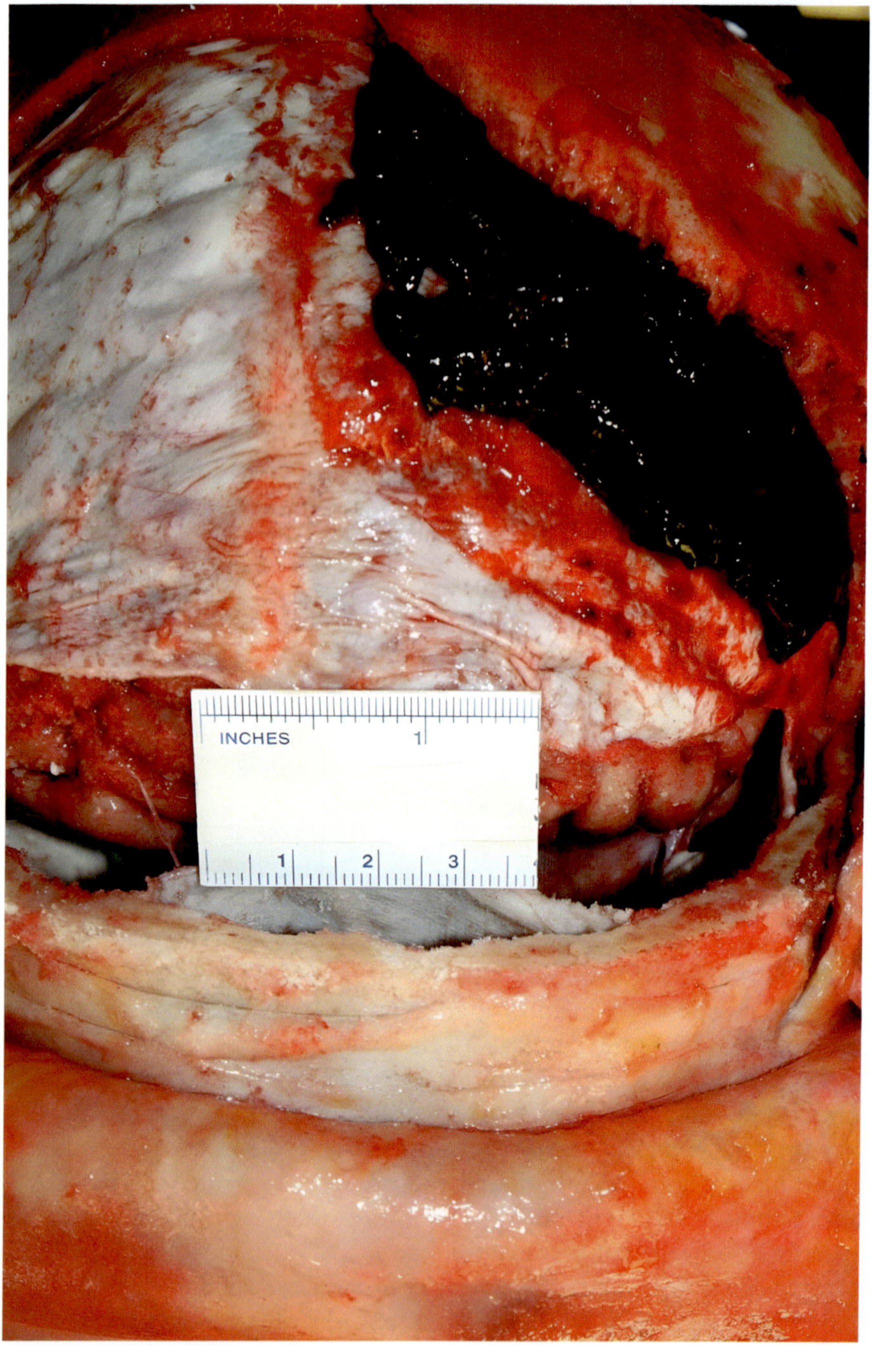

Figure 9.4 Epidural hemorrhage.

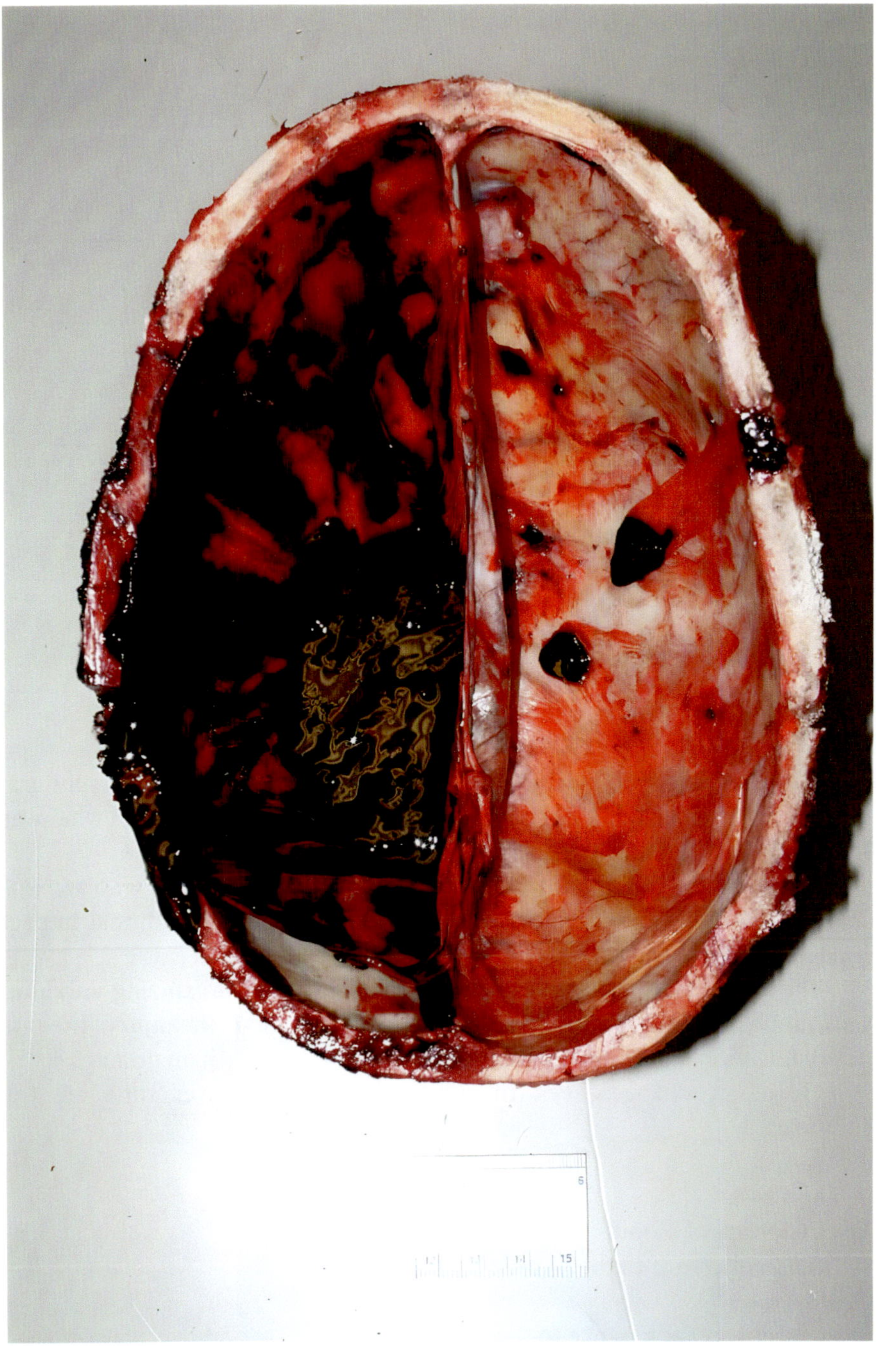

Figure 9.5 Subdural hemorrhage.

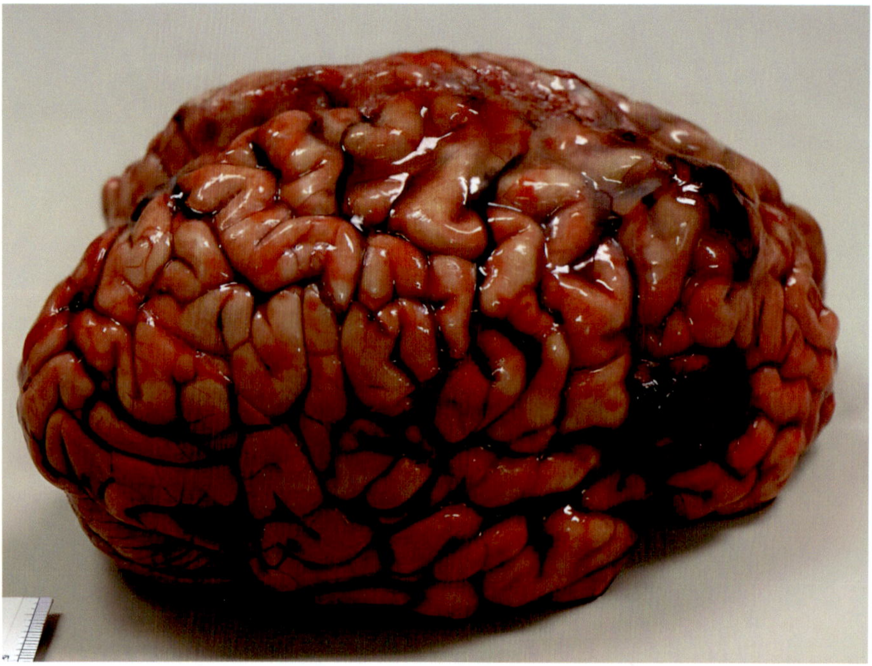

Figure 9.6 Compression of the brain from subdural hemorrhage.

use disorder. Since the bleeding occurred in a confined space, the subdural blood can be collected and sent for toxicology analysis reflective of what was in the blood at the time of injury.

Abusive head injury shows subdural hemorrhage in infants who are violently shaken and may strike a firm surface resulting in additional impact injuries (see Chapter 23).

The progression of a subdural hemorrhage to an organizing subdural hematoma on histology will aid MEs/coroners in "aging" the injury. The rate of organization and resorption is related to the size of the hematoma.

Histologic changes seen in subdural hematoma over time are the following:

- Days 1–4.
  - Clotting of blood.
  - No adherence to the dura.
- Day 5.
  - Multifocal adherence to the dura.
- Weeks 1–2.
  - Degeneration (brown discoloration). Inner membrane starts to form.
  - Hemosiderin is obvious. Hematoidin is negative.

- Weeks 2–4.
    - Outer membrane starts to form.
    - Hematoma looks like dirty motor oil, grossly. Appearance of hematoidin.
    - Foci of fresh hemorrhage common.
- Months 1–3.
    - Inner and outer membranes well formed.
- Months 3–6.
    - Fusion of inner and outer membranes. Maturation of collagen.

Chronic subdural hematoma shows new hemorrhage that occurs after encapsulation by membranes. A re-expanding subdural hematoma is similar to an epidural hematoma in that pressure is applied across a membrane in a non-uniform manner.

Subarachnoid Hemorrhage

A subarachnoid hemorrhage is a generalized diffuse arterial hemorrhage lying underneath the arachnoid covering (meninges) of the brain. It is caused by a ruptured berry aneurysm of the cerebral arteries spontaneously, traumatically, or from a tear of the vertebral arteries associated with displacement of the cervical vertebrae from a blunt force impact to the face, head, or neck (Table 9.1).

Brain Trauma

Concussions result in an instantaneous loss of consciousness of variable duration and show no evidence of structural damage to the brain. However, repeat concussions over time, as seen in football players or boxing, can have deleterious long-term effects. The effects may include seizure disorders, dementia,

Table 9.1 Hematoma Comparisons

	Epidural	Subdural	Subarachnoid
Skull fracture	Yes	Sometimes	Sometimes
Traumatic origin	Almost always	Almost always	Rarely/may be spontaneous
Source	Large arteries	Bridging veins, small arteries	Vertebral or basilar arteries
Development	Rapid (hours)	Slow (days)	Rapid (hours)
Distribution	Circumscribed	Hemispheric	Diffuse

behavioral changes, chronic traumatic encephalopathy (CTE), or secondary impact syndrome (SIS).

Contusions result in rupture of small cortical vessels that causes hemorrhagic necrosis of the brain cortex. Typically, a contusion involves the crests of gyri of the brain. Sometimes contusions may be associated with subarachnoid hemorrhage. Contusions can be independent or dependent relative to the motion status of the head. Independent contusions include fracture contusions (associated with skull fractures), herniation contusions (associated with cerebral edema or brain swelling), or gliding contusions (associated with movement of the brain). Coup contusions (where the fixed head is struck by a moving object) result in cortical contusions subjacent to the impact site. Conversely, contrecoup contusions are caused when a moving head impacts an unyielding or fixed surface, resulting in cortical contusions on the side of the brain opposite the impact site. Typically, contrecoup gliding contusions involve frontal and temporal lobes. Finally, intermediate contusions occur in locations intermediate to coup and contrecoup contusions at the corpus callosum (cerebral bridge connecting the right and left cerebral hemispheres), deep cerebral structures, or brainstem. Typically, these occur when the moving head impacts at the vertex.

Lacerations of the brain show as gross tears of the brain tissue and are usually associated with fractures or deceleration injuries, as seen in motor vehicle accidents. Subarachnoid hemorrhage frequently results. Penetrating brain injuries from bullets, knives, axes, shrapnel, or bone also tear brain tissues and may cause complications, including hemorrhage and infection. A crushing injury results in extensive fractures and lacerations, while contusions are minimal or absent when the head is compressed against an unyielding surface.

Diffuse axonal injury shows widespread shearing of axons caused by excessive force, occasionally from deceleration injuries. The victim is unconscious from the moment of injury and remains permanently in an unconscious, vegetative, or severely disabled state. Axonal injuries are commonly associated with hemorrhagic lesions in the corpus callosum, brainstem, or parasagittal white matter.

Secondary brain lesions result from cerebral edema (brain swelling) causing herniation or hypoxia. Herniation occurs transtentorially, either at the brainstem (central) or the uncus (lateral). Cerebellar tonsillar and subfalcial (cingulate gyrus) herniation also occur. Brain death occurs when the brain receives inadequate blood supply or oxygen due to compression of the cerebral vessels due to cerebral edema.

Brainstem or spinal cord injuries can be associated with fractures or dislocation of the vertebral column. Typically, contusions and lacerations are associated with cord injury and posttraumatic swelling, leading to secondary necrosis preceding to death. Subluxation of the head from the first cervical vertebrae is referred to as an atlanto-occipital dislocation and may cause a

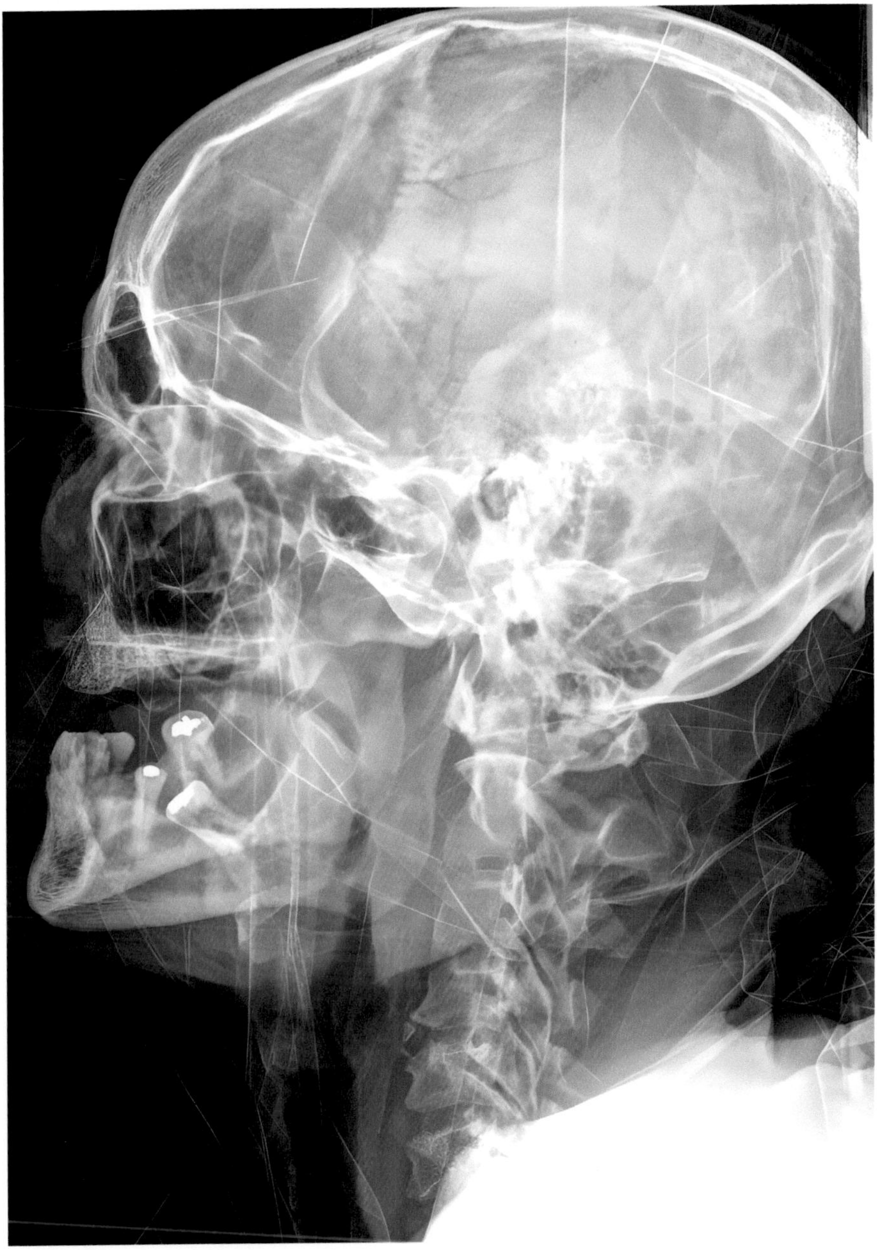

Figure 9.7 Cervical spinal column X-ray.

laceration of the brainstem. Cervical spinal column injuries can be visualized by postmortem imaging, such as X-ray (Figure 9.7).

A complete autopsy, including opening the head, is required to assess for the presence or absence of injury. Careful examination of the skull and dissection of the brain are key to determining the cause and manner of death.

Bibliography

Itabashi, H.H., Andrews, J., Tomiyasu, U., Erlich, S., and Sathyavagiswaran, L. 2007. *Forensic Neuropathology: A Practical Review of the Fundamentals* (1st ed.). Burlington, MA: Academic Press.

Leestma, J.E. (2014). *Forensic Neuropathology* (3rd ed.). CRC Press. https://doi.org/10.1201/b16882

Troncoso, J., Rubio, A., and Fowler, D. 2010. *Essential Forensic Neuropathology*. Baltimore, MD: Lippincott Williams and Wilkins.

Whitwell, H., Milroy, C., and du Plessis, D. (Eds.). (2021). *Forensic Neuropathology* (2nd ed.). CRC Press. https://doi.org/10.1201/9781003158035

Motor Vehicle Fatalities 10

MARY H. DUDLEY

OBJECTIVES

Upon completion of this chapter and corresponding reference material, the reader will be able to

- Describe the primary considerations of the investigator in a motor vehicle fatalities
- Discuss the differences in injury patterns related to fatal vehicle collisions in driver vs. passenger
- Describe the investigative aspects of motor vehicle fatalities to make a determination as to the manner of death
- Differentiate various types of injuries in pedestrian fatalities of children vs. adults

Introduction

Motor vehicle fatalities may cause immediate or delayed injuries to drivers, passengers, and/or pedestrians. The accident scene may be cleared by law enforcement and/or highway patrol. Subjects involved may be transported to the hospital. The medicolegal death investigator (MDI) must obtain information, reports, and photos from investigating agencies, paramedics, and/or emergency department staff. Information from the scene, clothing, vehicle, and medical records provides clues as to what occurred causing specific injuries. This chapter explains various injuries and causes related to motor vehicles, motorcycles, and pedestrians involved in traffic fatalities.

Role of the Medicolegal Death Investigator in Traffic Fatalities

Forensic investigators may be asked to examine the external injuries of motor vehicle accident victims and provide valuable information to the pathologist to formulate the cause and manner of death. This is often very difficult to do accurately on scene, unless obvious severe craniocerebral injury is sustained.

DOI: 10.4324/9781003538622-12

Subsequent autopsies in those cases frequently reveal unexpected injuries not diagnosed at the scene or in emergency rooms by external examination alone.

However, in some jurisdictions, the MDI may be called upon to examine the body externally when major injuries are visible that would explain death. In such cases, to help ensure accuracy of external examination under direction of the ME/coroner:

1. Photograph the decedent as is.
2. Remove all clothing from the victim.
3. Clean off blood.
4. Examine the body under good light.
5. Record all injuries, including photography documentation.

If there is insufficient injury to explain death, then an autopsy must be performed. Many forensic pathologists will autopsy all motor vehicle accident victims to photograph and document injuries, as criminal or civil litigation may follow.

Motor Vehicle Injuries

Head Injuries

Head injuries are among the largest group of serious injuries and the most important site of fatal injuries sustained in motor vehicle accidents. The primary traumatic lesions include skull fractures; subdural, epidural, or subarachnoid hematomas; or axonal injuries (see Chapter 9). Skull fractures are caused by direct force or transmitted force. Signs of skull fractures include the following:

- Blood/cerebral spinal fluid draining from the ears that indicates a fracture of the basilar skull (middle cranial fossa).
- Bilateral "black" or "raccoon" eyes indicating a fracture of the basilar skull (anterior cranial fossa).
- *Battle's sign* or bruising behind the ear indicating a fracture of temporal bone or middle cranial fossa resulting in a skull fracture.

The severity of injury varies from mild injury (linear fracture) to moderate to severe (depressed, basilar, or stellate skull fractures).

Subdural hematoma is defined as a hemorrhage between the dura and arachnoid membrane caused by torn bridging veins. Signs include a gradual increase in raised intracranial pressure, for example, bradycardia, gradual loss of consciousness, and fixed dilated pupils. Subdural hematoma is a common fatal injury associated with severe injury that occurs in 30% of serious head injuries. However, 50% occur without skull fractures.

Subarachnoid hemorrhage is defined as hemorrhage between the arachnoid membrane and pia (brain surface) caused by rupture of the vertebral or cerebral arteries associated with moderate-to-severe injury. Subarachnoid hemorrhage is a common injury in motor vehicle accidents and results in rapid loss of consciousness and cerebral edema.

Epidural hematoma is defined as hemorrhage between the skull and dura associated with extensive head injury, skull fractures, laceration of the middle meningeal artery, and rapid loss of consciousness.

Diffuse head injury or craniocerebral injury may include skull fractures, diffuse brain injury, diffuse vascular injury, and/or diffuse axonal injury. The brain is very vulnerable to rotational forces, with movement within the cranial vault causing shearing forces within the white matter. The skull may be intact, and the brain often looks extremely normal. Clinically, the victim is unconscious at the scene and never regains consciousness.

Spinal and Brainstem Injuries

High spinal and brainstem injuries include fatal ponto-midbrain or pontomedullary junction or high cervical spinal cord injuries (atlanto-occipital dislocation or high cervical fracture) caused by flexion injury and deceleration injuries. These injuries compromise vital respiratory function.

Midcervical fractures and associated spinal cord injuries are usually caused by flexion. Hypermobility of the neck is an unreliable method for diagnosis, especially if the victim is young or rigor is absent.

Thoracic spinal cord injuries are caused by flexion or compression injuries. The severity is mild to moderate. Unlike high cervical spinal cord or brainstem injury, compression of the cord at the thoracic level will not compromise vital respiratory functions.

Lumbar spinal cord injury severity is mild to moderate and is more common in vehicular pedestrian accidents.

Facial Injuries

Facial injuries include maxilla, mandible, and zygomatic bone fractures and cause external bruising of the anterior neck and face, intraoral hemorrhage, and/or avulsed teeth.

Chest Injuries

The chest is the second most important site of fatal injuries. Forty percent of motor vehicle accidents have severe chest injuries but often very little external bruising. Chest injuries include rib fractures resulting in cardiac, pulmonary aortic tears resulting in internal bleeding or pneumothoraces. Cardiac contusions/lacerations are usually fatal injuries and are caused by deceleration injuries (heart continues moving forward against fixed sternum) resulting in tearing at the thinnest parts—right ventricle, atria. Associated findings noted at autopsy include fractures of the sternum, bilateral rib fractures, and hemopericardium (blood in the heart sac), which may cause a cardiac tamponade.

Aortic laceration is a fatal deceleration injury associated with fractures of the sternum and/or rib fractures. The aorta is relatively fixed at junction with the left ventricle and at the junction of the arch with the left subclavian artery. Lacerations generally occur above the aortic valve or just distal to the left subclavian artery, resulting in cardiac tamponade or bilateral hemothoraces. Fractures and displacement of the thoracic and lumbar vertebrae often result in laceration or transection of the aorta, resulting in a hemothorax or hemoperitoneum.

Hemothorax is defined as blood in pleural cavity caused by aortic, intercostal artery, or pulmonary vessel lacerations.

Pneumothorax is defined as air in chest cavity caused by open chest wounds, torn bronchus, pulmonary laceration, or medical intervention, including cardiopulmonary resuscitation and mechanical ventilation. Signs include subcutaneous emphysema (bubbles of air under the skin of the chest, neck, and scrotum) and larynx shift from the midline with tension pneumothorax. Severity is moderate to severe, and rapid expansion of pneumothorax causes lungs to collapse, resulting in a tension pneumothorax, which is rapidly fatal.

Unstable rib fractures (flail chest*)* is defined as multiple ribs broken in more than one place. This creates a segment that collapses on inspiration, interfering with normal respiration. Signs include bruising, palpable rib fractures, and generalized "whiteout" of lungs on chest x-ray. Severity depends on the extent of injury and is more severe if more than four ribs are broken or if ribs are broken in more than one place.

Lung contusions/lacerations are associated with rib fractures and cause hemo-/pneumothoraces. Aspiration of blood or gastric contents occurs with head injuries that bleed and causes a depressed level of consciousness. Aspiration of blood or gastric contents may be the terminal event.

Abdominal Injuries

Severe abdominal injuries may show little or no external bruising. Aspirating the abdominal cavity with a syringe and needle may reveal blood (hemoperitoneum) with abdominal injuries. Severe abdominal injuries often occur in motor vehicle fatalities and often include pelvic fractures and/or lacerations of the liver, spleen, kidneys/bladder, pancreas, or intestines.

Pelvic fractures include anterior/posterior fractures and separation of symphysis pubis and sacroiliac joints. Fractures through sacroiliac joints tear small iliac veins, cause hemorrhage into pelvic soft tissue, and may cause bruising around the groin and instability of the pelvic girdle.

Liver laceration is caused by direct blunt impact and/or secondarily from rib fractures and may occur from seat belts, air bags, steering wheels, or direct crushing injury from the vehicle's frame. Severity depends on the extent of laceration and may be moderate to lethal.

Splenic laceration is caused by direct blunt impact and/or secondary rib fractures and is more likely to rupture if enlarged, resulting in internal bleeding. Severity depends on the extent of laceration and may be moderate to severe.

Renal/bladder lacerations cause blood in the urine and/or retroperitoneal hemorrhage.

Pancreatic contusion/laceration is caused by direct impact, commonly seen with lap seat belt use, and is often associated with duodenal rupture. Lower abdominal seat belt abrasion may be present.

Hollow viscus rupture includes rupture of the colon, small intestine, or stomach and is caused by direct impact. Hollow viscus rupture results in free air under the diaphragm seen on x-ray.

Injuries of the Extremities

Injuries of the extremities include femur fractures that may cause severe blood loss, fat emboli, deformity, and bruising.

Crush injuries cause acute blood loss and rhabdomyolysis (breakdown of muscle), causing acute renal failure and disseminated intravascular coagulation, where intravascular microthrombi and bleeding occur concurrently.

Degloving injury (stripping of flap of skin or tissue by abrasion) involves the hands and feet, caused by tire tread or road contact, and may be worse if the vehicle is braking at the time of impact.

Traumatic amputation is caused by direct force and may result in severe blood loss.

Superficial injuries include dicing incisions caused by tempered glass from side windows and may help "place" the occupant in the vehicle (driver vs. passenger), as the injuries occur on the side of the body closest to the side window (Figure 10.1). Parchment abrasions (brown or tan dry abrasions) occur during the postmortem or perimortem period. Tire tread abrasions are seen in pedestrian or ejected occupant rollover accidents.

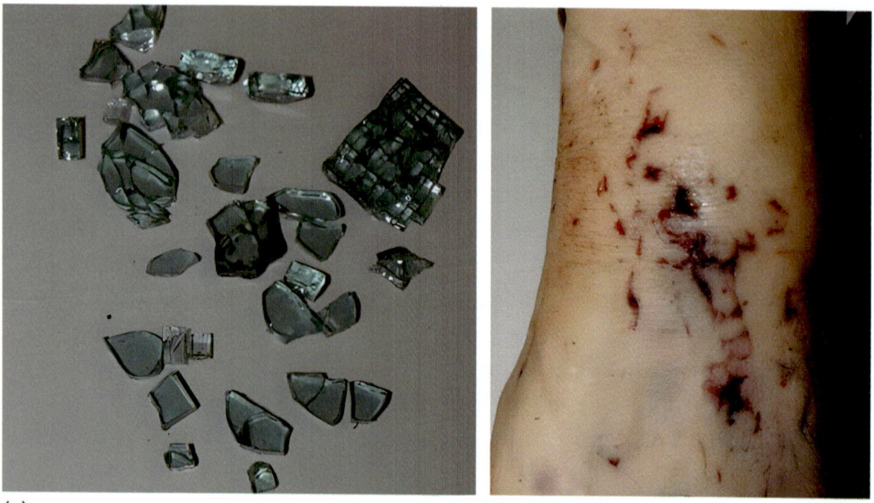

(a) (b)

Figure 10.1 Cubes of tempered glass (a) and (b) dicing injury.

Motor Vehicles and Trucks

Head-on Collisions

Head-on collisions result in different injuries to the occupants based on position within the vehicle.

Driver

Driver injury occurs when the face hits the windshield and causes facial lacerations (less common now that laminated glass is used in windshields) and/or facial and frontal skull fractures. Injuries from the head striking the steering wheel or roof of the vehicle result in frontal skull fractures (usually bilateral), periorbital contusions (black eyes), subdural and subarachnoid hemorrhages, and frontal and temporal lobe contusions. Contact of chest and abdomen hitting the steering wheel or column results in cardiac contusion and laceration, aortic laceration, fractures at sternum and ribs, liver lacerations, and splenic lacerations. Knees impacting the dashboard cause fractures of the femur, tibia, and pelvis, and posterior dislocation of the femur at the hips. Seat belts reduce but do not prevent these injuries, and air bags reduce injuries caused by steering wheel. (Seat belts must also be worn with air bags.)

Frequently, driver survives the crash and may be subject to charges for death of the passenger, especially if intoxicated. Investigation as to position in the vehicle includes the following:

- Pattern and type of blood in the vehicle or side window
- Trace evidence, hair, and fibers in the vehicle

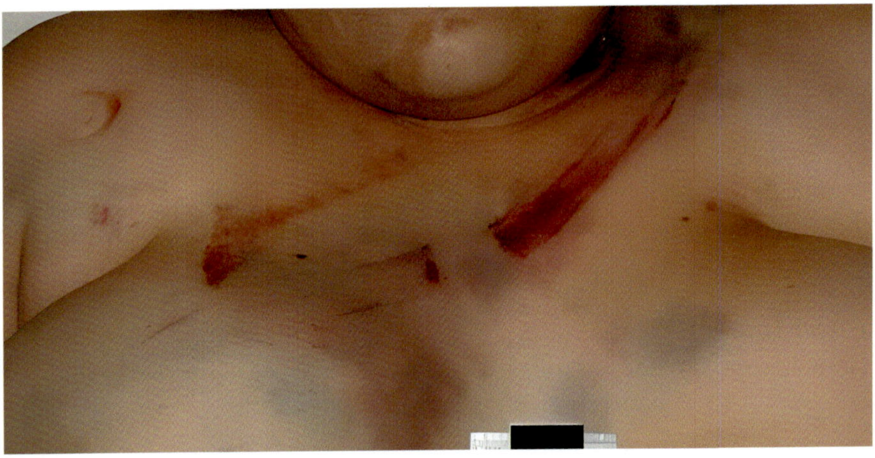

Figure 10.2 Seat belt abrasions.

- Brake or accelerator pedal impression on the sole of the driver's shoe
- Seat belt abrasions on the body (Figure 10.2)
- Pattern and location of dicing injury

Front Passenger

The front passenger has twice the incidence of serious injuries in motor vehicle accidents. Injury pattern is similar to that of the driver, but the front passenger does not have a steering wheel to hold onto to break forward movement and usually has less warning of the collision. Instead of the head, chest, and abdomen hitting the steering wheel, these body parts tend to hit the dashboard.

Rear Passenger

The rear passenger often sustains less severe injuries, as the back of the front seat acts as passive restraint, but often no seat belt or only lap seat belt is worn. However, unrestrained passengers tend to hit their heads on the vehicle roof, causing severe injury. Passengers wearing lap seat belts may show typical injuries such as lumbar spine fractures; pelvic fractures; and rupture of the duodenum, liver, and pancreas.

Side Impact Collisions

The modern car is designed for head-on impacts; they are very vulnerable to side impacts because doors and side panels are lighter. There is greater penetration into interior space. Seat belts and front compartment air bags may be less protective in side impacts than in head-on collisions. Side impacts may make front air bags unstable, and they may inflate up to 30 minutes after impact. Side air bags help reduce injuries from side impacts. Injuries tend to be lateralized by direct impact, and the victim may be forced against the door on the side opposite the impact.

Head Injuries

The brain is vulnerable to lateral rotation and may sustain injuries, including skull fractures, subdural/subarachnoid hemorrhages, and diffuse closed head injury.

Chest Injuries

Chest injuries include unstable rib fractures on the side of impact, pulmonary contusions, and frequently result in deceleration injuries.

Abdominal Injuries

Abdominal injuries include liver lacerations, splenic lacerations, and often lateral and unstable pelvic fractures.

External Injuries

Side windows are made of tempered glass that produces cuboidal sharp fragments; these cause multiple short linear or squared-off superficial cuts known as *dicing incisions* or injuries on the face and arms.

Injuries to the Extremities

Fractures of the femur and tibia on the impact side are not uncommon.

Rear Impact Collisions

The seat provides good protection to the body in rear impacts provided the vehicle itself is not crushed. The introduction of headrests has significantly reduced the incidence of hyperextension injuries of the cervical spine and whiplash injuries.

Rollover Vehicle Accidents

A complex pattern of injuries occurs with rollover accidents, as the victim may come into contact with many surfaces. Collapse of the roof may cause *traumatic asphyxia* due to compression of the chest or head and neck flexion, massive head injuries, fracture of the base of the skull, compression fractures of the spine, and chest and abdominal injuries.

Ejection Accidents

Unrestrained, ejected passengers (especially in rollover and head-on impacts) often die of massive head injuries, crush injuries to the chest, unstable rib fractures, or flexion injuries of the spinal cord.

Motorcycle Injuries

Motorcycle helmets decrease death and serious injury by 65%. With head-on impact, the rider is thrown forward over the handle bars striking head and chest and flexing the cervical and thoracic spine. Injuries seen with motorcycle injuries include severe head, spine, chest, abdominal, and leg injuries.

Head Injury

Severe head injuries include

- Skull fractures
- Subdural/subarachnoid hemorrhages
- Contusions
- Laceration of pontomedullary junction of the brainstem

Spinal Injury

Spinal injuries include

- Atlanto-occipital dislocation
- Cervical and thoracic fractures
- Spinal fractures

Chest Injury

Chest injuries often involve

- Multiple rib fractures
- Aortic laceration and cardiac laceration (deceleration injuries)

Abdominal Injury

Abdominal injuries involve

- Liver laceration
- Splenic laceration
- Pelvic fractures

Leg Injury

Leg injuries include

- Extensive abrasion, burns, and bruising of the thighs and legs
- Femoral fractures caused by the motorcycle hitting the legs

Pedestrians

Classic Impact Patterns

Primary impact is from the bumper strike as it hits the lower leg, resulting in bruising of the calf and fractures of the tibia and fibula. The height of the fracture above the heel reflects the height of the bumper at impact but is often lower because the vehicle is braking at the time of impact. If one foot is raised at the time of impact, fracture may be lower on one leg than on the other. Occasionally, the primary impact site is not obvious without dissection.

Secondary impact results when the body strikes the pavement or hood of the vehicle. Paint transfer or patterned abrasions from impact of the headlight, hood, or windshield may occur. On the buttocks, impact produces an avulsion pocket, a cavity of lacerated adipose tissue, which forms a large deep bruise; often the skin is intact. A diagram depicting primary vs. secondary impact is shown in Figure 10.3.

The head hits

- The windshield if the vehicle is traveling less than 30 miles per hour (mph)
- The top/back of car if the vehicle is traveling faster than 30 mph
- The road behind car if the vehicle is traveling faster than 60 mph

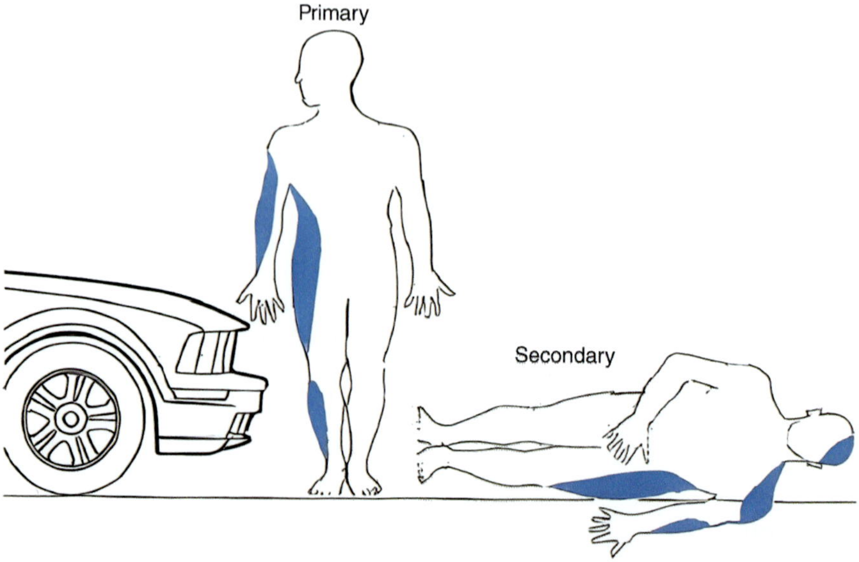

Figure 10.3 Diagram of primary vs. secondary impact sites.

Pickup Trucks and Higher Vehicle Accidents

Pickup trucks and higher vehicles tend to push the body under the vehicle rather than throw the body over it if primary impact is above the victim's center of gravity. Primary impact is often higher on the body than in an impact from a car. Often a van or truck has vertical or overhung grillwork that causes patterned abrasions.

Secondary impact may involve tire imprints (tire abrasions and "brush" abrasions), as the victim is often run over. "Crush" injuries of the head, chest, and abdomen may result in deep lacerations of organs and/or depressed fractures of the skull. Protruding objects under the vehicle may produce patterned injuries. Characteristically heavy grease stains may be observed on clothing or the body.

Children

Because of their lower centers of gravity, children tend to go under—not over—the car. Children are often hit by pickup trucks and vans backing out of driveways because they cannot be seen.

Children run over by a vehicle sustain crush injuries of the head, chest, and abdomen. Tire mark abrasions are often seen as patterned injuries on the body.

Atypical Pedestrian Patterns

Low-velocity impacts show bruising visible subcutaneously, but no obvious primary impact site on calf is seen.

Unusual pedestrian victim positions include lying, kneeling, or squatting. Individuals lying on the road include intoxicated individuals, suicides, individuals hit by previous car, and already dead or dumped bodies. A kneeling/squatting position shows the primary impact site on the arms or trunk. These victims have low centers of gravity; therefore, they tend to be run over. Injuries include crush injuries to the head, chest, and abdomen; tire and brush abrasions; and femoral, humeral, and pelvic fractures.

Vehicular Homicide

Vehicular homicide involves intentional high-acceleration impact of a pedestrian, cyclist, or other individual resulting in severe, fatal injuries. Multiple tire prints are usually present, and manner of death ultimately depends on evidence from the scene and eyewitness statements. "Hit-and-run fatalities" may also be considered homicides for manner of death, depending on the investigative circumstances of the case.

Accident vs. Natural Causes

Natural causes of death show no bruising or injury associated with typical motor vehicle pattern injuries. Typically, there is a low-velocity impact or single-vehicle accident with little damage to the vehicle. Autopsy will reveal natural disease with minimal or no injury to explain death, and the manner of death is thus best classified as natural. If the individual has natural disease but sustained injury from the accident and was alive at the time of the accident, the manner of death is best classified as accidental (e.g. natural disease in a "hostile environment").

Atherosclerotic Cardiovascular Disease

Frequently, the driver is noted to slow down prior to the accident, and the impact is often very low velocity. In addition, chances are that the cause of death is atherosclerotic cardiovascular disease (ASCVD) and the manner is natural if there is no good explanation for the crash, collapse was witnessed before the crash, injuries on the body and car are minor and superficial, and driver has severe ASCVD.

However, if there are extensive injuries with abundant bruising and bleeding and evidence of a recent heart attack, the manner of death should be accidental.

Cerebrovascular Accident

If there is a ruptured cerebral aneurysm or a bleeding vascular malformation, death may be sudden. Often it may be difficult to differentiate these natural causes of death from cerebral trauma due to the accident. Remote infarcts or a history of seizure activity in drivers may increase the risk of motor vehicle collisions, which may be fatal.

Motor Vehicle Suicide

Collisions with no explanation—for example, a single vehicle hitting a stationary object, driving off a bridge without evidence of braking, or pedestrians running in front of moving vehicles—may be a suicidal manner of death. Careful investigative clues may reveal previous suicide threats, previous suicide attempts such as scars on wrists, history of mental illness or anti-depression medication, and imprint of acceleration pedal on the sole of the shoe. A psychological autopsy may help sort out the intent and manner of death (see Chapter 14).

Fatal Pedestrian Investigation

There are two primary considerations at the scene of an automobile–pedestrian accident:

1. Preservation and security of the area
2. Analysis of the scene, vehicle, body, and circumstance

Auto–Pedestrian Collision

When an automobile and pedestrian collide, a complete description of the scene is necessary. This begins with road and weather conditions. The surface material and lighting at the point of collision are noted. The pedestrian's activity at the time of the accident is also described. For example, the pedestrian may be on a scooter, using in-line skates, pushing or pulling a cart or stroller, or carrying materials. Photographs of the scene indicate the items that might have been involved in the collision.

Observations at the scene include skid marks, spills, debris, and personal effects. Skid marks should be measured, photographed, and described. Spills at the scene are usually from the vehicle but might also be from objects that the victim was carrying. Samples of fluids should be either taken or positively identified on site. Automobile coolant, washer fluid, battery acid, and oil are frequently seen. Debris from under the victim's body and the vehicle, such as mud, dirt, rust, snow, or other material, should be identified as to the location found and type. Other debris might be from the automobile itself such as glass, plastic, chrome, or parts of the vehicle. (One chip of paint will reveal the color, year, make, and model of a vehicle that struck the victim and may have left the scene.) Clothing, shoes, tissue, blood smears, and personal effects are also often strewn about the scene and must be collected and properly preserved.

Driver and Vehicle Investigation

The automobile is photographed, measured, and diagrammed—usually on a standard form. The impact site shows transfer of material and pattern imprints. Hair, tissue, or fibers may be on the vehicle. If the windshield is broken, the patterns of breaks are important. Blood spattered on the automobile is analyzed for spatter pattern.

Driver behaviors contribute to the investigation. Activities in which the driver was involved prior to the crash are researched. The investigator notes the time when the driver first became aware of the pedestrian. A description of evasive actions taken is documented from the driver as well as any witnesses. Also, any obstructions described by the driver that interfered with a clear view of traffic are listed.

The driver and witnesses should describe post-crash actions. In the case of "hit-and-run" accidents, the time of flight related to acknowledgment of impact is important. If the driver began treatment of the pedestrian at the scene, all measures taken should be described. Additionally, a determination must be made as to whether or not the victim was moved; if so, how far and by whom. Medical information may be obtained from the driver, including blood analysis for alcohol and drugs. The presence or absence of drug paraphernalia at the scene or on the driver is also useful evidence to the investigator.

Finally, a forensic pathologist presents findings from the autopsy and toxicology results.

Adaptations of standard investigations of motor vehicle–pedestrian collisions can be made to collisions between people on moving sports equipment or large animals. Automobiles frequently collide with deer. In some instances, the driver is injured or killed. Many techniques of investigation can be used to assess damage and driver condition.

Collection and Preservation of Evidence

Evidence collection from other investigative techniques applies to the scene of a vehicle–pedestrian death. As in other situations, trace evidence from the victim, including hair, blood, skin, and clothing fragments, is collected. Specific evidence from the vehicle includes paint, vehicle parts, grease, and glass.

The autopsy and examination of evidence in motor vehicle impacts with pedestrians is surely to be included in any litigation surrounding liability. Consequently, the skills of the ME/coroner and death investigators will be challenged.

Motor Vehicle Injuries

Motor vehicles and pedestrians may collide without causing death. Whether the injuries lead to death or recovery, investigations of motor vehicle accident injuries are conducted to determine fault and extent of liability. Settlement of claims related to accidents is generally delayed until all parties to the accident have been satisfied with their independent investigations. In some cases, accidents involve buses, trolleys, or multiple passenger vehicles.

Type and Severity of Injuries

Speed, vehicle, and victim size are critical to determining type and severity of injuries. The victim's height, weight, sex, and age are obtained at the beginning of an investigation.

Speed of Vehicle

First, information should be obtained to determine if the vehicle was accelerating or braking. Measurements and configuration of tire marks aid in determining vehicle activity.

Speeds less than 25 mph

- Little vehicle damage.
- Victim is thrown forward or to the side of a moving car.

Speeds from 25 to 40 mph

- Front impact with victim thrown onto hood and/or windshield.
- Victim then either slides off hood or travels for some distance before falling off.

Speeds greater than 50 mph

- Impact launches the victim up and over hood with re-impact on the trunk, rear bumper, or pavement.
- Impact by a large truck, van, bus, or semitrailer creates impact site above the victim's center of gravity; the victim is launched forward or to the side or held against the grill until the vehicle stops.
- The victim is often run over by the vehicle.

Adults

Adult pedestrians sustain bumper fractures (fractures caused by front bumpers), pelvic fractures, or a variety of skin and soft tissue injuries (Figure 10.4). Notwithstanding variations in the type of vehicle, bumper height, victim's height, and victim position, one or more types of injury can result. Injuries from the impact of a braking MG Midget differ considerably from those caused by a Lincoln Town Car being driven at the speed limit.

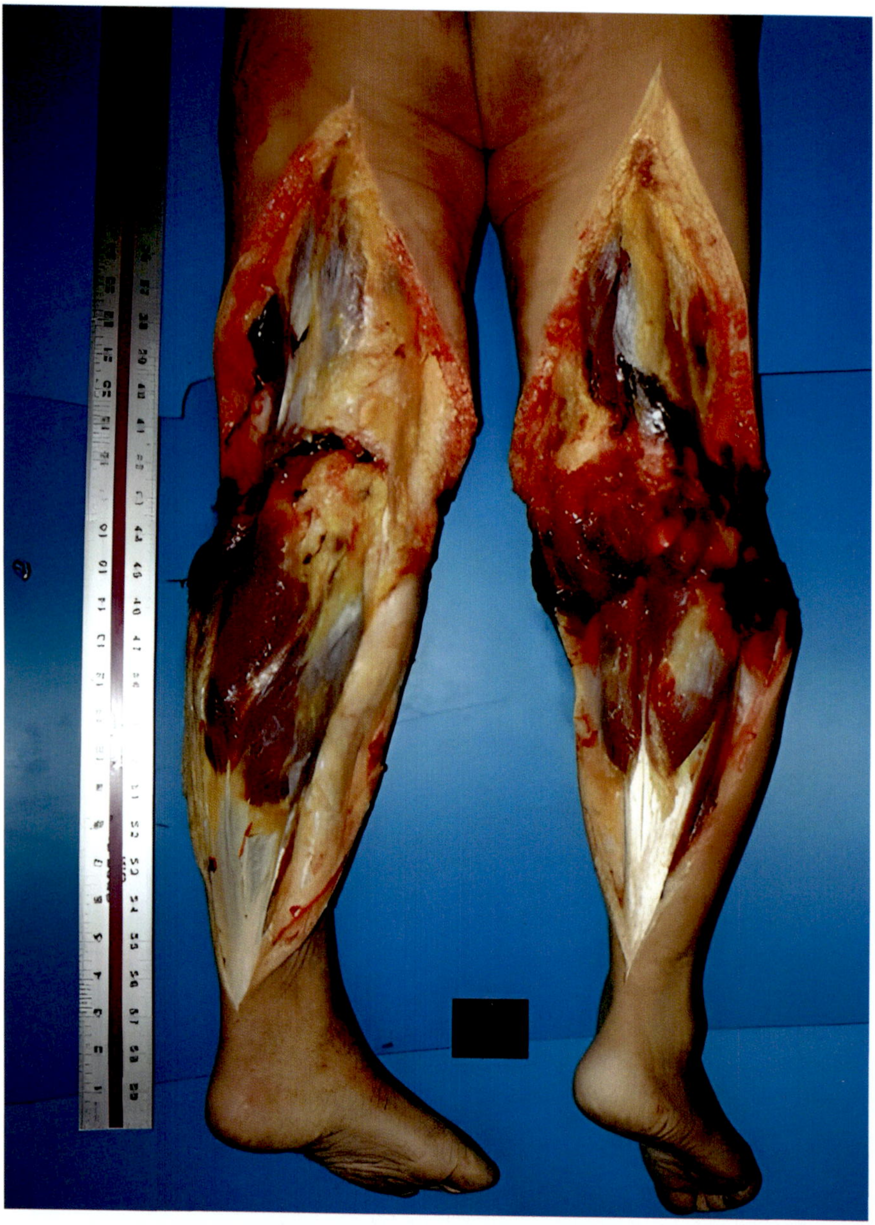

Figure 10.4 Leg cut-down demonstrating bumper injuries.

Adult pedestrians who are standing, running, or walking usually have an impact site below the center of gravity—that is, below the waistline at pelvic brim. A pelvic fracture occurs, frequently with a secondary injury where the body hits the edge of the hood. In addition to the fracture, hyperextension of the pelvis with stretch injuries to the groin may be sustained.

Abrasions and contusions are occasionally absent. Those likely to be seen show patterns that match the vehicle at the impact site. In addition to tire marks, patterns are created by the grill, headlights, mirrors, or emblems.

Bumper fractures are likely. These are wedge-shaped fractures of the tibia, fibula, or femur. Typically, the wedge points in the direction of vehicle travel. The average distance between the ground and fracture is 14–15 inches, including the heel height of the victim's shoes. Bumper fractures of different heights may indicate that the victim was walking or running.

Blunt trauma to the head often results from striking the windshield, windshield support, trunk, or rear bumper. Although few significant chest and abdominal injuries occur, cervical spine injuries are more common. Whiplash injuries can result from a rear strike to the pedestrian. Atlanto-occipital subluxations appear as part of injuries to the cervical spine.

Additional injuries might appear as avulsion pockets on body surfaces. Avulsion pockets are pockets of blood and/or liquefied fat beneath the skin at an impact site. That site can represent the impact with the vehicle or ground. Skin overlying the injury is usually intact without external evidence of injury but may be abraded.

Children

Children show impact sites similar to those seen on adults struck by a van or bus—that is, the child is hit above the waist and thrown forward or to the side and run over by the vehicle. Injuries may be more severe with children than adults due to size differences. However, the description, tire imprints, and types of injuries are similar.

Victims Lying in Roadway

Victims of automobile–pedestrian accidents may remain on a road awaiting emergency care or police response. These victims may be hit by a second vehicle. Single-vehicle victims may have an impact site from a "hit-and-run" incident or intoxicated driver. Victims, too, may be intoxicated while lying injured on a roadway.

Injuries to lying victims are commonly blunt injuries from under surfaces of the vehicle, "road rash" abrasions from being dragged, tire imprints, and crush injuries. Tire marks leave a patterned imprint on the skin and clothing (Figures 10.5 and 10.6). Photographs of the pattern or tracing the design onto paper or a plastic transparency can be useful to the investigation. Skin avulsions show tears in the direction of turning wheels, while severe lacerations result from braking tires. Abrasions occur on the skin where the body is dragged or scraped along the ground.

Figure 10.5 Clothing demonstrating a tire tread pattern.

Crush injuries, including lacerations to visceral organs and chest compression, occur when the victim is run over. There is an "overstretching" of skin (or striae) with resultant superficial tears.

Secondary Impact Injuries

Secondary impact injuries are incurred from striking the ground, other fixed objects, or another vehicle following the initial impact. Brush burns from sliding along pavement or blunt injuries of the head and extremities result from the momentum of the victim, as the body is tossed or dragged from the point of impact. Rollover injuries are generally a combination of primary, secondary, and crush injuries.

Sideswipes

Injuries caused by objects extending beyond the perimeter of a vehicle are considered sideswipe contacts. Pedestrians can incur sideswipe contacts from motor vehicles. In a brief contact, there may even be absence of a definite impact site. Major or minor injuries can be caused by objects affixed to the side of an automobile such as mirrors, tires, or even a roof.

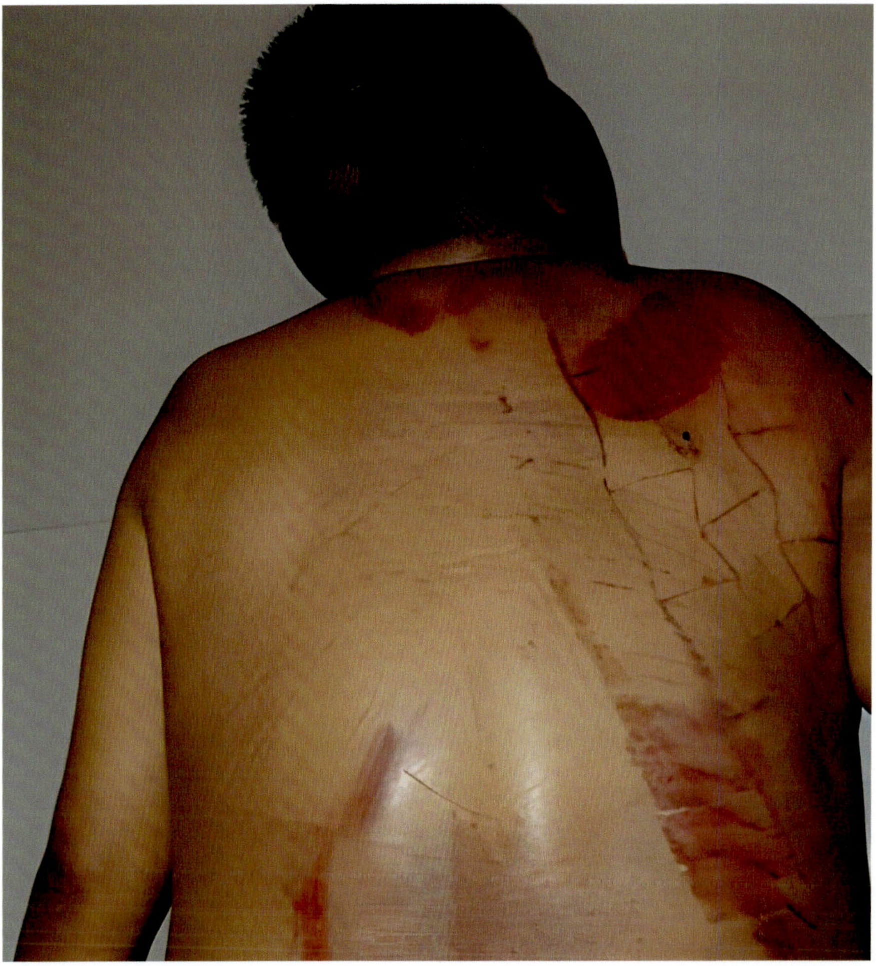

Figure 10.6 Tire mark, patterned injury on skin.

Head injuries often occur from being knocked to the ground. The types of injuries described earlier as secondary impacts also pertain to falls after a sideswipe.

Scene Analysis

Scene analysis focuses on determining what happened and how it happened. Most automobile collisions are related to accidents, but some are mechanisms of suicide or homicide. Scene analysis can help the ME/coroner determine whether a death is related to homicide, suicide, or natural causes. Photography preserves the scene for later reanalysis, and photographs provide some of the medicolegal evidence used to determine liability. Sketches and diagrams are also important. The police fill in a standard diagram on the police report. This includes information such as positions of vehicles, traffic light information, damage to vehicles, flow of traffic, and unusual obstructions or obstacles. Perspective sketches of the vehicle from a number of angles relate the vehicle to the scene. Position of the victim and evidence of external injuries can be included in a diagram. Later, the diagrams and photographs can validate one another.

Bibliography

DiMaio, V.J.M. and Molina, D.K. 2021. *DiMaio's Forensic Pathology* (3rd ed.). Boca Raton, FL: CRC Press. https://doi.org/10.4324/9780429318764

Dolinak, D., Matshes, E., and Lew, E. 2006. *Forensic Pathology: Principles and Practice*. Burlington, MA: Elsevier.

Firearms Identification 11

MARY H. DUDLEY

OBJECTIVES

Upon completion of this chapter and corresponding reference material, the reader will be able to

- Discuss the history and development of firearms
- Differentiate between a rifle and shotgun
- Identify various kinds of bullets
- Identify direction of rifling from recovered bullets
- Describe two types of handguns

Introduction

Law enforcement may move or remove weapons from the scene involved in firearm fatalities. It is important to have a basic understanding of the various types of firearms and ammunition as it relates to gunshot wounds and fatal injuries. The medicolegal death investigator (MDI) must obtain reports and photographs of the scene from other agencies involved. This chapter outlines basic terminology related to firearms and ballistics, including ammunition, handguns, rifles, and shotguns.

Firearms

History of Firearms

The first firearm was a fourteenth-century hand cannon. It was a crude weapon with a smooth, unified bore that was loaded with a variety of small hard objects like metal, rocks, or gravel. The matchlock was the standard firearm of the first settlers in North America. This firearm was named for the match, a wicked piece of material that was lit when lowered into a priming pan of loose gunpowder. The wheel lock was the first firearm to use flint and steel for lighting the primer—similar to a cigarette lighter. The flintlock fired when a flint clamped into the hammer, struck a metal plate, and sparks from the flint ignited the gunpowder. The flintlock was used from the 1600s until the 1800s.

DOI: 10.4324/9781003538622-13

In the early 1800s, fulminate of mercury was used as a primer in the percussion lock firearm. A small cap coated with fulminate of mercury was struck by the hammer causing a spark to ignite the gunpowder. This type of primer led to the self-contained cartridge and was an important step in the development of breech-loading (rear-loading) firearms. Rimfire and center-fire ammunition are used in breech-loading firearms. The breech-loader resulted in the ability to open and close the back of the barrel, permitting rapid firing.

Ammunition

Ammunition used in a rifle or pistol is generally called a cartridge. A cartridge contains powder, primer, and a bullet assembled in a case.

Gunpowder (propellant) drives in the bullet from the firearm as it burns. Types of powder include rolled ball, flake, lamel, and tubular. Primer usually consists of compounds of lead, barium, or antimony and is used to light the powder. It burns quickly when struck by a sharp blow of the firing pin. In center-fire ammunition, the primer is contained in a small metal cap that fits in the center bottom of the cartridge case. In rimfire ammunition, the primer is located in the rim of the cartridge case.

Common cartridges for rifle and pistol use are listed in chart form and by cartridge interchangeability. The ammunition must match the gun in which it is fired. The caliber is stamped on the head of the cartridge. Examples of caliber in inches and metric equivalent are listed in chart forms (Table 11.1).

Forensic pathologists generally categorize projectiles into three major groups.

1. Small caliber (.22 or .25)
2. Medium caliber (.357, .38, 9 mm)
3. Large caliber (.44)

Table 11.1 Common Cartridges for Rifles and Pistols

Common Cartridge	Cartridge Interchangeability
Caliber in Inches	Metric Equivalent in Millimeters
.22	5.56
.25	6.35
.30	7.62
.32	7.65
.40	10
.45	11.43

Bullets fall into two categories:

1. All-lead bullets
2. Metal-jacketed bullets

The configuration of a bullet may be

- Round nose
- Wadcutter (cylindrical)
- Semiwadcutter (a truncated cone with a flat tip and sharp shoulder)
- Hollow point
- Hydra-Shok (central post)
- Glazer round (composed of a lead core, snake shot metal pellets, and a blue Teflon plug)

All-lead bullets are constructed of lead to which antimony, tin, or both have been added to increase the hardness of the alloy. Some lead bullets are covered by a thin coating of copper or copper alloy that acts to harden and lubricate the bullet. This coating should not be confused with a copper jacket.

Metal-jacketed bullets may be either full metal-jacketed or partial metal-jacketed. As a rule, military ammunition is full metal-jacketed, while civilian ammunition is partial metal-jacketed. Jacketing usually consists of copper, although aluminum and steel (rarely) may be used. In partial metal-jacketed ammunition, the metal jacket is open at the tip to expose the core of the bullet.

Mechanism of a Firearm

With a cartridge in the chamber of a gun, the hammer falls, driving the fire pin to strike the primer at the base of the cartridge. This ignites the primer that explodes and ignites the powder. The powder burns and creates gas that expands in the case, forcing the bullet and gas down the barrel of the gun.

Safety

Most guns have a safety. One must learn exactly how it works. The safety blocks the trigger so that it cannot be pulled. The bottom or latch that puts in on or off is located close to the action on a firearm.

The safety must always be engaged whenever a gun is loaded. The safety is released only prior to firing the gun.

Be careful! Only the safety blocks the trigger—nothing else. A hard blow in the right place can still fire the gun. Also, a safety can wear out or may not work. Never depend on the safety to prevent a gun from firing by accident.

Handgun Actions

There are four types of handgun actions:

1. Bolt action—The bolt is a firearm in which the breech closure is in line with the bore at all times; manually reciprocates to load, unload, and cock; and is locked in place by breech bolt lugs and engaging abutments usually in the receiver. The two principal types of bolt actions are the turn bolt and the straight pull.
2. Single shot—The single-shot pistol is usually a break-open action. The cartridge is loaded and ejected by hand.
3. Revolver—The name revolver derives from the action of the revolver's round magazine or cylinder; each time the trigger is pulled or the hammer is cocked, the cylinder revolves. When the chamber in the cylinder is in line with the barrel, it becomes the firing chamber. Revolvers work by single or double action. With single action, the hammer must be cocked before each shot is fired, whereas with double action, the hammer is cocked and the cylinder rotates when the trigger is pulled (Figure 11.1).

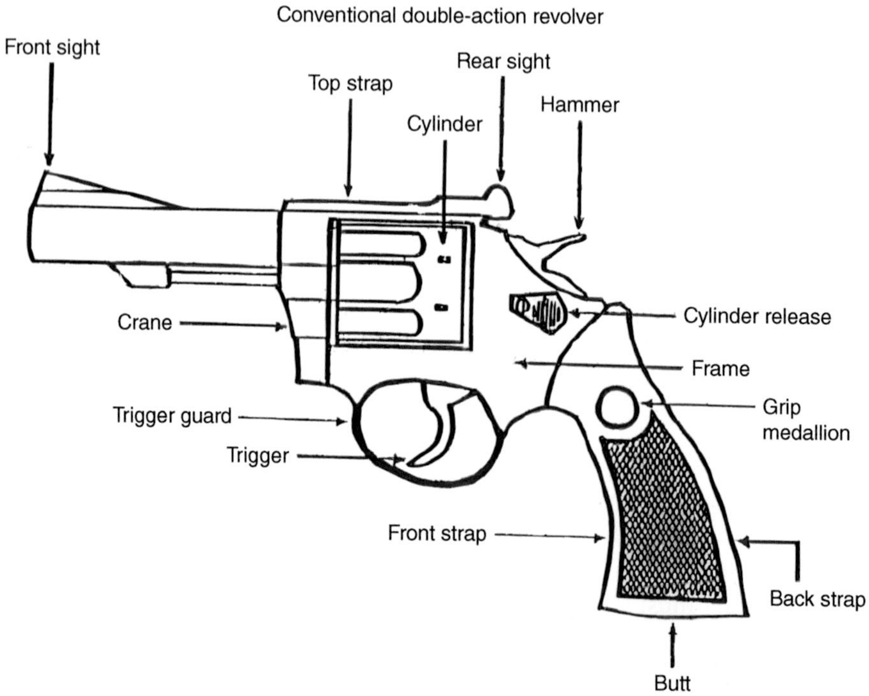

Figure 11.1 The drawing depicts a revolver.

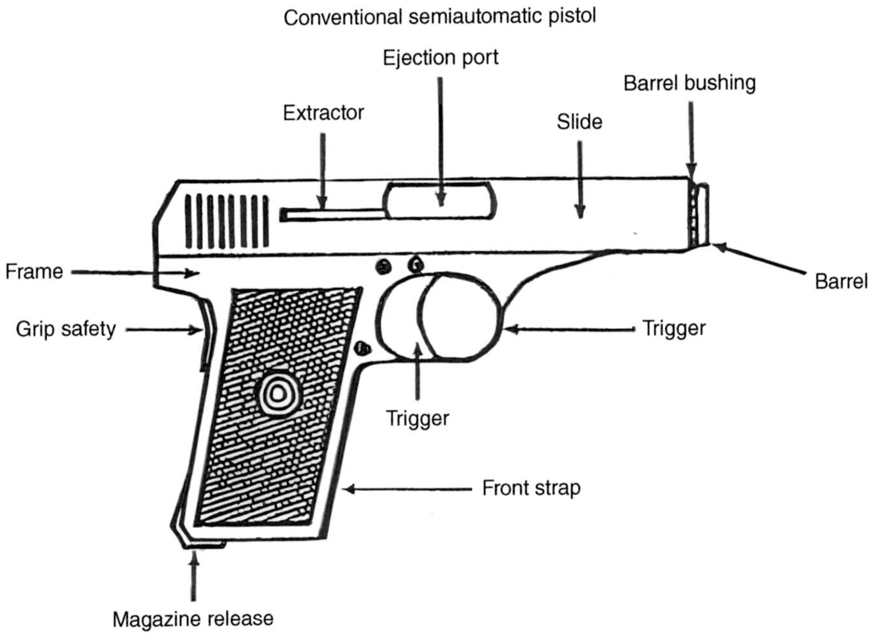

Figure 11.2 The drawing depicts a semiautomatic pistol.

4. Semiautomatic—Most semiautomatic pistols must be cocked for the first shot. Each time the trigger is pulled, an empty cartridge is ejected and a fresh one loaded. Extra cartridges are carried in the magazine or clip (Figure 11.2).

Basic Types of Handguns

Revolvers all possess a cylinder that revolves with each cocking and firing of the weapon. Cartridges are usually of the rimmed type and are not automatically ejected during firing. Revolver mechanisms may be either single action or double action. Single-action guns are typified by the frontier-style "six shooter." These weapons all have an external hammer that must be manually cocked before the gun can be fired by pulling the trigger. The term single action refers to the fact that pulling the trigger accomplishes only one thing—release of the cocked hammer. Double-action revolvers may possess an external hammer or be hammerless. Pulling the trigger of a double-action revolver accomplishes two things—it cocks the weapon and releases the hammer (whether internal or external). Most double-action revolvers with external hammers may also be operated in the single-action mode. The weight of a double-action trigger pull is always heavier than a single-action pull (typically 2×–3×).

Autoloading pistols or automatics all take cartridges from a magazine or clip located in the grip. Upon discharge, the slide moves rapidly rearward, extracting and ejecting the expended cartridge, as well as recocking the gun. As the slide is driven forward by an internal coil spring, a live cartridge is stripped from the magazine and loaded into the chamber. This cycle takes place with each pulling of the trigger until the ammunition supply in the magazine is exhausted. At this point, depending on the design of the particular pistol, the action may remain open, with the slide held back by a latch or follower in the magazine.

Rifling

Rifles and handguns have rifled barrels. A series of parallel spiral grooves are cut the length of the interior of the barrel. The grooves are called rifling and cause the bullet to spin and travel point first. The metal between these grooves are called lands, and the distance between the lands is referred to as bore diameter.

Rifle Actions

The action is the heart of the rifle. The stock and barrel are attached to the action. It includes all the small parts that load, fire, and eject the cartridge. There are five types of rifle actions, and types of rifles are depicted in Figure 11.3:

1. Hinge action
2. Bolt action
3. Lever action
4. Pump action
5. Semiautomatic

A gun is usually referred to by its action, for example, a bolt-action rifle or a semiautomatic shotgun.

The single shot is the simplest type of action. A shell or cartridge is loaded by hand. Modern single shots are generally bolt actions. Many older models are lever actions. In other words, they must be reloaded by hand after each shot.

The action works by operating the bolt, lever, or pump when shooting the bolt action, lever action, or pump action, respectively. It extracts or ejects the empty shell and then loads a fresh shell into the chamber and cocks the gun for the next shot.

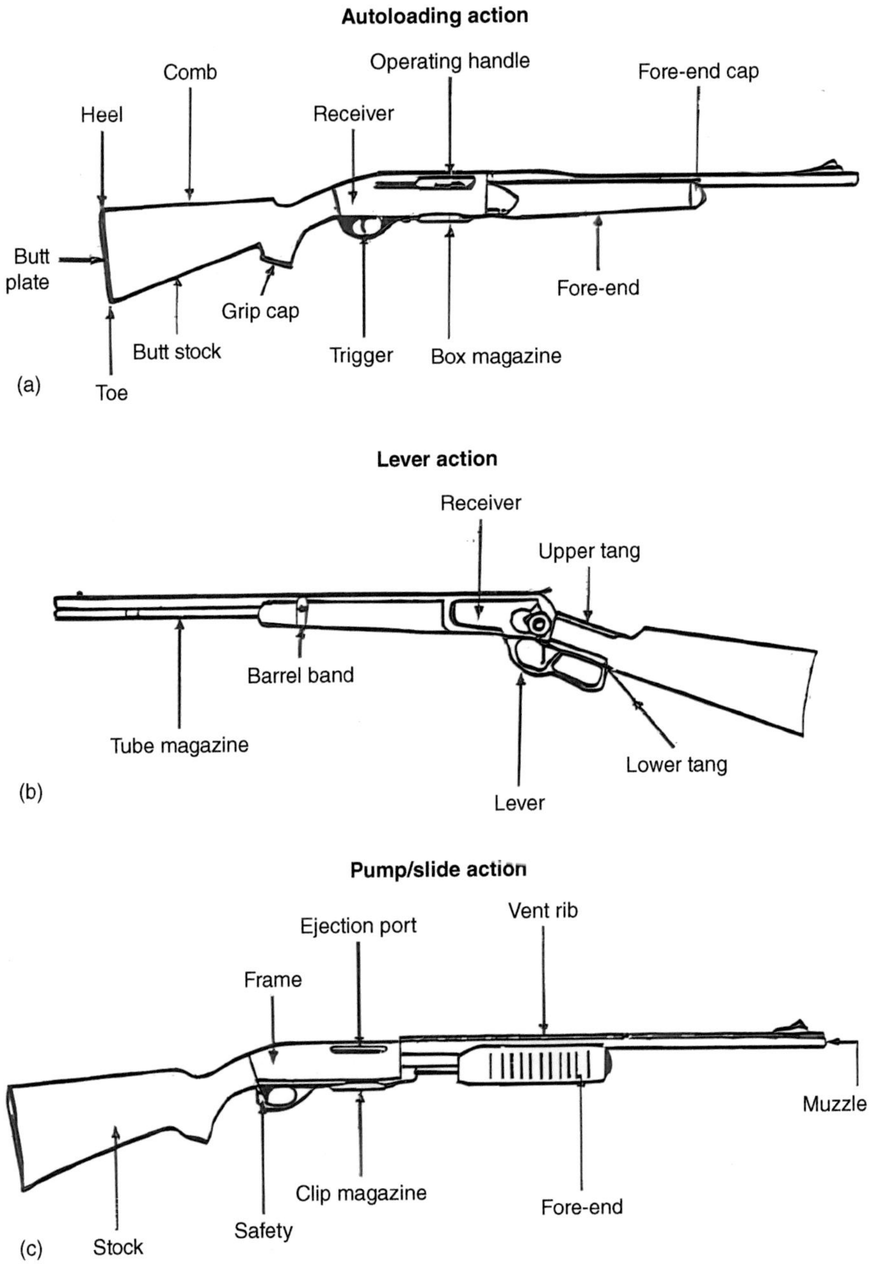

Figure 11.3 The drawing depicts different types of rifles: (a) autoloading, (b) levers, and (c) pump/slide.

Some hunting guns are called automatics; this is not correct. They are actually semiautomatics or autoloaders. In other words, the action does most of the work by itself. It reloads by itself, but the trigger must be pressed to fire each shot.

Machine guns are true automatics. They continue to fire as long as the trigger is held back or until ammunition is depleted. Machine guns are not legal hunting guns anywhere and are only legal if registered under federal law.

Shotguns

Shotguns differ from rifled weapons in that they have a smooth bore and are designed principally to fire multiple pellets down the barrel rather than a single projectile. The term gauge is used to describe the caliber of a shotgun. This refers to the number of lead balls of the given bore diameter that weigh 1 pound. In a 20-gauge shotgun, 20 lead balls that are the diameter of the bore weigh 1 pound. The only exception to this nomenclature is the 410 shotgun, which has a bore diameter of 0.410 inch.

Shotgun barrels all have some degree of choke. Choke refers to a partial constriction of the bore of the barrel at its muzzle end to control the size of the shot pattern. The choke, rather than the gauge of the shotgun, determines the size of the shot pattern at a specific distance. The tighter the choke, the smaller the pattern of pellets. Shotgun choke ranges from full choke to cylinder bore, with the tightest choke being the full choke weapon and the cylinder bore weapon having virtually no choke at all.

Modern shotgun ammunition consists of a plastic body or tube with a thin brass-coated steel or brass head, primer, powder, pellets, and wads. The end of the shell is usually closed in a wedge-shaped crimp. The only common exception to this is Federal 00 buckshot. This has a thin circular disk of plastic closing off the end of the shell that functions as an over-the-shot wad, with the edges of the mouth of the tube rolled into a crimp, holding the wad in place.

The shot loaded in shotgun shells is lead, lead with a thin copper coating, or steel. Shot can be divided into two categories—birdshot and buckshot. Birdshot is used to hunt birds and other small game. Buckshot is used for larger game and by police agencies.

Shotgun Range of Fire

1. Fire pellets, slugs, and rarely some specialized projectiles such as flechettes.
2. Per U.S. law, barrel must be greater than 18 inches or else is considered “sawed off” and illegal.

3. Barrel is not rifled.
4. Gauge describes caliber number of lead balls of the given bore diameter that weigh 1 pound—that is, with a 12-gauge shotgun, 12 balls of diameter 0.662 inch weigh 1 pound.
5. For 10–28-gauge shotguns, the larger the gauge, the smaller the bore (12 gauge is the most common weapon). The smallest bore size is 0.410 inch; it is not named by convention and has a 0.410 inch bore diameter.
6. Choke, a partial constriction of the barrel at the muzzle end to keep the shot together longer at long distances, has no practical meaning in terms of most shotgun injuries.
7. Shell components and materials recovered from wounds.
    a. Birdshot.
        i. Tube, paper, or plastic with brass head.
        ii. Powder.
        iii. Over-powder wad, cardboard and fiber filler wads, and over-shot wad, with or without plastic collar.
        iv. With or without polyethylene/polypropylene filler to cushion the shot.
        v. Plastic one-piece wads, "power piston," "triple plus," open to show petals.
        vi. Shot: the larger the number, the smaller the shot—that is, No. 12 is smaller than No. 2.
    b. Shot, wads, collars, and one-piece "power piston" type wads may be recovered from contact and close wounds.
    c. Buckshot.
        i. Larger pellets S4 small; 000 largest.
        ii. Filler color may vary, white or black.
        iii. Filler marks may look like stippling; filler travels out further than powder.
        iv. Scrape off residues to differentiate black filler from powder.
    d. Slugs.
        i. Most common are Foster, Brenneke, and Cabot.
        ii. Foster is hollow grooved metal; if close, Brenneke leaves screw, cardboard, wad, and slug; Foster and Cabot may have plastic inserts to keep shape.
    e. Special loads are made for special purposes.

Other Miscellaneous

1. Weapons.
    a. Air guns.
    b. Zip guns (home-made gun) (Figure 11.4).

Figure 11.4 Example of a zip gun as a crude, home-made firearm.

   c. Nail guns.

2. Bullets.
   a. Unrifled: consider smooth bore weapon.
3. Ammunitions with distinctive characteristics.
   a. Glazer round: a copper jacket with pellets and a plastic plug; X-rays of the pellets and plug show distinctive patterns.
   b. Exploding ammunition: X-rays show the primer cap and anvil.

c. KTW load green Teflon coating.
d. Nyclad black nylon coating.
e. Shotshell cartridges, "snake shot" fine pellets, lethal at close range to temporal bones.
f. Silvertip jacket is aluminum; jacket may be missed on X-ray.
g. Black talon hollow point that opens and looks like a flower, black-coated.

Bibliography

DiMaio, V.J.M. 2016. *Gunshot Wounds, Practical Aspects of Firearms Ballistics and Forensic Techniques.* Boca Raton, FL: CRC Press.

DiMaio, V.J.M. and Molina, D.K. (2021). *DiMaio's Forensic Pathology* (3rd ed.). Boca Raton, FL: CRC Press. https://doi.org/10.4324/9780429318764

Gunshot Wounds

12

MARY H. DUDLEY

OBJECTIVES

Upon completion of this chapter and corresponding reference material, the reader will be able to

- List five of the most common questions relating to gunshot wound deaths
- List types of observations required at a scene involving gunshot wounds
- Describe the characteristics of entrance wounds vs. exit wounds
- Discuss the range of fire, muzzle-to-target distance, and the associated characteristics of contact, intermediate, and distant range of fire
- Describe the characteristics of shotgun wounds according to the range of fire

Introduction

The scene investigation of gunshot wounds helps medical examiners correlate the circumstances of death with the autopsy findings. The medicolegal death investigator (MDI) can answer questions as to how the injury occurred by painting a history from witnesses, law enforcement, and medical records. Circumstances of death related to gunshot wounds determine the manner of death as accidental, homicide, suicide, or undetermined. Scene documentation, diagrams, and photography detail observations and findings. This chapter focuses on the MDI's role in firearm-related fatalities, the understanding specific types of firearm injury patterns, and the definition of terminology related to gunshot wounds as well as the range of fire. The forensic autopsy reveals important external and internal injuries related to the cause of death, including the range of fire, entrance and exit wounds, the trajectory path of the projectile, and, when retained, projectile recovery.

DOI: 10.4324/9781003538622-14

Medicolegal Investigation of Firearms Injuries

Common Questions

1. Where was the person shot?
2. How many times was the decedent shot?
3. Where are the entries and re-entries? Where are the exits?
4. Are there any bullets through clothes that did not penetrate the body?
5. What was the course or direction of each shot through the body?
6. What was the sequence of fire?
7. What is the mechanism of death due to gunshot?
8. What was the muzzle-to-target distance? Contact? Close? Intermediate? Distant? Any intermediate targets? Ricochet?
9. What was the direction of fire, especially in relation to the shooter?
10. In what position was the decedent when shot?
11. What is the estimated interval of survival between injury and death?
12. What was the capacity for movement and activity after being shot?
13. What kind of ammunition(s)?
14. What was the cause of death?
15. Any competing causes of death (e.g., body found in water or in fire)?

Mechanisms

1. Perforating vital structures and causing hemorrhage. Examples are perforations of the heart, great vessels, lung, or highly vascular solid organs.
2. Damaging organs that control vital body functions. Examples are brain injuries with swelling that interfere with breathing and cardiac control or injuries of the high cervical spine that impair breathing (Figure 12.1).
3. Causing complications that result, either immediately or remotely, in death. Examples are sepsis associated with gunshot injuries to the bowel, coma-induced complications of pneumonia, seizures due to gunshot injuries to the brain, or pulmonary emboli complicating recumbency due to injury. Some complications are lethal years after the injury (such as bowel obstruction due to adhesions caused by the injury).
4. High-velocity weapons may cause lethal injury due to blast injury to adjacent organs without directly perforating them. Injuries to the neck may result in injury to the cord (contusion) or airway (soft tissue swelling) without directly perforating them. This is due to the transfer and dispersion of the kinetic energy of the bullet to the tissue.

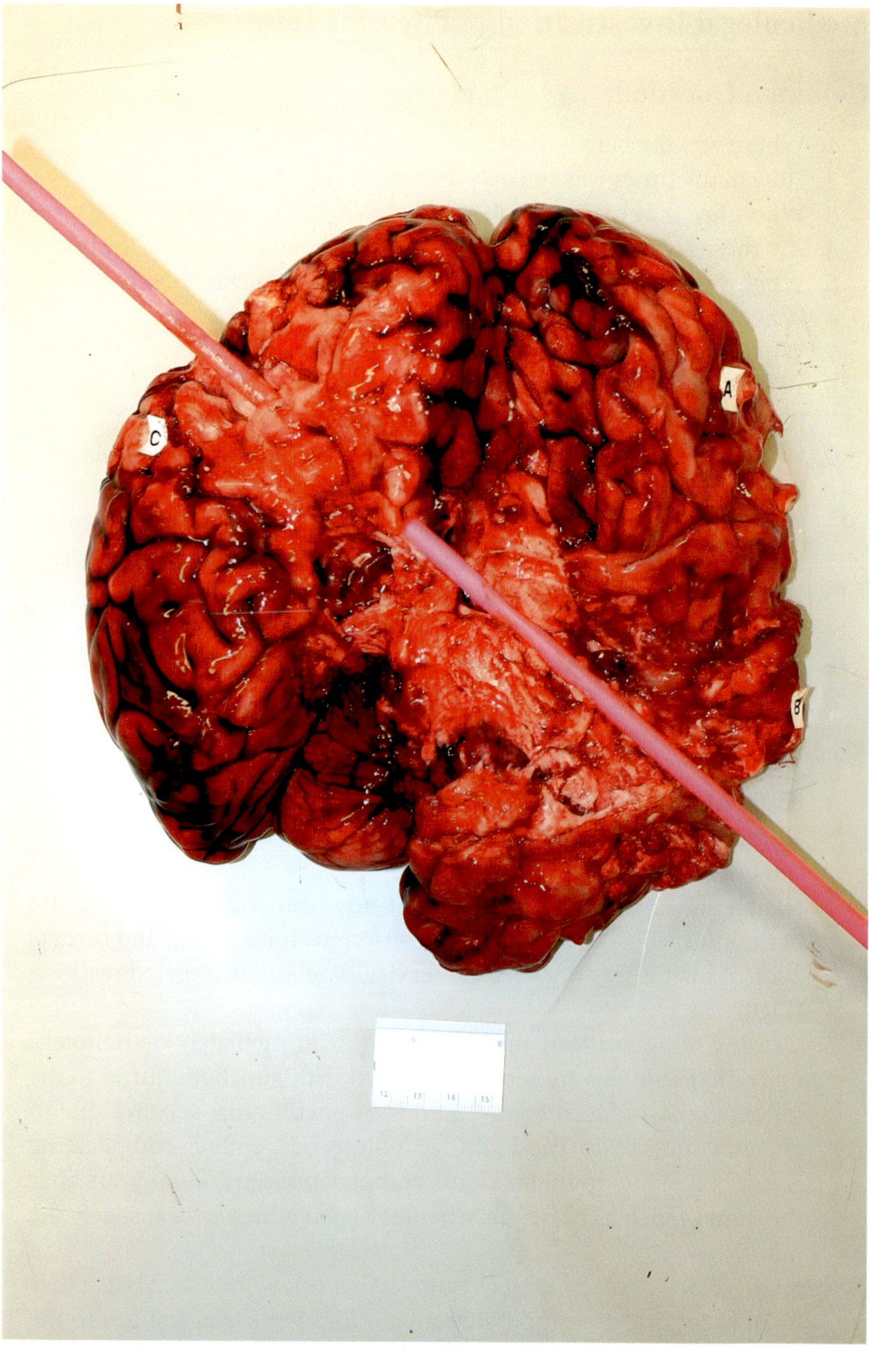

Figure 12.1 Gunshot wound trajectory through the brain.

5. Sites of fatal gunshot wounds include
   a. Brain 40%
   b. Heart 25%
   c. Aorta or other major vessel 25%
   d. Solid viscera 10%

Scene and Body Exam

1. Examination at the scene of death/circumstances:
   a. Observe and obtain the following information from the investigating officer and witnesses:
      i. Who is the decedent? Is the decedent a prominent person or person at risk?
      ii. Date last seen alive, when found, and by whom?
      iii. How did the person come to be found?
      iv. Evidence for time of injury and time of death.
      v. Where is the body? Open vs. concealed place? Known to the decedent?
      vi. Is the gun present? Is it the decedent's?
      vii. Where is the weapon, cartridge case, and spatter in relation to the decedent? Any bullets in walls, mattresses, chairs?
      viii. In what position was the person when shot? Sitting, standing, lying down, sleeping?
      ix. Any evidence of activity or motion after injury? Any evidence of struggle or sexual assault?
      x. Any evidence of forced entry? Anything missing?
      xi. Photograph the above and anything that will be disturbed during transport. Coordinate photography with investigator to ensure that all is covered.
      xii. Bag the hands in paper bags and secure with rubber bands to preserve any residues, spatter patterns, or trace evidence.
   b. Document the scene (body, gun, recovered bullets) through a scene sketch and narrative summary.
      i. Are any obvious inconsistencies apparent at the scene?

2. Examination of the clothed body and clothing.
   a. Recover all clothes from any intermediate treating agency such as emergency medical systems (EMS) or the emergency room.
   b. If received separately, examine clothes with the body.
   c. Identify entrances by powder or wipe, or in driven fibers.
   d. The body should be examined clothed and photographed as received. Residues present on clothing distinguish entrances from exits and indicate muzzle-to-target distance. Powder residues may

be present but not visible, requiring rhodizonate testing by a firearms examiner to document distance. Fragments of intermediate targets such as wood or ricochet surface material may also be recovered from clothes.

e. Refrain from cutting clothing. Clothing should be retained and hung to dry.
f. Note in the record any damage or residues deposited on clothes.
g. Note any bullet holes to clothes that are not associated with injury to the body—usually tangential grazing shots.

3. Radiography.
   a. Radiographs should be taken of the clothed body to avoid loss of bullets wedged between layers of clothes or within the lining of clothes.
   b. Radiographs should be taken even when it appears the bullet has exited because fragments of jacket or parts of special ammunition may be lost in the track.
   c. Be sure X-rays capture skin edges of the chest and abdomen to find bullets as they commonly become lodged just beneath the skin.
   d. Label films carefully. X-rays may be submitted as evidence in court to document the location of projectiles in the body.
   e. Radiographs may show the direction of bone fragments pointed in the direction the bullet was traveling.

4. Examination of the unclothed body.
   a. Order by number or letter each wound on a diagram and look at each one to characterize an entrance or exit. When tracks are sorted, label entrance and exit with the same number and "X" for projectile recovery.
   b. Look for residues using a hand lens or dissecting scope. Resect and block any ambiguous wounds for microscopic examination for powder at the end of the examination.
   c. Examine wounds before cleaning.
   d. If wounds do not clearly indicate entrance or exit, or if multiple surfaces are involved, a series of digital photographs for reference may help sort out possible tracks.
   e. Hypothesized tracks need confirmation by autopsy according to the policy outlined by the death investigation system.
   f. Depending on overall circumstances, other studies may be necessary before cleaning.

5. Special studies.
   a. Perform gunshot residue tests and trace metal tests before disturbing or washing the hands.

   b. Any tests for lead residues to distinguish blunt force injuries from grazing wounds should be performed prior to washing.
   c. Alternate light source examination for trace evidence.

6. Photography.
   a. Photograph body as received, clothed and unclothed.
   b. Photograph hands and wounds if residues and blood splatter patterns are present, or if pertinent to the case when residues and blood splatter patterns are not present (e.g., if the person is said to have "grabbed the gun").
   c. Photograph the body after cleansing to show wound locations.
   d. Photograph individual wounds to document entrance, exit, and distance characteristics.
   e. Photograph the body with trajectory rods following the autopsy and cover the autopsy incision with drapes.
   f. Shoot true anterior/posterior (AP) and lateral views plus any other views deemed meaningful. For example, reposition and photograph the arms to show the position of an entry and associated re-entry or impossibility of a self-inflicted shot.
   g. Photograph recovered bullets.

7. Internal examination.
   a. Document each wound by diagram and narrative, recording its size and wound characteristics; by measurements from the top of the head and the midline; and by anatomical location.
   b. Trace each track, recovering any trace evidence (fabric or intermediate targets) and metal.
   c. Compare completeness of recovered materials with radiographs.
   d. Document the location of each recovered missile by measurement.
   e. Identify pathological findings pertinent to survival (such as large hemothorax or hemoperitoneum) or capacity for activity (such as transection of the thoracic spinal cord that would have precluded running or any other motion).
   f. Recover any old bullets from previous injuries.
   g. Handle bullets with gloved hands (never use metal forceps).
   h. Correlate autopsy information with that of the investigating officer in the autopsy room to identify any inconsistencies not apparent at the scene.
   i. If a fetal death occurs, document its injuries as a separate case.

8. Collection of evidence on gunshot cases—items collected include the following:
   a. Gunshot residue, trace metal, or lead tests.
   b. Bullets and bullet fragments.

c. Material adherent to bullet.
d. All clothing.
e. Pertinent trace evidence such as recovered and exemplary hairs, fibers, glass, etc.
f. Radiographs.
g. Blood, vitreous and other body fluids, and liver for ethanol and drug testing.
h. Blood spots for DNA testing.
i. Hospital admission blood and body fluids, if death was delayed.
j. Clothes for DNA typing if multiple transfusions were administered (or collect from blood bank the initial hospital sample drawn for type and crossmatch).
k. Sexual assault kits if the decedent is a woman, or if circumstances or pathological findings are suspicious for recent sexual activity in a male shooting victim.
l. If a fetus is involved, collect serological evidence—fetal and placental blood and tissue from the fetus—for possible paternity testing.

Gunshot Wounds

1. Description of a wound includes the following:
   a. Size: a rough indication of caliber but not infallible.
   b. Shape: an indicator of direction.
   c. Characteristics: abraded, stippled, burned, lacerated, etc.
   d. Patterns of muzzles and intermediate targets.
   e. Contaminants: wood, glass, clothing
   f. Distance of the entrance, exit, or recovery from the top of the head to the left or right of the midline, front, or spine.
   g. Description in relation to anatomical location, for example, the right front shoulder.
   h. Its path through the body, listing the organs perforated.
   i. Evidence of vital reaction in the form of bleeding or inflammation.
   j. Location of recovery or exit.
2. Entrances vs. exits (Table 12.1).
3. Distance ("range of fire," "muzzle-to-target distance").
   a. Caveats: On clothed body surfaces, distance is best determined by firearms examiner and examination of the clothes—especially if the shot looks distant.
   b. Uncovered body surfaces.
      i. Look before washing and shaving.

Table 12.1 Entrances vs. Exits

Characteristic	Entrances	Exits
Burn	Yes	No
Powder	Yes	No[a]
Stippling	Yes	No
Abrasion	Yes	No, unless shored
Laceration	Yes, if contact[b]	Yes

[a] Unless the exit is close to a near shot, the margin will be free of burns and powder.
[b] Wounds to palms and soles are lacerated regardless of distance.

ii. Photograph close-up before and after any alteration if the wound is doubtful or critical to the interpretation of the case (when there is a discrepancy between the wound and the history).

c. Contact muzzle resting on the skin with or without muzzle marks (Figure 12.2a and b).

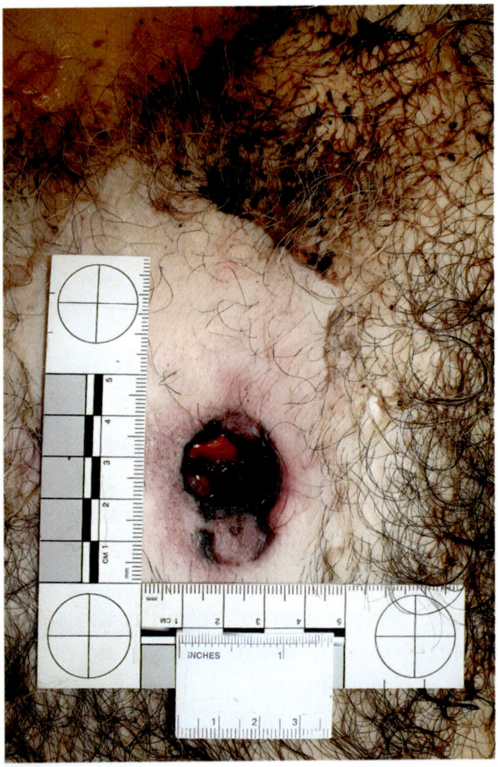

(a)

Figure 12.2 (a) Contact range gunshot wound and (b) gun used to cause muzzle imprint.

(b)

Figure 12.2 (Continued)

i. Zero to minimal powder, without stippling, on the outside.
ii. The margin is burned black.
iii. Usually lacerated—at least a little with 22s.
iv. Gunshot wound to the skull.
    A. In tissue over bone, such as the skull, larger calibers may show stellate laceration and entry wounds may be larger than exit wounds.
    B. Often associated with radial fractures at the entrance and sometimes at the exit.
    C. Entrances show soot residues on the bone and dura.
    D. Beveling of bone—inner table of entrance wound (Figure 12.3) and outer table of exit wound (Figure 12.4).
    E. Wounds to the temples are associated with fractures of the orbits and periocular ecchymoses, that is, "black eyes."
v. If angled, residues leak out onto the skin at edges that are not in contact—wound may be oval instead of round.
vi. Powder is blown into the subcutaneous tissue.
vii. Subcutaneous tissue may be pink due to carbon monoxide (CO) in gases combining locally with blood to form carboxyhemoglobin.
viii. Is visible microscopically as yellowish-black crystalline debris on the surface and in the track.

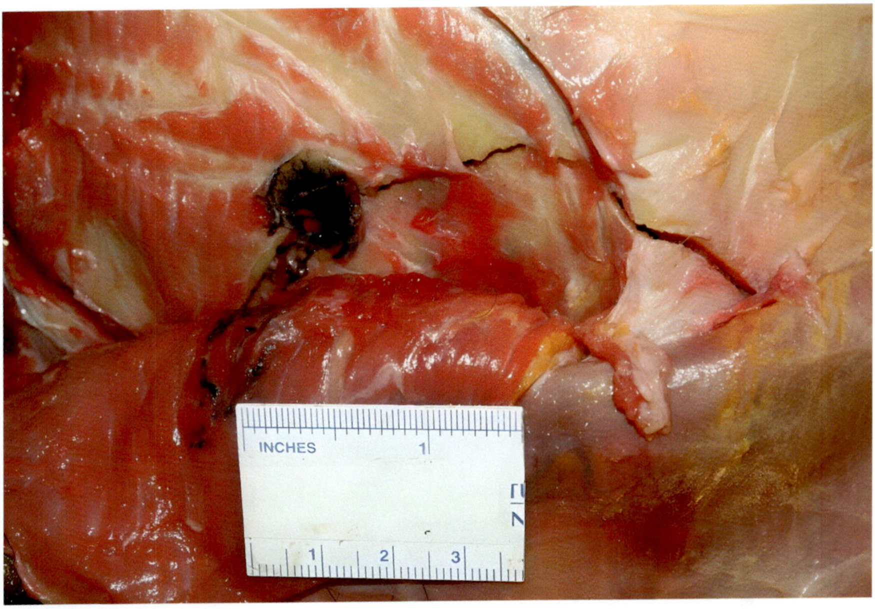

Figure 12.3 Internal beveling.

ix. Alizarin S stain may identify residues in decomposed entrances.
x. Difficult to determine in decomposed bodies.
xi. Powder may remain on bone in decomposed and skeletonized bodies and after skin is surgically resected.
xii. Consistent with homicides and suicides—rarely accidents.

d. Tight "hard" contact: weapon is pushed into the skin.
   i. Shows all of the above and often also a muzzle mark.
   ii. Muzzle marks often indicate muzzle configuration, showing sight marks, ejector rod marks, slide marks, etc. (Figure 12.5).

e. Near-contact range but not in contact; ½ inch away from the skin.
   i. Entrance has a wide zone of powder and burn (Figure 12.6).
   ii. If angled, residue will be eccentric, with the wider margin pointing toward the side where the muzzle was positioned.
   iii. May not be able to distinguish from an angled contact gunshot wound.
   iv. Scraping some of the residues on a cotton square may help determine the type of ammunition if no bullet or gun is available.

f. Intermediate range (Figure 12.7).
   i. Intermediate from ½ inch to 6–12 inches.
      A. Zone of powder increases but becomes less dense with increasing distance.

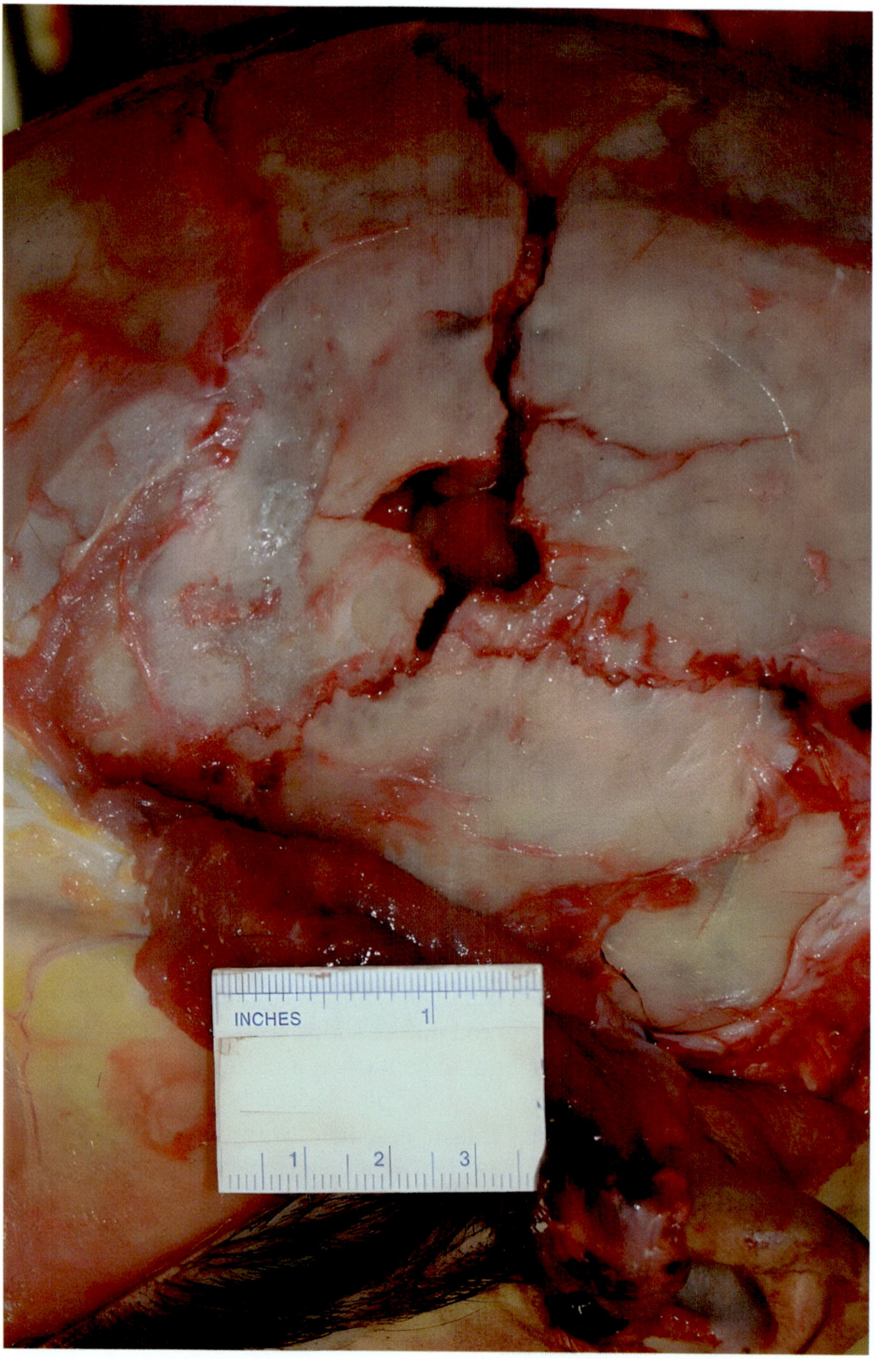

Figure 12.4 External beveling.

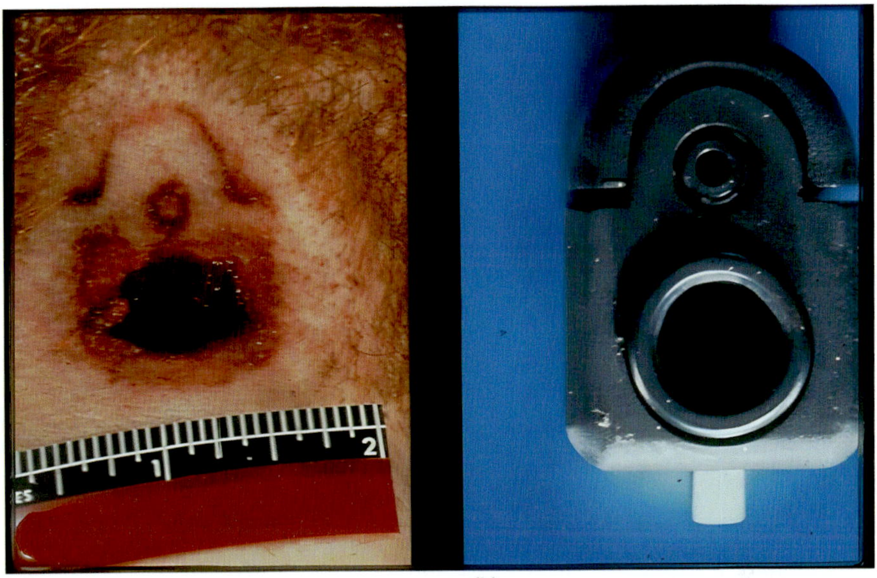

(a) (b)

Figure 12.5 (a) Muzzle imprint and (b) barrel of the gun causing the muzzle imprint.

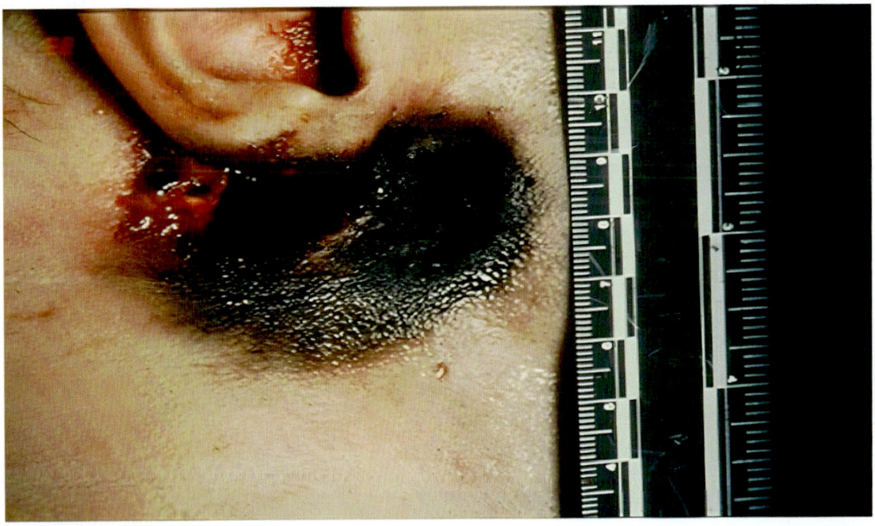

Figure 12.6 Soot around the wound.

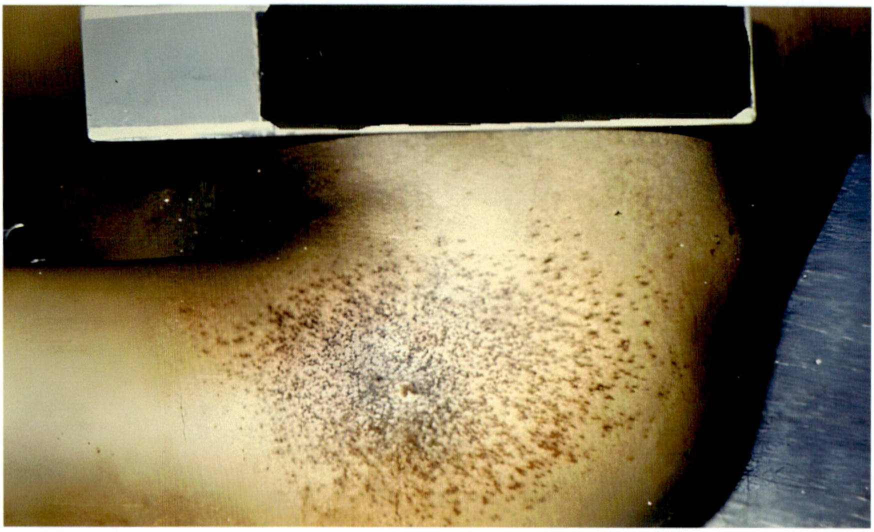

Figure 12.7 Stippling.

B. Shows tattooing or stippling by powder grains, with pattern and shape that reflect the type of powder and distance.
C. Beyond 1 foot, residues may not be visible unless examined very carefully, and perhaps not even then. Will be chemically visible on clothes.
D. Residues can indicate ball, flattened ball, or flake disk (Figure 12.8).

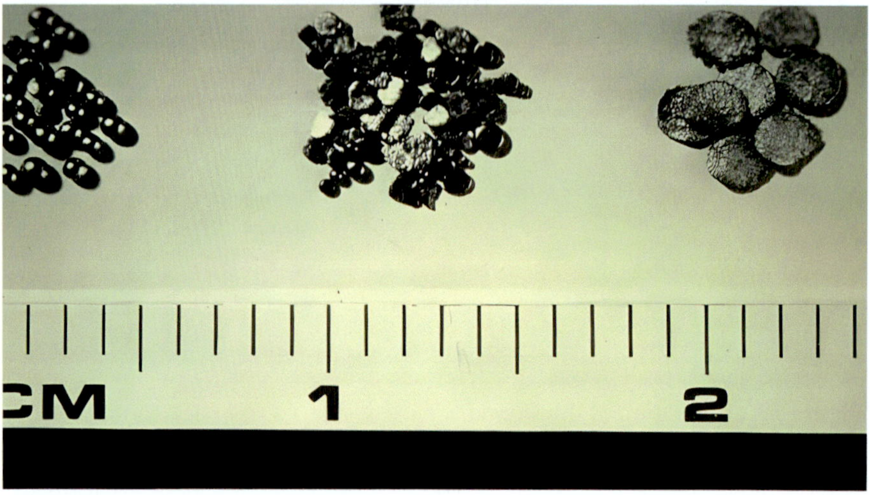

Figure 12.8 Different types of gunpowder.

E. The pattern can be duplicated by a firearms examiner for a closer estimate of distance.
F. "Pseudotattooing."
- Fragments of intermediate targets.
- Fragments of bullet shaved off by a poorly fitted cylinder to barrel.
- Fragments from bullet fragmenting after hitting another surface (i.e., asphalt).
- Suture marks.

ii. Intermediate greater than 6–12 inches or 1 foot.
A. Depending on weapon, slight residues may not be visible.
B. Ball powder may deposit visible powder up to 3 feet.
C. May see bullet wipe, grayish residues from barrel carried on the surface of the bullet.

g. Distant range: 2 feet or greater (Figure 12.9).
i. Usually no visible residues unless ball powder is present.
ii. Requires firearms examination of clothes to rule out residues.
iii. Wounds at 4 and 40 feet look the same.

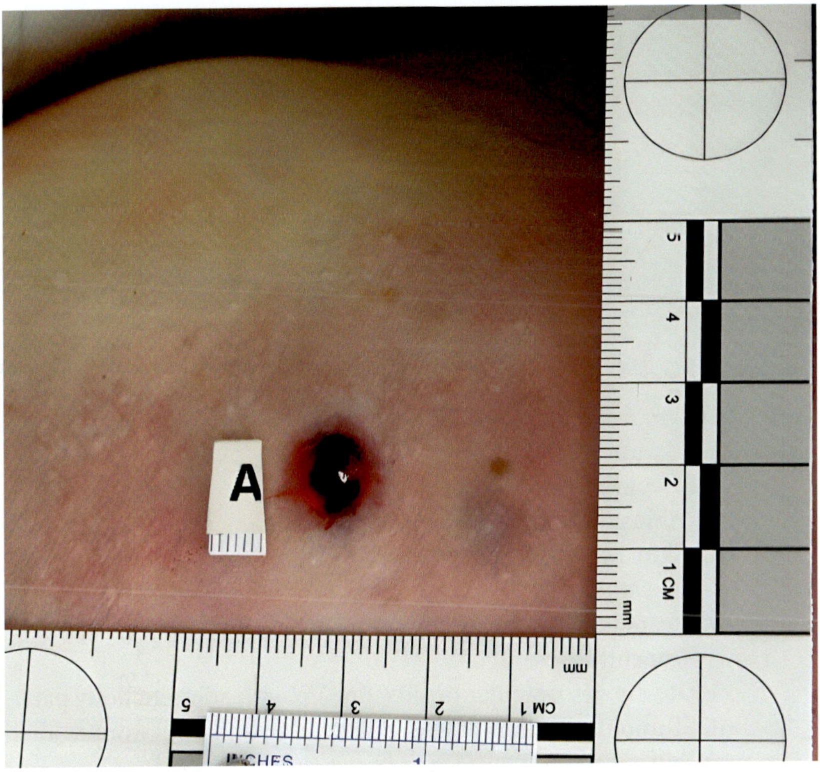

Figure 12.9 Distant-range wound.

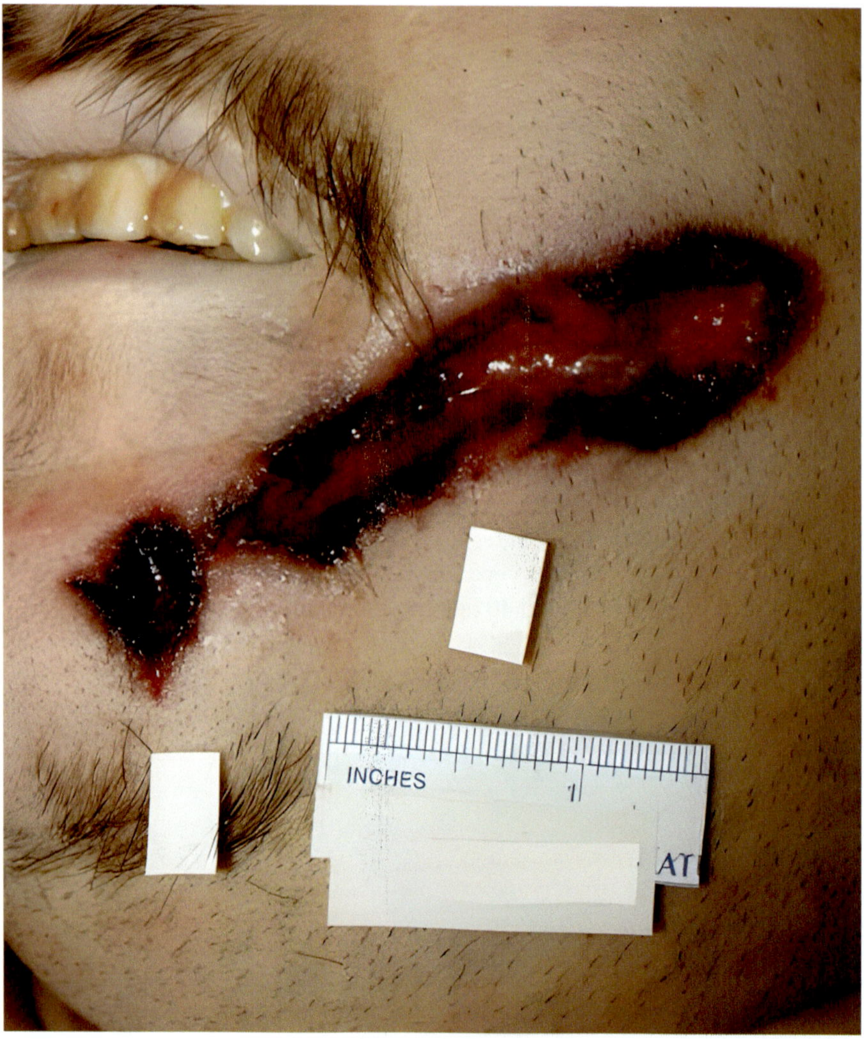

Figure 12.10 Graze wound.

h. Graze wounds (Figure 12.10).
    i. Abrasion at entrance end; split at exit.
    ii. Skin tag points may show direction from which the bullet came.
    iii. Tears point in the direction the bullet traveled.
i. Atypical entrances.
    i. Re-entries irregular or slits; line up with adjacent body part.
    ii. Tumbling entrances elongated or cylindrical wound after hitting another surface or tissue.
    iii. Irregular from semi-jacketed separating; may see two irregular holes.

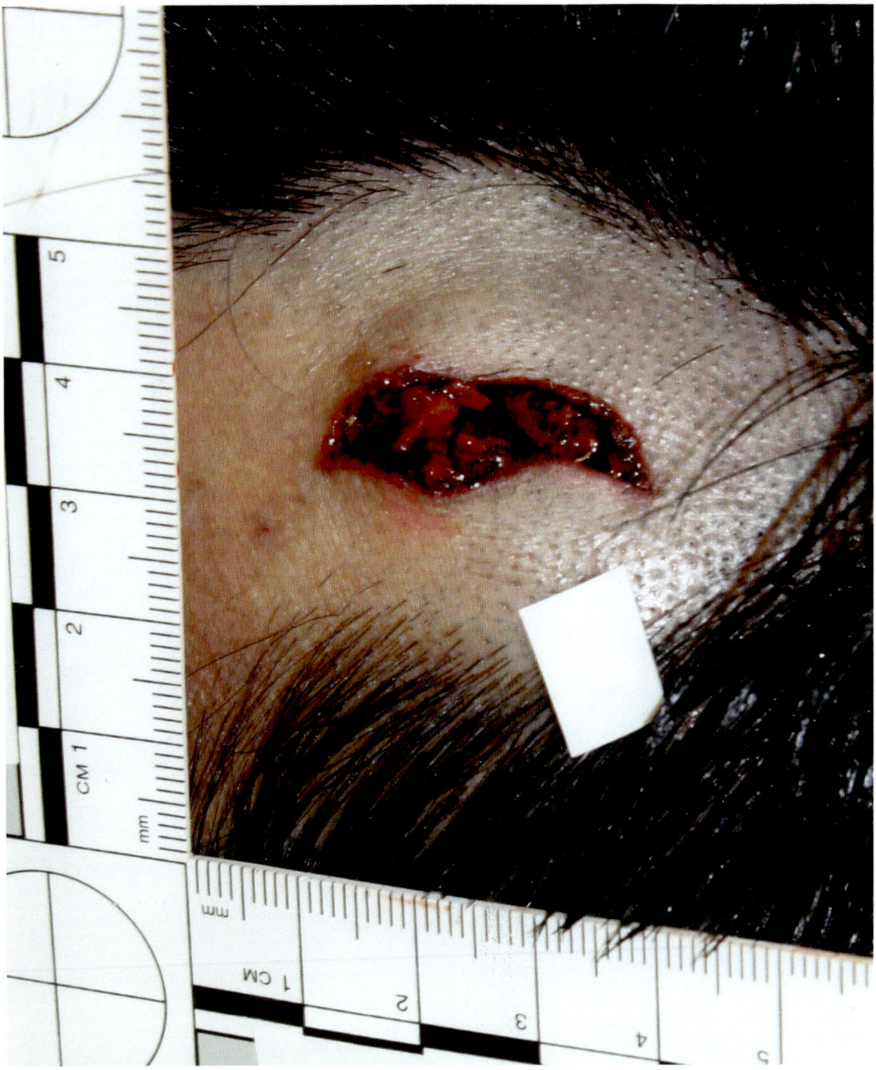

Figure 12.11 Exit wound.

- iv. Foreshortened entrances through belts or firm adjacent intermediate target, so that the entrance is widely abraded but clean except for traces of the target.
- v. Palm and sole entrances are stellate regardless of distance.
- vi. Star-shaped abrasions around the entrance; accelerator ammunition.
- vii. Stellate where skin is stretched tight over bone.

j. Gunshot wound exits.
- i. Slits in soft stretchy tissue areas (Figure 12.11).

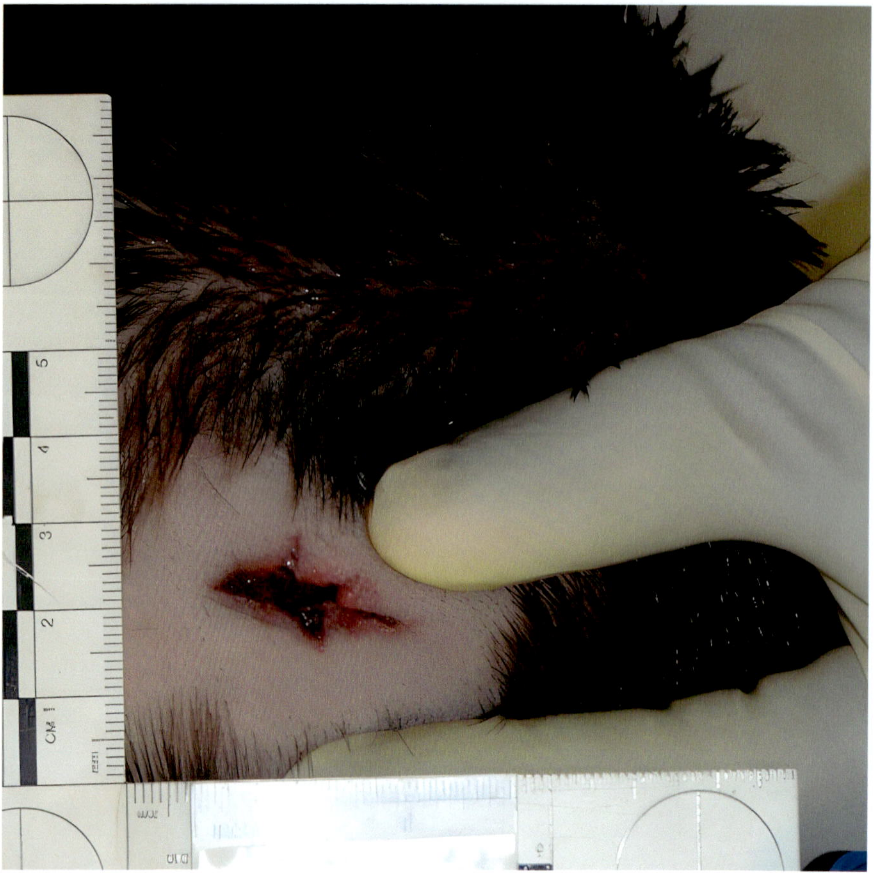

Figure 12.12 Stellate exit wound.

    ii. Stellate over tight skin of the skull or chin (Figure 12.12).
    iii. Shored exits: abrasion caused by skin being firmly in contact with a hard surface at the moment of exit. May resemble a distant-range entry wound.
k. Other marks associated with gunshot wounds.
    i. Cylinder gap marks: if the cylinder of a weapon is in close proximity to clothes or skin, residues escape from in front and sometimes from the rear of cylinder to form a roughly linear deposit of residues. Distance between hold and first mark is a measure of barrel length.
    ii. Patterns representing shapes of intermediate targets such as zipper teeth, religious medals, or coins.

Shotgun Wounds

1. Shotgun wounds/distance.
   a. Contact/close.
      i. Most devastating firearms injury at a close range.
      ii. Birdshot usually does not exit. Nearly all kinetic energy is expended in the body.
      iii. Buckshot and slugs may exit when tangential.
      iv. Contact head shots fragment the head.
      v. Determine entrance by reconstructing skin edges; otherwise, the head looks the same whether shot is to the back, mouth, or temple.
      vi. Intraoral shots may show lacerations at the corners of the mouth.
      vii. In right-handed persons, the left hand may show powder or rust from steadying the muzzle.
      viii. Contact shotgun wounds to the trunk produce a well-defined hole with extensive internal dispersion and damage.
      ix. In bodies where the skin surface is not intact, that is, decomposed or burned, the degree of dispersion will be the same whether contact or several yards ("billiard ball effect").
      x. Underlying soft tissue will be pink due to carboxyhemoglobin.
      xi. Recover pellets, plastic shot cup, and cardboard wadding from wound.
   b. Intermediate/distant (Figure 12.13).
      i. Pellets disperse with distance; axiom is distance in yards.
      ii. Inches of spread: 1 (discount flyers).
      iii. Margins show scalloping, then dispersion.
      iv. Buckshot scalloped at 3 feet, satellite holes at 9 feet.
      v. Definitive distance is determined by a firearms examiner shooting the weapon in question with the ammunition in question.
      vi. Dispersed buckshot may show an incomplete pattern and resemble multiple bullet injuries.
   c. Wad marks.
      i. Power piston four petals; .410 has 3 at 1–3 feet. Wad marks out to 20 feet.
      ii. Filler wad works to 15 feet.

Rifle Wounds

1. Low-velocity rifles.
   a. Entrance of contact wound may show "teardrop" burn.
   b. Fired bullet may show microgrooving, indicating a rifle shot.
   c. Damage is less than higher-velocity rifles.

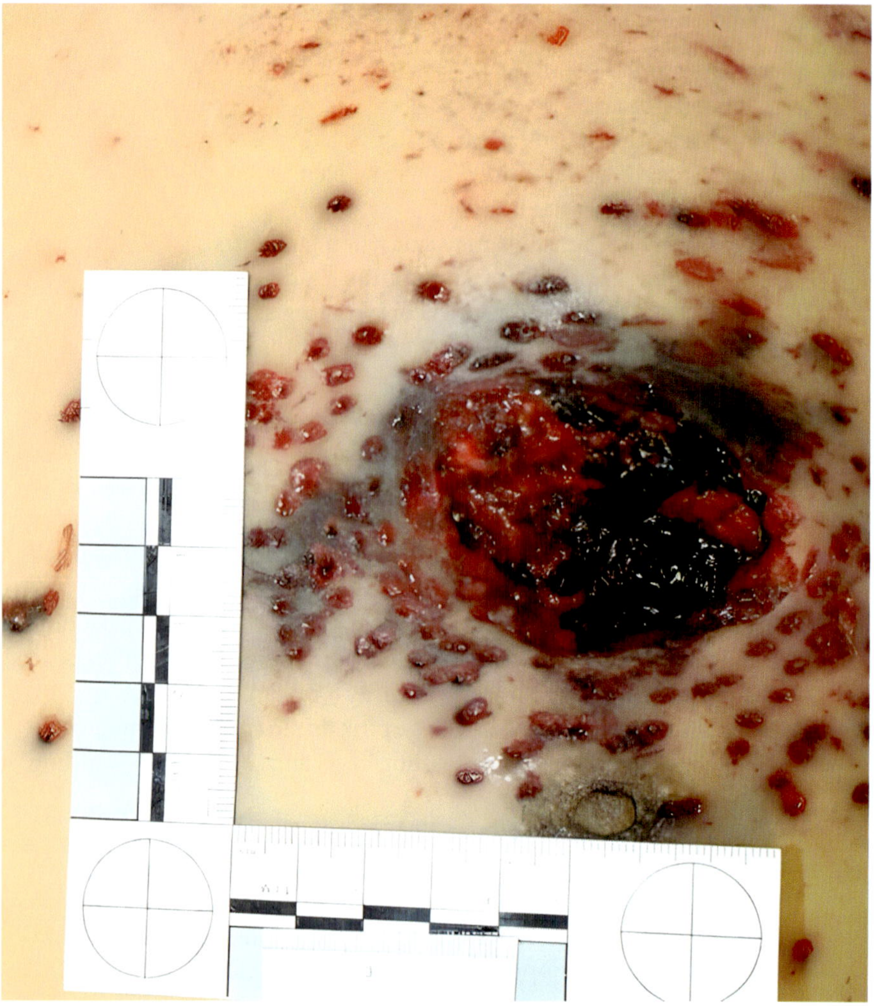

Figure 12.13 Shotgun wound showing spread of pellets.

2. High-velocity rifles.
   a. May injure structures without perforating them.
   b. Bullets are full or semi-jacketed.
   c. Military is full metal jacketed; it deforms and fragments less.
3. Distance: contact, intermediate, or distant.
   a. Contact wounds to the head.
      i. Gas expansion explodes head.
      ii. Entrance is at the origin of radial tears.
      iii. Residues may be minimal.

b. Wounds to the trunk do not disrupt like head wounds.
   i. If contact, may leave a muzzle mark.
   ii. Organs show more disruption than handgun.
   iii. Underlying tissues may be pink.
   iv. Bullets are more likely to tumble and fragment.
   v. Radiographs show a "lead snowstorm."
   vi. Entrances may show microtears.
   vii. Show less powder than handguns.
   viii. Exits are larger and more irregular than bullets from handguns.

Conduct after Injury

1. Only immediately incapacitating injury is a gunshot wound to the midbrain or basal ganglia of the brain.
2. Incapacitation does not mean death. Survival may be longer.
3. Only injuries that prevent return of fire are head shots and shots to the firing hand.
4. Behavior is limited only by blood flow to the brain; consciousness remains 10–15 seconds after the heart/carotid is disrupted.
5. Trunk shots may allow a person to walk, drive, run, or return fire.

Concealed Sites for Injury

1. Usually small caliber.
2. Axilla, back, nose, eye, base of skull, where the bullet may travel below the base and not be seen upon opening the skull or removing the neck.
3. Head and hair-bearing areas.
4. Areas already injured.
5. All orifices.
6. Always look at the back, axilla, and feel through the hair for swellings, blood, and holes.

Forensic Studies

1. Gunshot residue tests on hands, body parts, and clothes.
2. Distance patterns/proximity patterns for range of fire.
3. Comparison of recovered bullets with suspect weapons.
4. Comparison of bullets to link a firearm to more than one case, especially over a period of time.
5. Examination of bullets for:
   a. Residues of intermediate targets: fabric, tissue, wood.

b. Patterns from intermediate targets such as screening.
c. Cytology or immunology on recovered tissue from a bullet to determine through whom of several persons or objects (wood) it passed.
d. Classes of weapons of origin.

6. Comparison of muzzle mark patterns with exemplars.
7. Trigger pull.
8. Mechanical working order and safety devices, "gun just went off."
9. Defects that predispose gun to accident—does it go off when dropped?
10. Reconstructions using anatomical models.
11. Examination of gunshot residues from wounds for powder type.
12. Elemental analysis of recovered microfragments of bullets for ammunition manufacturer.

Manner of Death

1. Depends on correlation of all historical, scene, pathological, and forensic science evidence.
2. Caveats.
   a. Beware of premature assignment of accident or suicide to a shooting death until investigation is complete.
   b. True accidental shooting deaths are uncommon.
   c. Beware of "accident" while "cleaning a gun."
   d. Beware of accidental shooting while hunting.
   e. Guns do not just "go off." Weapons at risk for accidental discharge upon dropping or casual handling can be determined by firearms examiners.
   f. Distance, direction, and reconstruction are critical to determination of manner.
   g. Measure gunshot wounds from the heel up and midline to side.
   h. If there is concern of manner of death for a gunshot wound or shotgun wound, measure from the right middle finger to the entry wound.
   i. Self-inflicted gunshot wounds from "Russian Roulette" are generally ruled as suicide manner.

Bibliography

DiMaio, V.J.M. 2016. *Gunshot Wounds, Practical Aspects of Firearms Ballistics and Forensic Techniques*. Boca Raton, FL: CRC Press.

III

Natural, Suicidal, and Accidental Deaths

Natural Deaths

13

MARY H. DUDLEY AND
LAUREN E. DVORSCAK

OBJECTIVES

Upon completion of this chapter and corresponding reference material, the reader will be able to

- Describe and define the major natural causes of death by organ system
- Describe the common cardiovascular diseases responsible for sudden natural death
- List two types of cardiomyopathy
- Differentiate between nontraumatic and traumatic subarachnoid hemorrhages
- Identify diseases of the respiratory system, liver, and pancreas that may cause death
- Understand the role of the medicolegal death investigator in investigating apparent natural deaths

Introduction

Among the manners of death, the largest category is death from natural causes. Accurate determination of natural death is important to the family to identify familial conditions, as well as to regional and national data banks to identify causation. Funds for research, programs to change health practices, and patient education efforts hinge upon identified needs, that is, the number of people per 100,000 who die from a medical condition or its sequelae. The distinction between accidental and natural causes is also important. This becomes particularly significant when an individual with a chronic condition becomes involved in an accident. Insurance accidental death benefits may pay double compared to a natural death benefit. The medicolegal death investigator (MDI) plays an important role in obtaining history in deaths due to natural disease, collection and inventory of medications, as well as obtaining information to rule out other manners of death. This chapter outlines major causes of unexpected natural deaths by organ system.

DOI: 10.4324/9781003538622-16

Role of the Medicolegal Death Investigator

Most natural deaths handled by MDI are those cases where there may or may not be a prior medical history of natural disease, medical treatment, and medical care by a physician. If there is a physician willing to sign a death certificate for an unattended home death, and there is no sign of non-natural circumstances of death, the MDI may decline jurisdiction. Unattended natural deaths are often sudden and unexpected in individuals without a prior medical history.

MDIs must gather information about a decedent's prior medical history and rule out any potential for unnatural causes of death at the scene that would indicate the need for additional examination or testing by a pathologist. For instance, the presence of drug paraphernalia at the scene may indicate a potential unnatural manner of death. The death investigator must reasonably rule out any injuries, foul play, or drug use that would indicate a manner of death other than natural. Medical history is of paramount importance but may be unknown if the individual did not regularly see a healthcare provider or family is unavailable to interview. In such cases, medications, even if expired, at the scene can indicate pertinent medical history, such as the presence of hypertensive or anticonvulsant medication at the scene. With the absence of potential for other manners of death and the presence of significant medical history and/or medications at the scene, as well as a history of significant symptoms (e.g. severe wheezing, shortness of breath, and chest pain prior to death), the reason for death can be presumed natural.

MDIs must also consider natural death symptoms that have the potential to indicate reportable infectious disease processes. Deaths with a history of recent fever, chills, sudden-onset vomiting, diarrhea, or upper respiratory symptoms such as productive cough may indicate a potential infectious disease process that has implications for public health reporting. One such instance is surveillance of annual influenza and COVID-19 deaths. A history of such symptoms should always be documented and reported to the medical examiner/coroner, as further workup may be indicated, such as autopsy with ancillary testing, even in a suspected natural death.

The cause of natural deaths may include various organ systems, including the cardiovascular system, central nervous system, respiratory system, gastrointestinal system, and others.

Cardiovascular System

The most common cause of sudden, unexpected death in the United States is due to cardiovascular disease. Cardiovascular disease includes pathology of the coronary arteries and/or the aorta, including atherosclerotic cardiovascular disease, aortic aneurysms, and myocardial bridging. Valvular disease, cardiomyopathies, and infection of the heart valves or heart muscle can also cause sudden, unexpected cardiac death.

Atherosclerotic Cardiovascular Disease

The most common cause of death from cardiovascular disease is coronary atherosclerosis. Approximately half of individuals with coronary artery disease die suddenly. At autopsy, significant obstruction of the coronary artery lumen of 75% or greater is seen in one or more vessels. Atherosclerosis may also be seen in the aorta. Corresponding cardiomegaly (enlargement of the heart) often accompanies atherosclerotic cardiovascular disease and is typically an indication of hypertensive cardiovascular disease. In some individuals with a history of hypertension who die suddenly, the autopsy shows an enlarged heart with left ventricular thickening, or hypertrophy, and no significant atherosclerosis. The mechanism of death in these cases is a cardiac arrhythmia, ventricular fibrillation.

Aortic Aneurysm

Aortic aneurysm as a cause of death may include aortic dissection and abdominal aortic aneurysm. Both conditions result in thinning of the wall of the aorta, causing weakness and eventual rupture of the aorta and bleeding. Dissecting aortic aneurysm usually occurs in the arch of the aorta and is associated with hypertension, Marfan syndrome, and pregnancy. Abdominal aortic aneurysm (Figure 13.1) most commonly occurs in the distal abdominal aorta, near the bifurcation of the common iliac arteries, and is associated with atherosclerotic cardiovascular disease.

Myocardial Bridging

Myocardial bridging has been noted in cases of sudden, unexpected cardiac death of young-to-middle-aged adults. Normally, coronary arteries lie on the surface of the heart before entering the muscle at the apex. However, at autopsy, some individuals show a variant of the coronary arteries that tunnel under the heart muscle close to the coronary ostia. This variant has been associated with sudden, unexpected death related to the length and depth of the overlying myocardial tissue bridge covering the coronary artery. Atherosclerosis is also associated with the bridging segment, as well as fibrosis or scarring distal to the segment, which may cause cardiac arrhythmia.

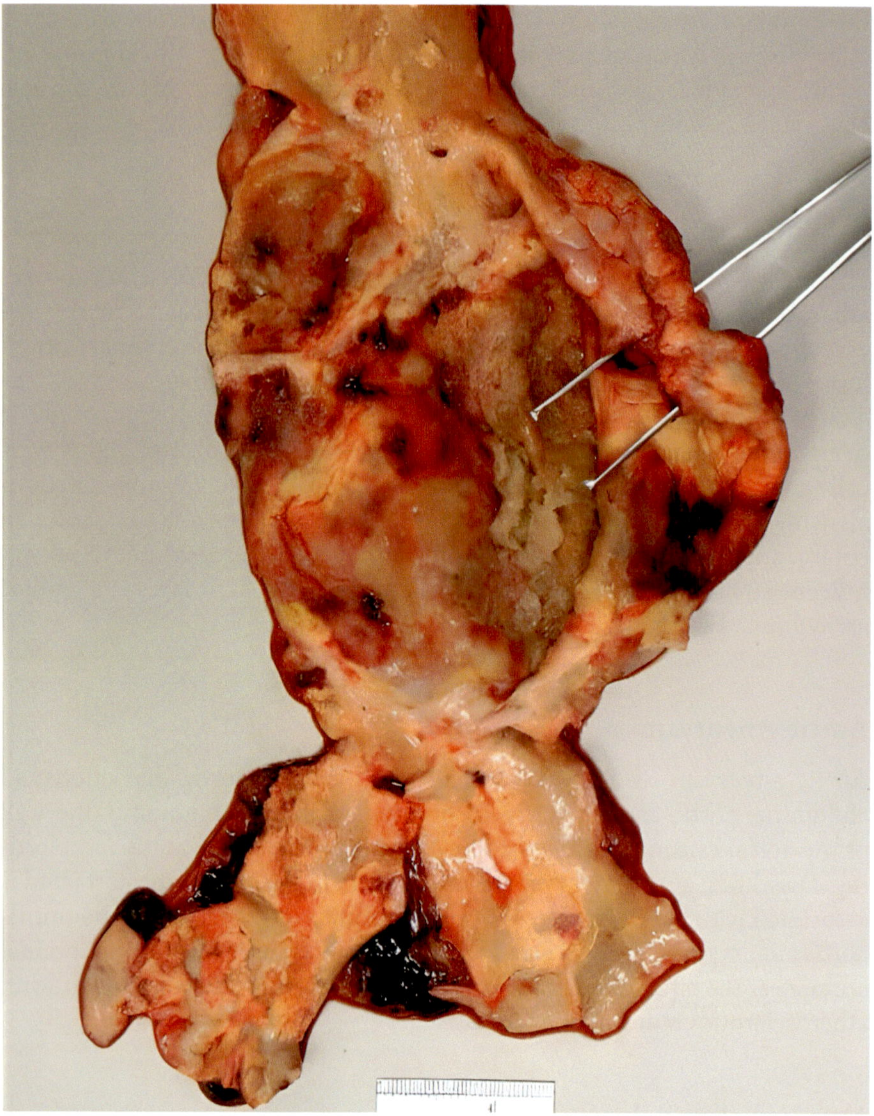

Figure 13.1 Aortic aneurysm.

Valvular Disease

Mitral Valve Prolapse

Mitral valve prolapse is associated with sudden cardiac death. The abnormal mitral valve located between the left atrium and ventricle shows cupping, redundancy, and thickening of the mitral valve, sometimes with ballooning into the left atrium. The thickening is caused by a gelatinous protein material, which weakens the valve and may be a marker for additional myxomatous changes in other areas of the heart, including the vessels, the myocardial system, and/or the left ventricle, leading to arrhythmia or death.

Cardiomyopathy

Cardiomyopathy is a general term for pathology of the heart. Cardiomyopathy types include dilated, hypertrophic, and infiltrative (restrictive) forms. Dilated cardiomyopathy involves weakness, thinning, and dilation of the ventricle walls that may be secondary to alcoholism or congestive heart failure. Hypertrophic cardiomyopathy (Figure 13.2) is defined by thickening of the left ventricle and interventricular septum that causes blockage of the outflow tract and restricts blood flow through the aortic valve. Infiltrative (restrictive) cardiomyopathy is caused by abnormal deposits of protein fibrosis, including conditions such as sarcoidosis or amyloidosis.

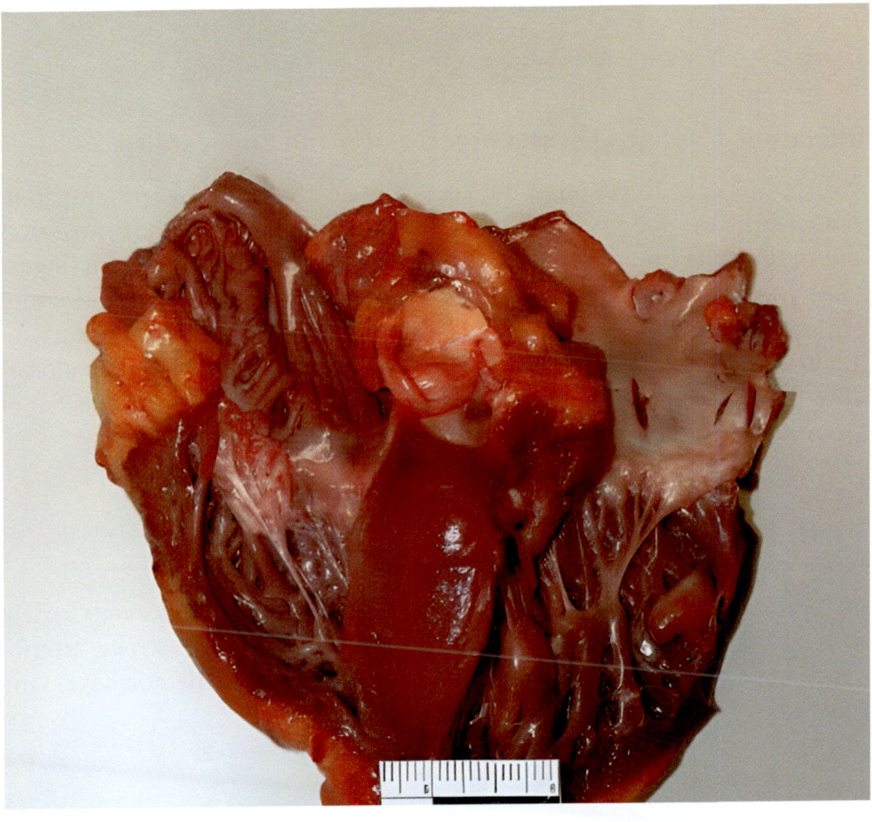

Figure 13.2 Hypertrophic cardiomyopathy.

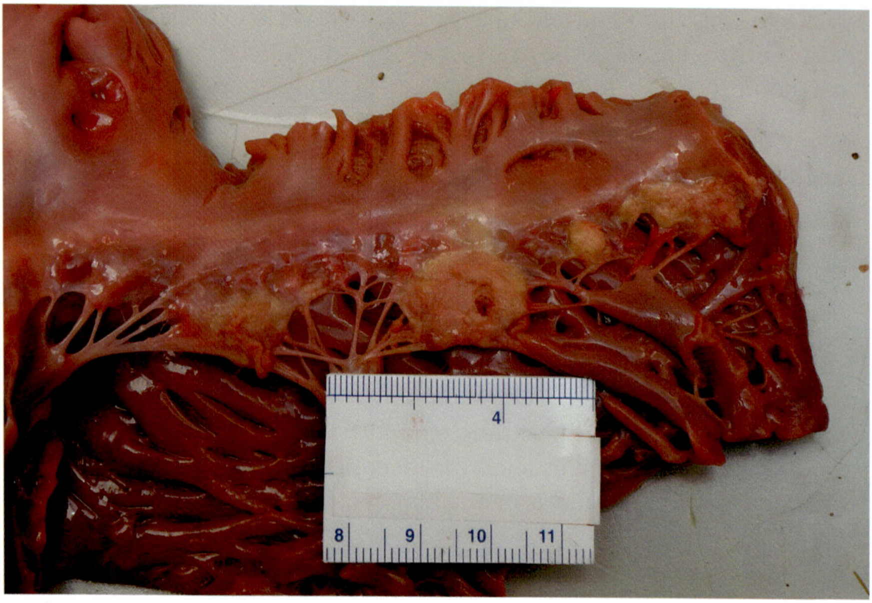

Figure 13.3 Vegetations on a heart valve.

Infectious Cardiac Disease: Myocarditis and Endocarditis

Myocarditis is an infection of the heart muscle caused by bacteria, fungi, or viral organisms. Endocarditis is infection or inflammation of the heart valves and/or the inner lining of the heart that may cause vegetations to form (Figure 13.3). Endocarditis may be noninfectious or caused by a variety of infectious organisms. Individuals with prosthetic heart valves, heart valve injury, or other cardiac abnormalities are at an increased risk of developing endocarditis. Subtle clues on the body may be a clue to endocarditis, such as flat or raised red lesions on the hands and feet or hemorrhages in the nails.

Central Nervous System

Sudden, unexpected natural deaths arising from the central nervous system may include seizure disorders, vascular pathology (including stroke, arteriovenous malformation, berry aneurysm, and hypertensive hemorrhage), and infections.

Epilepsy

Individuals who die from seizures may have a history of prior head injury or epilepsy. Seizures are periods of abnormal electrical signaling in the brain and can be due to prior trauma, low blood oxygen, drug use, alcohol withdrawal, or unknown causes. Epilepsy is a disorder defined as having recurrent seizures, specifically two or more unprovoked seizures occurring more than 1 day apart, or one unprovoked seizure with a high likelihood of recurrence. Autopsy may show softening and discoloration of the cerebral cortex in cases of prior trauma, whereas the gross lesions are not seen in epilepsy. The circumstances of death are important, as it will affect the manner of death as homicide, accident, or natural. Death from a terminal seizure may show injury from biting the tongue. Toxicology results may show subtherapeutic anticonvulsant medication levels. The mechanism of death may include positional asphyxia or a lethal cardiac arrhythmia due to adrenalin release secondary to seizure activity.

Vascular Pathology

Vascular pathology causing sudden death includes a cerebrovascular accident (stroke) caused by narrowing of the cerebral arteries and cerebral ischemia due to decreased blood flow to the brain. Hypertension can cause a hemorrhagic stroke of the brain. Other vascular abnormalities include a congenital weakness of the vessel wall, causing ballooning, or an aneurysm, which may rupture and cause rapid death. The aneurysms are generally of a small size located at the base of the brain and termed "berry" aneurysms (Figure 13.4). Another congenital anomaly of the cerebral vessels is an arteriovenous malformation, which is composed of a webbed network of thin-walled arteries and veins. This malformation may rupture and can be diagnosed at autopsy.

Infections

Infections of the central nervous system include bacterial invasion of the brain coverings, termed meningitis, or of the brain matter, including encephalitis or abscesses. Cultures help to identify the infectious organisms.

Tumors

Brain tumors may involve the meninges or brain tissue. Occasionally, an individual may die suddenly or unexpectedly from an undiagnosed primary or metastatic brain tumor. The mechanism of death includes seizures and increased intracranial pressure from the space-occupying lesion.

Respiratory System

Diseases of the respiratory system are another potential source of unexpected deaths due to natural causes. Significant causes of death due to respiratory

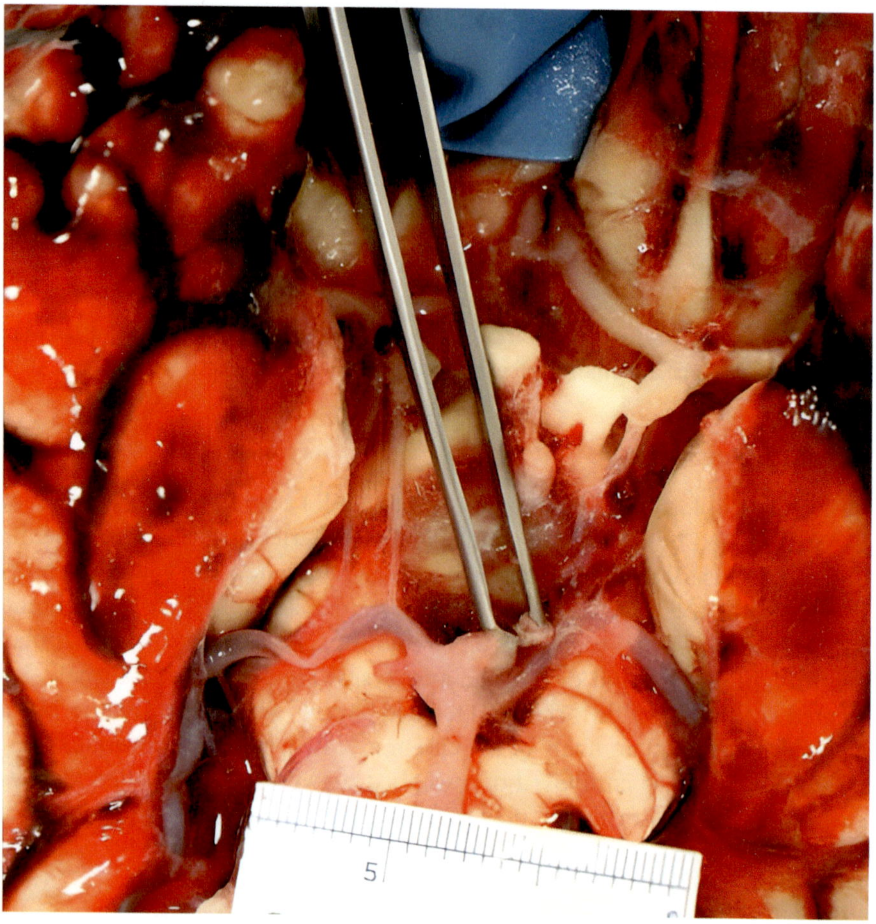

Figure 13.4 Berry aneurysm.

diseases include infections, restrictive diseases such as pulmonary fibrosis or obstructive diseases such as asthma, and emphysema or chronic obstructive pulmonary disease.

Infections

Bacteria, viruses, and fungi may infect the upper and lower respiratory tract. The upper respiratory tract consists of the airways above the vocal cords. Significant infection of the upper airway, such as laryngeal abscesses or inflammation of the epiglottis, can obstruct the airway and cause death by a lack of oxygen delivery to the lungs. The lower respiratory tract consists of the airways below the vocal cords. Pneumonia is a significant infection of the lower airways in the lungs that can be a result of bacteria or viruses. Pneumonia may also be a result of aspiration of oral or gastric contents into the airways. This may happen for a variety of reasons, and it is important to determine whether an individual had a history of difficulty swallowing, seizures, or any significant history that may predispose him or her to aspiration. Chronic pneumonia may lead to inflammation of the lung lining or pleurisy.

Common viral endemic infections that may cause death in susceptible populations with weakened immune systems include coronavirus (COVID-19) and influenza. Annual vaccines to these viruses are made commercially available based on predictions of the circulating strains of the virus. However, predictions may not always accurately account for the actual viral strains circulating, and infections with viruses may increase or fall from year to year with the efficacy and use of vaccines. COVID-19 is the contagious virus implicated in the recent pandemic and has now become more endemic. Most individuals infected with COVID-19 strains experience mild-to-moderate symptoms, including fever, fatigue, and cough, but susceptible individuals may experience severe respiratory symptoms, including respiratory failure or death. Loss of smell and taste, and an increased incidence of blood clots, have also been associated with COVID-19 infection. Influenza, commonly known as the flu, is also a respiratory virus that is highly contagious and can result in symptoms of fever, chills, body aches, cough, and congestion. Influenza can also be fatal in susceptible individuals.

Restrictive Lung Diseases

Restrictive lung diseases ultimately decrease the ability of the lungs to expand properly. The overall lung volume becomes decreased over time, and the work of breathing becomes increased. Often, in restrictive lung diseases, fibrosis or scarring of the lung is the end result. Scarring of the lungs can arise from a variety of causes and has been associated with allergic reactions to inhaled particles, a consequence of drug toxicity, long-term exposure to dust particles such as asbestos, and infections such as tuberculosis, among many others. Pulmonary fibrosis, or lung scarring, however, frequently has no known cause.

Obstructive Lung Diseases

Obstructive lung diseases are those that result from a blockage of the airways. Individuals with obstructive lung disease have problems exhaling, often due to collapse of the smaller airways and/or inflammation of the airways. Examples of obstructive lung diseases include asthma, emphysema, and chronic bronchitis.

Asthma

Asthma is a reactive airway disease where swelling and abundant mucous production are triggered by a variety of environmental or genetic factors.

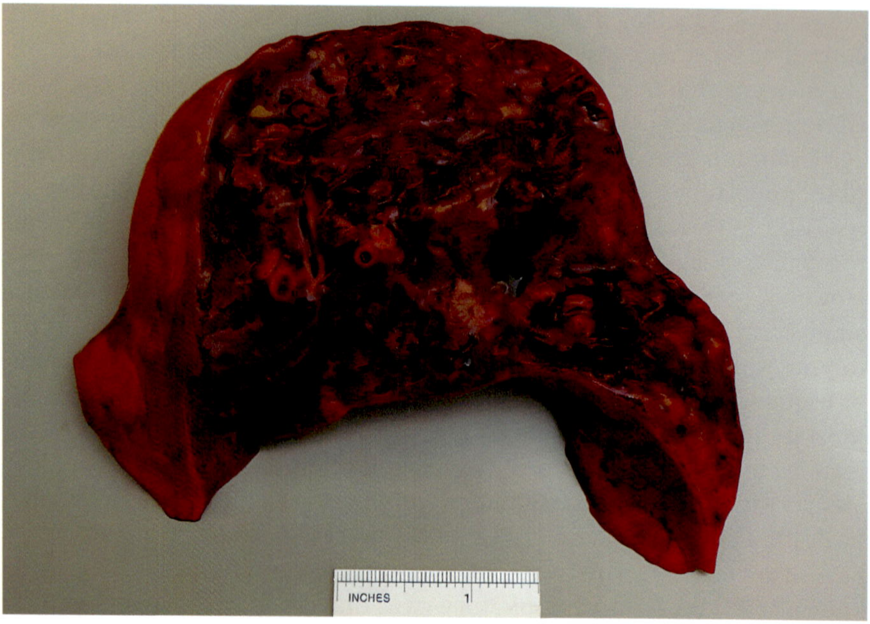

Figure 13.5 Cut surface of the lung demonstrating prominent bronchioles and mucus plugs.

Swelling of the airways can cause significant obstruction and inhibit gas exchange. Autopsy may reveal hyperinflation of the lungs as a result of air trapping in the lower airways. On cut sections, the lungs may demonstrate abundant mucous plugs and prominent bronchioles as a result of smooth muscle hyperplasia (Figure 13.5).

Chronic Obstructive Pulmonary Disease

Chronic obstructive pulmonary disease encompasses chronic bronchitis and emphysema, which are chronic, progressive diseases that affect the lungs. The most common cause for development of these diseases is cigarette smoking, although other environmental and genetic factors may also play an important role. Exposure over time to airway irritants causes the lung tissue to become thin and dilated. Autopsy may reveal grossly dilated alveoli and blebs on the surfaces of the lungs, which may rupture into the chest cavity. The mechanism of death in these cases is a result of air trapping in the lower airways, which hinders efficient gas exchange.

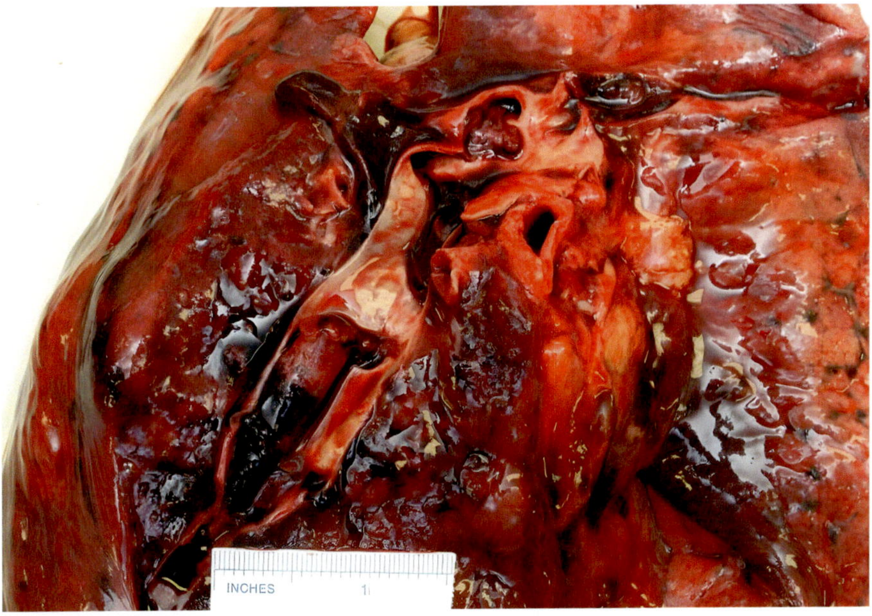

Figure 13.6 Pulmonary thromboembolism.

Pulmonary Embolism

Pulmonary embolism, or blood clot in the lungs, can be rapidly fatal and may not have preceding symptoms (Figure 13.6). Blood clots in the lungs often originate from other sites, such as the deep leg veins, known as deep venous thrombosis (DVT). If a thrombus or clot travels to the lungs, blood flow through the lungs can become severely obstructed, resulting in a mismatch between ventilation or breathing and oxygen delivery. Risk factors for the development of blood clots include long periods of immobility (such as after surgery), injuries, tobacco smoking, pregnancy, medical conditions (such as cancer), advancing age, oral contraceptive use, and genetic/heritable conditions that predispose the blood to clot. COVID-19 has also been associated with increased reports of blood clots.

Gastrointestinal Tract

Common natural diseases of the gastrointestinal tract that can cause death include cirrhosis of the liver, gastrointestinal ulcers, and pancreatitis.

Cirrhosis

Exposure of the liver to toxins such as alcohol or infections such as hepatitis causes repeated cycles of liver injury and regeneration. Over time, the pattern of injury and regeneration causes scarring of the liver, resulting in nodularity, or cirrhosis, seen at autopsy (Figure 13.7). Cirrhosis is an end-stage liver disease, where the liver can no longer function properly. The liver serves many purposes, such as filtering toxins, producing blood clotting factors, synthesizing proteins, and producing bile for digestion. When the liver is significantly damaged, bile flow may become blocked, toxins may build up in the bloodstream, and blood may not clot properly. Death may be due to a variety of mechanisms, including hepatic encephalopathy (toxic ammonia build-up in the bloodstream and brain) or gastrointestinal bleeding. An important clue to significant liver disease during death investigation is yellowing of the skin and eyes, termed jaundice of the skin and scleral icterus.

Gastrointestinal Ulcers

Ulcers in the gastrointestinal tract may be secondary to a variety of causes but are commonly a result of toxins, infections, or chronic irritation of the lining of the esophagus, stomach, or intestine. Ulcers may also be secondary

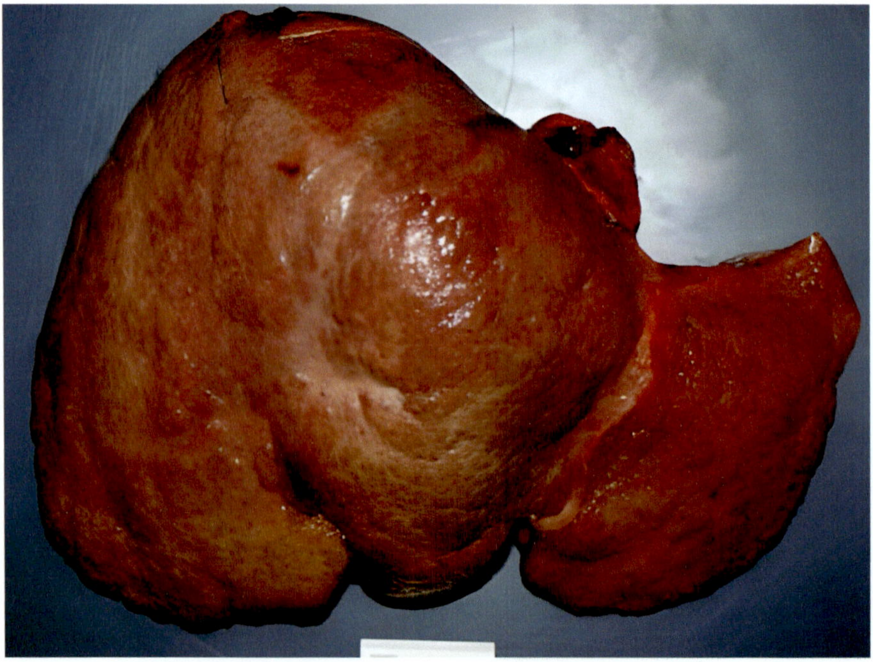

Figure 13.7 Hepatic cirrhosis.

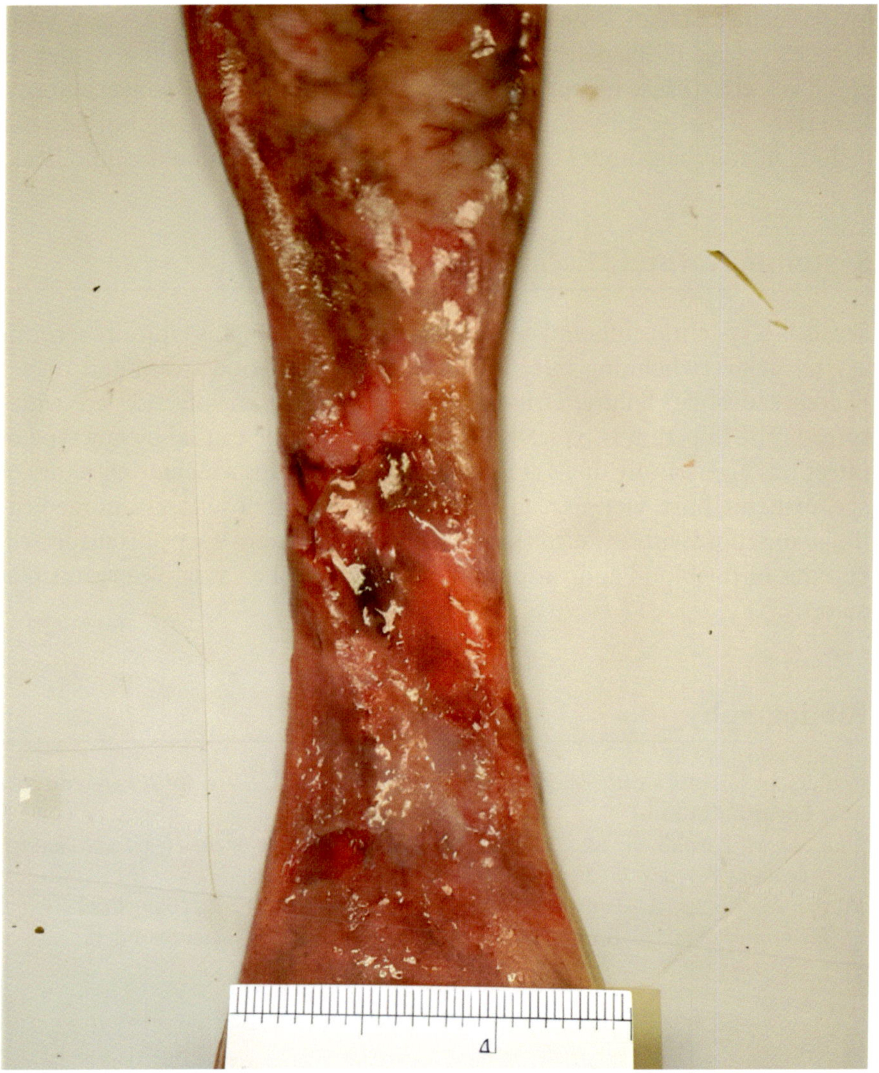

Figure 13.8 Esophageal ulcer.

to reflux of stomach acid into the esophagus or, more rarely, a tumor breaking through the inner lining of the gastrointestinal tract. Significant ulcers may cause death by eroding through a blood vessel to cause gastrointestinal bleeding (Figure 13.8).

Pancreatitis

Pancreatitis is a painful inflammatory condition of the pancreas that can be caused by infection, obstructing gallstones, high lipid levels in the blood, or toxins such as alcohol. When severe, inflammation of the pancreas may cause significant leakage of pancreatic enzymes into the surrounding tissues or blood vessels to cause hemorrhage or fat necrosis that may be seen at autopsy. Rare signs of pancreatitis may be seen on the external surfaces of the body and include hemorrhage under the skin of the left flank or around the umbilicus.

Systemic Natural Disease

Sepsis is a systemic, inflammatory, natural condition that is typically secondary to an overwhelming infection that enters the bloodstream and causes widespread organ failure. Original sources for such an infection are widespread. The infection is typically bacterial but may be caused by any type of infectious agent. Individuals at risk for developing sepsis include extremes of age, diabetes, burn victims, cancer patients on immunosuppressant medications, and those with any disorder of the immune system. If sepsis is suspected, cultures of the blood and various tissues may reveal a causative organism at autopsy.

Bibliography

Centers for Disease Control and Prevention. 2025. COVID-19. https://www.cdc.gov/covid/index.html

Fineschi, V., Baroldi, G., and Silver, M. D. 2006. *Pathology of the Heart and Sudden death in Forensic Medicine*. Boca Raton, FL: CRC Press.

Kumar, V., Abbas, A., Fausto, N., Robbins, S., and Cotran, R. 2005. *Robbins and Cotran Pathologic Basis of Disease*. Philadelphia, PA: Elsevier Saunders.

Suicide Deaths

14

MARY H. DUDLEY AND
LAUREN E. DVORSCAK

OBJECTIVES

- Define the medicolegal death investigator's role in scene investigation of apparent suicide deaths
- List five risk factors associated with suicide
- Identify two elements of suicide
- Describe the various methods of suicide deaths

Introduction

Suicide is the deliberate termination of one's life. After declining in rates from 2018 to 2020, suicide rates generally increased during the COVID-19 pandemic (Garnett and Curtin, 2024). Age varies by sex; peak age for males is over 75 years, whereas peak age for females is 45–54 years (Garnett and Curtin, 2024). Males are four times more successful in their suicide attempts than females. However, females make three times more attempts, and firearms are one of the leading means of suicide for both males and females (Garnett and Curtin, 2024). This chapter outlines risk factors, elements of suicide, determination of the manner of death as suicide, and methods of suicide. It also highlights the medicolegal death investigator's (MDI's) role in investigating suspected suicide. A case study is included.

Medicolegal Death Investigation of Suicide

The MDI plays an important role in helping the ME/coroner in determining the manner of death in cases of suspected suicide. Interviews of family and friends may provide important past medical and mental history of depression and/or previous suicide attempts. Scene documentation and photography provides additional information regarding circumstances surrounding death in ruling out other manners of death, such as accidental hanging (e.g. "the choking game" or autoerotic asphyxia). The MDI will document additional evidence such as notes of intent or medications at the scene that can provide important clues related to potential self-harm.

Death investigation often begins with obtaining a prior history through interviewing relatives and friends to create a "psychological autopsy", which is a

DOI: 10.4324/9781003538622-17

retrospective query of the decedent's life and stressors in an attempt to understand their motivations. Medical records are reviewed for physical or mental illness. The body is searched for signs of previous attempts or "hesitation marks" such as wrist scars, neck scars, or forearm scars. Tracheotomy scars, surgical cutdown scars, or other scars may indicate prior attempts or treatment. Approximately, one suicide occurs for every 25 attempts (Vitiello et al., 2009).

Signs of Risk

A sudden, unexpected mood change—particularly a change from a frantic or agitated state to one of calm deliberation—is often a clue. Other personality changes and signs of suicide risk include the following:

- Increased depression/exalted mood or "mood swings."
- Increased fatigue or listlessness.
- Sudden increase in alcohol use.
- Giving away one's treasured possessions.
- Making peace with family members and oneself.

Elements of Suicide

Two elements are required to cite suicide as a manner of death:

1. An intent to commit suicide.
2. A specific act that carries out that intent.

Proof of suicide may be demonstrated from one or more of the following:

- A suicide note in the victim's handwriting (however, fewer than half of all suicidal individuals actually write a note).
- Audio/video tape recording.
- Body in a locked room, possibly with deadbolt and/or chain in place.
- Firearm residue on hands.
- Evidence of prior rehearsal.
- Flag folded into a triangle and placed near suicidal veterans or patriots.
- Presence of the book *Final Exit* or use of any of its recommended suicide methods (*Final Exit* is a book about and for persons who want to end their lives because of age or sickness; it serves as an instruction manual on how to commit suicide).
- Recent membership or interest in the Hemlock Society, a national group that supports euthanasia, assisted suicide, or suicide. The mode of suicide is asphyxia with a plastic bag and/or overdose of a sleeping pill or sedative (Seconal [secobarbital] is often the drug of choice).

Probable Suicide

An ME/coroner's office often has to make some difficult decisions. Characteristics of wounds or overdose of ingested drugs suggest suicide. Locations of wounds, contact gunshot wounds, practice or hesitation marks (numerous superficial incised wounds on wrists or neck), or coexistence of multiple sublethal and/or lethal wounds may or may not indicate suicide. Drug ingestion can be validated by high stomach concentration of legal or illegal drugs, as distinguished from low or absent drug metabolite in body fluid.

Further, teenagers or adults who play Russian roulette are generally aware of the chances to live or die if they put a loaded gun to their head and pull the trigger. The manner of death in Russian roulette is considered suicide under most circumstances. Reckless acts such as "chicken", drug abuse, or volunteering for hazardous duty may also indicate a conscious or unconscious desire for death. The death investigation usually reveals related indications of suicidal intent.

Suspicion of Suicide

Suicidal behavior can be subtle or overt. When suicide is a suspicion, the decedent's present and past situations must be considered. For example, grief caused by recent losses or threats of losses can create feelings of hopelessness that prompt suicide. Grieving occurs not only from loss of a loved one through death or divorce but also from loss of one's professional reputation, personal reputation, financial security, or political position. A history of emotional illness (particularly depression), change of habits, and record of substance abuse can also raise suspicion of suicide. Physical findings supported by behavioral clues may be the only evidence available to an ME/coroner for a suicidal intent.

In addition, recent purchase of weapons or prior suicide attempt strongly supports suspicion of suicide. Among those who made an initial attempt, a second attempt occurred within 3 months.

Concealment of Suicide

Concealment of suicide by family members is a frequent behavior when the body is discovered. Concealment is often motivated by financial gain, religion, social stigmas, insurance, and fear. Families or friends may alter the body or scene or misinterpret events when they want to hide a suicide. Ways of altering the body include concealing a wound, cleaning the body, or taking down a hanging body. Further, concealment of suicide may occur by the individual, possibly in an attempt to make the scene appear as if it were some other manner of death.

A variety of methods are frequently employed in efforts to remove evidence or alter the scene or investigation. These include the following:

- Removal of any notes, weapons, or drug containers.
- Planting a gun cleaning kit.
- Emphasizing an illness of the deceased.
- Withholding the actual story.
- Introducing evidence of struggle to the scene.
- Sanitizing the scene.

Case Study—Contributed by Lauren E. Dvorscak

A 68-year-old man had not been heard from in a week, and family members requested a welfare check. When law enforcement arrived at the scene, nothing appeared out of order, and they left without incident. The next day, the family traveled to the location and could not locate the decedent but did find concerning messages that he may have harmed himself. Requesting additional support from law enforcement, the residence was searched. Investigators noticed a chest freezer that had items placed on top of it (Figure 14.1). On further inspection, the items on top of the chest freezer were glued.

An MDI was called in and confirmed that the chest freezer contained the missing family member (Figure 14.2). Opening the freezer showed that the

Figure 14.1 Chest freezer.

Figure 14.2 Decedent inside the chest freezer.

items on top were glued, indicating an attempt to conceal the fact that the decedent was in the freezer. The decedent was wearing a modified motorcycle helmet and was holding a shotgun.

The decedent was transported to the medical examiner's office with the helmet intact, which showed modification allowing for an intraoral shotgun injury through the helmet (Figure 14.3).

The scene was thoroughly documented by the MDI, who relayed specific details about the scene to the medical investigator in a complete narrative report. The MDI played a crucial role in documenting the pieces of the case that aided the medical examiner in the ultimate conclusion of cause and manner of death. This case highlights the importance of thoroughly examining the scene, as glued items on top of the chest freezer may have concealed the decedent for much longer had investigators not thought to check inside.

Suicide Methods

Gunshot Wounds

The majority of suicidal deaths in the United States occur as a result of gunshot wounds, accounting for approximately 55% (CDC, 2025). A gunshot either in contact or at close range to an easily accessible body area often indicates a self-inflicted injury. A working knowledge of both suicide patterns and gunshot wounds is necessary when treating patients in the emergency department or

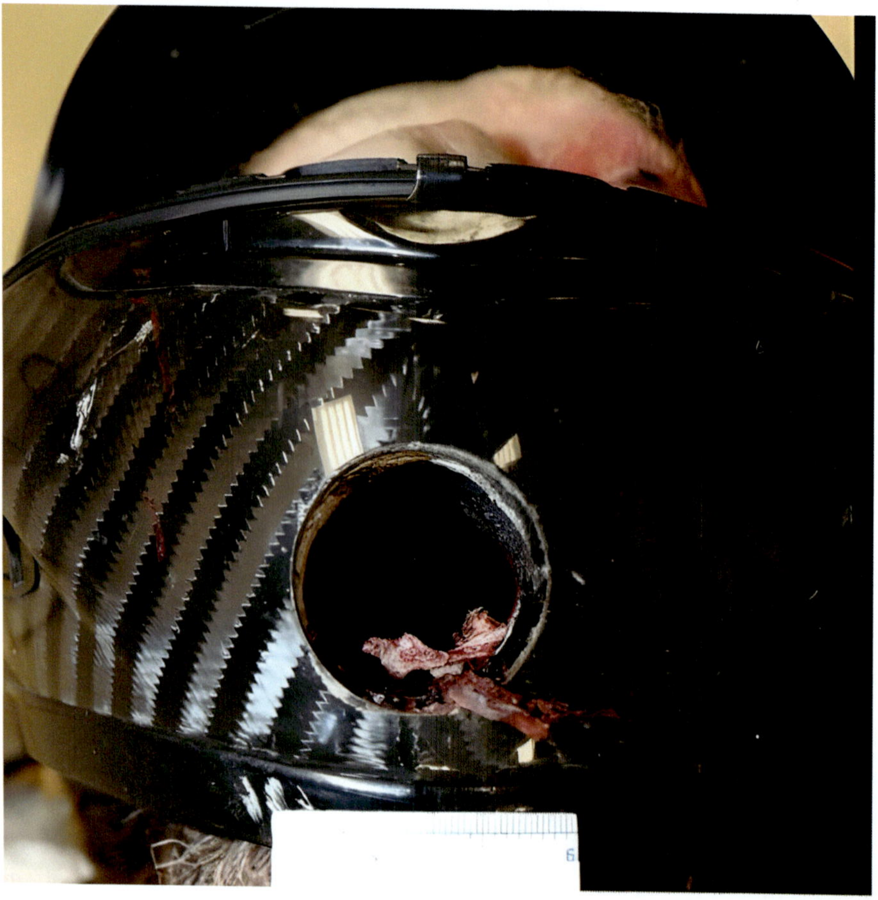

Figure 14.3 Autopsy photograph of modified helmet.

evaluating a body at a death scene in order to determine whether a homicide, suicide, or accident was the manner of death. In many instances, it is difficult to discern one from the other.

Suicide by firearms has increased to the highest number recorded in 2023, at a total of 27,300 in the United States, according to the Centers for Disease Control and Prevention. The ME/coroner needs to consider suicide when dealing with contact gunshot wounds to the head (particularly the forehead or temporal area) or mouth (intraoral).

Contact entry gunshot wounds can be identified by gunshot residue or soot surrounding the wound. The size and shape of a gunshot wound are unreliable indicators as to whether a wound is an entry or exit wound. However, if soot is present, it is an entry wound; residue is never associated with exit wounds. An intermediate-range wound shows the deposit of burnt and unburnt gunpowder stippling or tattooing surrounding the entrance wound. The circumference of gunpowder stippling relates to the range of fire—the closer to the skin that the barrel of the weapon is at the time of firing, the smaller the circumference of gunpowder stippling. The range of fire is determined by the firearms examiner firing the weapon with similar ammunition.

Stellate splitting of the skin, particularly over bone, also indicates a close contact gunshot wound. The in-rushing propellant gases that accompany a bullet through the skull and into the brain blow back and are trapped between the skull and skin, ripping and tearing the skin in a stellate manner.

Blow-back and gunshot residue will also remain on the hand of the individual who pulls the trigger (Figure 14.4). Thus, the victim's hands should be protected with paper bags until the ME/coroner can examine them for residue.

Drugs

Twelve percent of suicides in the United States are due to drugs or poisons (CDC, 2025). Suicide by drug overdose is more common among females. Multiple drugs and/or alcohol may be involved. Other poisons such as arsenic or ethylene glycol (antifreeze) may be intentionally ingested. Scene investigators should be alert for empty prescription bottles; those bottles may have patient names other than the victim's name on the label (Figure 14.5). Thorough background investigation and complete toxicology analysis are indicated in suspicious cases. All medication bottles should be collected at

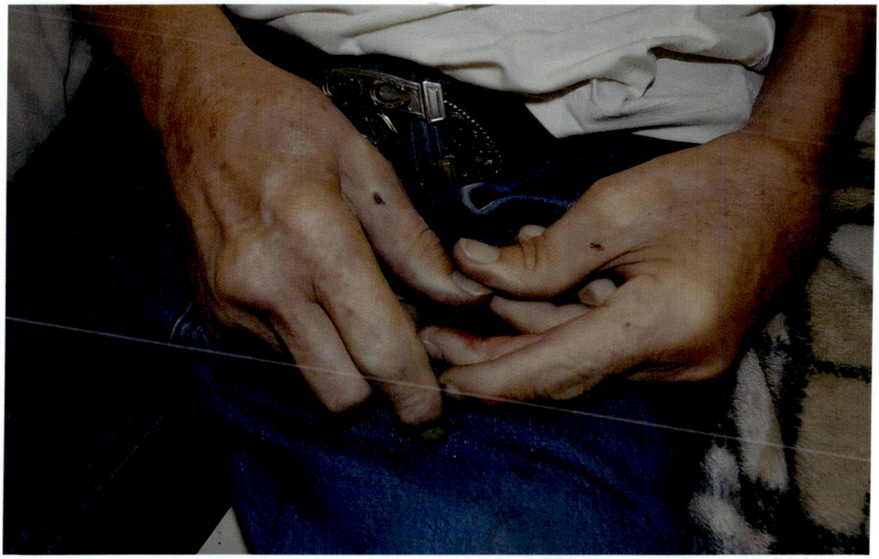

Figure 14.4 Blood on the hands of a decedent who had a self-inflicted firearm injury.

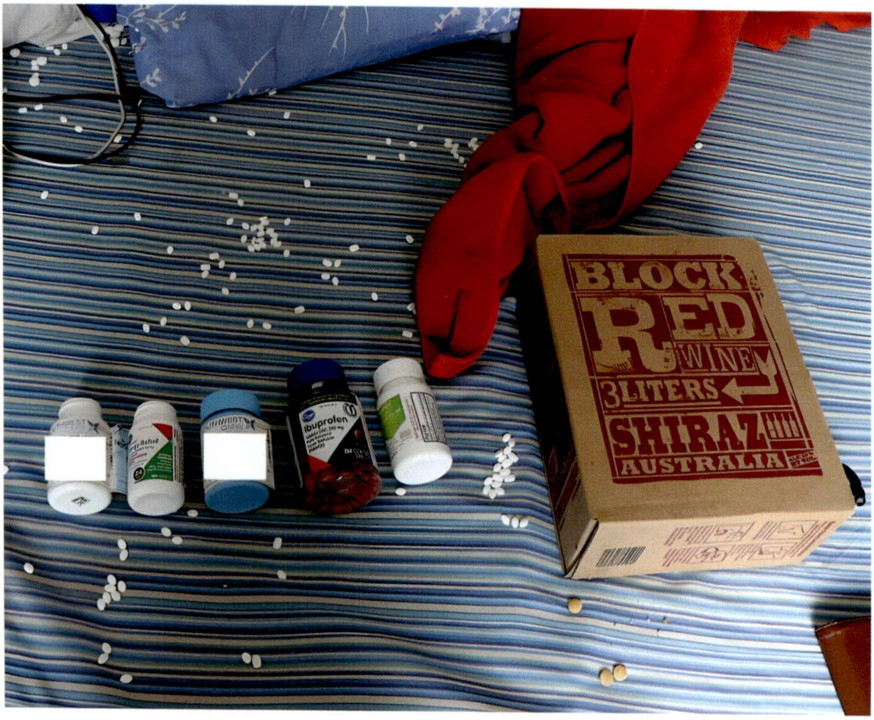

Figure 14.5 Scene photograph of medications and loose pills in a suicidal overdose.

the scene and documented on the medication log brought back to the ME/coroner's office.

Asphyxia

Asphyxia and suffocation are the second most frequent type of suicidal manner of death, accounting for 25% of cases in the United States (CDC, 2025). Types of asphyxia include suffocation (including inhalation of toxic substances), strangulation, hanging, and drowning. A plastic bag found around the decedent's head may indicate suicide by asphyxia or suffocation (Figure 14.6), but not conclusively. Often, an overdose of a sedative in addition to a plastic bag around the head and chronic illness indicate an intention of self-harm. Scene investigation is an important adjunct to determining the manner of death in cases of suspected intentional asphyxia. Plastic bags near the body, postural asphyxia, or body position give additional clues to the manner of death.

Suicide by hanging does not require total suspension. The victim's position at time of death is variable—the body can be kneeling, sitting, or lying down (Figure 14.7). If the body is hanging, it is frequently cut down by the

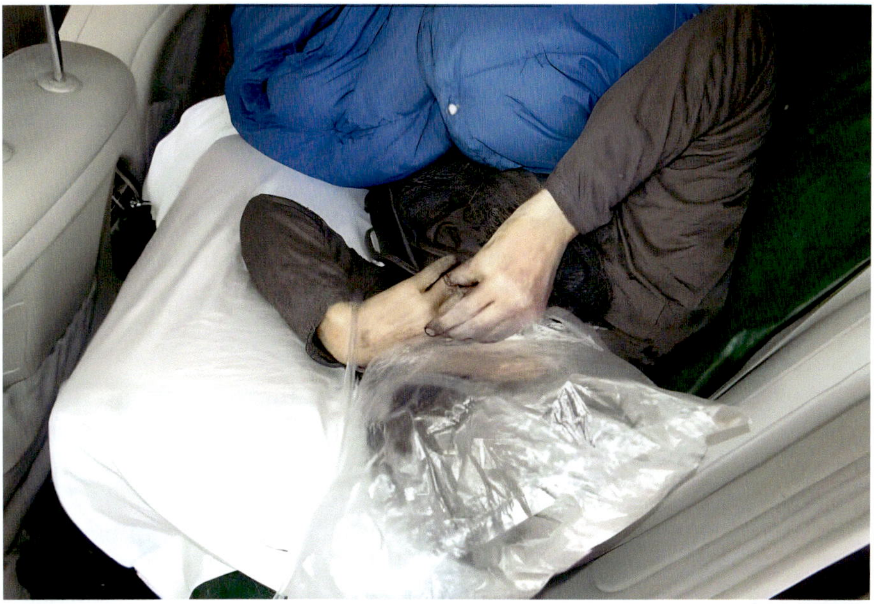

Figure 14.6 Plastic bag over head.

Figure 14.7 Hanging scene photo.

person who discovers the body. Ligatures used are variable and a noose can be a T-shirt, sheet, shoestring, or even braided dental floss. Anything that can constrict the carotid arteries is sufficient to cause death. For example, the weight of the head alone is approximately 8–10 pounds; the pressure of the weight of the head against the neck ligature is sufficient to constrict the carotid arteries and cause death.

In a hanging case, the noose is the most valuable piece of evidence to the investigation. The investigator should completely photograph and preserve the noose without disturbing the knot. To do this, remove the noose by making a cut away from the knot (see Chapter 15 for additional details regarding death investigation in asphyxia).

Asphyxial suicides by carbon monoxide inhalation occur from a running vehicle in a closed garage, from car exhaust fumes directed into the vehicle through a hose or other pipe, from burning fuel in an enclosed space, or from chemical reactions that produce carbon monoxide (Figure 14.8). Carbon monoxide is an odorless, colorless gas that has a high affinity of binding to hemoglobin within red blood cells, much greater than that of oxygen. This displaces oxygen from the red blood cells and prevents normal oxygen delivery to tissues, ultimately preventing cellular respiration. This is reflected on examination as a cherry-pink discoloration of the skin or underlying tissues.

Cutting or Stabbing

Suicide by cutting or stabbing is recognized by multiple incised wounds or hesitation marks. Favored sites are the neck, wrists, and chest. The nondominant wrist and forearm are frequently involved (Figure 14.9). Suicide by stabbing or wounds that cause exsanguination are more prevalent in countries where firearms are banned.

Electrocution

As with suicides by cutting or stabbing, suicides by electrocution are more prevalent in countries where firearms are banned. For example, firearms are banned in Australia; thus, a popular way to commit suicide is by electrocution. Electrical wires are separated and attached to the wrists; then the electrical cord is plugged into an outlet.

Blunt Trauma

Intentional blunt trauma and self-injury may be seen in individuals who jumped from tall buildings or bridges. Other (accidents) with no explanation

Figure 14.8 Carbon monoxide toxicity by burning coal in an enclosed space.

may be a suicidal manner of death, for example, a single vehicle hitting a stationary object or driving off a bridge without evidence of breaking, or a pedestrian running into traffic. The scene investigation, physical evidence, autopsy findings, and toxicology results are key to determine the manner of death as suicide.

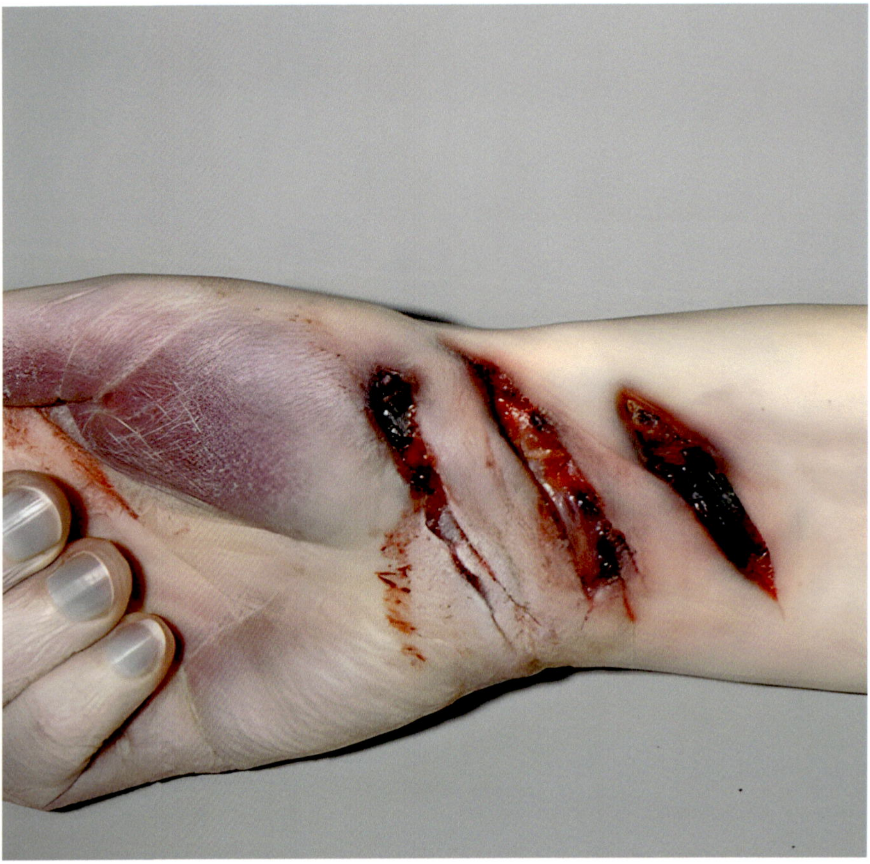

Figure 14.9 Incised wounds on wrist and forearm.

References

CDC National Center for Health Statistics- Fast Stats. 2025. https://www.cdc.gov/nchs/fastats/suicide.htm

Garnett, M. and Curtin, S. 2024. *Suicide Mortality in the United States, 2002–2022, NCHS Data Brief No 509, 2024*. Atlanta, GA: Centers for Disease Control and Statistics.

Vitiello B, Silva SG, Rohde P, Kratochvil CJ, Kennard BD, Reinecke MA, Mayes TL, Posner K, May DE, March JS. Suicidal events in the Treatment for Adolescents With Depression Study (TADS). *J Clin Psychiatry*. 2009 Apr 21;70(5):741–747. doi: 10.4088/jcp.08m04607. PMID: 19552869; PMCID: PMC2702701.

Asphyxia and Drowning Deaths

15

MARY H. DUDLEY

OBJECTIVES

Upon completion of this chapter and corresponding reference material, the reader will be able to

- Describe the role of the medicolegal death investigator for asphyxial and drowning deaths
- Describe the autopsy findings associated with asphyxia and drowning deaths
- Discuss asphyxia as a cause of death
- Describe evidence that may be gathered at the scene of a death by asphyxia
- Differentiate between hanging and strangulation deaths
- Discuss the key points associated with drowning deaths

Introduction

Asphyxia refers to any condition in which the body or any vital organ is deprived of oxygen by any means. Extrinsic causes of asphyxia may include electrocution, drugs, or anesthesia. Intrinsic natural causes may include hemorrhage, pneumothorax, ruptured aneurysm, pulmonary edema, cardiac insufficiency, or obstructive tumors. Forensic pathologists may classify asphyxia into three types, including compression of the chest or neck, obstruction of the airway, and exclusion of oxygen. Compression of the chest must be sufficient to prevent adequate respiratory movement. Compression of the neck can occur with or without blockage of the airway as with hanging or strangulation, causing the obstruction of blood flow to and from the brain. Smothering, aspiration of foreign material, and swelling of the respiratory tract cause airway obstruction. Allergic reactions can also cause sufficient swelling and obstruction of the airways. Oxygen depletion, drowning, replacement by toxic gases (carbon monoxide) and chemicals (cyanide poisoning) may cause asphyxia by exclusion of oxygen.

DOI: 10.4324/9781003538622-18

This chapter identifies the role of the medicolegal death investigator (MDI) in asphyxial and drowning deaths, autopsy findings, and key points of drowning deaths.

Medicolegal Death Investigator Scene Investigation for Asphyxial Deaths

The role of the MDI at the asphyxial death scene is to document findings, interview witnesses, photograph the scene, and collect evidence. Asphyxial deaths may fall under the manner of death as natural, accident, homicide, suicide, or undetermined, depending on the circumstances surrounding the death. Accidental manner of death is the most common, followed by suicide, homicide, and natural. Because of the many causes and types of asphyxial deaths, as well as few specific autopsy findings, the scene investigation, event history, and evidence collection are extremely important.

The history of the event of sudden collapse may reveal choking while eating related to poor dentition or alcohol use. Children while eating or playing with small toys may choke on food or other objects, causing airway obstruction. Sudden infant death may be associated with soft bedding, co-sleeping, or positional asphyxia. Risk factors for asphyxia include age (infants and elderly), immobility, paralysis, seizure disorder, drugs, and alcohol.

Asphyxia may occur in industrial or farm accidents when clothing is caught in machinery, and the individual becomes trapped. Individuals working under raised vehicles or other heavy machinery can become entrapped if the jack fails or the machinery slips from raised platforms. Accidental ligature strangulation or asphyxial deaths may occur during autoerotic activities.

Suicidal asphyxial deaths may be caused by hanging, suffocation (plastic bags), or carbon monoxide. Twenty percent of suicide deaths are by hanging. Hanging may occur with various positions of the body, and most don't require full suspension (e.g. kneeling, sitting, or lying down). The weight of the head and neck against the ligature is enough force to occlude blood flow to or from the brain. The ligature should remain on the body, and the body should be photographed as found at the scene. If the ligature must be removed (or was removed for life-saving attempts), it should be cut away from the knot, with the knot undisturbed, and should accompany the body to the medical examiner/coroner's office.

The MDI must take precaution for individual safety when investigating deaths suspected to be from carbon monoxide. Carbon monoxide toxicity may be classified as accidental or suicidal manner of death. Carbon monoxide is an odorless, colorless gas that can build up in indoor spaces, confined spaces, or outdoors. Common sources of carbon monoxide toxicity include motor exhaust, gas stoves, furnaces, gas water heaters, grills, and generators.

Carbon monoxide binds more readily to hemoglobin, reducing oxygen transport to vital organs. The severity of symptoms depends on the carbon monoxide concentration, exposure duration, and individual health factors. Early (flu-like) symptoms include dizziness and tiredness within 2 hours of exposure. Longer exposure will cause nausea, confusion, unconsciousness, and death.

Homicidal asphyxial deaths include smothering, manual strangulation, and ligature strangulation. The decedent may be a rape victim, child, frail/elderly adult, or an otherwise incapacitated adult (e.g. under the influence of drugs or alcohol).

Autopsy Findings

Imaging studies, autopsy with external and internal examination, and neck examination may support scene investigation in determination of the cause and manner of asphyxial deaths. Prior to examination, imaging studies may reveal the cause of asphyxia (e.g. fractures, aspiration of radio-opaque foreign bodies, etc.). External examination may show cherry-red lividity related to carbon monoxide or cyanide toxicity. Congestion and/or cyanosis of the face and eyes may be seen in asphyxial deaths associated with neck or chest compression. The tongue may protrude and show drying artifact. Bloody mucus is often dried at the nose and/or mouth. Petechiae, small pinpoint hemorrhages, may be observed on the scalp, face, mucus membranes of the mouth, eye sclera, and/or conjunctiva (Figure 15.1). Depending on the position of the body, dependent portions may be engorged, including the hands, feet, or genitalia.

A pressure abrasion around the neck can indicate the presence and nature of a ligature in cases of hanging. Different types of ligatures can include belts, ropes, leashes, electrical cords, wires, clothing, or sheets, among others, and may leave patterned impressions on the neck, depending on the material used. A ligature mark with hanging is usually upward canting, either toward the back or front of the neck, depending on the location of the knot and method of suspension (Figure 15.2). Ligature strangulation creates a more horizontal mark on the neck (Figure 15.3). Manual strangulation may show finger indentations, fingernail marks, or other abrasions on the neck (Figure 15.4). There may be defensive injuries or signs of a struggle with homicidal asphyxia.

Differences exist between strangulation by ligature (usually a homicide) and hanging. In ligature strangulation, a horizontal neck pressure abrasion is commonly below the level of the thyroid cartilage. In hanging, the neck mark cants upward toward the knot, but it may be horizontal as in strangulation if the hanging occurs while lying. The mark in hanging is usually at or above the

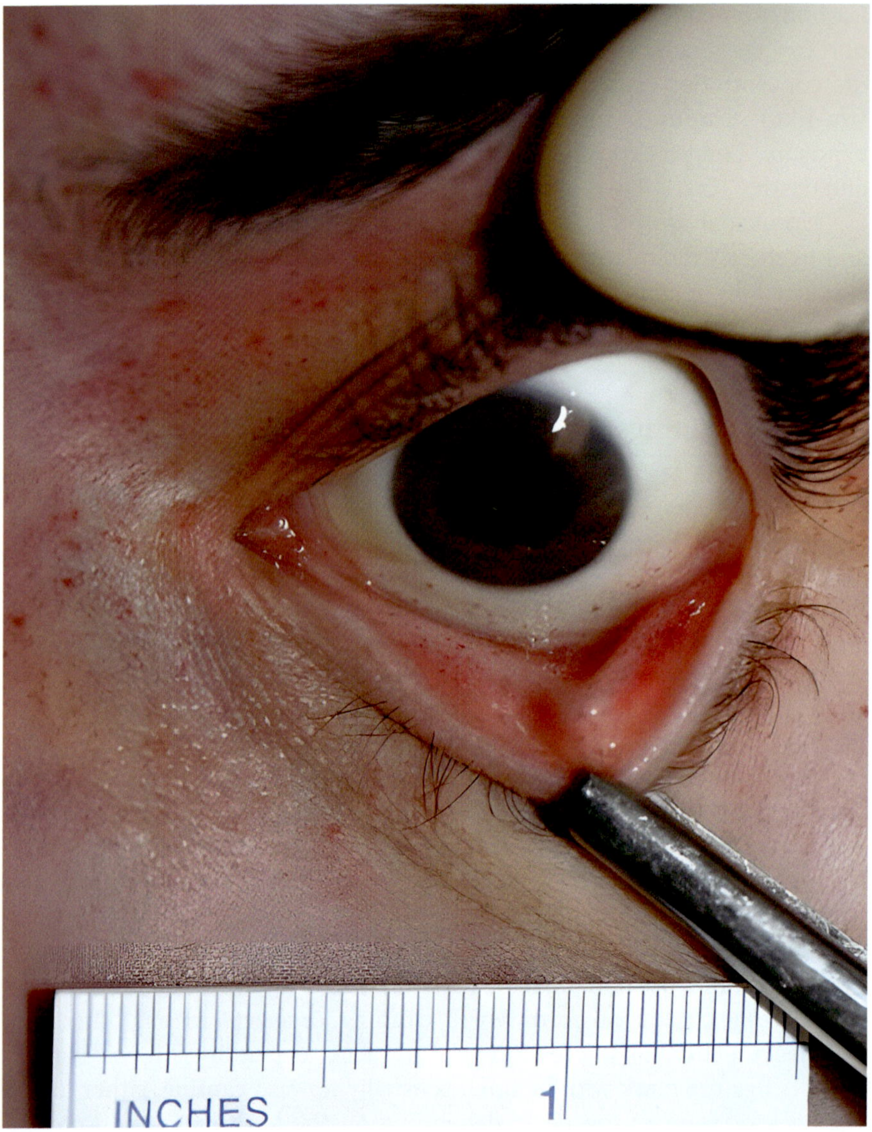

Figure 15.1 Petechial hemorrhages in the conjunctivae.

level of the thyroid cartilage. Fractures seldom occur with hanging, except with a long drop or in the elderly. Pressure abrasions and/or petechiae may fade with a period of survival. Skin folds may be seen in babies, obese individuals, or in decomposition, which may mimic ligature marks.

Asphyxia may be a diagnosis of exclusion, as autopsy may not show external or internal injury depending on the nature of the case. The internal examination may demonstrate little evidence of injury of the subcutaneous tissue

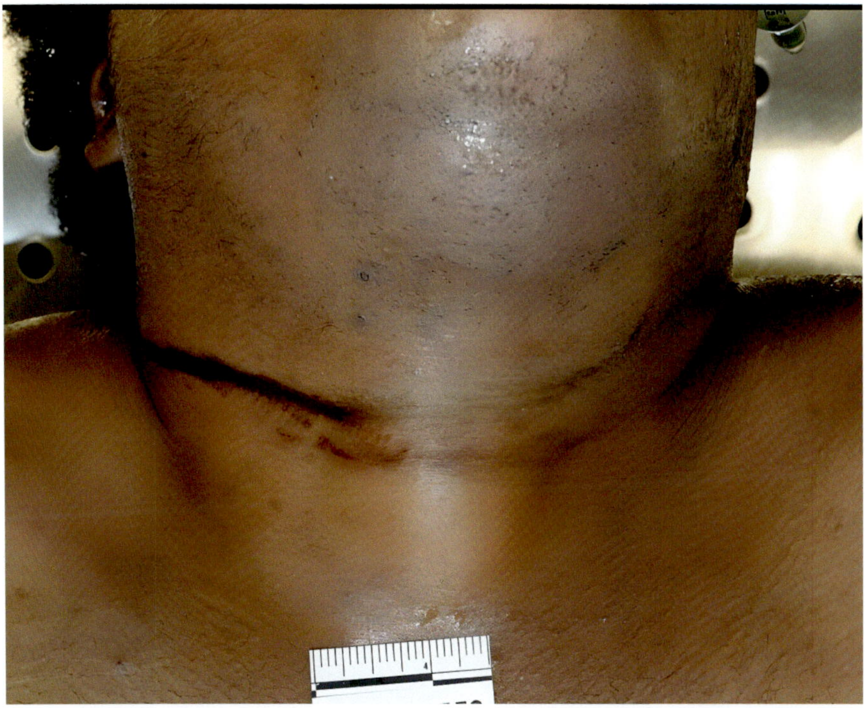

Figure 15.2 Ligature mark in hanging.

immediately beneath the skin in cases of hanging or accidental asphyxia. However, deep injury of the neck can occur in homicidal strangulation. Middle ear hemorrhage or petechiae of the pleura and epicardium may be seen. Cerebral and pulmonary edema (swelling of the brain and fluid build-up in the lungs) are common autopsy findings in deaths from low-oxygen states, as in asphyxia. Thoracic and abdominal injuries may be seen with compression or mechanical asphyxia.

Dissection of the neck should not begin until the chest cavity and cranial vault have been removed and examined. The strap muscles of the anterior neck should be examined in a layered fashion from outer to inner muscle groups. Adequate exposure is required, and the skin incision should extend up the posterolateral aspect of the neck. Careful removal of the larynx, hyoid bone, base of the tongue, and upper trachea is performed en bloc with adjacent soft tissues, leaving behind the blood vessels of the carotid sheath. Manual strangulation may cause fractures of the hyoid bone with surrounding hemorrhage. Removal of the hyoid bone from the neck bloc allows for clearer photography of injury (or lack thereof) and additional imaging to document any fractures (Figure 15.5). Careful inspection of the upper and lower airways in situ, in cases of suspected aspiration or choking,

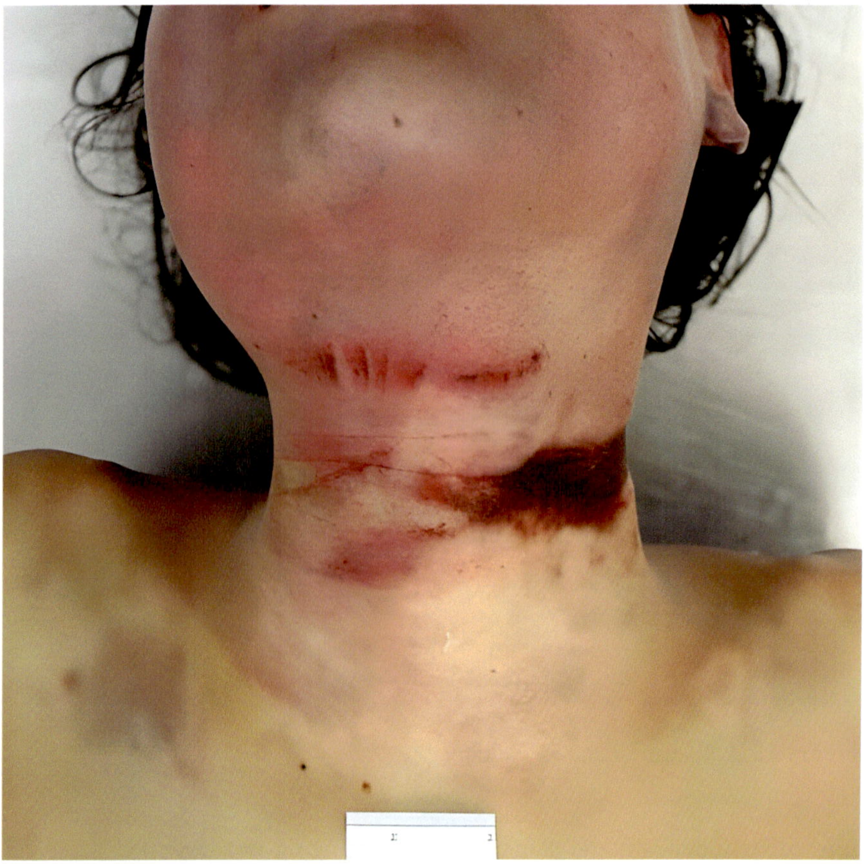

Figure 15.3 Ligature strangulation mark.

can more accurately document the location and/or presence of foreign bodies (Figure 15.6).

Respiratory Choke Holds and Vascular Neck Restraint

Respiratory choke holds or vascular neck restraint is mainly used by law enforcement or security personnel to temporarily subdue and control a combative individual or uncooperative suspect from harming himself/herself or others. Neck compression can produce transient cerebral ischemia and unconsciousness. Stimulation of the carotid sinus by pressure on the neck causes bradycardia (slowed heart rate) and a decrease in arterial blood pressure. The arm and forearm, a baton, large metal flashlight, or other devices are used to compress the neck. Compression can also be done by hand if the

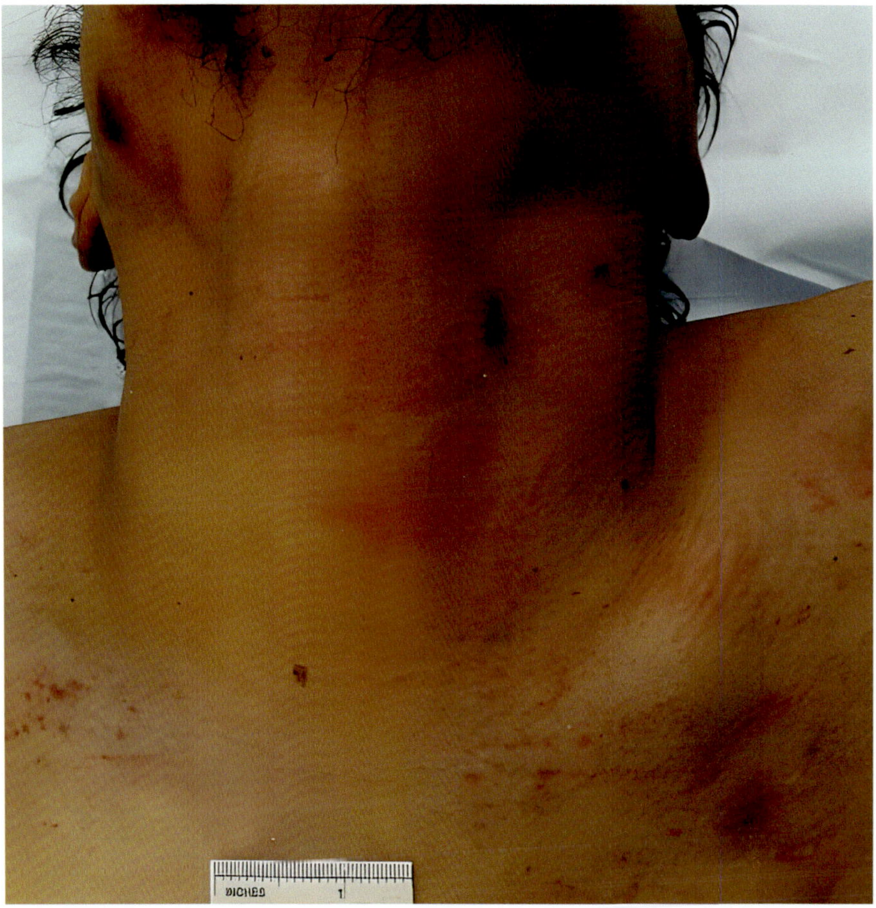

Figure 15.4 Manual strangulation marks.

person applying the hold is strong and is able to reach both carotid arteries on the neck with the thumb and index finger.

In a respiratory choke hold, the forearm compresses the neck, which can restrict air and/or blood flow. In this hold, the forearm is placed straight across the front of the neck. The free hand grips the wrist and pulls the wrist back. Loss of function is due to collapse of the airway and carotid arteries, subsequently decreasing oxygen to the brain. However, if too much force is used, the larynx or hyoid bone can be fractured. The resulting hypoxia sensitizes the heart to arrhythmias.

The vascular neck restraint applies continuous symmetrical force to the sides of the neck, compressing the carotid arteries and jugular veins. The arm is placed around the neck, with the antecubital fossa or crook of the arm centered at the midline of the neck. The free hand grips the other wrist and pulls it backward, creating a pincer effect. Compression of the carotid arteries

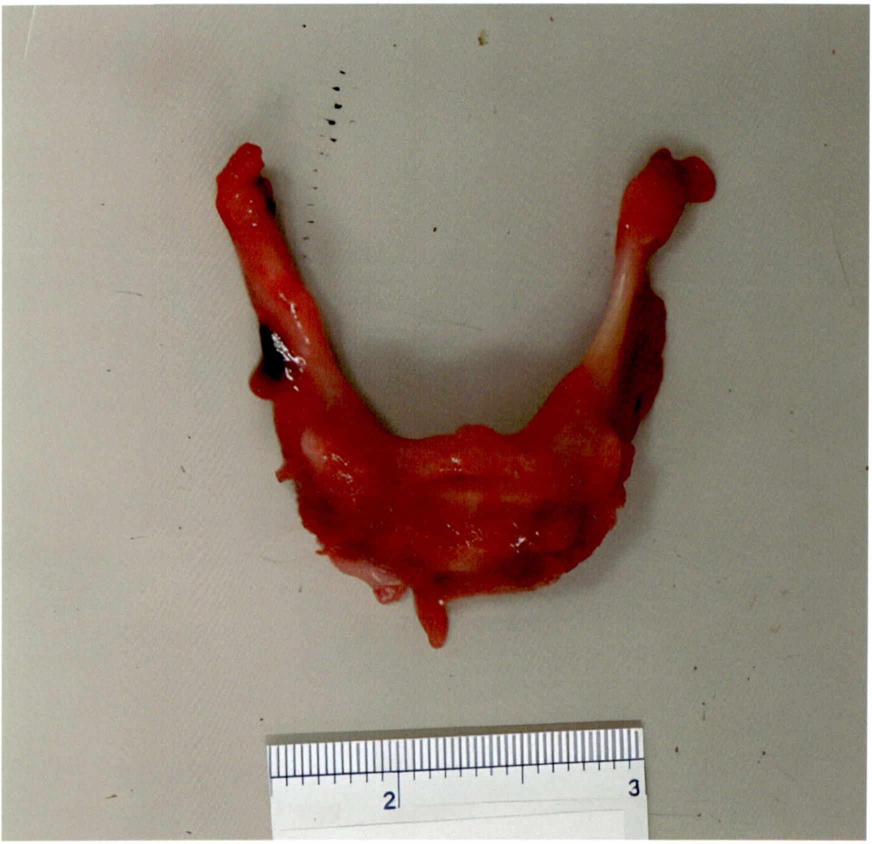

Figure 15.5 Hyoid bone separated from neck bloc.

causes the loss of consciousness in approximately 10–15 seconds. Vascular neck restraints can easily and unintentionally become a respiratory choke hold on a violently struggling individual. There is rarely any finding of trauma to the structure of the neck with pathological examination. Compression of the carotid arteries with decreased cerebral blood flow may cause a stroke in an individual with atherosclerotic disease.

Drowning Deaths (Contributed by James L. Caruso)

An average of 3600 fatal, unintentional drownings (non-boating related) occur annually in the United States. An additional 332 individuals die each year in boating-related incidents. Men are more likely to die of drowning than women, with an approximately 4:1 ratio in adult drownings. Drownings are more common in freshwater than seawater and occur more commonly in the

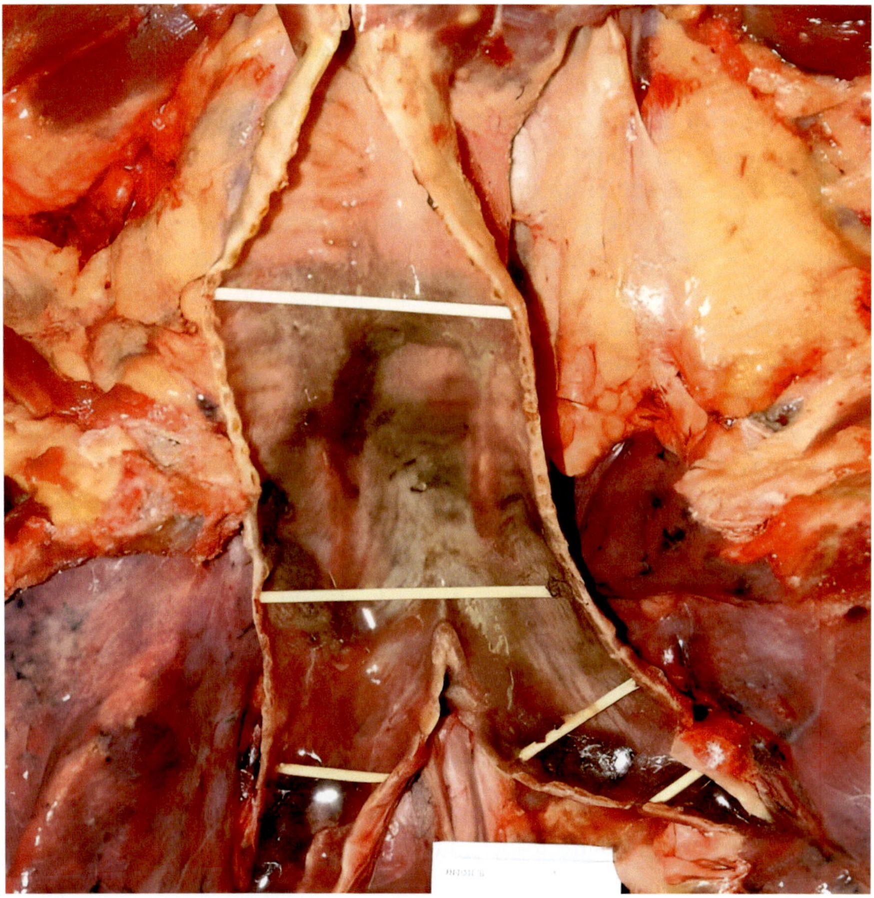

Figure 15.6 Autopsy in situ dissection of lower airways.

spring/summer months. For adolescents and adults, 70% of water recreation deaths involve alcohol.

Children ages 1–4 years have the highest drowning rates. An average of 22 nonfatal, near-drowning incidents occur each day. Among children ages ranging 1–14 years, fatal drowning remains the second leading cause of injury-related death behind motor vehicle accidents.

Medicolegal Death Investigator Scene Investigation for Drowning Deaths

Medicolegal death scene investigation, including history, photography, and evidence collection, is extremely important when a body is found in water. The manner of death may be natural, accident suicide, homicide, or undetermined. Most drowning deaths are an accidental manner of death. The most common location of drownings includes swimming pools, open water (ocean or lake), and rivers. Drownings can occur in bathtubs or hot tubs. A child can drown in a tub or bucket of water. Drowning is an asphyxial death due to submersion, at least of the airway, in a liquid medium, causing hypoxic injury of the heart and brain.

The body may be removed from the location where the drowning occurred and may have undergone resuscitation and/or transported to the hospital. The MDI will need to obtain information from emergency personnel and return to the location of the incident to obtain information regarding the circumstances of the drowning.

Some bodies intentionally weighted down in water are homicides or suicides. As decomposition progresses, it becomes more difficult to determine the cause and manner of death. Animal artifact can appear similarly to antemortem injury on the body. Bodies disposed in water may be an accidental drug death or homicide. Items on the body should not be removed, unless prior permission was granted by the ME/coroner's office. Clothing, wraps, bindings, and other evidence near the body should be documented, photographed, collected as evidence, and transported to the ME/coroner's office.

The following investigation questions should be considered in collecting information related to drowning deaths:

- Where did the death occur?
- Was the body moved?
- Was cardiopulmonary resuscitation attempted?
- If bathtub, was decedent's airway immersed? (Water may no longer be in the tub upon MDI's arrival.)
- How long were they submerged, or when were they last seen alive?
- Is the setting appropriate? (e.g. if in bathtub, is the decedent clothed?)
- If swimming pool or beach setting, did the decedent know how to swim?
- Is boating or SCUBA (self-contained underwater breathing apparatus) diving involved?
- Was the decedent near an electrical or exhaust source?
- If adolescent or adult, what barriers exist to exiting the water safely?
- Is there evidence of alcohol, prescription, or illicit substance use at the scene?
- Did the decedent have a significant medical history? (e.g. seizures, immobility, cardiovascular disease)

A comprehensive water-related death scene investigation protocol is recommended by the National Center for Fatality Review and Prevention, which includes additional questions for data gathering in drowning deaths (NCFRP, 2024).

Key Points

1. Drowning is a diagnosis of exclusion. Prior to arriving at this conclusion, one must rule out other causes or contributory factors in death (e.g. trauma, natural disease processes, drug overdose, disposal of a homicide in water). A complete autopsy, imaging studies, and toxicology are always indicated.
2. A drowning death is death by asphyxiation with subsequent hypoxemia and cerebral anoxia. The amount of water inhaled is variable, and in 10%–15% of cases, laryngeal spasm can result in dry drowning.
3. Absorption of large amounts of water—which especially occurs in cases of freshwater drowning—was once thought to cause serious electrolyte abnormalities and potentially fatal dysrhythmia. This is no longer assumed to be the case as it is likely that a healthy heart and kidneys would compensate for the increase in volume, and electrolyte abnormalities do not seem to play a large role.
4. The "break point" is defined as the time when a person can no longer voluntarily hold his or her breath. This occurs in response to blood levels of carbon dioxide (CO_2) and oxygen (O_2). The person breathes regardless of his or her immersion status, and if submerged, continued inhalation of water occurs.
5. The type of water inhaled—fresh or saltwater—usually has little bearing on survival. Freshwater drowning can result in large amounts of fluid absorbed, resulting in damage to pulmonary surfactant, causing alveolar collapse. This may become clinically important if the individual survives. Saltwater drowning draws fluid into the alveoli, causing pulmonary edema, pleural effusions, and hemoconcentration.
6. Near drowning is defined as resuscitation of a submersion victim with subsequent survival of at least 24 hours, regardless of whether or not death occurs after this period.
7. External findings that may occur prior to or after death include a foam cone from the nose and mouth, wrinkled skin from water immersion, and predation artifact.
8. Because individuals who drown usually struggle, rigor mortis sets in earlier, and rapid cooling slows the decomposition process. Immersion leaches blood from wounds, so determining antemortem or postmortem wounds may be difficult.
9. Autopsy should include thorough cardiovascular, respiratory, musculoskeletal, sinus, and middle ear examinations. Special attention should be made to the airways, gastric contents, and skull (temporal bone). Imaging studies of the head and neck may show evidence of trauma, and a posterior neck dissection may be indicated.

10. Nonspecific autopsy findings may include fluid or debris in the airways, esophagus, and stomach.
11. Various chemical tests, electrolyte studies, and diatom analysis have not been shown to be useful in evaluating drowning deaths.

Bibliography

Caruso, J. L. 2013. The forensic pathology of drowning and pulmonary overexpansion injury. *Academic Forensic Pathology*, 3(4):435–445.

DiMaio, V. J. M. and Molina, D. K. 2021. *DiMaio's Forensic Pathology* (3rd ed.). Boca Raton, FL: CRC Press.

Dolinak, D., Matshes, E., and Lew, E. 2006. *Forensic Pathology: Principles and Practice.* Burlington, MA: Elsevier.

Edmonds, C. and Caruso, J. 2014. Diving fatality investigations: Recent changes. *Diving Hyperbaric Medicine* Jun;44(2):91–96. PMID: 24986727.

National Center for Fatality Review and Prevention. June 2024. Review of drowning fatalities. Accessed 2025. https://ncfrp.org/wp-content/uploads/Drowning_Guidance_Update_June2024.pdf

National Center for Fatality Review and Prevention. Water-related death scene investigation protocol. Accessed 2025. https://ncfrp.org/wp-content/uploads/Water-Related-Death-Scene-Investigation-Protocol.pdf

Environmental Deaths 16

MARY H. DUDLEY AND LAUREN E. DVORSCAK

OBJECTIVES

Upon completion of this chapter and corresponding reference material, the reader will be able to

- Understand the role of the medicolegal death investigator in the scene investigation of environmental deaths
  - Name the criteria for hypothermia and hyperthermia as causes of death
- Identify environmental factors that contribute to hyperthermia and hypothermia
- List medical conditions that predispose an individual to exposure deaths
- Describe autopsy findings associated with exposure death

Introduction

The effect of extreme heat or cold environmental factors can result in heat exhaustion, hypothermia, and/or death. Normal body temperature is generally considered to be 98.6°F or 37°C. Individual body temperature can vary by age, time of day, physical activity, dehydration, and environmental factors, such as ambient temperature, clothing, humidity, and exposure time. Risk factors for exposure deaths include alcohol intoxication, very young or advanced age, unhoused status, injuries, and blood loss. The circumstances surrounding the death and the medicolegal death investigator's (MDI's) examination assist the medical examiner in determining the cause and manner of death. Hyperthermia and hypothermia are diagnoses of exclusion made after ruling out other causes of death and require assimilation of scene information, autopsy findings, and ancillary study results. This chapter will discuss scene investigation, manner of death, predisposing factors, and autopsy findings in deaths from environmental exposure. Two case studies are included.

DOI: 10.4324/9781003538622-19

Medicolegal Investigation of Environmental Exposure Deaths

MDIs must gather information from various sources when investigating deaths potentially related to exposure to hot or cold temperatures. Such information includes weather condition data, living conditions, location of death, and environmental factors. Witnesses and family interviews assist in the collection of background medical and social history and events leading up to the environmental exposure. Hypothermia- and hyperthermia-related deaths can occur in indoor or outdoor settings. Indoor variables include functional heating or cooling regulation or lack thereof. Environmental factors also include the temperature, humidity, windchill for dates last seen alive.

Other significant factors in exposure deaths include obesity, mobility, strenuous activity, water availability, appropriate clothing, and suspicion of drug or alcohol use or foul play. If emergency services were activated, a body temperature may have been documented by the clinical team. It is important to collect any medical records in deaths that occurred after transport to a hospital, where temperature around the admission should be documented.

Photography at the scene should include the heating and/or cooling source, if present. Photograph the thermostat if one is on scene or measure the room temperature if one is not available. Additional photographs should include documentation of the body and surrounding areas as related to injuries or other pertinent findings. Clothing and other materials such as drugs are also important to document by photography and collect at a potential exposure scene.

Scene investigation, physical evidence, radiology, autopsy findings, and toxicology results are key to determining the cause and manner of death.

Hypothermia-Related Deaths

Approximately 1000 hypothermia-related fatalities occur in the United States annually, most commonly among individuals aged 30–50 years and more common in men (CDC, 2019). Hypothermia is defined as a body temperature of below 95°F (35°C). Symptoms may include shivering, confusion, hallucinations, and cardiac arrest. Immersion in water can drastically increase susceptibility to cold temperatures.

Hypothermia deaths result from several circumstances, including individuals exposed to cold environments when intoxicated and the elderly. Elderly individuals at home in poorly heated homes and an increasing number of unhoused individuals die of "exposure." Elderly individuals have been found to wander away from home or a nursing home and die of hypothermia. Another category includes individuals trapped by severe winter storms or other natural disasters such as flash floods. Other exposure deaths include outdoor sports enthusiasts—skiers, hikers, and participants in water sports who miscalculate their exposure and get caught by a change in weather.

Medical conditions that contribute to hypothermia include low body weight, cardiovascular disease, dementia, and other neurodegenerative disorders. Hypothermia is generally considered an accidental manner of death; however, the underlying cause of death during cold weather may be initiated by natural disease. An example of which includes an individual with a history of heart disease dying in the cold while shovelling snow.

Since there are no diagnostic anatomic abnormalities characteristic of hypothermia, a determination of exposure as cause of death depends on the recognition of associated—but not diagnostic—anatomic findings coupled with circumstantial evidence and toxicology. It is important to exclude other causes of death such as trauma, blunt force injury, or asphyxia (including drowning). Fatal drug and alcohol intoxication, as well as natural disease, must be excluded.

The autopsy may show external and internal findings that contribute to the diagnostic criteria of hypothermia as the cause of death. External manifestations include careful inspection for appropriate clothing for weather conditions, such as wet/frozen clothing or paradoxical undressing (Figure 16.1). Paradoxical undressing is frequently seen in cases of lethal hypothermia. As compensatory mechanisms are overcome when out in the cold for too long,

Figure 16.1 A photograph of a death scene with evidence of paradoxical undressing.

dilation of the peripheral blood vessels may cause an individual to feel warm despite the cold. This may result in the paradoxical act of undressing. Individuals found nude in the cold are not uncommon but require additional care in investigation to ensure no foul play has occurred.

Evaluation of the skin surface for abrasions, contusions, or lacerations is necessary. A characteristic bright pink to red lividity is seen with a cold body. It is important to distinguish postmortem cold artifacts from injury. Sometimes previous evidence of hypothermia such as frostbite or absence of digits may suggest an at-risk individual.

Internal manifestations may include gastric ulcers and hemorrhagic pancreatitis, sometimes seen in individuals who initially survive for 24–48 hours. Classic gastric ulcers (Wishnevsky ulcers) are often seen in hypothermia deaths and show surface ulcerations with a dark, well-demarcated appearance (Figure 16.2). Microinfarcts of major organs, pulmonary congestion, and an enlarged right atrium of the heart may be due to bradycardia and congestive heart failure associated with hypothermia deaths.

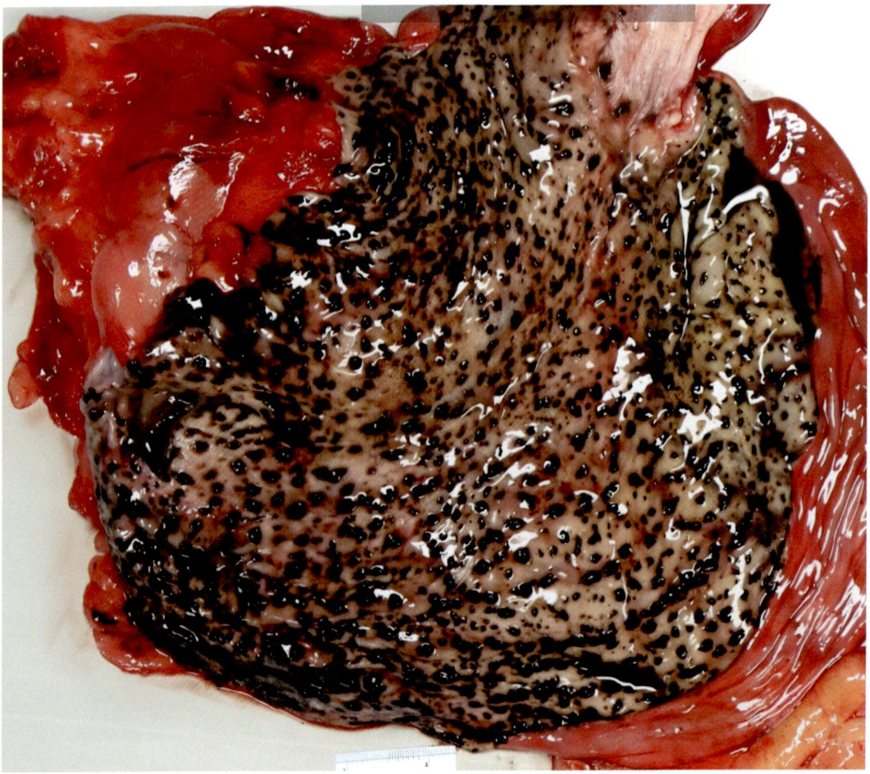

Figure 16.2 Wishnevsky ulcers in the stomach at autopsy.

Toxicology and postmortem chemistries may be helpful in evaluating hypothermia cases. Alcohol and other drugs such as phenothiazines, opiates, and central nervous system depressants (barbiturates) are contributing factors to hypothermia deaths. John Coe reported high vitreous glucose levels in hypothermia deaths. Higher glucose levels may be seen with longer survival period related to cold stress response. A study of iatrogenic hypothermia during cardiopulmonary bypass surgery suggested that hypothermia blocks insulin secretion.

Hypothermia is a diagnosis of exclusion. Therefore, to determine hypothermia as a cause of death, one must evaluate environmental circumstances, anatomic findings, and toxicology results.

Hypothermia Case Study—Contributed by Lauren E. Dvorscak

An 85-year-old woman was noticed to be on the ground in her driveway by a neighbor one morning, who called for a welfare check. She was wearing shorts, no shoes, and the outdoor temperatures overnight were reported to be 30°F. Death investigators were dispatched to the scene by law enforcement, and the MDI noted some blood stains on the concrete. When she was rolled over, the MDI noted red abrasions on her knees as a potential source of the blood (Figure 16.3). Other scene findings included a secured driveway gate,

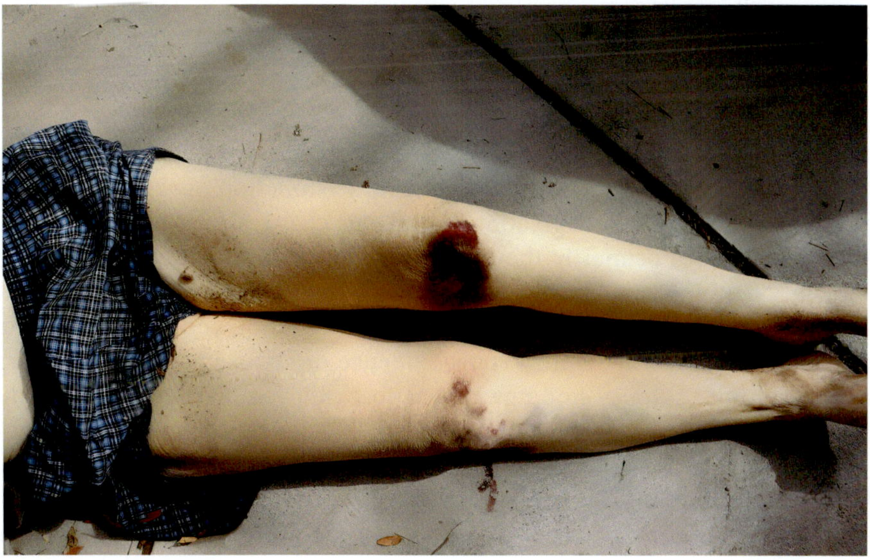

Figure 16.3 Abrasions on the knees with blood on the ground.

but unsecured residence, and access to heat within the residence. Recent history was significant for increased forgetfulness described by her family.

Autopsy revealed subtle signs of hypothermia, including Wischnevsky ulcers and evidence of a right hip fracture. It remained most likely that she fell outside in her driveway, sustained hip trauma and could not get up, leading to abrasions on her knees and the blood on the ground. She ultimately died of hypothermia, with blunt hip trauma and dementia as significant contributory factors.

This case study highlights the importance of documenting the scene completely by the MDI. Clues that the pathologist should be suspicious for more significant trauma were highlighted by the MDI who investigated this scene by documenting both in narrative and photograph the visible injury at the time of the scene investigation.

Hyperthermia Deaths

Seventy percent of hyperthermia-related fatalities tend to involve males over the age of 65 years, and the vast majority of cases occur during the summer months (May to September). Susceptible groups at risk include infants (particularly when left in vehicles), athletes with strenuous activity in the heat, socially isolated/unhoused individuals, individuals with drug/ or alcohol use, individuals with obesity or cardiovascular disease, and the elderly. The temperature of the human body is approximately 98.6°F (37°C), generally regardless of the environmental temperature. A lack of thermoregulation or dehydration because of exercise, age, illness, or disease can increase susceptibility to heat exposure. Extreme summer heat, especially with high humidity, can contribute to increased numbers of heat-related illnesses, including death.

Classic hyperthermia is manifested by a core body temperature greater than 105.8°F (41°C), hot and dry skin, and dysfunction of the central nervous system and thermoregulation. Pathologic changes at autopsy from heat exposure involve primarily the central nervous system and cardiovascular system. Neurological changes include cerebral edema, petechiae, and gross hemorrhage. Cerebellar signs of neuronal degeneration and necrosis can be evident. Some decedents may show evidence of seizure activity, including tongue biting. Autopsy findings related to cardiovascular changes include signs of fluid volume deficiency, decreased vascular resistance, and myocardial degeneration. Some decedents are in varying stages of decomposition when discovered. Others may have died of exposure, but the external temperature has cooled and reduced the core temperature. Consequently, some findings at heat exposure scenes may be unclear, highlighting the importance in documentation of all environmental findings.

Preexisting natural disease might be attributed as the primary cause of death when the criteria for heat-related death are not met and the decedent dies during a heat wave. In such instances, exposure to the hot environment may be listed as a contributing cause of death. The manner of death in heat exposure cases is usually cited as "accidental." However, context is important. There are cases where children have died in closed, hot automobiles when left there by a parent. Homicide may then be considered if abuse and neglect enter the investigation.

Because epidemic heat stroke occurs in a predictable manner during a period of sustained high outdoor temperatures, the public should be informed of the prevention measures, including staying cool and hydrated or making use of public/community centers during peak heat times of the day. In smaller communities, the ME/coroner may take the initiative to inform people if the public health agency has not done so. Persons who decrease physical activity, use air conditioners, and can provide self-care during extended high temperatures are at lower risk for heat stroke and subsequent death.

Hyperthermia Case Study—Contributed by Lauren E. Dvorscak

A park ranger for the White Sands National Park found a 51-year-old woman down while patrol in the park in the summer months, where temperatures were over 100°F. The MDI was called in to investigate the death. Upon initial inspection, the decedent appeared to be a tourist and had a digital camera around her neck (Figure 16.4). While she was dressed for the weather, no water was located nearby. It appeared, and was assumed initially, that she was there alone, exploring the park.

After photographing the scene and the decedent, the MDI attempted to gain more information about the decedent by looking at her camera. After reviewing the photographs that she had taken, it was discovered that her family members had been with her at the park (Figure 16.5). A search and rescue immediately commenced for the missing family members, who were found approximately mile away, in need of medical assistance. The surviving family members indicated that they had gone in search of water after getting lost in the park and that the decedent wasn't feeling well, so had stayed behind to wait for them.

Autopsy revealed accelerated decomposition changes for the time interval since death and evidence of postmortem tanning of the skin, but was

Figure 16.4 Photograph of the decedent in the sand with a camera visible.

otherwise unremarkable. Vitreous electrolyte analysis showed evidence of dehydration. The cause of death was hyperthermia and dehydration due to environmental heat exposure. The manner of death was accidental.

This case study highlights the importance of the MDI to think critically at the scene and examine the evidence in front of them, keeping an open mind about searching for clues. Had the MDI not thought to look through the camera, the other family members may have also succumbed to the heat.

Figure 16.5 A photograph of the digital camera, showing a photograph the decedent had taken.

References and Bibliography

Centers for Disease Control and Prevention, 2019. *QuickStats*: Death Rates Attributed to Excessive Cold or Hypothermia Among Persons Aged ≥15 Years, by Urban-Rural Status and Age Group — National Vital Statistics System, United States. *MMWR Morbidity and Mortality Weekly Report* 2021;70:258. DOI: https://doi.org/10.15585/mmwr.mm7007a6

DiMaio, V. J. M. and Molina, D. K. 2022. *DiMaio's Forensic Pathology* (3rd ed.). Boca Raton, FL: CRC Press

Dolinak, D., Matshes, E., and Lew, E. 2006. *Forensic Pathology: Principles and Practice.* Burlington, MA: Elsevier.

Dudley, M. H. and Zumwalt, R. E. 1992. Hypothermia deaths: Diagnostic criteria. Abstract presentation at *AAFS National Meeting 1992*, New Orleans, L.A.

Duong, Hieu and Patel, Gaurav. 2024 NIH. Hypothermia Deaths.

Mirchandani, H. G. and McDonald, G. 1996. Heat-related deaths in Philadelphia-1996. *The American Journal of Forensic Medicine and Pathology*, 17(2):106–108.

Todd, K. H. 1994. Environmental emergencies, bites, and stings. In Stein, J.H., ed., *Internal Medicine*, 4th ed. St. Louis, MA: Mosby.

Fire Deaths

17

MARY H. DUDLEY AND LAUREN E. DVORSCAK

OBJECTIVES

- Describe the role of the medicolegal death investigator in fire-related deaths
- List six common causes of house fires
- Differentiate between positive scientific means of identification and unreliable identifiers
- Describe the possible causes and manners of fire-related deaths
- Discuss the various components of a complete death investigation for fire-related deaths
- Compare the pertinent autopsy findings to artifactual findings in fire deaths

Introduction

In 2023, 1.39 million fires were reported in the United States (National Fire Protection Association, 2025). Approximately 3,670 deaths in the United States per year are attributable to burns or injuries sustained in destructive fires (National Fire Protection Association, 2025). While only one-fourth of fires occurs in residential structures, these types of fires account for over 60% of deaths in the United States (National Fire Protection Association, 2025). Common causes of residential or structure fires include defective electrical wiring, smoking, improper use of electric heaters, kitchen and cooking accidents, and children playing with matches.

Forensic issues in fire-related deaths not only involve the determination of the cause and manner of death but often involve severely disrupted and damaged remains, making the identification of the decedent a challenge. The determination of whether the decedent was alive or dead at the time of the fire is also of significant importance. Fires may be accidentally or intentionally set by the decedent or another individual in an attempt to destroy evidence. This chapter highlights findings in fire investigations and fire-related fatalities, as well as the role of the medicolegal death investigator in scene investigation. It also covers autopsy findings, toxicology, and firefighter fatalities.

DOI: 10.4324/9781003538622-20

Role of the Medicolegal Death Investigator

Death investigation in fire-related fatalities includes careful assessment of the decedent and the scene in conjunction with other agencies (such as law enforcement and the fire department). Deaths attributable to fire may be immediate or delayed. Immediate mechanisms causing death in fires include thermal burns and inhalation of products of combustion (importantly, carbon monoxide). Delayed deaths are typically a result of burn complications, such as fluid and electrolyte losses through damaged skin, chronic respiratory failure from thermal lung injury, or sepsis and subsequent shock from infections that can complicate thermal burns.

Contributory conditions in fire deaths must also be considered. If it seems as though the decedent could have escaped the fire, other factors may have played a role in the death. For example, drug or alcohol intoxication, young or advanced age, significant underlying natural disease, hyperthermia/heat exhaustion, or trauma are conditions that increase the likelihood of fatality in a fire.

The scene investigation helps to establish the manner of death determined by the circumstances of the fire event. Evidence at the scene for medicolegal death investigators to document may include the presence of accelerants (e.g. gasoline canisters), exposed wires, space heaters, and even the absence or presence of smoke alarms. Although the cause of death is related to fire injuries, the manner of death may be homicide, suicide, or accident. Homicide manner includes arson as direct injury or to conceal gunshot wounds, blunt injury, or sharp force injuries. Arson is also seen for profit, revenge, or pyromania. If arson is suspected, clothing should be preserved and tested for the presence of accelerants, and depending on the jurisdiction, is best collected at the scene, as off-gassing in the body bag can affect this testing. Volatile analysis may also be done on soil or carpet under the body. Samples are collected and placed into airtight containers made of glass or metal to be sent in for analysis. Plastic bags are never used for this purpose. Suicide is rarely seen from self-emulation or incidental entrapment. Accident is the most common manner of death in fires related to adult smoking, cooking, candles, faulty electrical wiring or equipment, or children playing with matches.

Autopsy Findings

Forensic examination of the body includes a complete external and internal examination.

External examination should include an estimation of the percentage of body surface area burned and the degree (depth) of thermal injury. It is also important for the investigator to be aware of artifacts that may occur in fire deaths.

Complete external examination will determine the percentage and degree of thermal injuries. The percentage of body surface area burns is based on the "Rule of Nines" as follows:

- Head – 9%
- Chest – 18%
- Back – 18%
- Upper extremities – 9% each
- Lower extremities – 18% each
- Groin – 1%

This formula is typically used for adults and does not correlate well with the body surface area in children due to their relatively large head, which accounts for approximately 18% of the body surface area in a child. The percentage of burns can predict survivability by adding the percentage burned to the age of the victim. If that number is near 100, the mortality rate is significantly high. For example, a 60-year-old adult with approximately 50% of the body burned has a very poor survival rate when compared to a 5-year-old child with 60% of the body burned.

The degree of thermal burns is assessed by thickness, or tissue depth, and may be designated as first, second, or third degree. First-degree burns involve the skin surface, causing redness and pain. Sunburns are a typical example of first-degree burns. Second-degree burns cause blistering of the epidermis or outer layer of the skin. These burns are considered partial thickness. Third-degree burns involve full skin thickness and require emergent medical attention. In the forensic external examination, it is important to document the degree of burns sustained and the extent of underlying tissues such as muscle or bone that is exposed.

Fire deaths may be due to thermal burns, smoke inhalation, or carbon monoxide toxicity. Any intact skin should be evaluated for discoloration. In particular, a cherry-red appearance of the skin or tissue may indicate significant carbon monoxide exposure (Figure 17.1).

The forensic autopsy continues the examination in greater depth. Internal examination of the organs involves special attention to the upper and lower airways, microscopic examination of the organs for thermal injuries, and collection of toxicology samples. A complete autopsy rules out trauma and natural diseases in fire-related deaths. It is important to establish if the subject was alive at the time of the fire or died prior to the fire. This is determined by examining the upper and lower airways, including the trachea and lungs. If the individual was breathing at the time of the fire, soot and burns may be seen in the trachea (Figure 17.2). Microscopic sections of the lung can show dark foreign material consistent with soot in the alveoli, or air sacs, which supports smoke and soot inhalation.

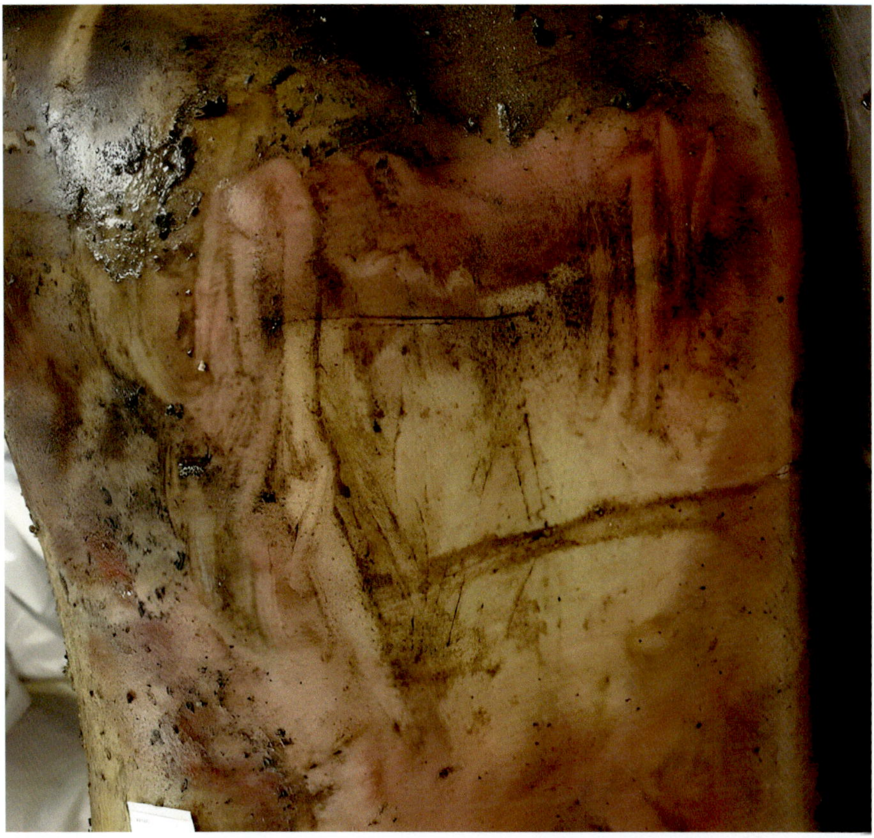

Figure 17.1 Pink-red livor mortis coloration in a decedent with thermal injury.

Artifacts of Thermal Injuries

Postmortem artifactual changes from heat may be evident on examination and may be unrelated to trauma. Artifacts encountered in extreme heat injury include a characteristic pugilistic posture of the body. Pugilistic posturing resembles a fencing or fetal body position. The arms and legs may be flexed and contracted due to intense heat and cause fractures of the extremities (Figure 17.3). The wrists may be bent and digits may be missing. Skull or facial fractures may also be secondary to intense heat. Charring of the external body surfaces, clouding of the corneas, splitting of the skin, and variable exposure of the internal organs unrelated to trauma are common findings on external examination of fire deaths.

Another artifactual finding seen at autopsy is epidural hemorrhage (Figure 17.4) unrelated to trauma. Congealed blood in the epidural space may be an artifact of boiling blood and bone marrow from the thin bones of the skull.

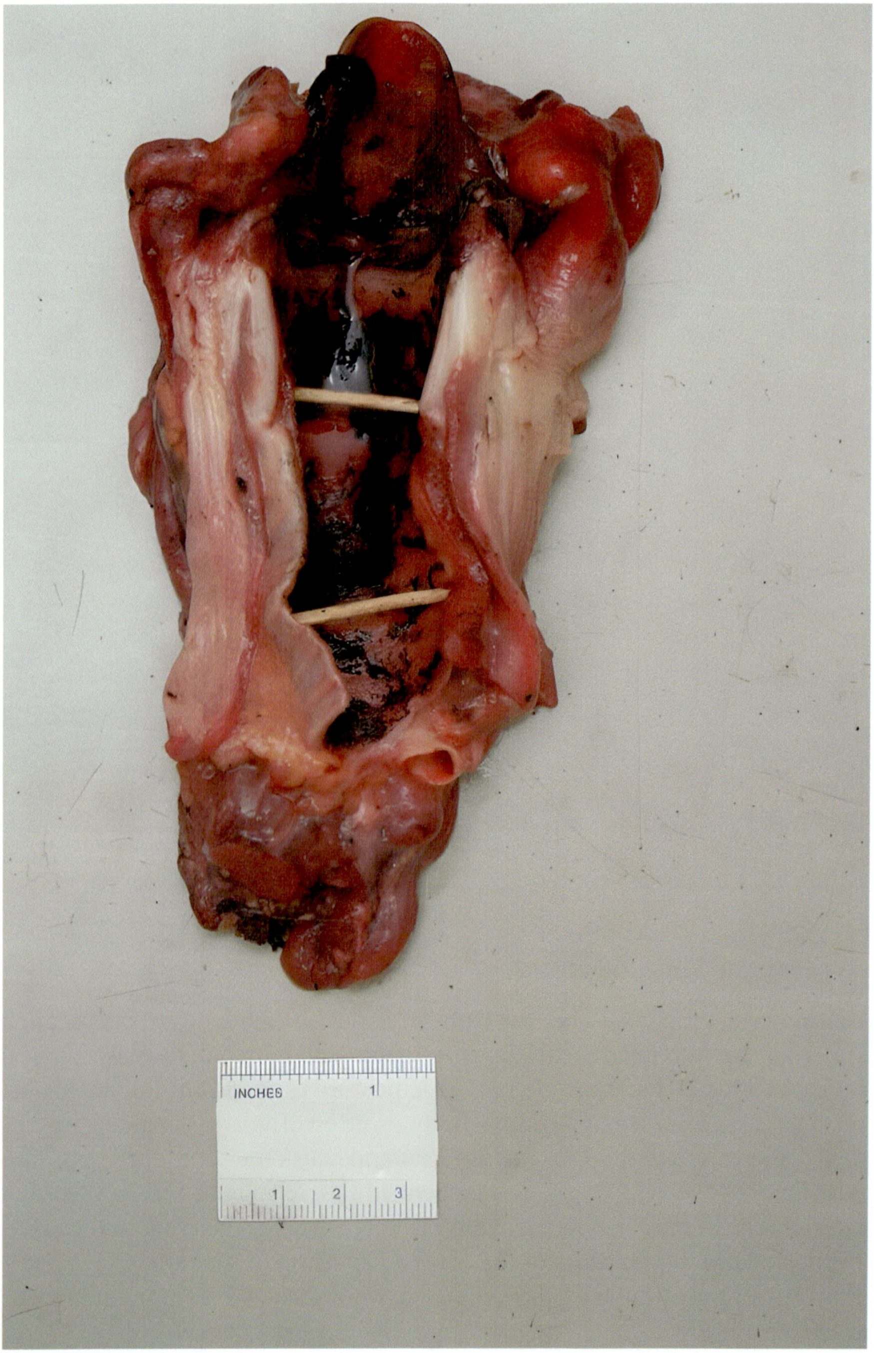

Figure 17.2 Soot in the airways.

Figure 17.3 Pugilistic posture.

Dental restorations may undergo changes under intense heat, such as vaporization or deposition of metal in the facial soft tissue. These metal deposits can mimic fragments of missiles from gunshot wounds. Postmortem injuries may also be uncovered on examination as a result of falling fire debris, or recovery efforts, and may be unrelated to antemortem injuries.

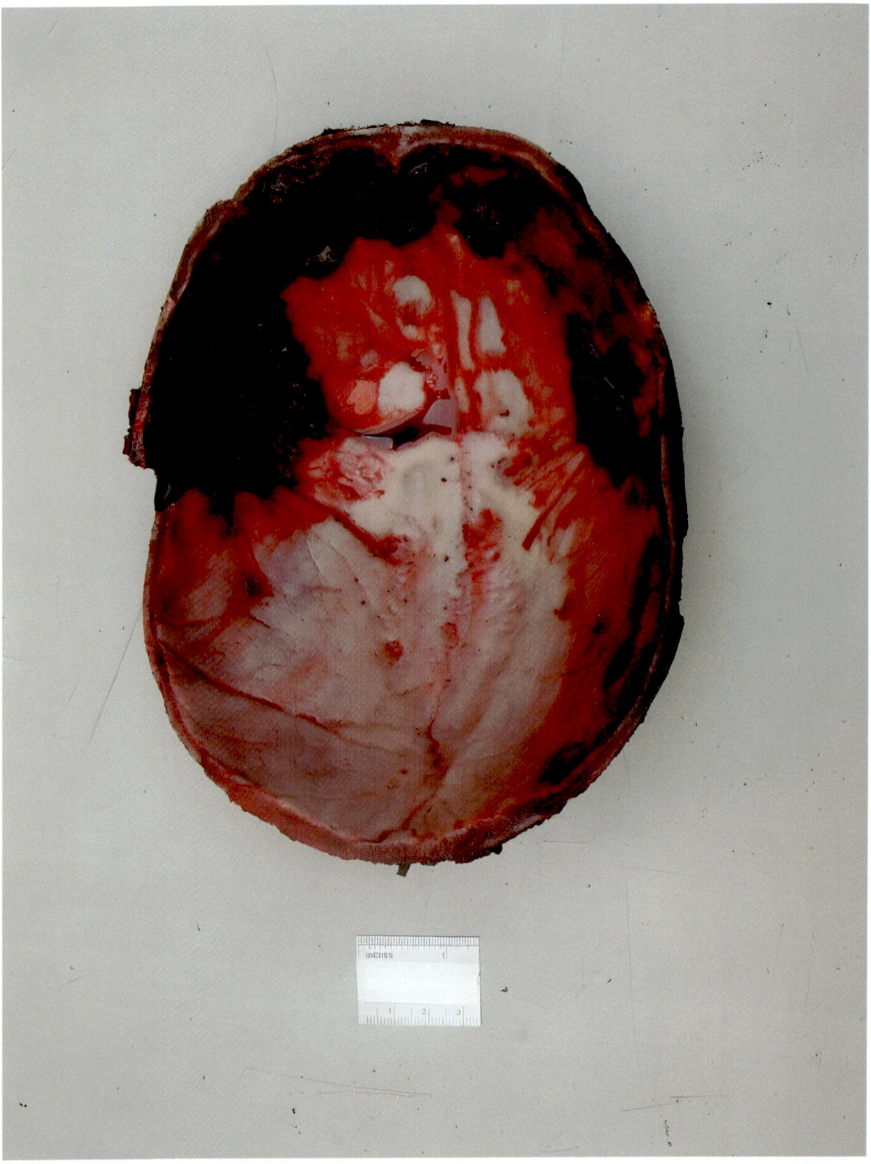

Figure 17.4 Thermal epidural hemorrhage.

Identification

Positive identification of fire death victims is difficult secondary to disruption of the body tissues by thermal injuries. Thermal injuries obscure presumptive identifying features, such as scars, marks, or tattoos. A visual identification or comparison to a photo may not be possible in severely burned remains. Additionally, charring or loss of the digits in the fire often precludes adequate identification by fingerprints. Other means of identification for victims of fire can include postmortem X-rays for comparison of intact bone features, identify prosthetic implants, or compare facial sinus cavities. Dental examination and comparison of records are also an important avenue for identifying disrupted remains. DNA samples can also be compared to antemortem data or family members for identification purposes.

Toxicology

Blood, urine, and vitreous fluid samples are collected for toxicology analysis. Of particular interest are drugs, alcohol, and carbon monoxide levels in the blood. Increased levels of carbon monoxide, typically above 10%–15%, are also indicative that the individual was alive at the time of the fire. However, smokers in particular may have higher resting levels of carbon monoxide, typically less than 10%, but this value should be interpreted in the context of the additional findings in each case. If significantly increased, carbon monoxide toxicity should be listed as a cause of death. The presence of drugs and/or ethanol may be contributory factors to the cause of death.

Firefighter Fatalities

Firefighter fatalities occur related to work-related deaths from failure of protective equipment, carbon monoxide toxicity, smoke inhalation, blunt injury, hyperthermia/heat exhaustion, and natural causes. Also, delayed, work-related deaths include respiratory failure and exposure to harmful particulates causing various cancers. In 2008, the US Fire Administration and the Federal Emergency Management Agency (FEMA) published a firefighters autopsy protocol as guidelines for scene investigation and medicolegal autopsy procedures for all firefighter fatalities where the line of duty death occurred (Stull, 2008).

References and Bibliography

Dolinak, D., Matshes, E., and Lew, E. 2006. *Forensic Pathology: Principles and Practice*. Burlington, MA: Elsevier.

National Fire Protection Association. 2025. Fires in the U.S. Website accessed at https://www.nfpa.org/education-and-research/research/nfpa-research/fire-statistical-reports/fire-loss-in-the-united-states

National Safety Council. 2015. *Injury Facts*, 2015 ed. Itasca, IL: National Safety Council.

Stull, Jeffery. March 2008. *Firefighter Autopsy Protocol*. Austin, TX: US Fire Administration, FEMA, International Personal Protection, Inc.

Electrical Deaths 18

MARY H. DUDLEY

OBJECTIVES

Upon completion of this chapter and corresponding reference material, the reader will be able to

- Understand the role of the medicolegal death investigator in the scene investigation of electrical deaths
  - Differentiate between low-voltage and high-voltage electrocutions
- List postmortem findings of electrical death
- Identify dangers of investigation in electrical deaths

Introduction

Electrical hazards account for approximately 1,000 deaths annually. The causes of electrical deaths are high-voltage current, lightning, and low-voltage current. Accidental electrocution is the most commonly seen death by electrocution. Suicide by electrocution is rare, and homicide is even more uncommon. The majority of electrical deaths are instantaneous and occur at the scene without transport to a medical facility. Any electrical death scene poses a danger to the first responders. If an electrical death is suspected, the scene must be secured, the source of the current shut off, and any faulty appliances should be removed for later testing. Lightning strikes can occur directly, by side flash, or by conduction through another object. Death is due to cardiopulmonary arrest, hyperthermia, and/or electrical injuries. Safety of the investigator and prevention of any additional fatalities is of upmost importance. The chapter includes the role of the medicolegal death investigator (MDI) at the scene, defines terminology, and discusses types of electrical deaths, as well as autopsy findings. A case study is also included.

Role of the Medicolegal Death Investigator

A large number of electrical deaths are discovered at the scene. Any electrical death scene poses a danger to the first people to reach the scene. The immediate action when an electrical death is suspected is to ensure that all questionable equipment, appliances, tools, and the site are secured by the appropriate

 DOI: 10.4324/9781003538622-21

agency until it can be made safe. The local power company is summoned to provide the exact location of the suspected electrical problem and to shut off the power. The possibility of electrocution exists when wires or electrical appliances are evident and electrical repairs or installation is in progress. If an electrical death is suspected, the scene must be secured and the faulty appliance removed and later tested.

Investigation of electrical deaths and injuries requires the basic skills of a certified electrician regarding testing and electricity. These include basic testing techniques for hot and ground wires, altered wiring, and correct installation. Investigators should also be able to test the amount of current available.

After the scene is secured, the MDI must gather information through witness and family interviews regarding the decedent's prior medical history, when last seen alive, activities prior to death, and how the death occurred. Scene and body photography, as well as documentation, includes the faulty electrical appliance or tools at the scene and any injuries or thermal burns on the body or clothing (including work gloves, hats, shoes, and socks). All clothing and evidence should be documented and accompany the body to the medical examiner/coroner's office.

Electrical Terms

Electrical terms are described as volts, current (amperes), and resistance. Alternating current (AC) is more commonly encountered than direct current (DC) because humans are four to six times more sensitive to AC than DC. Ohm's law states that resistance equals voltage divided by amperes (R = V/A). Amperes are calculated by dividing volts by resistance (A = V/R). Hertz (Hz) refers to 1 cycle/second or the frequency of polarity change/time. AC alternates polarity 60 times/second or 60 Hz. Any investigation of a scene should contain as much information as possible about the circuitry to enable further calculations.

Low voltage refers to less than 1,000 V of AC, while high voltage is over 1,000 V and can be either AC or DC. Currents within a United States household are 120 V for most appliances and 220 V for clothes dryers, stoves, and some washing machines. A typical urban or suburban power line supplies approximately 7,500 V; transcontinental cable supplies roughly 100,000 V. Commonly used outlet plugs have two or three slots for appliance cords. Plugs have a hot wire, neutral wire, and a ground. The two-prong plugs have an internal ground.

Types of Outlets/Receptacles

Electrical current runs from the point of contact to the point of grounding and follows the shortest path. This also applies to current that enters the body.

Electrical burns are found at the entry and exit sites in approximately half of low-voltage electrocutions and essentially all high-voltage electrocutions. The time when the burn was caused—antemortem or postmortem—is difficult if not impossible to differentiate. Minute metal particles may be deposited at the entry or exit contact site.

Electrical Deaths

Low-Voltage Electrocution

Low-voltage electrocution requires direct contact with the electrical circuit. The amperage is the most important electrical measurement for damage assessment. Fatal ventricular fibrillation can be caused by 70 mA of electricity. Involuntary muscle contractions are caused by as little as 15 mA, commonly known as "shock." Dry calloused skin presents a higher resistance than moist skin. Less than 2 A can cause ventricular arrest, although when the current is turned off, the heart should begin a normal sinus rhythm.

High-Voltage Electrocution

Direct contact with a hot wire is not necessary with high-voltage electrocution because the current can arc or jump across a distance. With 1,000 V, the electric arc is but a few millimeters. However, a current of 100,000 V can arc about 1 yard. High voltage can cause irreversible electrothermal injury to the heart and brain, where the temperature generated can be as high as 4000°C (7232°F).

Lightning

Approximately 40 million lightning strikes occur in the United States per year, and the odds of being struck are reportedly less than one in a million. The majority of individuals struck by lightning survive, and recent data indicate approximately 15–20 deaths from lightning occur annually (CDC, 2024). Lightning strikes are high-voltage DC. The strike can occur directly, by a side flash, or by conduction through another object. Lightning strikes generally occur during a thunderstorm, in open fields, near water, shelters, or metal objects. The decedent may show thermal skin burns on the entrance and exit sites of the lightning strike or from metal objects in contact with the body (for example, metal coins in pockets) (Figure 18.1a). The clothing, including hats, shoes, and socks, may show burn marks or tearing (Figure 18.1b). All clothing must accompany the body to the medical examiner/coroner's office. An arborescent (fernlike) pattern may transiently be on the skin in individuals that are struck by lightning, known as ferning. Death is due to cardiopulmonary arrest, hyperthermia, or electrical injuries.

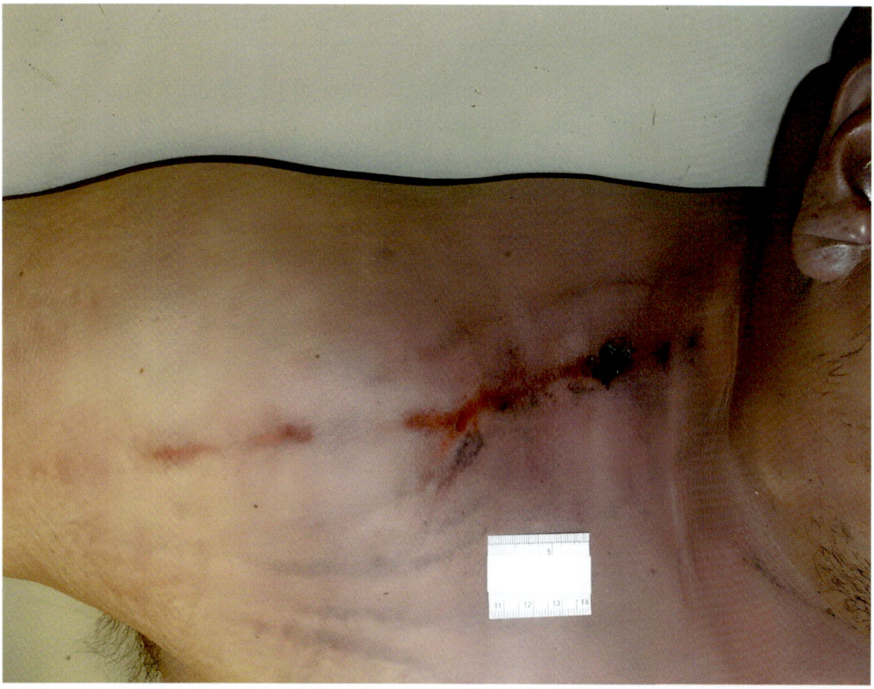

(a)

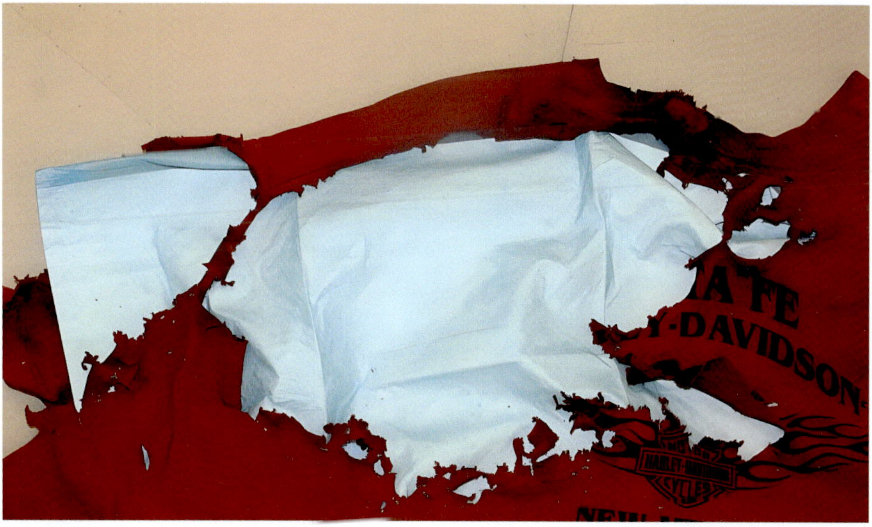

(b)

Figure 18.1 (a) Right shoulder demonstrating linear burn from lightning. (b) Clothing demonstrating tearing and burns from lightning.

Autopsy Findings

At autopsy, nonspecific gross findings may resemble an asphyxial death in appearance. Externally, skin changes at the area of electrical contact show a targetoid burn appearance, with central brown or black necrosis (skin destruction) surrounded by an area of clearing or pallor and an outside rim of hyperemia (redness) (Figure 18.2). The skin and blood vessel walls may show

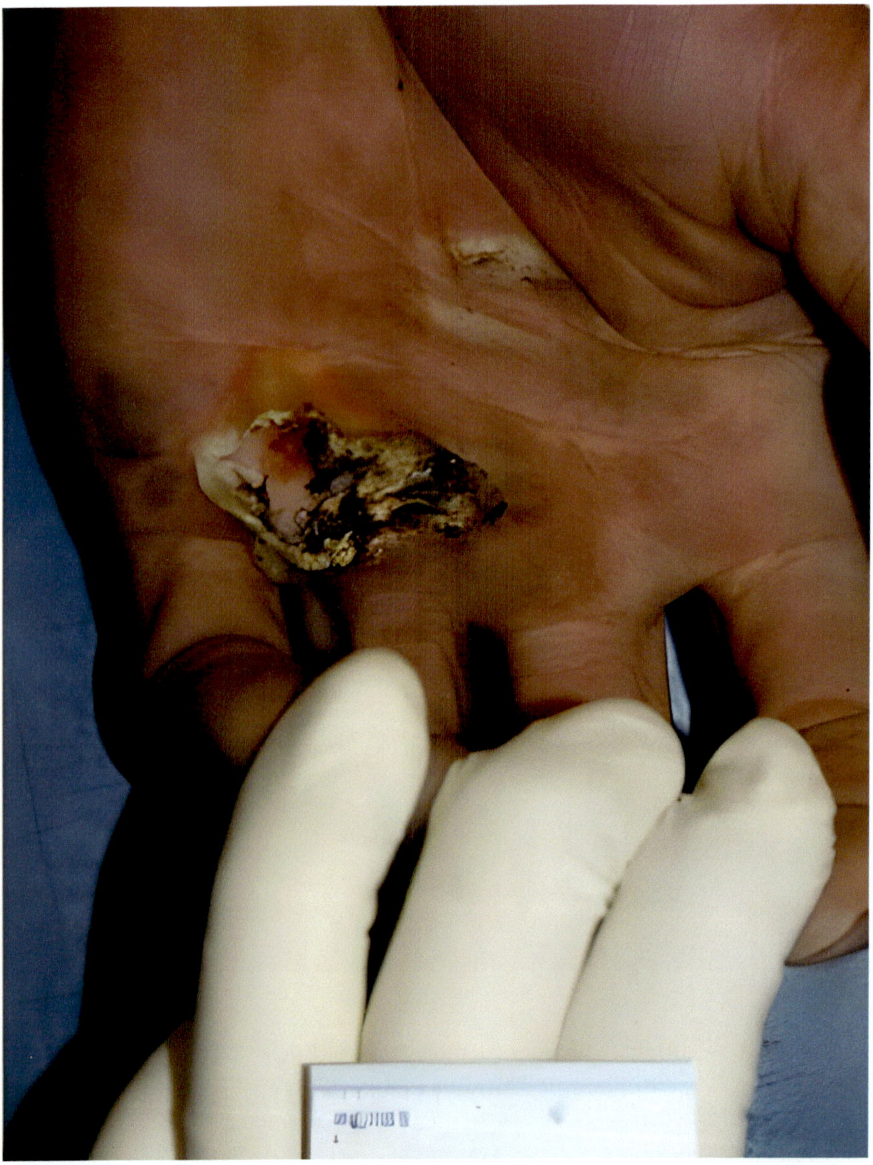

Figure 18.2 Electrical burn on the hand.

gross microscopic changes from the electrical burn. Microscopic changes in the heart are manifested by a contraction band necrosis in the sinoatrial and atrioventricular nodal areas, as well as in the heart muscle.

Electrocution Case Study—Contributed by Lauren E. Dvorscak

Two oil-field workers aged 35 and 38 years were working with a lift near some high-voltage electrical lines after a rainstorm (Figure 18.3). They were found near the equipment, unresponsive, with apparent injuries (Figure 18.4). After initial investigators rendered the scene safe, the MDI was called to investigate as part of a multidisciplinary team. The MDI thoroughly documented the

Figure 18.3 Oil field with lift and raised basket.

Figure 18.4 Mid-range photograph showing the position of decedents next to the lift.

placement of the equipment through overall, mid-range, and close-up photographs, as well as preliminary findings on the decedents.

Autopsy revealed both subtle and overt signs of electrocution on both decedents (Figure 18.5), corresponding to additional information received that the lift had made contact with the high-voltage power lines at the scene while both men were in contact with the lift. The cause of death for both individuals was electrocution, and the manner of death was accidental.

This case study highlights the importance of safety at the scene and thorough documentation by the MDI.

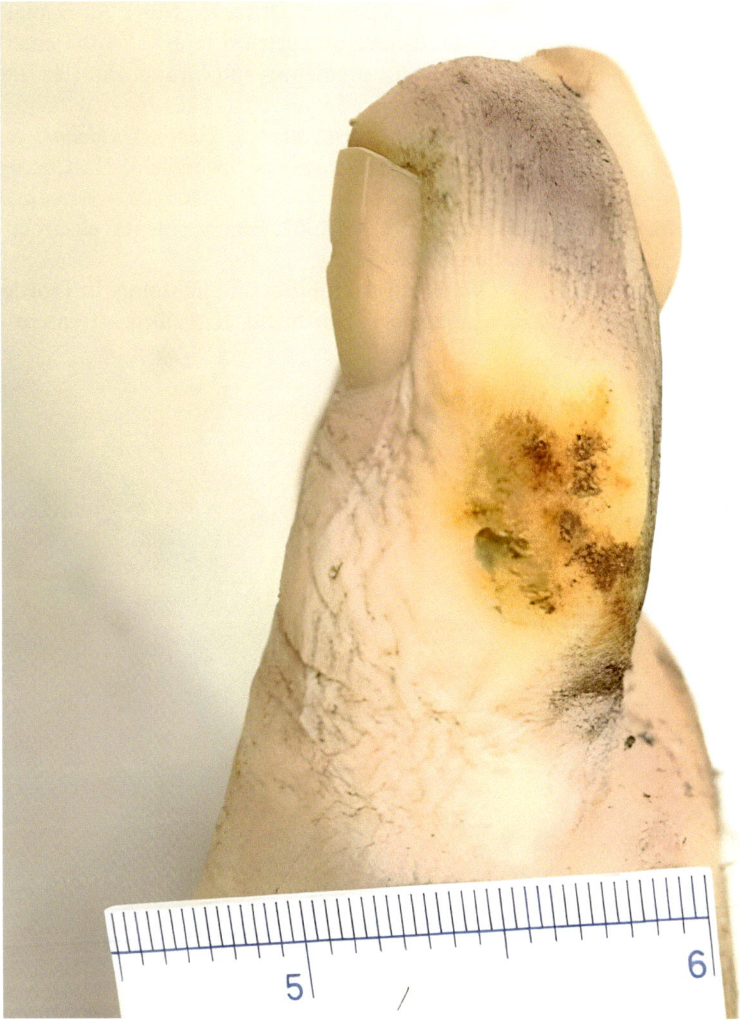

Figure 18.5 More subtle signs of electrocution at autopsy included electrical burns on the fingers of the decedents.

Bibliography

Centers for Disease Control and Prevention. 2024. Lightning strike victim data. https://www.cdc.gov/lightning/data-research/index.html

DiMaio, V. J. M. and Molina, D. K. (2022). *DiMaio's Forensic Pathology* (3rd ed.). Boca Raton: CRC Press

Dolinak, D., Matshes, E., and Lew, E. 2006. *Forensic Pathology: Principles and Practice.* Burlington, MA: Elsevier.

Karray, R., Chakroun-Walha, O., Mechri, F., Salem, I., Drira, H., Nasri, A., Damak, A., and Rekik, N. 2025 Jan, 27. Outcomes of electrical injuries in the emergency department: Epidemiology, severity predictors, and chronic sequelae. *The European Journal of Trauma and Emergency Surgery*, 51(1):85.

Spitz, W. and Fischer, R. 1993. *Medicolegal Investigation of Death: Guidelines for the Application of Pathology to Crime Investigation*. Springfield, IL: Charles C. Thomas Press.

Taylor, A., McGwin, G., Valent, F., and Rue, L. W. 2002. Fatal accidental electrocutions in the US. *Injury Prevention*, 8:306–312.

Wright, R. K. and Gantner, G. E. 1990. Electrical injuries and lightning. In Froede, R.C., ed., *Handbook of Forensic Pathology*. Northfield, IL: College of Forensic Pathologists.

Drug and Alcohol Deaths

19

MARY H. DUDLEY

OBJECTIVES

Upon completion of this chapter and corresponding reference material, the reader will be able to

- Describe external findings and long-term complication of intravenous drug abuse
- Discuss the major drug categories and drug effects on the body
- Estimate blood alcohol levels from number and type of alcoholic beverages ingested over an identified period of time
- List individual variables that affect the levels of alcohol in the body
- State the blood alcohol level for legal definition in the state where you live or where you work of "driving under the influence of alcohol," "driving while intoxicated," "drunk driving," or other reference to operating a motorized vehicle while drinking
- Discuss the difference between vitreous and blood alcohol levels
- Describe the impact of putrefaction on blood alcohol content
  - Describe the role of the medicolegal death investigator at the death scene of possible drug- or alcohol-related deaths

Introduction

In a 20-year period from 2003 to 2023, the rate of drug overdose deaths nationwide increased from 8.9/100,000 to 31.3, and approximately 60,000 deaths annually have been attributed to the acute effects of alcohol (CDC, 2024). Alcohol and drugs may be the main cause of death due to toxicity. The forensic autopsy may not reveal injury or natural causes of death and will often rely on toxicology results. The medicolegal death investigator (MDI) scene investigation, documentation, photography, and evidence collection contain vital information for the determination of manner in drug and alcohol-related deaths. This chapter covers the major categories of drugs, including opiates, stimulants, volatiles, sedatives/antidepressants. Information related to alcohol deaths and a case study are also included.

DOI: 10.4324/9781003538622-22

Role of the Medicolegal Death Investigator in Scene Investigation

When investigating the scene in drug- and/or alcohol-related deaths, the MDI will be able to obtain important information from witness statements regarding the circumstances of death, history of drug and/or alcohol use, medical history, and a list of current medications. Documentation of the scene through concise narrative report and photographs of the overall scene may also show the presence or absence of illicit drugs and/or paraphernalia (Figure 19.1).

In any case of drug overdose where the patient dies in the emergency room or hospital, it is important to keep everything connected to the patient in place. This means that all Intravenous (IV) lines are sent intact, as well as all fluids in urine or nasogastric collectors. Antemortem specimens are helpful in determining the cause of death. All admission hospital specimens should be saved. Too often an initial specimen is collected (blood or urine) and forgotten during the course of treatment or when the patient dies.

If illicit drugs and/or drug paraphernalia are found, they are often secured as evidence by law enforcement. Drug paraphernalia refers to any equipment used to produce, conceal, or consume illicit drugs (Figure 19.2). Paraphernalia may include items such as bongs, roach clips, spoons, various pipes, tourniquets, syringes, and needles. Prescription drugs may also be found at the

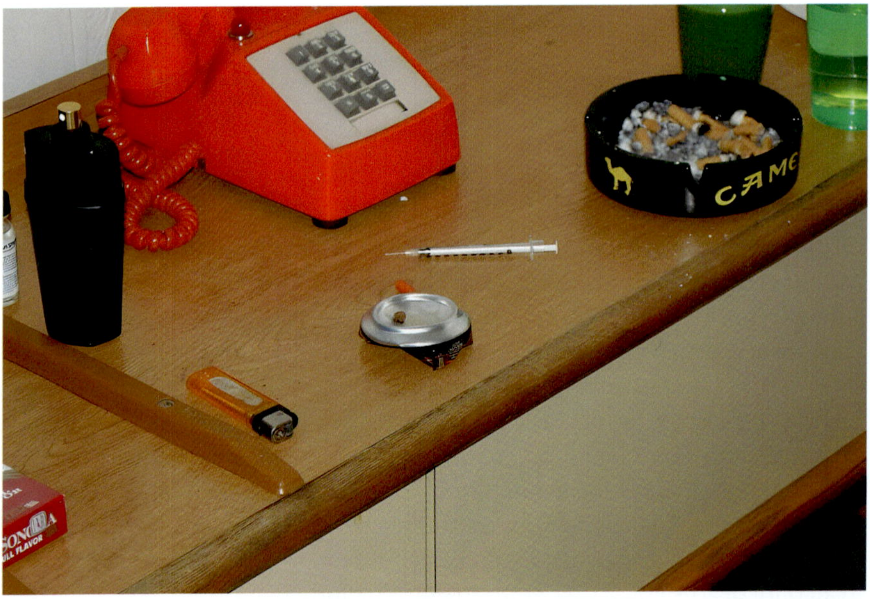

Figure 19.1 Drug paraphernalia at a scene.

Figure 19.2 Illicit drug paraphernalia.

scene related to a drug overdose (Figure 19.3) and should be documented via a complete medication log, including prescription drug name, prescriber, pharmacy, date filled, number issued, dosage prescribed, and number of pills left. Scene investigation in alcohol-related deaths may include full and/or empty containers of alcohol (including mouthwash, rubbing alcohol, or hand sanitizer) at the residence (Figure 19.4). Any evidence collected by the MDI at the scene must be carefully documented, photographed, collected, and secured with associated chain of custody forms.

Drug-Related Fatalities

Illegal drug use causes accidents and is often the cause of homicides. Opiates, stimulants, volatiles, and sedatives/antidepressants are major drug categories associated with fatalities. Ingestion, inhalation, and injection are usual routes of drug abuse.

IV drug use carries complications related to both the drug itself and to the route of administration. Sudden death can occur from overdose. Systemic infections, including HIV/AIDS, hepatitis, tetanus, and bacterial sepsis, are common from shared needle use and contaminated supplies.

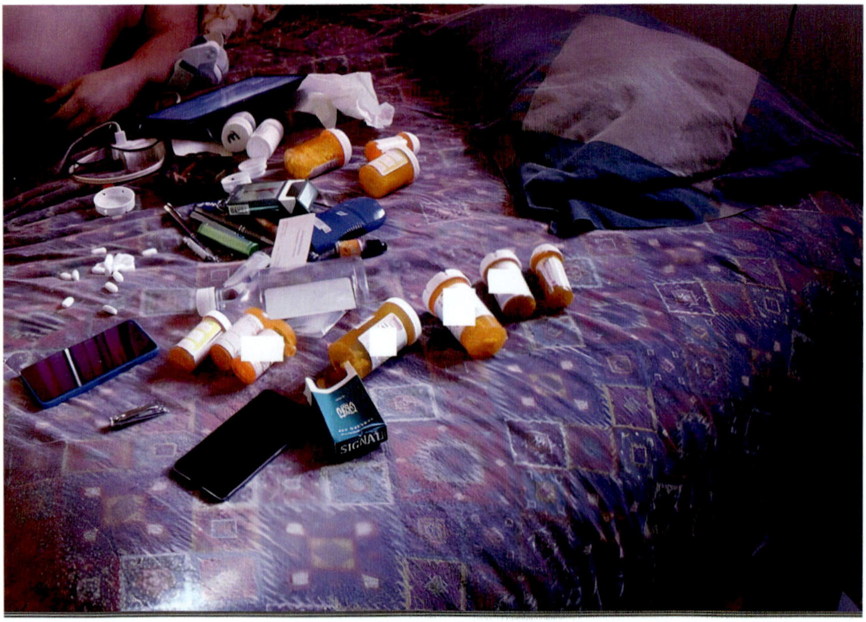

Figure 19.3 Prescription bottles and loose pills at a scene.

Indications of IV drug use are needle punctures over veins. Puncture marks may be visible on the arms, hands, legs, feet, or neck. Sites between the toes or along the bones may show bruising or inflammation. Tattoos frequently conceal puncture sites. Needle "tracks" over veins are the result of scarring from repeated needle punctures (Figure 19.5); these represent long-term drug abuse. Cutaneous "skin pop" ulcers result from injection of nonsterile drug preparations into the subcutaneous tissue. This can be purposeful or accidental if a vein is missed. Ulcers heal as round or oval-pressed scars. Skin popping is the last resort of IV drug users run out of accessible veins.

In the emergency room or with ambulance crews, it is important to circle any existing puncture sites before or immediately after IV infusions are started. It can be confusing at autopsy to differentiate between attempts to insert a vascular catheter and recent needle puncture marks.

Opiates

Opiates provide pain relief with feelings of euphoria but may also cause respiratory and central nervous system depression. Morphine and codeine are derived from the opium poppy. Semisynthetic variations are heroin, oxycodone, and hydromorphone. Synthetic preparations are meperidine (Demerol), propoxyphene (Darvon), pentazocine (Talwin), methadone, and

Figure 19.4 Alcohol-containing mouthwash.

fentanyl. Opiates can be inhaled, ingested, or injected. Some forms are available orally for long-term pain control.

Heroin is generally injected into peripheral veins. Chronic use causes scarring of the veins and surrounding soft tissue, resulting in "needle track marks" generally found in the arm or hand veins. Occasionally, the marks are covered by elaborate tattoos in an attempt to conceal the injection sites.

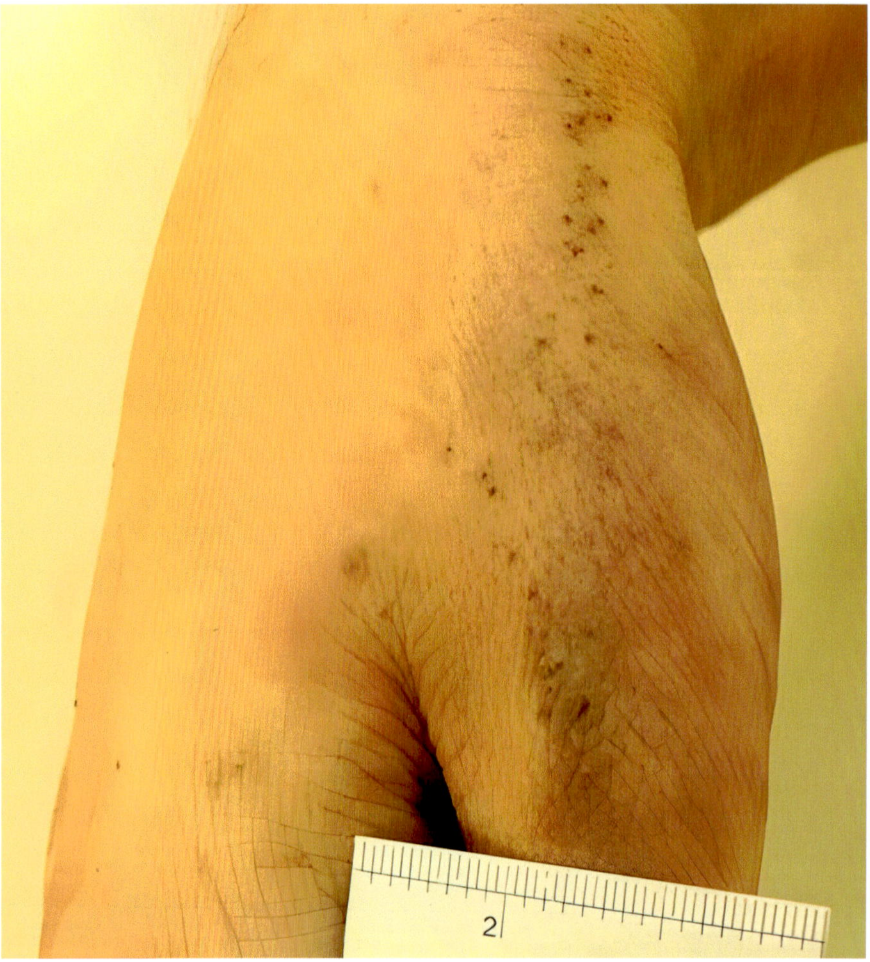

Figure 19.5 Needle track marks.

Fatalities can occur when packages of heroin are transported in condoms in the gastrointestinal tract of an individual. Sometimes they leak into the bloodstream, causing fatal drug overdose.

Stimulants

Cocaine, amphetamines, and hallucinogens are classified as stimulants. As with opiates, swallowing, "shooting up," and snorting are the usual methods of use. Cocaine and amphetamines come in a variety of forms, including powder, crystal, crack, and pill form. Dexedrine and Ritalin are prescribed stimulants that may also be abused. Lysergic acid, peyote, mushrooms, and phencyclidine are common hallucinogens. The common response of all stimulants is euphoria, agitation, hallucinations, hyperthermia, and tachycardia.

Cocaine and methamphetamine are commonly used stimulants nationwide. Cocaine is extracted from the leaves of the *Erythroxylon coca* plant and the alkaloid. Cocaine hydrochloride results from dissolving the alkaloid in hydrochloric acid to produce heat-labile white crystals. Freebase or crack is made from the cocaine hydrochloride crystals and can be smoked. The pharmacologic action of cocaine affects every body system. Seizures, deliriums, fevers, hemorrhages, and changes in hematological makeup are frequent. Cocaine is metabolized by the liver rapidly (half-life of 30 minutes) into benzoylecgonine, norcocaine, and ecgonine methyl ester. Concurrent use of ethanol and cocaine produces the product cocaethylene, which has toxic properties by itself in addition to its two components. Cocaine can be consumed by chewing, snorting, smoking, or IV injection. Skin popping is another method of administration. Cocaine is a vasoconstrictor, and chronic snorting can cause perforation of the nasal septum resulting from repeated nasal inhalation. Erosion of dental enamel can occur due to the high acidity of cocaine upon ingestion.

Body packers and/or stuffers try to illegally transport cocaine in plastic bags or balloons by swallowing the balloons or inserting them into the rectum or vagina. If a bag leaks, the individual can overdose or die. Similar in properties to cocaine, methamphetamine is also a stimulant with a half-life of 3 hours. It is metabolized by the liver to amphetamine.

Sedatives/Antidepressants

Sedatives, sometimes known as "sleeping pills" or "hypnotics," belong to a number of drug classifications. Many of these drugs are prescribed reluctantly because of low therapeutic index and high addiction liability. Barbiturates, known as "blues," "yellows," or "reds," and phenobarbital are available by prescription and often found on the illegal market. Drugs taken for sedation and sleep disorders can result in a longer period of sedation than anticipated, depending on the dose and potency of the drug. This can lead to accidental overdose. Coupled with alcohol, the effects can result in a deadly overdose. The ME/coroner's office must determine whether the overdose was intentional or accidental.

Antidepressant medications include selective serotonin reuptake inhibitors (e.g. fluoxetine, sertraline), serotonin-norepinephrine reuptake inhibitors (e.g. duloxetine), tricyclic antidepressants (amitriptyline), and monoamine oxidase inhibitors. These medications are not typically abused for any euphoric or other effects and most commonly implicated in intentional ingestions. Both sedatives and antidepressants are generally ingested. Therefore, stomach contents, vomitus, pills, or bottles at the scene assist in determining the cause of death. Blood samples and solid organ tissue are examined at autopsy to determine if alcohol was associated with the drugs.

Volatiles

Volatiles are usually suspected at the scene of a huffing death when volatile containers are found at the scene (Figure 19.6). Evidence at the scene may show paint stains, smears on the hands, face, hair, or clothing of the decedent. Huffing refers to inhalation of chemical vapors to produce a "high." When inhaled, they depress the central nervous system, causing slurred speech, drowsiness, dizziness, impaired coordination, hallucinations, and euphoria.

Inhalants used for huffing may include solvents, fuels, nitrites, or canned gas dusters containing hydrocarbon alkanes or hydrofluorocarbons, among several toxic chemicals. Solvents become gases via energy input (usually heat) or by reducing pressure. Aerosol or liquid forms include hair spray, cleaning supplies, or paint. Inhaled fuels or gases include propane, gasoline, refrigerants, and nitrous oxide. Aerosols have a similar effect as solvents.

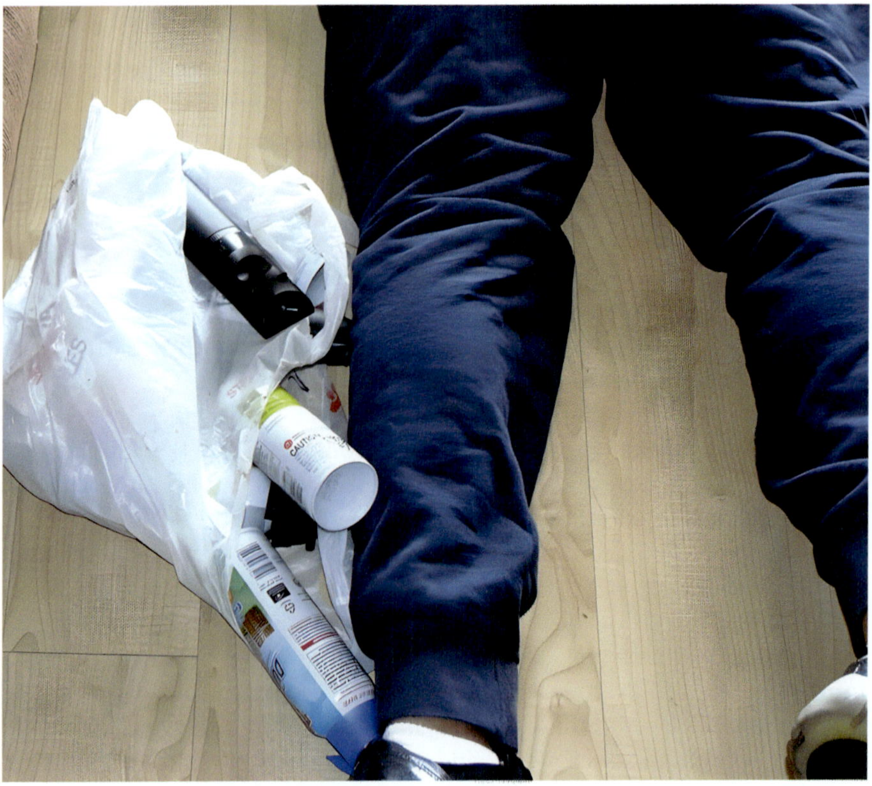

Figure 19.6 Electronics duster found at a scene.

Huffing any fuel is extremely dangerous, as the hydrocarbons in fuels are directly toxic. Nitrites differ from solvents and aerosols, as they act to relax muscles and dilate blood vessels rather than have effects directly on the central nervous system. Compressed air dusters can produce psychoactive effects but have the danger of resulting in cardiac toxicity, inducing arrythmias.

The effects of huffing last only a few minutes, and the action must be repeated to maintain euphoric effects. The initial effects of huffing include feelings of euphoria and intoxication. The dangers increase with each inhalation, which may include central nervous system depression, brain injuries, coma, and death.

Alcohol Fatalities

Forty-two percent of the general population abstain from drinking alcohol or rarely drink alcohol. Thirty-one percent consider themselves to be light drinkers; that is, they have an average of less than one drink per day. Eighteen percent are classified as moderate drinkers who drink one or two drinks daily, and approximately 9% of the population are heavy drinkers who consume more than two drinks per day.

A "drink" is a 12-ounce can of beer (4% alcohol), 4-ounce glass of wine (12% alcohol), or 1 ounce of 100-proof liquor (50% alcohol). Rubbing alcohol, mouthwash, and hand sanitizer have been implicated in toxic ingestions, especially when other sources of alcohol are not readily available. Each standard drink typically increases blood alcohol levels by 0.02%, depending on a number of variables that affect the rate of alcohol absorption through the stomach and upper small bowel. Most alcohol is absorbed in 1 hour, but the rate of absorption depends on

- Concentration and total quantity of alcohol in the stomach
- Nature of food already in the stomach
- Length of time stomach contents remain in the stomach
- Permeability of the stomach and intestinal membranes

In most states, blood alcohol level for intoxication for driving is 0.08%–0.10%. Five drinks of any substance within an hour will enable almost anyone to become legally drunk, using the current 0.1% level. If the body metabolizes alcohol at 0.02% an hour, the measured blood level still varies individually primarily due to body weight.

Alcohol is absorbed unaltered through the gastrointestinal tract, and its presence is detected in the blood within 5 minutes. The maximum concentration is within 30–90 minutes. Alcohol is metabolized in the liver to carbon dioxide and water and is excreted by the kidneys and lungs. Alcohol absorption begins immediately in an empty stomach. However, absorption is delayed when the stomach is full.

Blood levels of ingested alcohol cause different mental and physical responses. Mild euphoria and relaxation occur with less than 0.05% ethanol in the blood. Deterioration of judgment and control of inhibitions begin at 0.05%–0.15%. Emotional liability, crying, or outbursts of anger occur at 0.15%–0.25%. Mental confusion leading to stupor, coma, and death occur at 0.25%–0.35% blood level. Translated to the ability to drive a motor vehicle, probable impairment and poor judgment begin after the first few drinks at 0.05%. The driver shows decreased reflexes and impaired coordination from 0.05% to 0.1%. Severe impairment occurs after 0.1% blood alcohol level, and the person is "legally drunk."

Blood alcohol concentration affects clinical symptoms as follows:

Blood Alcohol Concentration (g/100 mL)	Stages	Symptom
0.01–0.05	Subclinical	Little effect
0.03–0.12	Euphoria	Beginning sensory/motor impairment
0.09–0.25	Excitement	Impairment, incoordination, drowsiness
0.18–0.35	Confusion	Disorientation, lethargy
0.25–0.40	Stupor	Impaired consciousness
0.35–0.50	Coma	Possible death

In the laboratory, samples are measured using the gas chromatogram, and the various volatiles represent a peak on a graph depending on the time of release from the "head space" of the specimen.

Alcohol is distributed to various tissues in proportion to the water content of the individual tissues. Tissues with low water content have low alcohol content. Equilibrium is usually reached within 1 hour after drinking. The relative concentrations of alcohol in body fluids and tissues are

- Whole blood, 1.0%–1.15%
- Urine, 1.2%–1.4%
- Cerebral spinal fluid (CSF), 1.10%
- Vitreous humor, 1.15%
- Brain, 0.85%–0.90%

Alcohol is eliminated from the body through the lungs, liver, urine, and perspiration. The liver metabolizes 90%–95% of alcohol. Liver disease interferes with metabolism and delays elimination from the body. Some drugs compete with alcohol for liver function and excretion. Excretion from other pathways totals 5%.

Blood and Vitreous Alcohol Levels

Vitreous alcohol levels trail behind blood alcohol levels during alcohol consumption until equilibrium is reached, but then vitreous levels are higher than blood levels once drinking ceases. Ordinarily, the vitreous fluid alcohol value lags behind the blood value by approximately 1 hour. That is, the vitreous level is lower during the pre-absorption state and higher during the post-absorption state. Therefore, both vitreous and blood alcohol levels should be obtained to determine if an individual has just started or stopped drinking.

Postmortem vitreous alcohol levels may be more accurate than blood alcohol levels in hospitalized trauma cases. For example, blood alcohol can be diluted if the patient is given transfusions of IV fluids. Blood alcohol levels may also vary if the patient has bled profusely due to depletion factors.

Postmortem Changes and Generation of Ethanol

Postmortem changes do not cause increase or deterioration in blood alcohol concentrations until putrefaction starts. Putrefaction may cause increase, decrease, or no change in blood alcohol levels. Analysis of vitreous humor or urine in decomposing bodies helps the ME/coroner determine whether alcohol found in the blood was ingested before death or formed after death.

Ethanol may be generated through the action of microbes on sugars in the blood during the postmortem period—both in situ and during specimen storage. Reports indicate that one-half to two-thirds of blood specimens taken at autopsy contain microbes—primarily yeast and *Escherichia coli*—that are capable of producing alcohol through fermentation. This fermentation requires sugar (glucose) and is promoted by elevated temperatures. Heart blood has particularly high glucose values immediately after death, probably due to agonal glycogenolysis.

If the body is placed at 4°C within a few hours of death, and if the collected specimen is adequately preserved (1% sodium fluoride), fermentation is inhibited, and the alcohol value measured in the collected specimen reflects the immediate premortem value. An exception may be for low alcohol values such as 0.05% or less. Such values must be interpreted with caution because fermentation during the postmortem period can easily produce such low levels of alcohol.

The vitreous specimen is somewhat protected from postmortem ethanol production by bacteria. Thus, vitreous ethanol levels may be more accurate than blood levels in decomposed, severely traumatized, embalmed, or burned bodies. Vitreous fluid behind the lens of the eye can be a very accurate measurement, especially if decomposition has occurred, and blood alcohol is higher as a result of postmortem ethanol production. However, if the eye is intact and the vitreous humor is clear, vitreous ethanol levels may be quite accurate.

Collection of Samples for Alcohol

Proper collection of blood alcohol samples during autopsy is important in determining both the cause and manner of death. Studies have shown significant differences in blood alcohol concentrations between blood samples taken from different parts of the body. Collection of postmortem blood samples for alcohol concentrations can also cause inaccuracies or errors. For example, drawing heart blood through the chest wall may result in contaminated samples—especially if there are internal injuries. Blood levels should be substantiated by analysis of vitreous humor, urine, CSF, and bile for ethanol content.

The first consideration is whether collection from the heart is as adequate as collection from a peripheral site such as the femoral vessels. When collection is carefully performed, alcohol results from these two sites are not significantly different. However, if pericardial fluid is included in the collection from the heart, the alcohol value may be falsely elevated due to postmortem diffusion of alcohol from the stomach. This is especially true in cases of decomposition and trauma where the usual barriers to diffusion from the stomach may be more easily breached during the postmortem period. In studies of alcohol diffusion from the stomach, alcohol values up to 0.23% were found in pericardial fluid at the same time that carefully collected heart blood was negative for alcohol. In cases where the integrity of the blood specimen is in question, a vitreous fluid specimen may be useful in corroborating the blood alcohol value.

The ME/coroner is often asked to testify in court as to the condition of the person at the time of an accident or death: "How many drinks did the person have?" That is difficult to determine because the exact length of time the person was drinking is often unknown—all that may be known is the blood alcohol level. As noted earlier, the concentration could be 1% in the blood and higher in the urine. Sometimes, there is no ethanol in the blood, but there is a very high level in the urine due to metabolism over time. The levels are never equivalent, and it is sometimes hard to determine alcohol levels. Therefore, the toxicology report states the laboratory values, and the interpretation of those values is best left to the toxicologist for legal purposes.

Toxicology Case Study—Contributed by Lauren E. Dvorscak

A 34-year-old man with a history of heavy alcohol use complained of visual difficulties and was found unresponsive several hours later. Following his death, MDI interview with his partner revealed that empty hand sanitizer containers had been recently found around the house (Figure 19.7). There were no other sources of alcohol found within the residence. An example sanitizer bottle was photographed by the MDI at the scene.

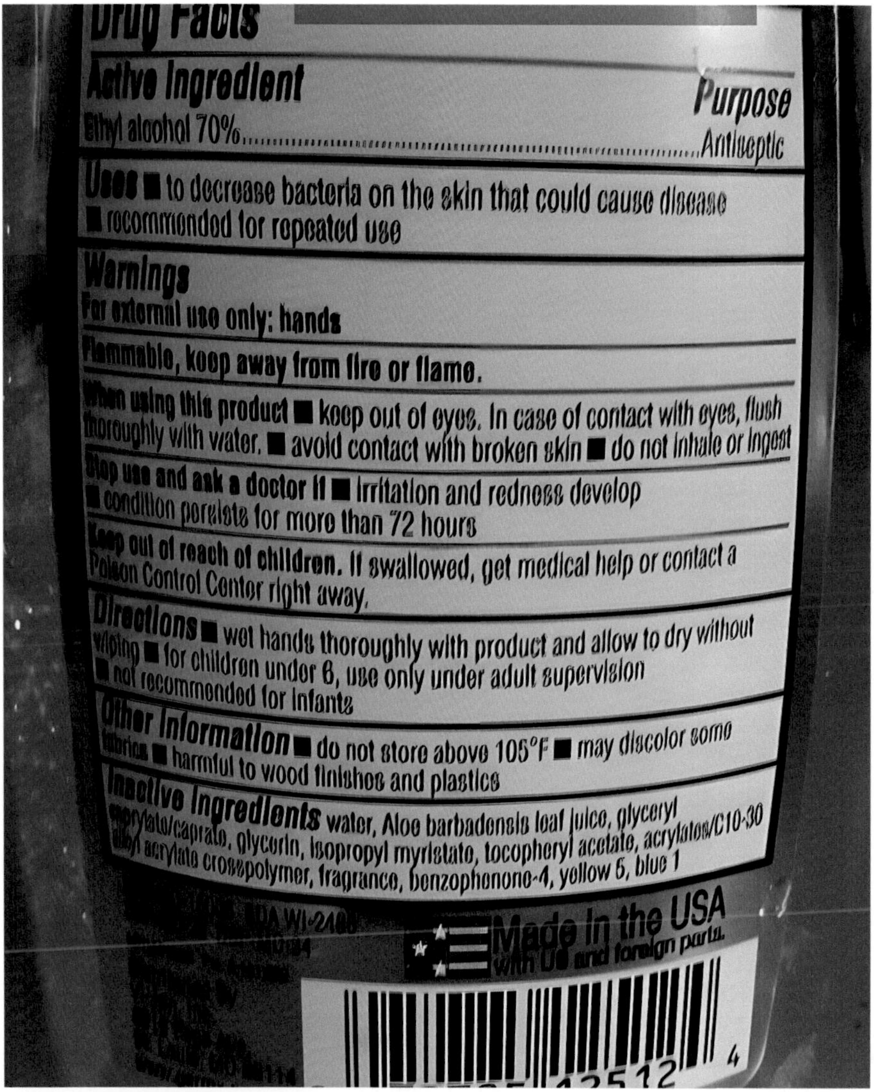

Figure 19.7 Hand sanitizer bottle photographed at the scene.

Autopsy revealed a well-developed man with a bicuspid aortic valve but no other significant abnormalities. Toxicology analysis of postmortem femoral blood detected a significantly elevated level of methanol (370 mg/dL). No other substances were present on postmortem toxicology analysis, including a screen for ethylene glycol. These findings were consistent with a history of visual disturbances.

The cause of death was attributed to the toxic effects of methanol, and the manner of death was accidental. The source of the methanol was believed to be contaminated hand sanitizer, which has been reported to occur. Given this information, the case was reported to the National Consumer Product Safety Commission. The case highlights the importance of the MDI in scene investigation and interview of witnesses and increases awareness of the possibility of methanol as a contaminating or unlisted ingredient in products on the market.

Conclusion

Autopsy samples obtained from blood, vitreous, or organs, including liver, lung, brain, and kidney, are sent for toxicology analysis. In the toxicology laboratory, most substances are detected by initial direct method (radioimmunoassay). Confirmatory testing generally involves a gas chromatogram-mass spectrometer that breaks the compound into its molecular components. The components can be charted on a graph and compared to a computer match.

Alcohol and drugs are found in many forensic-related deaths such as motor vehicle accidents, homicides, and suicides. Alcohol and drugs may also be the sole cause of death by intoxication. Unless otherwise supported by scene investigation, an illicit drug death is generally classified as an accidental manner of death. The cause of death is generally "acute drug intoxication." Two or more drugs are classified as "mixed drug intoxication." A death involving drugs and alcohol is signed out as a "combined drug and ethanol intoxication."

Legal medications can be used in illegal ways. Consequently, both legal and illegal drug use can result in accident, suicide, or homicide. Scene investigation and complete toxicology evaluation and autopsy findings are needed to provide complete information in the death investigation.

Bibliography

Baselt, R. C. 1995. *Disposition of Toxic Drugs and Chemicals in Man*, 4th ed. Foster City, CA: Chemical Toxicology Institute.

Baskin, S. I. 1991. *Principles of Cardiac Toxicology*. Boca Raton, FL: CRC Press.

Centers for Disease Control and Prevention. 2024. Facts about US deaths from excessive alcohol use. https://www.cdc.gov/alcohol/facts-stats/index.html

Centers for Disease Control and Prevention n.d. Drug overdose deaths in the United States 2003–2023. https://www.cdc.gov/nchs/products/databriefs/db522.htm

Cravey, R. H. and Baselt, R. C. 1981. *Introduction to Forensic Toxicology*. Davis, CA: Biomedical Publications.

Dolinak, D. 2013. *Forensic Toxicology: A Physiologic Perspective*. Calgary, Alberta, Canada: Academic Forensic Pathology, Inc.

Karch, S. B. 1996. *The Pathology of Drug Abuse*, 2nd ed. Boca Raton, FL: CRC Press.

O'Neil, M. J. 2013. *The Merck Index*, 15th ed. Cambridge, UK: Royal Society of Chemistry.

Reed, S.. Inhalants. https://www.addictioncenter.com/drugs/inhalants/huffing. Accessed 2025.

Workplace Injury and Death

20

MARY H. DUDLEY AND
CHERYL L. POZZI

OBJECTIVES

Upon completion of this chapter and corresponding reference material, the reader will be able to

- Understand the role of the medicolegal death investigator in scene investigation of workplace fatalities
  - List five areas of concern in the workplace where lack of information regarding forensic issues can have serious consequences
- Identify six components of a basic accident/investigation plan for the workplace
- Describe the need for proper occupational and safety forensic techniques in the workplace
- Discuss proper use and function of components of the forensic evidence kit for the workplace
- Describe the purpose and differences among close-up, midrange, and distance photography used in scene investigation in the workplace

Introduction

Approximately 5300 work-related fatalities were recorded in the United States in 2023, which was a slight decrease from 2022 (Bureau of Labor Statistics, 2024). Workplace-related injuries and/or death may require internal investigations from the place of employment, or external investigations from occupational agencies, law enforcement, or medical examiner (ME)/coroner offices. Workplace accidents may result from equipment failure, process failure, or hazardous material exposure. Workplace investigations have broadened their scope and can encompass causation factors to include mental health issues, shooter-suicide deaths of employees, and infectious diseases to include COVID-19-related deaths. Advances in photography, onsite security cameras, communication systems, community awareness, use of drones for

 DOI: 10.4324/9781003538622-23

broader site investigations, and various agencies' intelligence systems have improved techniques for all investigators involved. This chapter includes workplace accident investigation planning, evidence collection, and the role of the medicolegal death investigator (MDI) in scene investigation of workplace fatalities. A case study is included.

Workplace Accident Investigation Planning

Occupational health and safety personnel are frequently involved in accident investigations. These personnel include occupational health nurses or physicians, industrial hygienists, company-trained safety investigators, internal security personnel, fire protection personnel, and hazardous management personnel. Any of these people may be the first to be called to an accident scene or may be called in at a later time for additional investigations. There may also be a designated company emergency response team that responds to emergencies. This team may comprise employees with various skills who "volunteer" their expertise during a crisis. To respond to accident scenes is not necessarily part of their job duties or descriptions.

Companies are often concerned with the safety and welfare of employees, as well as visitors, neighboring companies and citizens, and the environment. They may have a communication and action plan in place with the regional fire and police departments, depending on the types of chemicals used and potential hazards. The local fire department and/or the internal safety/security or fire department may be responsible for conducting periodic evaluations to determine if various safety regulations set forth by the National Institute for Occupational Safety and Health and Occupational Safety and Health Administration (OSHA) are being met.

They may also perform duties during crises such as

- Identifying hazardous substances
- Evacuating people
- Securing the premises
- Neutralizing chemicals
- Properly disposing hazardous materials
- Testing for safety before allowing re-entry to the environment

During an accident, there may be injured persons requiring treatment or possible fatalities. In the occupational setting, it is imperative to know the following:

- The plant layout
- Hazardous substances with which employees work

- Locations of any hazardous processes or equipment
- Typical signs and symptoms of exposure to any of those hazards

Occupational personnel responding to the accident scene could easily be disabled by toxic gases, electricity, or other hazards. As critical as forensic investigations are, additional fatalities or injuries are unnecessary and preventable. Outside investigators should employ a communication force with company safety personnel to better understand substances involved and potential consequences.

It is important for occupational personnel to understand forensic techniques. Issues where lack of information about forensic techniques can create serious consequences include

- Destruction or loss of evidence
- Improper documentation
- Lack of or poor photography
- Breaking chain of evidence rules
- Improper investigative procedures

The best measures that safety or occupational personnel can take are to be informed about proper forensic techniques and then to develop accident plans that incorporate these skills. Good communication with other professionals that may be involved is also necessary.

An accident investigation plan should recognize all important persons who may be involved from different disciplines. It should also define roles and responsibilities for each job without redundancy or confusion. There should be internal investigators and external investigators to interview witnesses, as well as a command center to direct personnel and provide information to families and outside agencies.

A checklist is helpful to outline policies and procedures to follow during an accident investigation. This ensures that proper equipment and resources are available, that personnel are notified, and that details are not overlooked.

Evidence Collection

Law enforcement and ME/coroner office usually have their own systems to collet forensic evidence at the scene. During smaller incidents, where external agencies may not be notified, proper supplies are critical for the company's investigation. An internal investigation kit may include the following items:

- Envelopes and self-sealing plastic bags ranging from sandwich to garbage bag size, with means of permanent marking and sealing (to identify evidence without damage).

- Absorbent cotton or gauze (for drying wet evidence inside paper bags).
- Identification tags labeled to include date, time, location description, and investigator's name. These should be completed and attached to evidence and then collated with a master list.
- Paper bags from sandwich to grocery store sizes (for some organic evidence that cannot be sealed in plastic bags due to moisture concerns).
- Wide-mouthed plastic containers with screw-on lids in various sizes up to 1 gallon (to protect fragile or other evidence that should be in a closed, rigid container).
- Flashlights and extra batteries.
- Auxiliary lighting for outdoor situations. A portable generator with extension cords is helpful and is essential at remote sites or during power outages.
- Digital camera, flash unit, and extra batteries.
- Camcorder with a tripod and auxiliary lighting, several fresh tapes, and extra batteries. The camcorder taping provides a visual and audible record and can be used to record interviews.
- Permanent marker fine enough to write on evidence tags.
- Pen that will not bleed onto fabric.
- Chain of evidence form. (No one touches, observes, or photographs evidence without signing, dating, and noting the appropriate time on the forms.)
- Personal protective gear, including gloves, masks, eye wear, clothing, and shoes, appropriate for the area. Blood-borne pathogens are always a potential hazard.
- Designated vehicle if the accident is at a remote site or not within walking distance. (Four-wheel drive or golf carts may be appropriate.)
- Crime or accident scene tape, traffic cones, barricades, etc.
- Voice-activated, handheld tape recorder with extra batteries and tapes.

Record basic information when the accident is reported. A recording device is the easiest and best means of documentation. Perform a voice test prior to proceeding. Note time of day, weather conditions, lighting, if the surface of the flooring was previously wet with another substance, if construction is taking place in the area, etc. Capture all pertinent information. Use the recording device to interview witnesses and document all findings. After returning to your office, transcribe the recorded tape as soon as possible and duplicate the master tape. Store these as permanent records in two secure locations.

Conduct an initial survey of the scene. Determine whether hazardous conditions persist. Is it safe to proceed with the investigation? Notify ancillary support if necessary for protection or evacuation. Determine the need for health-care assistance. Can the company health department manage the level of injuries or is the situation more extensive with greater numbers of victims requiring additional support?

Rope off the scene for evidence protection. Privacy screens may also be required. Protect evidence from destruction by the environment, people, insects, or animals.

Photographs of the scene should include distance shots to record the complete perspective, midrange shots, and close-up, detailed shots. Use of a ruler or scale in the photographs may be necessary for accuracy. A bold pocket rod as used by surveyors is ideal in photographs. Date notation can be helpful. Permission need not be obtained when photographing persons involved in an accident. Consider photographing groups of bystanders who might have witnessed the accident. There can never be too many photographs. Label and keep photographs with the case file.

Evidence items should be photographed before collection, labeled, and transferred following the chain of evidence rules. If evidence items must be stored, ensure they are kept in a locked area where access is limited.

Safety and occupational health personnel must realize their jobs are critical. The injured employee may have a legal claim against the manufacturer of a vehicle, tooling product, office chair, or chemical substance. The company may have to prove that they were not negligent in supplying proper safety instruction or devices to employees who subsequently hurt themselves on the job. An employee may have a legal suit against the company for lack of warning about hazardous materials. There might be a workplace violence situation with a resulting death or injury. This might involve investigation from various perspectives. Accurate documentation of these incidents can assist those involved. Occupational health and safety personnel must strive to provide a competent and complete internal investigation.

Role of the Medicolegal Death Investigator in Workplace-Related Deaths

The MDI must work closely with occupational health personnel to obtain information about the employee, the work environment, and duties at the time of injury and/or death. The MDI plays an important role in the scene investigation that occurs in the workplace. The scene investigation includes documentation of the incident and circumstances of death, photography, and evidence collection. The circumstances of death may be related to the work environment or unrelated, including natural deaths (cardiovascular disease), accidental death (alcohol or drug-related), or violent deaths (suicide or homicide).

Workplace Death Case Study—Contributed by Lauren E. Dvorscak

Two related men, aged 34 and 66 years old, were found at the bottom of a manhole after pumping drainage from a leach line while working at a Solid Waste Authority facility (Figures 20.1a and b). A witness stated one man dropped a cellular phone into the hole as they were switching out the pump for a new one. The witness left to retrieve a tool from a nearby shed to remove the phone from the hole. Upon his return, both men were at the bottom of the 18-foot-deep hole. Emergency services were called, and the decedents were ultimately retrieved by a hazmat unit member wearing appropriate personal protective equipment, using a sling lowered into the manhole and tying the wrists of each decedent together with gauze.

Scene Investigation

The scene was located at a solid waste facility. The manhole was positioned south of a trash cell, which was designed to capture drainage from the garbage dumped into the cell. The cover of the manhole was reportedly off upon arrival of the death investigator, and pumps, piping, and tools were nearby. A utility truck with hoist was positioned near the hole as part of rescue efforts. The decedents had been found on top of one another, in supine and partially seated positions at the bottom of the hole, partially positioned on ladder rungs. Responding emergency personnel confirmed the death of both men and measured levels of gases at the scene in the hole as part of safety efforts for rescuers. The oxygen reading at the bottom of the hole was 9%–12% as measured via a probe lowered into the environment. The methane level in the same environment was measured at 600 parts per million. The hydrogen sulfide levels were also extremely elevated at reported toxic levels, although the parts per million remain unknown.

The decedents were warm to the touch at the time of recovery from the manhole and at death investigator examination, without outward evidence of trauma.

Autopsy

External examinations of both individuals revealed fully clad, well-developed, well-nourished men without evidence of significant injuries to otherwise explain death. Only rare petechial hemorrhages were in the right palpebral conjunctiva of the 34-year-old man.

Internal examination of the 34-year-old man revealed nonspecific findings of cerebral and pulmonary edema. Evidence of natural disease included

(a)

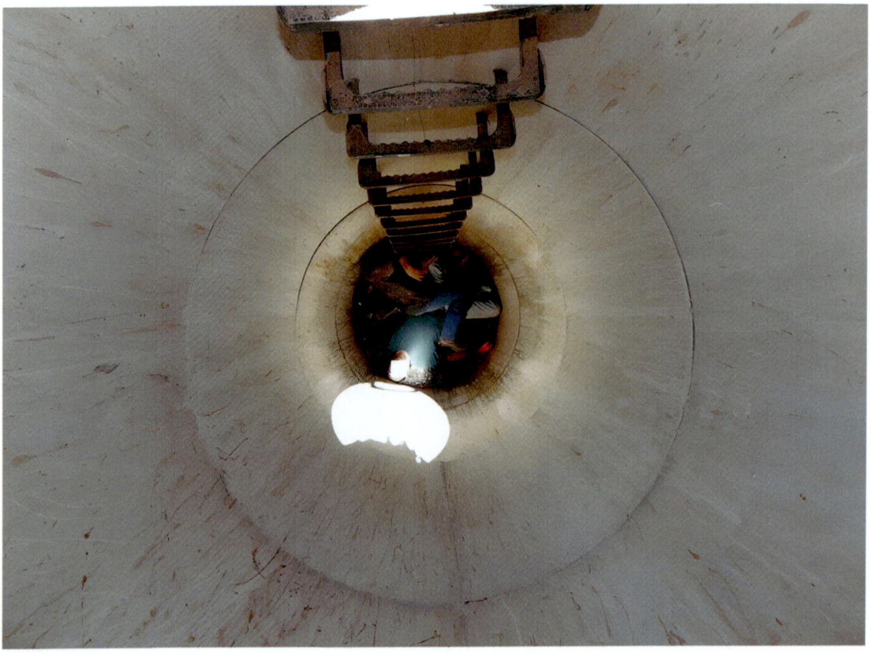

(b)

Figure 20.1 (a) The outside and (b) inside views of the manhole at a waste treatment facility.

moderate atherosclerotic cardiovascular disease, with up to 50% stenosis of the left anterior descending coronary artery.

Internal examination of the 66-year-old man revealed evidence of severe atherosclerotic cardiovascular disease, with up to 90% focal stenosis of the left anterior coronary artery. Mild hepatic steatosis was also present at autopsy.

Samples of femoral and heart blood were collected from both individuals at the time of autopsy examination and sent for basic screens as well as environmental exposure panels, which overall did not reveal high levels of methane nor significantly elevated percentage saturations of methemoglobin or sulfhemoglobin.

The cause of death for both individuals was gaseous suffocation, and displacement of oxygen in the environment was the most likely mechanism. The manner of death for both individuals was accidental. This case highlights the importance of scene safety and proper retrieval of decedents from hazardous situations, which may occur at the workplace.

Bibliography

Bureau of Labor Statistics, National Census of fatal Occupation Injuries in 2023. 2024. USDL-24-2564. https://www.bls.gov/news.release/pdf/cfoi.pdf Accessed 2025.

US Department of Labor Occupational Safety and Health Administration. February 10, 2016. Website accessed at https://www.osha.gov

IV

Domestic Violence, Child Fatalities, and Elder Fatalities

Domestic Violence

21

MARY H. DUDLEY

OBJECTIVES

Upon completion of this chapter and corresponding reference material, the reader will be able to

- Describe physical injuries seen with domestic violence
- Discuss major components of the domestic violence protocol
- Understand the issues surrounding a history of domestic violence leading to a fatality and the role of the medicolegal death investigator in scene investigation

Introduction

Domestic violence crosses all ages, gender, ethnicity, and socioeconomic status. Domestic abuse can take place over years and remain undetected, unrecognized, and untreated. The terminology of domestic abuse includes physical, sexual, emotional, economic, psychological abuse, and threats to harm another person. The Joint Commission on Accreditation of Healthcare Organizations mandated standards for identification of victims and collection of evidence. In the past 20 years, these standards have improved awareness of domestic violence, intimate partner violence, and human trafficking. Programs include education for healthcare workers to recognize signs of abuse and establish community support, as well as resources for abuse victims. This chapter includes information regarding crimes against women and men, human trafficking, and domestic violence protocol for the primary care setting. The role of the medicolegal death investigator (MDI) in domestic violence fatalities is also included.

Crimes Against Women and Men

Physical assault is a major cause of injury sustained by women, and sexual assault is a significant proportion of those crimes. Women are much more likely to be injured in an assault than men. In particular, intimate partner violence (IPV) is cited as a cause of injury for every 4 out of 1000 women. IPV is

DOI: 10.4324/9781003538622-25

abuse or aggression that occurs in a romantic relationship and refers to both current and former spouses and/or dating partners. It often starts in the early years of teen dating. Ninety-five percent of individuals who physically abuse their partners also psychologically abuse them. One in ten women are sexually assaulted by an intimate partner. One in four women and one in seven men experience physical violence by an intimate partner.

One in three women and one in 20 men are killed by intimate partners. IPV accounts for 72% of murder–suicides. Between 2014 and 2019, a 2021 study found that IPV was involved in 68.2% of mass shootings (Geller et al., 2021).

Human Trafficking

Human trafficking is the recruitment, transportation, and solicitation of a person with a purpose of a commercial sex act. In such cases, the sex act is induced by force, fraud, or involves a minor. Awareness of human trafficking has increased and can intersect with IPV. Intimate partner trafficking occurs when an abuser "compels their partner to engage in commercial sex, forced labor, or involuntary servitude" and may involve fraudulent marriages for this purpose.

Domestic Violence Protocol for Primary Care Setting

1. Obtain/document
    a. Incident history (quotes) from battered woman
    b. Address of occurrence
    c. Name/relationship of person she states caused injury/injuries
2. Perform complete physical/neurological exam
    a. Document injuries (body map/trauma sheet, sites of injuries). Indicate old/new injuries
    b. Identify presence of bruises, cuts, lacerations, burns, abrasions, etc.
    c. Determine extent or type of injuries inconsistent with patient's explanation
    d. Assess multiple injuries in different stages of healing
    e. Document problems during pregnancy, specifically preterm abortion, bleeding, intrauterine growth retardation, and hyperemesis
    f. Document other related problems
        i. Evidence of alcohol/drug abuse
        ii. Eating disorders

   iii. Vague or nonspecific physical or psychological complaints (fatigue, anxiety, rage, loss of appetite, dissociation, chronic irritable bowel syndrome, pelvic inflammatory disease, ulcers)
   iv. Repeated use of emergency services
   v. X-ray if indicated (to determine old/new fractures)

3. Mental health examination
   a. Assess emotional abuse
   b. Look for other related problems
      i. Depression, sleep disturbances, nightmares, and social problems
      ii. Suicidal ideation, suicide attempts/threats, patient, and/or partner
   c. Determine treatment/referral mental health department if indicated

4. If the victim has been sexually abused or raped, do a physical exam or refer to sexual assault response team/emergency department. Also collect forensic evidence
   a. Assess safety of patient/children

5. Informed consent (photography): make copy of consent for chart
   a. Photograph injuries (multiple photographs)
   b. Determine wound size with ruler—include in photograph
   c. Include patient's name and date of birth, date, photographer's name with all photographs

6. Rights/access to medical records
   a. Inform battered woman of her rights to her medical records and how to access them in case of future medical and/or forensic needs

7. Referrals
   a. Domestic violence center
   b. Child Protective Services (CPS) child abuse
   c. Children's Advocacy Center sexual abuse

8. Call 911 to report domestic violence crime
9. Reporting
   a. Healthcare provider should discuss reporting requirements and solicit cooperation of the patient. However, the patient's consent is not required to make a report—patient's safety must be considered at all times
   b. Information reported to a law enforcement agency should not include the complete medical record but should be limited to information that is necessary for the agency to respond

10. Documentation
    a. SOAP format is one that may be used to record information from the patient's description of the incident
        i. Subjective: quote the patient as much as possible. Record the patient's description of the incident
        ii. Objective: record objective findings, information must be accurate. In a court of law, the medical records are presumed to be correct when there is a discrepancy between the chart and the patient's testimony. Complete a body map
        iii. Assessment: assess the situation for immediate safety of the patient and lethality of the situation (lethality checklist and danger assessment tool)
        iv. Plan: make a report when appropriate, provide resources, aftercare actions, and consider immediate safety issues. Document police involvement to include the police department called/responded and name of the officer to whom information/evidence was given
    b. Document information given for referrals to counseling crisis centers, safe houses, etc.

11. Treatment
    a. Treat medical injuries as indicated. Use caution in administering/prescribing medications, especially if the patient is returning home and the abuser has not been determined or apprehended; medication may make the patient unable to avoid assault

12. Aftercare
    a. Assess immediate safety of patient/children, respecting the victim's evaluation of the situation; determine if she feels safe
    b. Assess lethality; inform patient if her situation is potentially lethal
    c. Remind her that battering is a crime and that she is protected by law
    d. Ask her what help she would like to receive
    e. Furnish her with a list of area shelters and crisis lines
    f. Explore available options for the patient/children
    g. Can patient/children stay with family/friends?
    h. Does patient need or want immediate access to a shelter?
    i. Provide copy of a safety plan if needed
    j. Contact CPS for child safety issues

The Role of the Medicolegal Death Investigator in Domestic Violence-Related Fatalities

If repeated abuse results in death, it is important for the MDI to obtain the past medical and social history from witness interviews and to obtain past medical records of injury. External examination of the body may show injuries of past or recent physical abuse, including petechial hemorrhages of the eyes or face, neck abrasions or contusions, or defensive injuries. Documentation of the scene investigation and body examination through written report and photographs helps determine the circumstances of death for proper manner of death classification.

References

Geller, L. B., Booty, M., and Crifasi, C. K. 2021. The role of domestic violence in fatal mass shootings in the United States, 2014–2019. *Injury Epidemiology* 8, 38. https://doi.org/10.1186/s40621-021-00330-0

National Sexual Violence Resource Center. https://www.nsvrc.org/statistics. Accessed 2025.

Tjaden, P. and Thoennes, N. 2006. *Extent, Nature, and Consequences of Rape Victimization: Findings from the National Violence against Women Survey.* Washington, DC: Department of Justice.

Sexual Assault

22

MARY H. DUDLEY

OBJECTIVES

Upon completion of this chapter and corresponding reference material, the reader will be able to

- State the legal definitions of rape, consensual sex, and statutory rape
- Describe the process of scene investigation of sexual assault-related deaths
- Identify pathological evidence of assault and identify the functions of sexual assault nurse examiners and the sexual assault response team

Introduction

Deaths related to sexual activity and crimes involving sexual assaults make up a significant proportion of deaths encountered by medicolegal death investigators (MDIs). Approximately 1 in 5 women and 1 in 71 men report experiencing rape (Black et al., 2011). Along with the increase in crimes, there is an increase in demand for investigation and pathological examination of specimens and victims of sex-related crimes. Sexual assault has evolved into a much broader scope over the past 20 years on a world-wide level. It is not gender-specific, nor does it profile education, cultures, age, ethnicity, or socioeconomic status. This chapter includes the role of the MDI, the sexual assault-related death scene, autopsy findings, definition of rape, profile of rapist, and role of the sexual assault nurse examiners (SANE) and the sexual assault response team (SART) in the clinical setting.

Role of the Medicolegal Death Investigator at Sexual Assault-Related Fatality Scenes

The role of the MDI at the death scene of a sex-related death is to obtain information regarding the circumstances of death and to accurately provide information and scene photographs to the medical examiner (ME)/C to determine

 DOI: 10.4324/9781003538622-26

the manner of death. Sex-related deaths can be classified into numerous entities and involve several manners of death. Occasionally, the sudden death of a male involved in sexual activity can be attributed to natural causes; the cause of death is usually cardiovascular disease, including atherosclerosis, cardiomyopathy, and berry aneurysm. It is important to note that fecal soiling and fluid discharge from the penis can be seen normally as a postmortem change and should not be misinterpreted as evidence of sexual activity in an otherwise natural death.

Accidental deaths and injuries sometimes result from sexual activity. Death scenes involving naked or partially clothed bodies and the presence of sexually explicit literature should be documented. Scene investigation and evidence collection are very important in autoerotic asphyxial deaths. Sex-associated asphyxia from hanging in autoerotic asphyxia associated with solitary masturbation is usually accidental. Death results from constriction of the carotid arteries during orgasm for the purpose of increasing the perceived pleasure. This can result in direct brain anoxia or cardiac arrhythmias when the usual escape mechanism fails. Other associated findings are evidence of repeated behavior, secluded location, sexually explicit literature at the scene, padded ligatures, binding of the limbs, an escape mechanism, and sometimes, crossdressing. Sexual assault may be associated with homicides where the cause of death is from head trauma, strangulation, or suffocation.

At the scene the body should not be touched or manipulated prior to photography. Prior to transportation, the hands are covered in paper bags, secured at the wrists with tape. The body is then sealed in a clean body bag with unique, labelled body bag seal for transportation.

Scene Investigation and Evidence Collection

Scene investigation of sex-related deaths, including rape homicides, usually involves law enforcement and crime lab personnel to look for and document evidence of forced entry or struggle. They may also preserve fingerprint evidence on items such as cigarette butts, beer cans, drugs, drug paraphernalia, and/or weapons. Law enforcement is responsible to secure the residence, obtain permission via warrant to investigate the scene, and to look for weapons or instruments. Stains from blood, semen, or saliva may be collected and analyzed for serological analysis.

Examination of the body involves the collection of evidence, description of clothing and injuries, and documentation of findings. The ultimate goal of the examination is to properly interpret the findings and reconstruct the events that occurred around the time of the death.

Clothing should be examined while on the body to document the degree of disarray and which parts of the body, if any, are exposed. The presence of obvious tears in the clothing should be noted for possible correlation with injuries on the body. Trace evidence such as fibers and hairs may be collected at the scene (with permission) or at autopsy.

Autopsy Findings

Forensic examination of the body includes a complete external examination. Prior to examination, complete radiographic imaging should be performed while the body is still within the body bag. The body should be photographed in the body bag as is, prior to manipulation of the clothing or body. Further, prior to removing the body from the body bag, any swabs for DNA analysis and/or fingernails should be collected to minimize risk of DNA contamination.

External examination should include close inspection, documentation, and photographs of injury of the head, neck, torso, genitalia, and extremities. Areas of particular concern are the genitals, anus, and breast where abrasions, lacerations, contusions, and bite marks could be present. Bite marks are associated with sexual assaults and leave important forensic evidence (e.g. saliva for DNA) to identify the suspect. If a bite mark is noted, a forensic odontologist can assist in evaluation, photography, and evidence collection (i.e. swabbing the area and/or removal of the bite mark) (Figure 22.1).

Hands and arms may show defensive-type wounds, such as broken fingernails, and the extremities may show marks related to forcible restraint. Nail clippings and scrapings are usually routine evidence collection in homicide cases. The neck should be inspected for ligature or finger marks, and the mouth and eyes may show petechial hemorrhages, as indications of asphyxia.

Further examination should not proceed until specimens have been collected from the vagina/penis, anus, and mouth. This process is facilitated by the use of a "sexual assault kit" (refer to Appendix F) because it involves collection of evidence that may indicate recent sexual activity. Both smears and swabs are collected along with blood for serology and hair from various parts of the body. A mechanism for the maintenance of a "chain of custody" is usually provided in commercially prepared kits. A scope may also be used to document trauma to the vagina or cervix prior to internal examination.

Smears can be examined for the presence of sperm, and a wet smear can be evaluated for the presence of motility. Sperm usually retain their motility for ½–2 hours after intercourse but lose their ability to move due to exposure to the acid pH of vaginal secretions. Sperm have been reported in

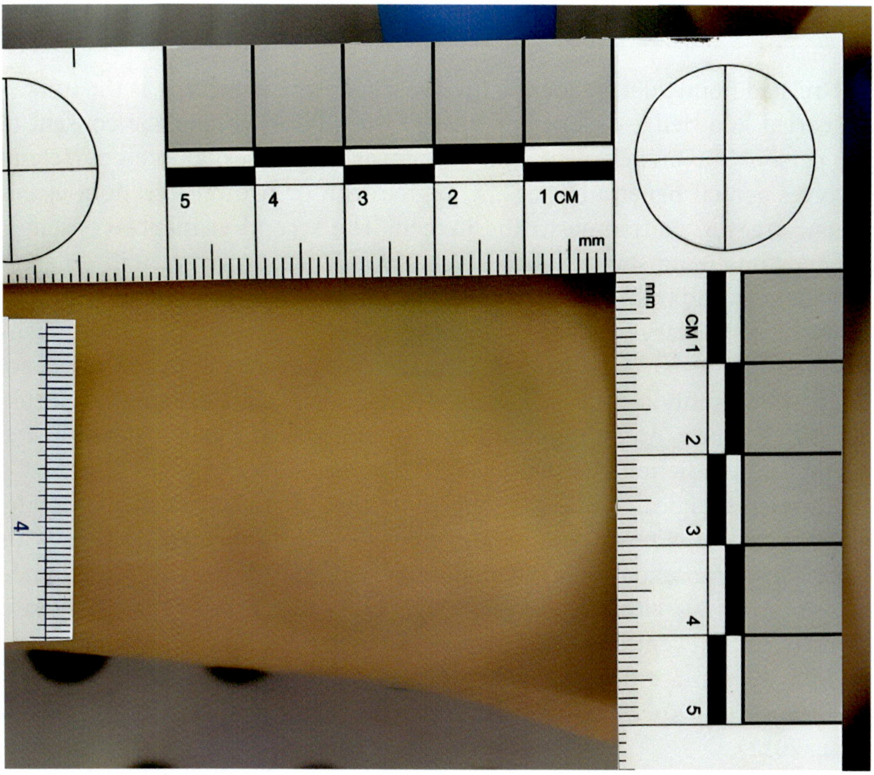

Figure 22.1 Bite mark.

approximately half of women who have had intercourse within the preceding 24 hours, but that percentage drops significantly as time passes (Hazelwood and Burgess, 2009). Sperm may be identified in samples taken from women who have showered, bathed, douched, or used various barrier methods of birth control. In the deceased victim, there are reports of recognizable sperm in samples taken weeks after death. A negative examination does not exclude recent sexual activity because a negative result may be due to the normal dissolution of sperm over time or sterility of the male partner.

The internal examination of the body at autopsy should include special attention to the brain, neck block, and any evidence of internal pelvic trauma. Even if there are no external signs of strangulation, in a sexual assault-related fatality, the internal neck examination includes a layered dissection of the strap muscles and removal of the hyoid bone to document presence or absence of any injuries. Additional ancillary studies in these fatalities include histology and toxicology.

Definitions of Rape

Sex-related homicides frequently involve rape. Rape is defined as the unlawful carnal knowledge of a person against the will or without the consent of the person. The first element—carnal knowledge—is sexual intercourse and involves genital penetration of any degree with or without erection, ejaculation, orgasm, or trauma to the hymen. The second element—consent—depends on circumstances of the event; its definition may vary in different jurisdictions and from case to case. The definitions of consensual sex and statutory rape also vary between jurisdictions. Consensual sex generally means that both parties involved willfully consented to intercourse or the sexual act in question. Statutory rape is typically defined as an adult engaging in a sexual act with a minor, or with an individual younger than legally defined in the particular jurisdiction's statute.

Epidemiological studies of rape show that victims are usually female, although there is much less careful documentation of male victims with regard to homosexual rapes. Female rape victims are usually in their late teens or early 20s, although there is a wide range of ages (Centers for Disease Control and Prevention, 2012). According to national survey results, nearly 40% of women are first raped between the ages of 18, but approximately 42% reported experiencing their first rape before the age of 18 (Black et al., 2011).

Rape is most frequent in areas where income is low and unemployment rate is high (Black et al., 2011). Rape is perpetrated in a context of violence rather than passion.

Profiles of Rapists

There is no single stereotypical rapist. General typologies of sex offenders may include compensatory, sadistic, power/control, and opportunistic (Robertiello and Terry, 2007). Even though the motivation behind rape is varied, there are some similarities between types of offenders. Many offenders have personalities that identify with masculinity, condone violence, have negative views of the opposite sex, have substance abuse problems, low self-esteem, and have not found an alternative outlet to manage aggression (Robertiello and Terry, 2007). At some point, these individuals lose control of their thoughts and act on their plans.

Rape murderers have also been divided into two types that display different behaviors and characteristics, according to Federal Bureau of Investigation criminal profiles:

1. Organized offenders are more apt to plan, use restraints, commit sexual acts with live victims, show or display control over their victims, and use vehicles to transport themselves to and from the crime scene.
2. Disorganized offenders are more apt to leave a weapon at the scene, position the dead body, perform sexual acts on the dead body, keep the dead body, try to depersonalize the body, and not use a vehicle.

Theories have been proposed to explain the behaviors of rapists; these include psychodynamic, behavioral, and biologic factors.

SANE/SART

The use of SANE to collect evidence from live victims in emergency rooms began in the early 1990s. SANE and SART are trained with specific knowledge and skills to identify injuries, gather, and preserve evidence related to sexual assault crimes from live victims in the clinical setting. They cooperate and share information with law enforcement and social service agencies that may pertain to sexual assault, domestic violence, exploitation, and human trafficking. Prompt collection and preservation of evidence has increased the conviction rates of sex offenders. Forensic nurses can provide necessary psychological support for sexual assault victims and are trained in legal issues to testify as expert witnesses in court.

The United States has experienced persistent shortages of SANE and SART personnel, especially in rural areas. This recognition of need in under served areas without emergency department-based forensic units and other resources has now prompted the use of telehealth as an option for sexual assault healthcare.

References

Black, M. C., Basile, K. C., Breiding, M. J., Smith, S. G., Walters, M. L., Merrick, M. R. et al. 2011. *The National Intimate Partner and Sexual Violence Survey (NISVS): 2010 summary report.* Atlanta, GA: National Center for Injury Prevention and control, Centers for Disease Control and Prevention.

Centers for Disease Control and Prevention. 2012. *Sexual Violence Facts at a Glance.* Atlanta, GA: National Center for Injury Prevention and Control, Division of Violence Prevention.

Hazelwood, R. R. and Burgess, A. W. 2009. *Practical Aspects of Rape Investigation: A Multidisciplinary Approach.* Boca Raton, FL: CRC Press.

https://pubmed.ncbi.nlm.nih.gov/31436683/

https://www.health.ny.gov/professionals/safe/
https://www.ovcttac.gov/saneguide/multidisciplinary-response-and-the-community/
https://www.safeta.org/wp-content/uploads/2021/08/Indiana-Guidelines.pdf
Robertiello, G. and Terry, K. T. 2007. Can we profile sex offenders? A review of sex offender typologies. *Aggress Violent Behav 12*(5):508–518.

Child Abuse and Infanticide

23

MARY H. DUDLEY

OBJECTIVES

Upon completion of this chapter and corresponding reference material, the reader will be able to

- Understand the medicolegal death investigator's (MDI)'s role in scene investigation of child abuse fatalities
  - Define child abuse and infanticide
- Identify state legislation related to reporting child abuse and/or neglect
- Discuss the pathological finding of abusive head injury
- Discuss five types of nonaccidental trauma
- Compare and contrast Resnick's five basic classifications of infanticide

Introduction

Child abuse is the purposefully inflicted injury of a child through physical, sexual, or emotional abuse or neglect. Child abuse and neglect includes all types of abuse and neglect of a child under 18 years old, by a parent, caregiver, or person in a custodial role (e.g. teacher or coach) that results in harm, potential for harm, or a threat to harm a child. One in seven children in the United States is estimated to experience some form of maltreatment in their lifetimes (Leeb, et al. 2008). This is likely an underestimate because many cases are not reported. Children under 1 year of age have the highest rates of victimization, and approximately one-third of those abused are under the age of 3 years. In 2021, 1820 children died of abuse and neglect in the United States (CDC, 2013). Child fatalities may occur with a single episode of abusive injury, multiple injuries of various ages, or subtle forms of abuse. This chapter includes historical perspectives, characteristics of child abusers, the role of the medicolegal death investigator (MDI) in scene investigation, types of child abuse, and infanticide.

DOI: 10.4324/9781003538622-27

Historical Perspectives

Historically, there have been few laws governing child abuse. While child labor laws were passed in the 1800s, the extent of fatal child abuse in this country was not fully appreciated either medically or publicly until the 1960s. In 1961, Adelson published an article in the *New England Journal of Medicine* on fatally abused children called "The Slaughter of the Innocents." In 1962, Kempe published a radiological study of infants having multiple bone fractures in various stages of healing and postulated that these were due to repeated assaults. In this article he coined the term "battered baby syndrome." In response to these medical studies and increased public awareness, by 1968, all states had enacted laws concerning child abuse that required all physicians and medical personnel to report suspected cases of abuse.

All states have a child fatality review board that comprises a multidisciplinary group of individuals, including representation from healthcare professionals, social work, law enforcement/legal community, and medical examiner/coroners. The purpose is to review all child fatalities on a regular basis to compile findings with a focus on data collection and preventability.

Characteristics of Child Abusers

Child abuse cuts across cultural, intellectual, and socioeconomic boundaries, but there are some well-known parental characteristics of child abusers. Abusing parents or guardians often have emotional disturbances and sociopathic personalities but seldom are psychotic. They are often young and immature and frequently were abused children themselves. Dependency, age inappropriateness, sadomasochism, egocentricity, and narcissism have been described. When seen in a clinical situation, abusive parents may be impulsive, demanding, withdrawn, depressed, or angry. There is often a stressful precipitating event. Since the precipitating event is often financial, it could explain the higher instance of child abuse among lower socioeconomic classes. More females than males abuse children, probably due to increased access to the children as a primary caregiver. Males, however, are more frequently involved in cases of fatal child abuse.

Role of the Medicolegal Death Investigator in Scene Investigation of Child Abuse Fatalities

The role of the MDI in child deaths, as in all deaths, is to fully document the scene, without speculation or bias. The MDI in scene investigation of child abuse death includes the documentation of the reported circumstances in death through witness (e.g. parent or caregiver) interview, observations, photography, and evidence collection. It is important to obtain family history, developmental and past medical history, pediatrician and immunization records, history of recent illnesses, falls, exposure, injury, recent history of hospitalization, and imaging studies. The following lists include external features of abuse and criteria for suspicion of inflicted injury.

External Features of Abuse

- Abrasions often patterned
- Contusions of different ages
- Lacerations
- Fractures or deformity
- There can be internal injuries without external manifestation
- Burns and scalds
- Scalds from hot water may be deliberate or accidental

Criteria for Suspicion of Inflicted Injury

- Multiple bruises/scars
- Concurrent injuries/neglect
- History of prior hospitalization
- Delay in seeking medical treatment for injury
- Injury appearing older than alleged
- Account of injury incompatible with age
- No witness to the "accident"
- Relative versus parent transports child
- Injury attributed to sibling
- History of being excessively withdrawn, submissive, polite, or does not cry during painful treatment
- Scalds of hands and feet, symmetrical full-thickness or isolated burns of the buttocks
- The history of how the injury occurred does not match the injury noted on examination

It is important to know who cares for the child, who discovered the child, and any attempts to revive the child. If the child is transported to the hospital, the primary scene where injury occurred should also be investigated. Scene investigation includes documentation, photography, evidence collection, and should include documentation of any safety hazards that may have contributed to injury. Objects that can result in patterned injuries include sharp objects, tools, toys, ligatures, furniture, or playground equipment.

Types of Child Abuse

Types of child abuse include a single-episode event or multiple injuries that may result in fatalities. Physical abuse includes blunt force injuries, burns, sexual abuse, poisoning, and neglect. Subtle forms of abuse include Munchausen syndrome by proxy and asphyxial deaths. Physical abuse should be suspected when there is any inflicted injury on a child requiring medical therapy, where there are inflicted bruises or abrasions on an infant, or where there are inflicted bruises or injury to the face of a child.

Blunt Trauma

Inflicted blunt force injuries include abrasions, contusions, lacerations, fractures, and/or a combination of injuries as seen with craniocerebral injuries. Determining the time of injury can be instrumental in eliminating or including a suspect in child abuse. Unfortunately, there is no known way to determine the age of an injury with scientific certainty. Among the uncontrollable variables that affect the speed of healing are size and location of the injury, whether the injury is contaminated or clean, and individual factors such as age and nutritional and immunological statuses.

Abrasions and Contusions

Abrasions or scraping away of the outer skin surface can occur after death and can appear identical to an injury sustained before death. Only after a number of hours of survival following an abrasion will there be microscopic evidence that the abrasion occurred before death.

Fresh bruises may be red, purple, blue, brown, or various combinations of those colors. The color of a bruise depends on its size and depth, density of hemorrhage, and normal pigmentation of the skin. The normal process of healing generally leads to color changes through yellow and green. Determination of age of a bruise by its color is variable and unreliable.

Abrasions or contusions located over bony prominences may occur with a history of falls, especially with toddlers learning to walk. Bruises of the midportions of the extremities (not over bony prominences), or bruising involving the scalp, face, or ears, may be indictive of inflicted trauma (Figure 23.1). Patterned injuries such as slap, pinch, grab marks, or fingernail marks are suspicious for abuse.

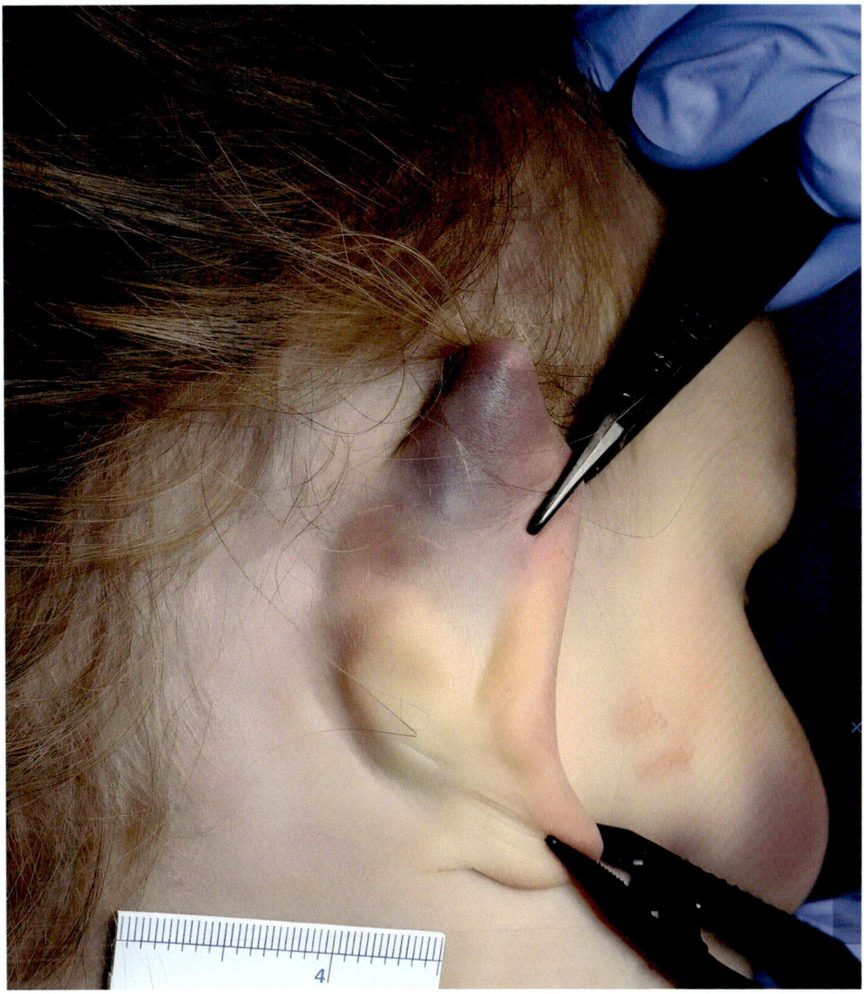

Figure 23.1 Contusion on the ear.

Lacerations

Lacerations or tears of the skin or mucosa may indicate inflicted injuries. A torn frenulum in the mouth or oral lacerations (Figure 23.2) may be seen with suffocation, blunt trauma involving the mouth, or from an object being forced into the mouth.

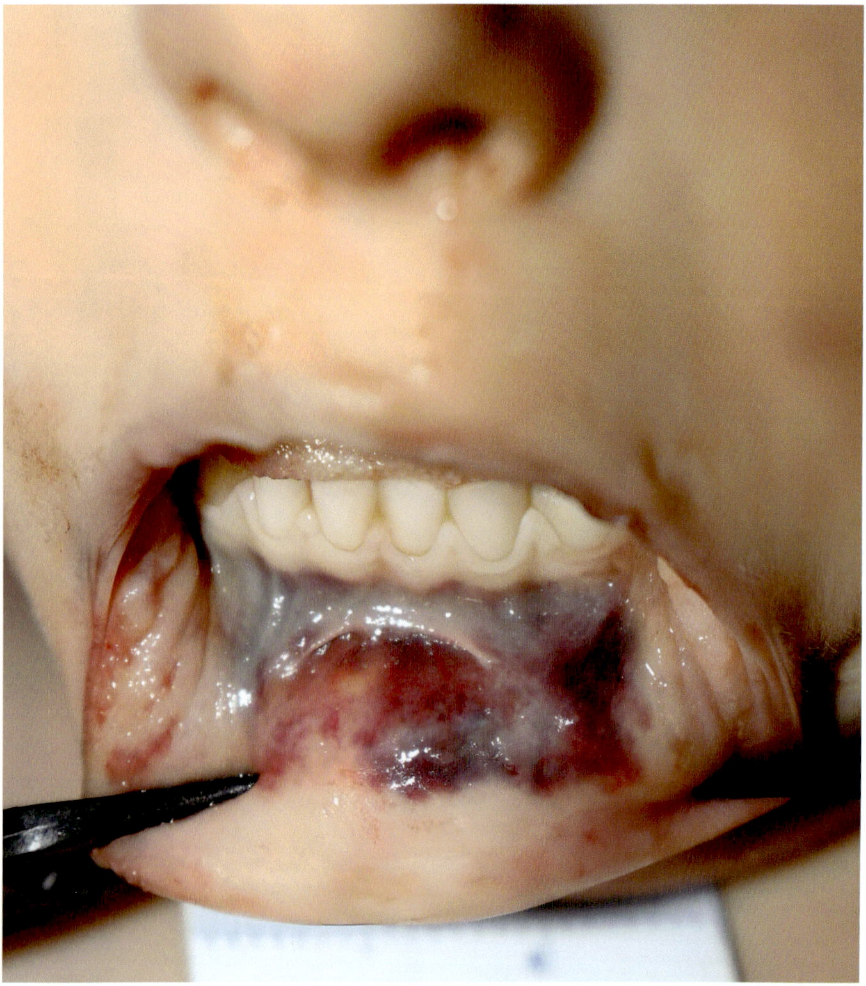

Figure 23.2 Oral lacerations from inflicted head injury.

Fractures

An infant or child who has sustained repeated episodes of blunt injury may have fractures in various stages of healing. Imaging studies are helpful to identify fractures of various stages. Bones heal in a logical sequence, but the speed of healing is variable and depends on the age of the individual, location of the fracture, stability of the fracture, and individual characteristics. The healing changes can be seen microscopically as early as 24–36 hours after injury. Calcification of the healing fracture is seen within 5–7 days microscopically but cannot be seen on X-ray until after 7 days at the earliest and usually not until 10–20 days.

Head Trauma

Nonaccidental head trauma (abusive head injury) often is associated with attempts at quieting a crying baby. The mechanism of injury can be due to a combination of factors, such as the child's relatively large head, weak neck muscles, immature skull and brain in movement, and impact of the head against a fixed object. Blunt impacts to the head may cause concussions in children with the rapid onset of cerebral edema and death. On imaging or at autopsy, cerebral edema may be the only finding. Nonaccidental head injury may cause severe cerebral damage or even death. Autopsy findings may show an impact site with abrasions, contusions, subscapular hemorrhage, subdural hemorrhage, cerebral edema, retinal/optic nerve sheath hemorrhages, and/or axonal injury.

In fatal and nonfatal child abuse cases that involve severe head injuries, the most common question asked is, "What is the degree of force necessary to cause the injury?" This question is often raised as a variation of, "Could the injury have been sustained by an accidental fall of three feet from a changing table or sofa onto a carpeted floor?" Several factors are involved related to the amount of force necessary to cause a skull fracture or other serious head injury in an infant or small child. These factors include the area or point of impact, whether the head is moving or stationary at impact, the type of surface on impact, and the amount of force involved.

Skull fractures are characterized as linear, a thin fracture line, or complex. Complex includes multiple (at least two fractures), diastatic (a fracture wider than a thin line), bilateral, or depressed (an indentation of the bony cortex). Force categories include crush (compression between two solid objects), rotational (a moving head impacting a fixed object), and translational (fixed head impacted by another object) injuries.

A 12-year retrospective review of clinical and autopsy cases of children under 2 years old compared head injuries and the forces involved. Fracture characteristics provide clues in determining the cause and manner of death between accidents and child abuse. Using university hospital cases over a 5-year period and 15 years of state medical examiner autopsy records, deaths attributed to accident and injury of children under 2 years old were reviewed. Four groups established for analysis included fatal and nonfatal accidents and fatal and nonfatal child abuse. The fatal accident group showed mainly complex skull fractures, external and internal head injuries, loss of consciousness, and crush or rotational force injuries, consistent with the reported circumstances of the incident causing injury. In the nonfatal accident group, most children had linear fractures and most cases had external head injury, minor brain trauma, and transient loss of consciousness, consistent with the reported history. Rotational forces injuries were common in nonfatal injuries, and crush force occurred more frequently in fatal situations.

In both fatal abuse and nonfatal abuse injury categories, all children were under 1 year old, demonstrating lower body weight and less overall development in comparison to the accidental trauma groups. The fatal abuse group demonstrated both complex and linear skull fractures. All cases had external head injury, brain injury, and immediate loss of consciousness. Rotational and crush force injuries were also present, and other body injuries were consistent with child abuse despite lack of corresponding history. The nonfatal abuse cases showed both mixed and complex fractures, as well as subdural hemorrhages, but did not experience loss of consciousness.

There were fracture characteristic differences between abuse and accident cases, with abuse cases showing more complex, stellate, diastatic, and biparietal fractures. Fatal accident cases with high-force calculation accounted for severe craniocerebral injuries and immediate loss of consciousness, similar to injuries seen in fatal abuse cases. Study findings showed that accidental falls from low heights may cause skull fractures; however, they were not shown to result in fatal intracranial injury. Nonfatal skull fractures from falls had fewer long-term sequalae than nonfatal abuse cases. The study concluded that force related to skull fractures and craniocerebral injuries with loss of consciousness relates significantly to the outcomes of head injuries in infants and young children.

Survival of severely injured children with head injury who receive aggressive medical care can incur lasting sequalae such as severe handicaps, seizure disorders, developmental delays, increased risk of infection, or other life-threatening complications. When these children die, one cannot ignore that immediate cause of death is inseparable from the original injury, which is the appropriate proximate cause of death. Careful investigation of circumstances surrounding the original head injury by the MDI is important to ultimately allow the pathologist to apply the correct manner of death, even if the original injury occurred years or decades earlier.

Sexual Assault

Sexual abuse is probably the most underreported form of child abuse, often occurring in the home and involving a family member. Approximately 9% of abused children have been victims of sexual abuse (Centers for Disease Control and Statistics, 2013). Blunt trauma, including abrasions, contusions, and/or lacerations, may be present on the genitalia. A sexual assault examination should be performed with evidence collection in cases of suspected sexual abuse and/or visible genital trauma. Bite marks can be associated with sexual abuse.

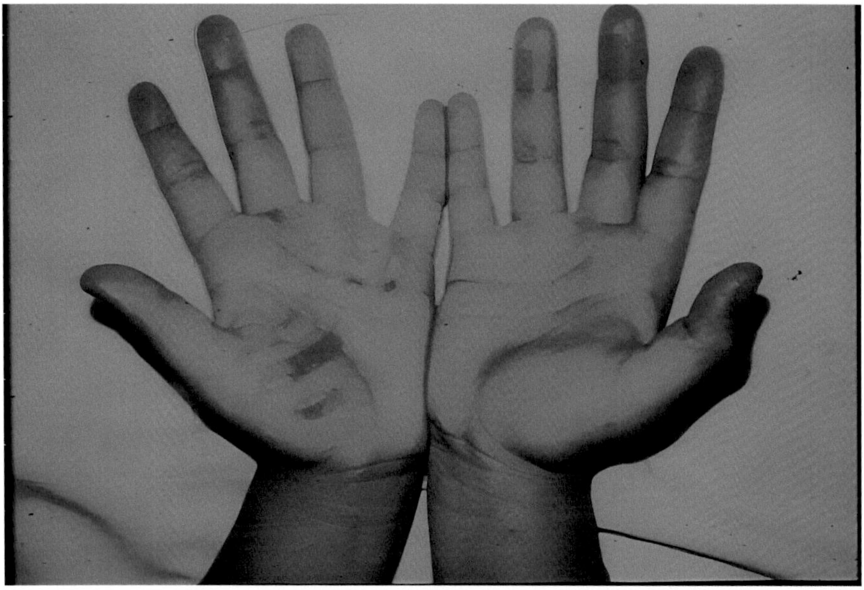

Figure 23.3 Contact thermal patterned burn.

Burns

Burns account for a high number of hospitalized children. Burn injuries occur in approximately 10% of child abuse cases, and 10% of hospital admissions are the result of child abuse (United States Department of Justice, 2001). Burns can be described as contact or scald. Contact burns are the result of the skin coming in direct contact with a hot object. Objects include cigarettes, irons, stove tops, heater grates, or curling irons. Patterned contact burns may involve the palms of the hands or soles of the feet (Figure 23.3). Scald burns are caused by hot liquid or steam. Tap water is the most frequent cause of abusive burns. As water temperature increases over 120°F, the rapidity of scalding increases dramatically. Maximum water temperature needs to be checked to determine the length of exposure needed to cause the burn. The developmental age, strength, and coordination of the child should be considered in determining willful versus accidental scalding.

Abusive tap water burns can be distinguished from accidental burns when the following characteristics are seen:

- Clear immersion lines
- Absent "splash" marks
- Stocking and/or glove pattern on the hand(s) or feet (Figure 23.4)

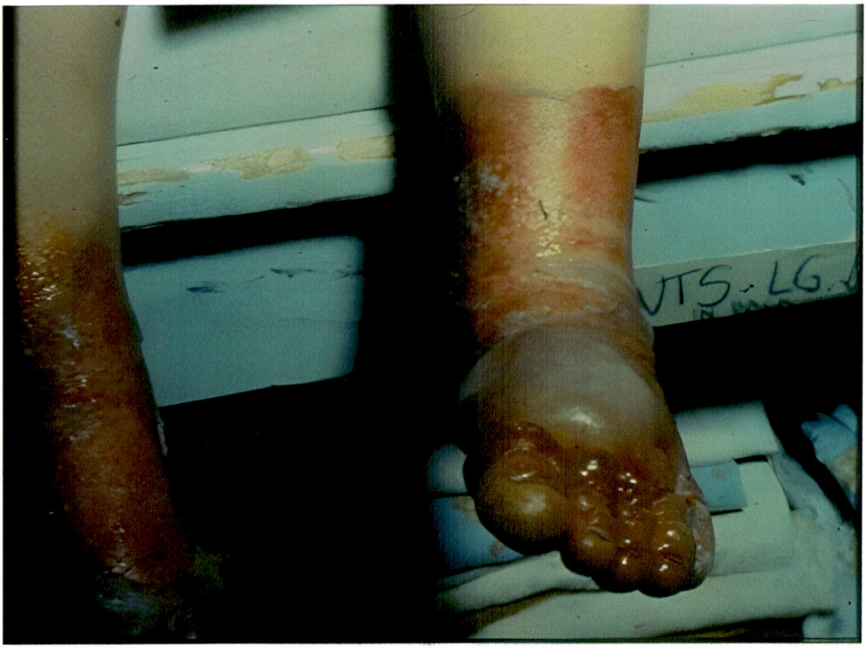

Figure 23.4 Scalding injury of child's feet.

- Protected flexion areas at the elbow, knee, or groin
- Absent "downward flow" pattern, as when a child accidentally pulls a container of hot liquid from height
- Mirror image burns
- Full-thickness burns

Poisoning

Poisoning is a less common form of child abuse than physical assault. When it does occur, it is extremely difficult to detect and prove. Few drugs or poisons produce pathognomonic or even characteristic lesions. Thus, a correct diagnosis usually requires prior suspicion and confirmation via toxicology testing. The offending agent need not be a classic poison or drug because almost any substance is potentially dangerous to an infant or child if taken in sufficient quantity. The assault may be a deliberate attempt to kill the child or an attempt to quiet or discipline the child.

Neglect

Neglect occurs when there is failure to act where the law places responsibility on the parents or guardian to provide food, shelter, protection, clothing, and medical care for their children. Neglect may include starvation, malnutrition, failure to thrive, dehydration, exposure to a dangerous environment, and failure to provide needed medical care. Emotional abuse and neglect are probably the largest area of child abuse. A neglected child may show learning disabilities, developmental lags, or abrupt/inappropriate changes in behavior or mood.

Subtle Forms of Abuse

Subtle fatal child abuse occurs when a child or infant is willfully killed or seriously injured in such a way that there are few or no external or internal findings that would explain the death or debility. The small size and fragility of infants and small children render them vulnerable to death and serious injury by a variety of subtle means. Types of subtle abuse include Munchausen syndrome by proxy and nonaccidental asphyxia.

Munchausen Syndrome by Proxy

A distinctly unusual form of subtle child abuse is Munchausen syndrome by proxy. The Munchausen syndrome is a psychiatric condition in which an individual deliberately produces symptoms of illness to be hospitalized or gain sympathy/attention. The Munchausen syndrome by proxy occurs when parents or guardians cause numerous hospitalizations or procedures for their children either through repeated physical assault or poisoning, by falsifying medical history, or by altering diagnostic tests to gain sympathy and attention. The child may die from complications of continuous, inflicted physical abuse and poisoning.

Asphyxia

Nonaccidental asphyxial deaths include smothering, suffocation, strangulation, and drowning. The circumstances and scene investigation are important in asphyxial death as there may be few diagnostic autopsy findings. A lack of suspicion in approaching these cases can obscure recognition of their willfully inflicted nature.

Smothering and suffocation of an infant can be accomplished without causing external injuries. Obstruction of the airway may cause death without demonstrable evidence, especially if the obstruction is removed prior to examination. Manual or ligature strangulation and compression of the chest (traumatic asphyxia) may be accomplished without leaving marks.

Deliberate drowning of infants and small children is often unwitnessed and occurs in the home. The child may be held under water until they become unconscious. The result may be a period of survival after removal from the water (near drowning). Drowning of an infant or child may leave no specific anatomic findings. If the child is removed from the water prior to investigation, the outward circumstances of the death may be elusive, highlighting the importance of thorough scene investigation. The diagnosis of homicidal drowning requires suspicion; thorough investigation of the circumstances; and an autopsy directed toward confirmation of immersion, evaluation of any survival interval, and identification of any injury. The pathologist should seek evidence of aspirated foreign material, especially if the immersion may have occurred in something other than tap water, and evidence of any bruises or abrasions of the face suggesting forceful submersion of the head.

Infanticide

Infanticide, the killing of infants and newborns, dates back to ancient Greece. Historically, infanticide involved disposing of deformed or sickly infants. The female infant was valued less than the male. However, the practice continues in many contemporary cultures—including our own—of disposing of unwanted but otherwise healthy infants and children.

Infanticide has been condemned by the church and the state, but little was done in the way of prosecution of offenders until the sixteenth century in England and New England. In the United States today, there are no separate statutes that deal exclusively with infanticide and filicide (specific term used when the offender is a parent of the child). Neonaticide, by strict definition, is the murder of a newborn within the first 24 hours of life. Charges vary from state to state. In ancient Rome, the father had the right to kill his children.

Several research studies are aimed at possible causation and prevention. Resnick's classification system includes five basic categories of infanticide and filicide. Twice as many mothers, compared to fathers, killed their infants. Mothers who kill their children are generally 16–38 years of age. Less than 20% of them are married, and the majority are not seen as being psychotic or depressed. Many of these young women are poor and have concealed their pregnancy and then killed and disposed of the infant secretly.

The most common methods used to kill the infants are asphyxial (strangulation, smothering, or suffocation), which leaves little physical evidence on the body and is difficult to prove. Infants are frequently delivered into toilets and allowed to drown. Occasional cases involve significant blunt force injuries to the head. The most dangerous time for a child is during the first 6 months of life. This is the time period when postpartum depression and psychoses may be encountered.

In 1969, Phillip Resnick published a study on children murdered by parents. He reviewed world literature from 1951 to 1967 and found 155 case reports (24 neonaticides were excluded from the study).

According to Resnick, the five basic classifications of apparent motive are

1. Altruistic, involving association with maternal suicide, the need to relieve real or imagined suffering, and twin infanticide
2. Acute psychoses, usually postpartum depression and psychoses, delirium, or hallucinations
3. Unwanted child of either a married or an unmarried mother or involving "secret pregnancies"
4. "Accidental" deaths, which include a violent single outburst, chronic child abuse, and neglect
5. Spouse revenge, also called the Medea complex

Altruistic child murders include those when a parent kills the child as a prelude to committing suicide. Possible explanations are that the mother projects her own identity onto the child or has concerns regarding who will care for the child after the parent is dead. The second type of altruistic filicide is committed to put the child out of imagined or real suffering such as chronic, debilitating illness. Twin infanticide occurs when a parent is unable to provide adequately for both twins and feels compelled to sacrifice one twin.

Resnick's second classification describes the parent under the influence of hallucinations, delirium, or postpartum depression. Emotional responses range from the "baby blues" that nearly all new mothers experience to deeper depressions and finally to massive psychotic reactions. The mother's relationship with the child is affected and can result in death of the child.

Unwanted child filicides are those that occur when the child is not wanted or was not planned. Unmarried teenage mothers frequently hide their pregnancies and will occasionally kill the child at birth, delivering the child alone in secrecy and disposing of the body as though the pregnancy never happened. Married women may kill a child that is illegitimate or was unplanned and presents a financial burden for the family.

"Accidental" filicides are not accidents but are unplanned, unintentional deaths of children during violent outbursts. They are accidental in that homicidal intent is absent. The mother may not have an active role in the abuse; she may merely stand by and watch her husband or boyfriend abuse the child. At other times, the mother is the one who has been abusing the child and causes the death. Deaths due to maternal neglect also fit into this category. Many cases of neglect are the result of poverty, ignorance, and chemical dependency. Munchausen syndrome by proxy is the unintentional death of a child that results from the actions of the mother inducing illness or reporting symptoms of disease, which she has caused in order to get sympathy. One common practice is to smother the child until the child stops breathing and loses consciousness. Sometimes there is a miscalculation, and the child dies.

Resnick's last category includes children who are killed by one parent in an attempt to punish the spouse. This is the classic Medea complex named after Medea, Jason's wife, who killed his sons to punish him for his infidelity.

Bibliography

Centers for Disease Control and Statistics. 2013. *Child Maltreatment: Facts at a Glance.* Atlanta, GA: National Center for Injury Prevention and Control, Division of Violence Prevention.

DiMaio, V. J. M. and Molina, D. K. (2021). *DiMaio's Forensic Pathology* (3rd ed.). Boca Raton, FL: CRC Press.

Dolinak, D., Matshes, E., and Lew, E. 2006. *Forensic Pathology: Principles and Practice.* Burlington, MA: Elsevier.

Dudley, M. H., Zumwalt, R. E. et al. 1993. Skull fractures under the age of 2 years: Accident vs. child abuse. Abstract presentation at *AAFS National Meeting 1993*, Boston, MA.

Leeb RT, et al. 2008. *Child Maltreatment Surveillance: Uniform Definitions for Public Health and Recommended Data Elements, Version 1.0.* CDC

Resnick, P. 1969. Child Murder by Parents: A psychiatric review of filicide. *American Journal of Psychiatry*, 126 (3) 325–334

United States Department of Justice. 2001. *Burn Injuries in Child Abuse: Portable Guides to Investigating Child Abuse.* Washington, DC: United States Department of Justice.

Zumwalt, R. E. and Hirsch, C. S. 1980. Subtle fatal child abuse. *Hum Pathol* 11:167–174.

Sudden Unexpected Infant Deaths

24

MARY H. DUDLEY AND LAUREN E. DVORSCAK

OBJECTIVES

Upon completion of this chapter and corresponding reference material, the reader will be able to

- Define sudden unexpected infant death (SUID)
- Discuss the components of a thorough SUID investigation
- Describe the reasons for the change in terminology by medical examiners from sudden infant death syndrome
- List the risk factors for unsafe sleep conditions
- Identify the preventative aspects for parent education to reduce unsafe sleep conditions

Introduction

The classification "sudden infant death syndrome" (SIDS) was created from a National Institutes of Health consensus committee who recognized that some infant deaths shared similar features and were otherwise unexplained. The SIDS classification is assigned to infant deaths that cannot be explained after a thorough investigation, autopsy, and review of the clinical history (Willinger et al., 1991). The term was originally intended to place sudden unexpected deaths of infants into a category of exclusion to facilitate case tracking and research. In practical use, the classification became a diagnosis and implied that SIDS was due to underlying natural disease processes. However, as scene investigation improved, forensic pathologists have realized that this is a far more heterogeneous group of infants, consisting of cases of undiagnosed natural diseases, accidental suffocations associated with unsafe sleep environments, and even covert homicides. This chapters includes historical perspectives, reclassification of infant deaths, role of the medicolegal death investigator, sudden unexpected infant death investigation (SUIDI), and infant sleep environment.

DOI: 10.4324/9781003538622-28

Historical Perspective

The incidence of SIDS experienced a major decline following the 1992 American Academy of Pediatrics recommendation (back-to-sleep campaign) that infants be placed for sleep in a non-prone position (Kattwinkel, 1992). This was followed by a plateau until the introduction of the SUID classification, after which deaths attributed to SIDS appeared to decline again. However, this recent decline is most likely attributable to a diagnostic shift away from terminology like SIDS in the field of forensic pathology and may not accurately represent a continued decline in infant mortality (Senter et al., 2011).

The National Association of Medical Examiners attempted to update the original SIDS classification and recommended the term "sudden unexpected infant death" or SUID. The 2006 SUID cause of death classification is used to describe any sudden and unexpected infant death, including deaths previously classified as SIDS. SUIDs can be attributed to a variety of different causes, such as suffocation, asphyxia, or entrapment, associated with the infant sleep environment. Thus, medical examiner/coroner practices of certifying SUIDs have shifted significantly over time, which may account for a large proportion of the decline in deaths certified as SIDS (Dvorscak et al., 2015).

Sleep Environment

Infant death due to an unsafe sleep environment is postulated to be due to unsafe sleep surface, overlay, positional asphyxia, hyperthermia, suffocation, and/or wedging/entrapment. These conditions may occur when the infant is sleeping on the same surface with another person. Although unsafe sleep environments are recognized as a contributing factor to infant deaths, it is apparent that further clarification is needed in order to avoid preventable infant mortality.

A retrospective review of infant deaths over a 12-year period at a large medical examiner's office found that more than 80% of infant deaths due to asphyxia/overlay were associated with an infant sleeping on the same surface with another individual (Dudley et al., 2011). In the same study, bed-sharing in a bed was documented more than twice as often as sleeping on a couch or chair. Of infants who died while sharing a sleeping surface, one-third had been sleeping with their mothers (Dudley et al., 2011).

Research indicates the frequency of bed-sharing for infants ranges from 14% to 24% of the time; thus, children do sleep alone more often than bed-sharing (Ruys et al., 2007). This suggests that the risk of infant death is three to seven times greater while bed-sharing. Data also found that infant mortality during bed-sharing at 1 month of age was nine times greater than those infants sleeping alone (Ruys et al., 2007).

Theories

There are several theories as to risk factors and cause of unexpected infant deaths during sleep. Early studies suggest a triple risk model associated with SIDS, which included vulnerability of the infant, exogenous stressors, and a critical development period (Trachtenberg et al., 2012). These same risk factors may help explain the increased risks associated with infant deaths in an unsafe sleep environment. The vulnerable infant less than 6 months of age may be more subject to environmental stressors of heat or hypoxic conditions, both of which may be present during co-sleeping, bed-sharing, positional asphyxia, prone sleeping position, or wedging and entrapment. The highly vulnerable infant, such as the low-birth-weight or premature infant, may be more susceptible to environmental stressors in the sleeping environment.

Unsafe sleep conditions may lead to asphyxia and hypoxia and may cause overheating and hypothermia. One study found that 90% of SIDS cases were exposed to one or more exogenous stressors near the time of death. Expression of heat shock protein was also found as a biomarker for overheating in the overwhelming majority of SIDS cases. Minor inflammation in the respiratory tract in 60% of SUID cases was also notable (Berry, 1989). If the infants had a fever associated with infection, they are more at risk in a hot environment due to immature cooling mechanisms.

Asphyxia, prone sleeping, and hyperthermia all play a role in infant death related to unsafe sleep environments. The underlying mechanism is likely multifactorial, similar to heart disease in adults, but may also be related to additional unknown intrinsic risk factors. However, awareness of the external, preventable risk factors may be significant in reducing the number of infant deaths related to unsafe sleep environments. Ruling an infant death as positional asphyxia or suffocation based on scene investigation and autopsy findings with an accidental manner is often a more accurate classification.

Role of the Medicolegal Death Investigator

Forensic death investigators play an important role in the evaluation of SUIDs by conducting death scene investigations, interviews to obtain vital information, and doll re-enactments to assist the medical examiner in determining the cause and manner of death. The role of the medicolegal death investigator in infant deaths, as in all deaths, is to fully document the scene, without speculation or bias. Descriptions of the scene and thorough documentation of facts, rather than interpretations of observations, are the essential role of the medicolegal death investigator at the infant death scene.

At the scene, death investigators must work closely with law enforcement to secure access to independently interview witnesses and investigate the primary death scene, especially if the infant has been transported to the hospital for resuscitation efforts. In such cases, death investigators should ask law enforcement to keep the scene of the incident secured, or request access to the primary scene as soon as possible to prevent alteration of the scene and preserve any possible evidence.

The Centers for Disease Control and Prevention (CDC) has published a valuable tool (SUIDI reporting form or SUIDIRF) for investigating infant death scenes (all infants under 1 year of age), which was most recently updated in 2024. The SUIDIRF collects critical information on the demographics of the infant, the infant's medical history (including any prenatal or neonatal diagnoses), caregiver/witness accounts, sleep environment, scene documentation before movement, a reconstruction of the scene, details of a doll re-enactment with the caregiver/witness, and description of the infant. To standardize and fully document infant death scenes, this form is highly recommended as a way to accurately and routinely obtain data necessary for medicolegal death investigators to certify infant deaths as accurately as possible. The SUIDIRF also serves to guide investigators through the steps involved in an investigation and allows for clear, consistent documentation. Ultimately, the SUIDIRF may also serve a purpose to recognize risk factors for SUID and aid in prevention of these deaths.

The SUIDIRF is voluntary and may not apply to all infant deaths under the medical examiner/coroner jurisdiction. In cases where the circumstances of death are clear (e.g. obvious injuries as a passenger in a motor vehicle collision), the form is not necessary. However, in the vast majority of infant deaths, the SUIDIRF is an extremely useful tool and is recommended to guide the investigation and ensure that essential information is not forgotten.

Regardless of the use of the SUIDIRF, a doll re-enactment is a critical element of SUID death scene investigations in infants where the death is otherwise unexpected or unexplained. A doll re-enactment is a visual representation of how the decedent's body was placed prior to death, and how they were found, and can often more accurately relay positioning of the body than words can, especially when the infant has been previously moved (e.g. for resuscitation attempts) (Figures 24.1a and 24.1b). In a doll re-enactment, a doll represents the infant, rather than re-introducing the decedent's body into a scene. The doll should have movable head, arms, and legs, and clearly be marked what is the front or back.

In performing a doll re-enactment, the caregiver/witnesses who placed and found the decedent should be present and informed as to what steps will be taken in the re-enactment.

General recommended steps in the re-enactment process are outlined below and referenced from the CDC's training manual titled *Sudden Unexplained Infant Death Investigation: A Systematic Training Program for the Professional Infant Death Investigation Specialist.*

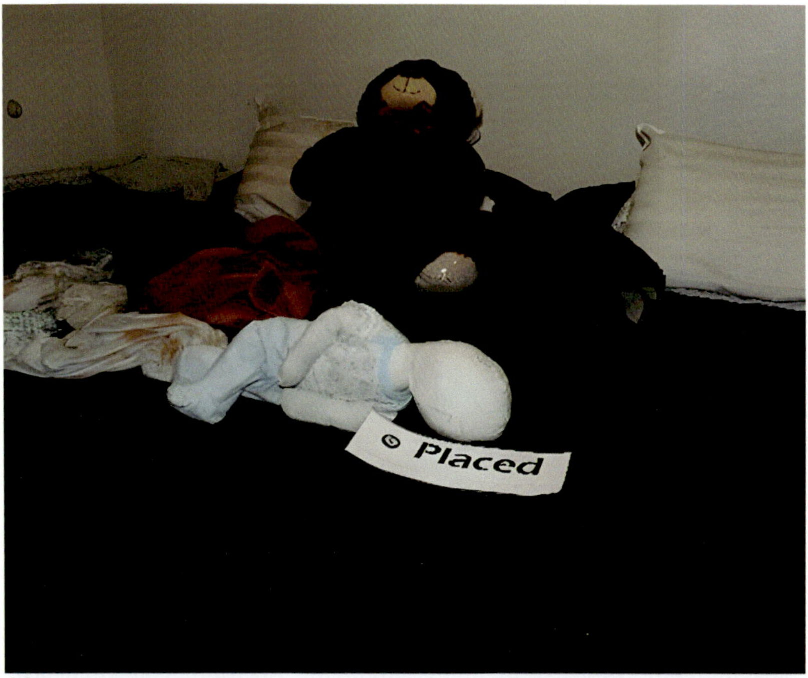

(a)

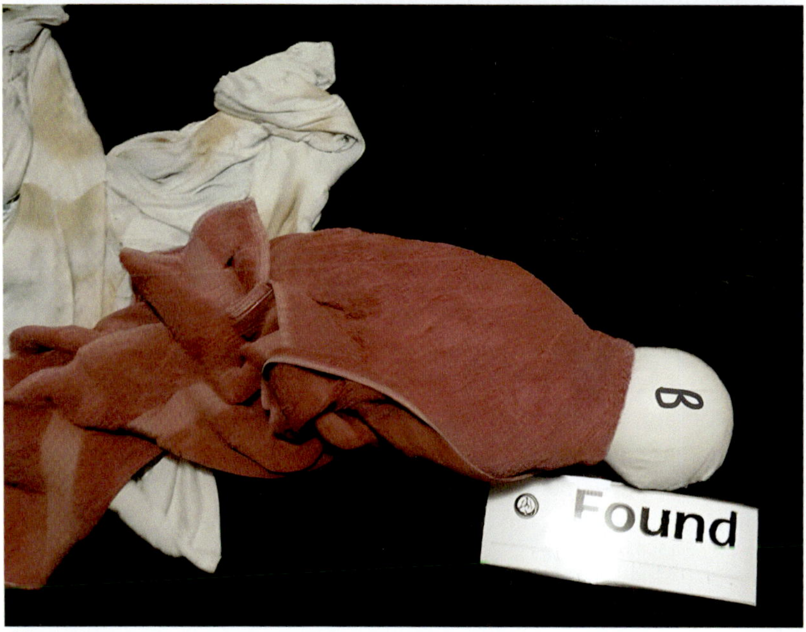

(b)

Figure 24.1 Placed and found photographs of a doll re-enactment.

1. Verify and document the information of the participating witness/caregiver, including relationship to the infant.
2. Review the goal of the re-enactment with the caregiver and/or witness, explain the process of re-enactment, and show them the prop (doll) used in the re-enactment. Reiterate the need for photographic documentation for the pathologist to ultimately determine the cause and manner of death.

   The goal is to provide a thorough and complete investigation, accurately depicting the exact environment where the infant was placed and found. Explain the importance of photography in clearly depicting the events to the pathologist, who will ultimately determine the cause and manner of death.
3. Answer any questions about the process.
4. Based on the description given by the participant about how the infant was placed when last alive, instruct the participant(s) to position the doll the exact same way, noting details such as face up versus down position, placement of arms/legs, positioning of bedding or other materials, based on the participant's best recollection of events. If the decedent was bed-sharing the same sleeping surface with other individuals, those individuals should be positioned as they were when the decedent was placed to sleep.
5. Use a placard or other marker to distinguish that the photograph will be as the decedent was placed.
6. Photograph the scene as it was when the decedent was last seen alive, using the doll as a prop in place of the decedent.
7. Based on the description given by the participant about how the infant was found deceased, instruct the participant (s) to position the doll in the exact same way, again paying attention to details about placement of the body (e.g. face up or down), any bedding, or any additional individuals present in close proximity.
8. Use a placard or other marker to distinguish that the photograph will be as the decedent was found.
9. Photograph the scene as it was when the decedent was found, using the doll as a prop in place of the decedent.
10. Thank the participant(s) for their cooperation and assistance, debrief them on next steps, and answer any remaining questions.

Autopsy Findings

Autopsy findings described in SIDS deaths as incidental observations may be physiological findings of hypoxia or stress. Tissue markers of hypoxia have been described to include extramedullary hematopoiesis in the liver and brain stem gliosis. Autopsy findings of persistence of fetal hemoglobin and raised hypoxanthine values in postmortem vitreous samples may indicate perimortem hypoxia (Berry, 1989). Neuropathology findings of delayed myelination and maturation of dendrite spines may explain a link between antemortem factors such as smoking and SUID (Berry, 1989). Also of interest are the findings of petechial hemorrhage in many of these infant deaths. One study concluded that a significant increase in thoracic petechiae in SUID and extension below the diaphragm were associated with hypoxemia and other conditions (Goldwater, 2011).

Conclusion

The cause of sudden unexpected infant deaths and exclusion of natural disease is revealed during a complete forensic autopsy, including review of medical history, cultures, imaging studies, toxicology, metabolic studies, and histological findings. The manner of death is based upon the circumstances at the death scene as documented by a thorough scene investigation, doll re-enactment, and witness interviews. Deaths related to unsafe sleep environments that are ruled as accidents may be preventable.

References and Bibliography

Berry, P. J. 1989. Pathological findings in SIDS. *The Journal of Perinatology* 9:180–183.

Centers for Disease Control and Prevention. 2024. Sudden unexplained infant death investigation: A systematic training program for the profession infant death investigation specialist. https://www.cdc.gov/sudden-infant-death/php/training/index.html

Dudley, M. H. and Hensley, S. T. et al. 2011. Infant death and unsafe sleep environment. Poster presentation at *NAME meeting 2011*, Seattle, WA.

Dvorscak, L., Lathrop, S., and Pinckard, J. K. 2015. Reclassification of sudden infant deaths in New Mexico. Abstract presentation at *AAFS National Meeting 2015*, Orlando, FL.

Goldwater, P. N. 2011. Intrathoracic petechial hemorrhages in sudden infant death syndrome and other infant deaths: Time for re-examination. *Pediatric and Developmental Pathology*, 11:450–455.

Kattwinkel, J. 1992. Positioning and SIDS. *Pediatrics* 89:1120–1126.

Öztürk, T. B., Gökçe, Ş., Tosyalı, M., and Umay Koç, F. 2023. Evaluation of the association between sleeping arrangements and breastfeeding in infants: A cross-sectional, Single Unit Study. *The Journal of Pediatric Research* Sep 14;10(3):195–204. https://doi.org/10.4274/jpr.galenos.2023.98965

Ruys, J. H., de Jonge, G. A., Brand, R., Engelberts, A. C., and Semmekrot, B. A. 2007. Bed-sharing in the first four months of life: A risk factor for sudden infant death. *Acta Paediatrica* 96:1399–1403.

Senter, L., Sackoff, J., Landi, K., and Boyd, L. 2011. Studying sudden and unexpected infant death in a time of changing death certification and investigative practices: Evaluating sleep related risk factors for infant death in New York City. *Maternal and Child Health Journal* 15:242–248.

Shapiro-Mendoza, C. K., Kimball, M., Tomashek, K. M., Anderson, R. N., and Blanding, S. 2009. US infant mortality trends attributable to accidental suffocation and strangulation in bed from 1984 through 2004: Are rates increasing. *Pediatrics* 123:533–539.

Trachtenberg, F. L., Haas, E. A., Kinney, H. C., Stanley, C., and Krous, H. F. 2012. Risk factor changes for sudden infant death syndrome after initiation of back to sleep campaign. *Pediatrics* 129:630–638.

Willinger, M., James, L. S., and Catz, C. 1991. Defining the sudden infant death syndrome (SIDS): Deliberations of an expert panel convened by the National Institute of Child Health and Human Development. *Pediatric Pathology* 11:677–684.

Elder Abuse

25

ROSS E. ZUMWALT

OBJECTIVES

- Understand additional guidelines for investigation of deaths in the elderly
- Identify common mistakes made in the investigation of deaths in the elderly
- Identify unique types of accidental deaths in the elderly
- List characteristics of potential abuse of the elderly
- Describe the potential victims of elder abuse
- Differentiate between signs of abuse and signs of neglect
- List differences between classical fall injuries versus abuse injuries in the elderly

Introduction

The medicolegal investigation of deaths in the elderly poses some unique challenges for the forensic death investigator. If an old person is found dead unexpectedly, a lack of suspicion that the death is something other than from natural causes can lead to an incomplete or insufficient investigation of the circumstances of death or an evaluation of the scene of death. Old people are often frail and vulnerable to die from minor injuries, accidental or inflicted, that would be easily handled by a younger person. This chapter focuses on deaths in the elderly that need particular care in investigation to provide adequate information for proper determination of the cause and manner of death. The chapter also emphasizes the particular characteristics involved in elder abuse deaths and includes a case study.

Geriatric Pathology in Death Investigation

Clearly, it is expected that old people will die, and when they do, it often comes as no surprise. Because the death is not unexpected, it is often concluded that the cause of death is from natural causes. This can be a dangerous

DOI: 10.4324/9781003538622-29

assumption for those involved in medicolegal death investigation. Old people can be injured as well as be ill. In fact, many old people are particularly vulnerable to injury because of their frailty, confusion, or unsteady gait. A minor injury that would be inconsequential to a healthy young adult might be fatal to an old person. Therefore, the investigation into deaths of the elderly requires more care, rather than less, in seeking history of prior injury or environmental exposure of an injurious agent. It may also require more care in the examination of the body for evidence of injury.

Common mistakes made in the investigation of deaths of the elderly are similar to those made in the investigation of decomposed bodies. The examination of the scene may be unpleasant—the elderly may be soiled with urine or feces, and the environment may be dirty and squalid. Consequently, a superficial examination of the scene and the body may be made. The body may be examined in poor light, uncleaned, and partially clothed.

The elderly are not immune to common forms of violent death, such as gunshot wounds and motor vehicle accident trauma, and their injuries correspond to those seen in the younger population. In addition, the elderly are susceptible to fatal injuries not usually seen in the young.

Natural Deaths

A superficial death investigation can lead to the misinterpretation of a nonnatural death as accidental or inflicted; the opposite can also occur. Some natural deaths can have the appearance of an accidental or homicidal death. This is particularly a problem if there is evidence of bleeding or blood stains at the scene.

Natural deaths with terminal bleeding can occur due to upper or lower gastrointestinal hemorrhage, eroded large arteries, or varicose veins, or erosion of cutaneous or pulmonary metastases. Decomposition with postmortem purging can mimic intrathoracic effusion with bleeding. End-stage cardiovascular disease and acute myocardial disease can result in the postmortem escape of various types of pulmonary edema. Finally, a terminal collapse can result in an injury, particularly of the head, that can mimic an assault. Old people are often frail and fall or bruise easily and at death may have numerous contusions, abrasions, and lacerations, both acute and chronic. In these cases, the scene investigation must be accompanied by an investigation of medical history, including medical records, and the circumstances leading to the death or the discovery of the body.

Accidents

Simple falls may trigger fatal complications. A fall from standing height may result in a fractured hip or ribs. The pain and immobility from the injury may aggravate underlying natural disease or provide the setting for pulmonary emboli or bronchopneumonia. When these natural disease complications result in death, the underlying cause of death remains the injury; the manner of death depends on how the injury occurred.

The elderly frequently take prescription medications. There is a great potential for fatal drug reactions and true overdoses among the elderly because of their ages, their frequently altered mental states, and the number and amount of medications often prescribed. The death investigator must be mindful of the need for careful documentation of medications at the death scene, as well as careful review of the medical history and whether or not prescribed medications are listed in an inventory of the deceased's medications.

Hypothermia, hyperthermia, and asphyxia are additional conditions that may result from environmental exposure that can cause death in the elderly. The manner of death in these situations is unnatural and depends on the circumstances of the exposure. Careful scene investigation, including environmental temperature, is important.

Case Report—Accidental Elder Death

An 87-year-old woman was found dead, sitting in her wheelchair at an assisted living center by a nurse's aide and was moved to her bed. Since the physician assigned to the facility was unavailable to make the pronouncement and sign a death certificate, the medical examiner was notified. The medicolegal death investigator responded to the scene and was informed that the woman had a history of congestive heart failure and previous strokes.

The death investigator viewed the body and noticed linear abrasions on the neck (Figure 25.1). She then interviewed the nurse's aide, who relayed that the deceased woman had been restrained in a posey (Figure 25.2) in the wheelchair and had slipped partway out of the chair but had been prevented from falling completely out of the chair by the posey.

The death investigator had the chair brought from another room and documented that the chair was unsafe because the seat was not secure, revealing a broken snap and torn seat (Figure 25.3).

The autopsy the following day confirmed the chronic natural disease of the heart and brain, but also showed injury in the left-sided strap muscles of the neck.

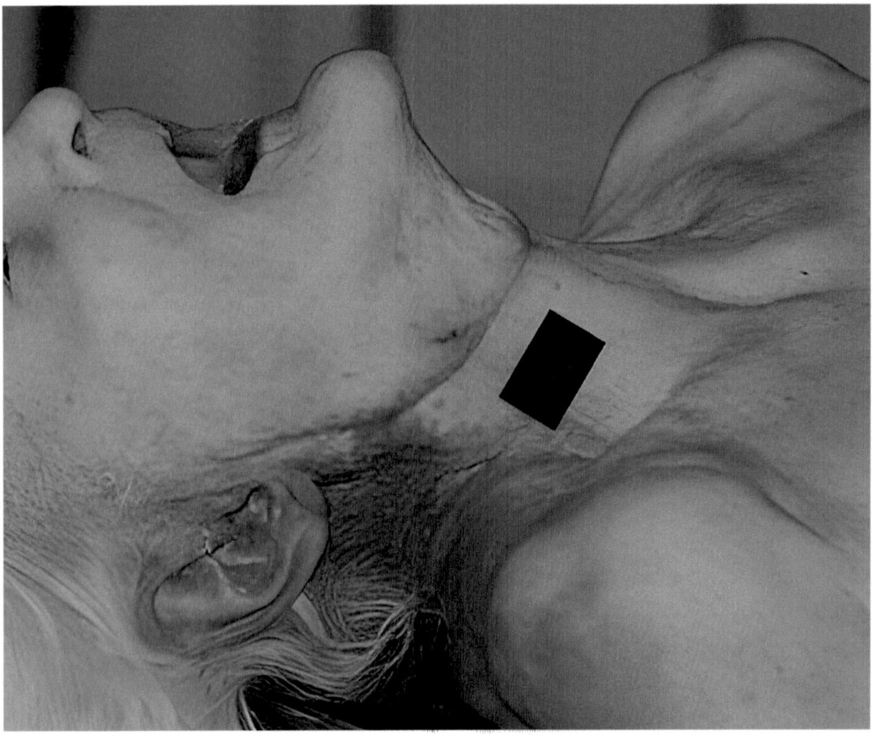

Figure 25.1 Linear marks on neck.

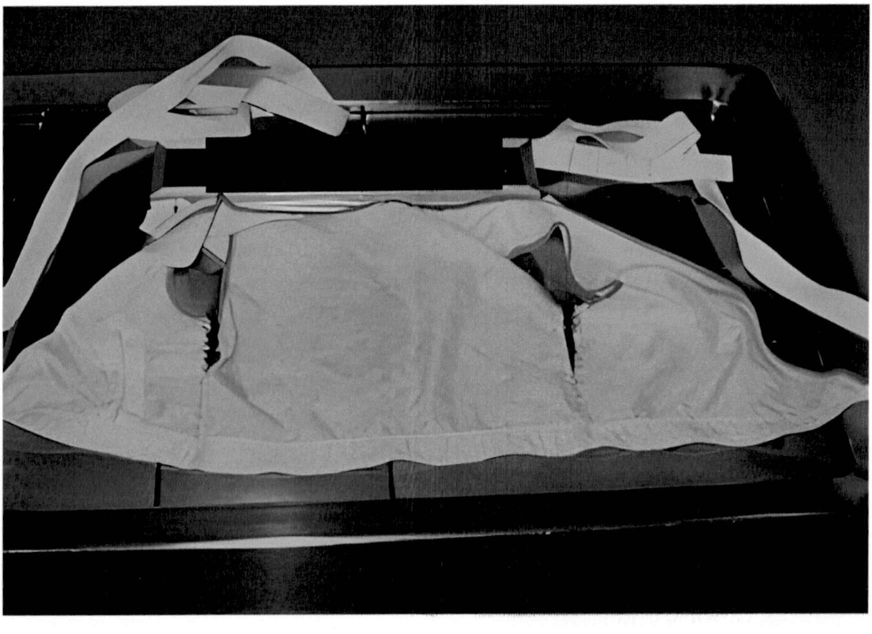

Figure 25.2 Posey.

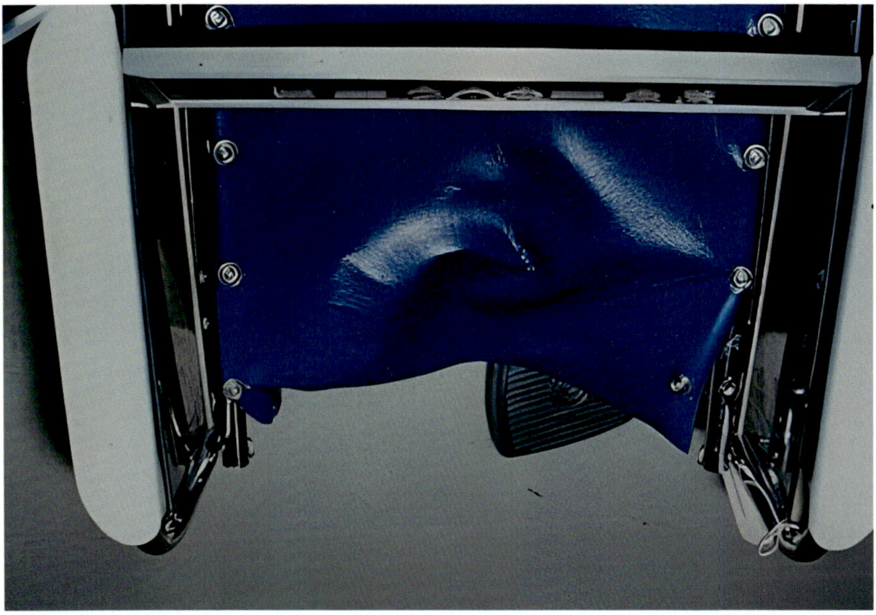

Figure 25.3 Wheelchair with torn seat.

The cause of death was certified as ligature strangulation with generalized arteriolosclerosis as a contributory factor. The manner of death was certified as accidental.

Therapeutic Complications

The elderly are particularly vulnerable to injury and death from therapeutic complications because of their frailty. When death is potentially the result of a therapeutic complication, there is the possibility that the death could be accidental, and the certification of that death is assigned to medical examiners and the medicolegal death investigator.

A death from a therapeutic complication is considered natural if the therapeutic complication was a recognized complication of that particular treatment and not the result of gross mismanagement.

Recognition of cases that are considered a legitimate therapeutic complication may vary from one medicolegal jurisdiction to another or from one forensic pathologist to another.

Therapeutic complications include surgical complications, drug effects, complications of diagnostic tests, radiation effects, blood transfusions, dialysis complications, and anesthesia.

Evaluation of therapeutic complications includes review of medical records, direct conversations with medical and medical support personnel, and often information from the family.

Suicide

Old people can and do commit suicide. A soft ligature around the neck, hanging from a seated position or placing a plastic bag over the head may cause death with few or no marks on the face or neck. If the scene has been altered by relatives, the investigator must be particularly attentive to detail to detect the violent nature of the death. Similarly, accidental asphyxia in the elderly may be hidden by caretakers.

Homicide

There are several categories of murder of elderly persons that are not generally seen in younger adults. Much attention has been directed to serial murders in medical institutions such as hospitals and nursing care facilities. The idea of a health-care worker as an "avenging angel" who poisons or otherwise kills the chronically ill, often moribund patients, is a common profile. The death investigator must take seriously any rumor that such activity is occurring so that deaths at that institution are monitored.

Isolated euthanasia is occasionally suspected but seldom confirmed. Assisted suicide and medical euthanasia are currently widely discussed. In situations where life-support equipment is inexplicably disconnected or too much pain medication is taken, the distinction between accident, suicide, and homicide becomes blurred and depends on an elucidation of the circumstances of death and not the autopsy findings.

Neglect

Elder neglect occurs when a person who has responsibility for the elder fails to fulfill that responsibility. This failure can be intentional or unintentional. Neglect can be seen in dehydration, malnutrition, lack of appropriate clothing, poor hygiene, inadequate or inappropriate care for medical conditions, unattended decubitus ulcer, injuries that have not been treated, or lack of access to support.

Elder Abuse

Elder abuse is a social problem with many similarities to child abuse and spouse abuse. These forms of family or domestic violence are common and involve all cultures and economic levels. Public awareness of child abuse began in the 1960s. Studies of spouse abuse followed in the late 1970s. By the end of the 1990s, a great deal of attention focused on elder abuse. Elder abuse may take the form of physical abuse, sexual abuse, psychological abuse, neglect, and material abuse.

Physical abuse is the willful physical assault on an old person and may take the form of beating, slapping, shoving, or forcible restraint by tying. Psychological, emotional, or mental abuse is often represented by repeated insults or threats. Other forms of psychological abuse include confinement to small spaces, isolation from human contact, or humiliation.

Incidence

The National Center on Elder Abuse reported that 7%–10% of adults suffer from some form of abuse (2015). Elder abuse is more difficult to identify than child abuse because of lack of professional and public awareness, relative isolation of the victims, and reluctance of the elderly to report abuse. One study estimated that only 1 in 14 cases of elder abuse comes to the attention of authorities (National Research Council, 2003).

The reasons for elder abuse are complex and rooted in the intricate interactions within families and cultures. Maladaptive families can resort to abuse during times of stress. Alcoholism, substance abuse, mental illness, mental retardation, and a history of violent intrafamily behavior can trigger overt abuse.

Characteristics of Victims

No group of the elderly is immune to the possibility of abusive behavior. However, several characteristics of abuse victims include biological sex, impairment, provocative behavior, past abuse, substance abuse, social isolation, and financial dependence. More older women than men are victims of abuse, and women are less likely to resist abusive behavior. Many studies report that abuse correlates with the extent and severity of physical or mental impairment. This produces greater demands and responsibilities for the caregiver, which can result in stress and frustration. Individuals who are overly demeaning, ungrateful, or otherwise unpleasant can aggravate already stressed and overburdened caregivers.

Older persons who have been abused in the past are candidates for further abuse when they display increasing impairments and dependency. As with child abuse, the parent who abuses his own child teaches the child a behavior pattern and may be abused by that adult child. An older person who is a problem drinker or drug abuser is susceptible to abusive behavior due to an inability to care for or tend to himself, particularly if he lives with an alcoholic caregiver. The elderly person who depends on his caregiver for all social interaction is more vulnerable to abuse. Economic dependency can result in hostility by a caregiver.

Characteristics of Abusers

The following characteristics, singly or in combination, are used to identify caretakers at risk for abusing the elderly, including alcohol/drug use, as well as history of physical or mental illness. Other factors include caregiving inexperience, financial issues, personality disorders, social isolation, and/or history of being abused as a child. For instance, a problem drinker may act out in hostility under the influence of alcohol. An individual with drug use may not only overtly abuse an elderly person but may also be unaware of the consequences of poor care. Some caregivers are themselves physically or psychologically impaired and cannot provide needed care. A caregiver with mental illness may be unable to care for a frail, older person.

It cannot be assumed that all individuals know how to care for an elderly person. Such persons can be ineffective or hostile in their roles as caretakers. If a caretaker views the older person as a financial drain on limited resources, he may develop hostility and become an abuser. In some cases, the abuse may result from resentment from being economically dependent upon the older person. Further, adult children who were abused as children are more likely to abuse the elderly through learned behavior or unconscious hostility. A caretaker unengaged outside of the home may not have family or friends from whom he can receive emotional support. Lastly, individuals with personality problems such as lack of understanding, lack of sympathy, and being hypercritical and chronic blamers often have unrealistic expectations about their roles in caregiving.

Fatal Elder Abuse

Fatal elder abuse occurs when death follows complications of injury or neglect received from caretakers. This definition excludes premeditated murder of competent independent elderly persons because of rage or for financial gain.

Investigation of possible fatal elder abuse requires a detailed account of the circumstances of the death and a thorough medical and psychosocial history. History of the circumstances of the death should be elicited from as many informants as possible—caregiver, other family members, neighbors, emergency medical systems, police, and others. If different histories are given, documentation of what is said by each informant is important.

In discussing the case with caretakers, ask them to describe a typical day for the deceased. Ask for a history of any injuries. Listen for clues that the caretaker feels overwhelmed, particularly when the patient cannot perform such tasks as toileting, bathing, or feeding himself. Be on the lookout for inconsistencies in the explanations. Specific questions to ask about the deceased include the following:

- Was he or she intellectually or severely mentally impaired?
- Does he or she need help bathing, dressing, or eating?
- Was he or she incontinent or needed help toileting?
- Does he or she depend on the caretaker for all social interactions?
- Does he or she have friends or social interactions outside the home?
- Was he or she demanding or authoritative to the caretaker?

Scene Investigation

At the scene, apply the appropriate death scene investigation techniques described in Chapter 3. The role of the medicolegal death investigator in elder deaths, as in all deaths, is to fully document the scene without speculation or bias. If the body has been transferred to a hospital for resuscitation attempts or for pronouncement of death, and there is any concern over establishing the cause or manner of death, an attempt to go to the home or the scene of death should be made. Are there characteristics of the living environment that restrict movement or freedom or accessibility to outside support? What is the condition of the home? Is it dirty, is it adequately heated, is there sufficient food and medicine available?

If the death occurs in a nursing home, learn as much information of the circumstances from the first responders, the person or persons who first found the elderly person dead, the roommates, the nurses, or the paramedics called to the scene. The original version of events as documented when first occurred are of utmost importance (e.g. incident report).

Physical Signs of Abuse and Neglect

Signs of abuse might be seen in head injuries, absence of hair, hemorrhage below the scalp, broken teeth, or eye injuries. Unexplained bruises about the face, lips, mouth, back, or buttocks, and bruises that are in various stages of healing, clustered, or form patterns are all causes for suspicion. Unexplained burns that look like cigar or cigarette burns, immersion burns, or friction burns from restraints should be investigated.

Neglect can be seen in dehydration, malnutrition, inappropriate or soiled clothing, poor hygiene, inappropriate care, decubiti, or injuries that have not been treated.

Conclusion

As average life spans increase, there will be a large number of elderly deaths requiring professional medicolegal death investigation. These investigations will be integral in correct determination of cause and manner of death. In particular, they will be crucial in distinguishing natural from unnatural causes of death, especially in cases suspicious for elder abuse or neglect.

Bibliography

Collins, K. A. 2006. Elder maltreatment: A review. *Archives of Pathology & Laboratory Medicine* 130:1290–1296.

National Center on Elder Abuse Administration on Aging. 2015. Statistics/data: elder abuse: The size of the problem. Website accessed December 2015, at https://www.ncea.aoa.gov/library/data/index.aspx. Washington, DC: Department of Health and Human Services.

National Institute of Justice. (2024). Death Investigation: A Guide for the Scene Investigator. https://nij.ojp.gov/library/publications/death-investigation-guide-scene-investigator-2024

National Research Council. 2003. *Elder Mistreatment: Abuse, Neglect, and Exploitation in Aging America*. Washington, DC: The National Academics Press.

Patel, K., Bansalathi, S., Chin, H., Suresh, P., Patel, U.K. 2021. Elder Abuse: A comprehensive overview and physician-associated challenges. *Cures*. https://doi.org/10.7759/cureus.14325

Rosen, T. et al. 2020. Identifying injury patterns associated with physical elder abuse: Analysis of legally adjudicated cases. *Annals of Emergency Medicine*. 76(3):266–276.

Appendices

Appendix A
Report Writing

LAURAMAE WILLIAMS

Introduction

Every medicolegal system has their own reporting format for the medicolegal death investigator to follow. Whether your office uses a checklist or narrative format, or a combination of both, it is essential that you gather accurate and detailed information and complete and submit a thorough and organize report so that the forensic pathologist/coroner can use the information to assist them in determining cause and manner of death.

Scene Interviews

After arriving on scene meet with the law enforcement agency in charge or the medical professional at the medical facility for a briefing on the events that led to the decedent's death. As appropriate also interview witnesses and/or family members for additional information regarding the decedent's health status or complaints prior to death. Confirm with the family the decedent's demographic and next of kin information. Photograph the scene thoroughly, taking notice of items such as tobacco products, including electronic devices, drug paraphernalia, alcohol, medications, medical equipment, or signs of violence. These may generate additional follow-up questions to ask the family as well as suggest possible related causes. When interviewing the family and witnesses, be sure to use terms they understand and avoid using technical and medical language so that you don't intimidate them. They will be more willing to cooperate and provide information if they feel comfortable speaking with you. Of course, you can use medical terminology in your narrative as it pertains to the decedent but be sure to use the terms correctly. Only use abbreviations that your agency has approved (e.g., *A-Fib, HLD*). Ask clear, open-ended questions; listen to the answers given; and ask for clarification when needed. A good way to clarify is to summarize back to the informant what they have stated. Interviewing law enforcement, witnesses, and family along with your scene investigation will provide you with the information needed to determine the circumstances that contributed to or caused the death. Document when the person was last known alive, any procedures administered after the discovery of the body, and other information as to what happened. All of this information will be written into your narrative.

Documentation

Document completely and accurately the information obtained through your interviews. When documenting the information provided, be sure to do so accurately, factually, and unbiased. Your biases and opinions are not necessary in your report. The narrative should answer the five Ws; Who, What, Why, Where, When, and How questions. This is a professional document and should always be written in full paragraphs.

Use your scene notes to write a comprehensive, well-written, and structured report. Your documentation will provide the pathologist information to assist them in determining the cause and manner of death. Your scene notes are usually quickly written and out of order as you conduct your interviews, but they will be helpful in writing your narrative. Try asking questions in the same manner on each scene so that there is continuity and ease when writing your narrative components. Abbreviations are ok here as long as you know what they mean. You'll want to write the word out in the narrative, so it is clearly understood by everyone who might review your report. If your agency has an approved list of medical abbreviations, then it would be permissible to include them in your report after initially identifying them. Remember that your report may be seen by other agencies at a later date, so write in a manner that is organized, factual, and objective. A well-written report will clearly paint a picture of the information the scene, witnesses, and the decedent provided, as well as be a useful resource for you should you be called to testify.

Photography and documentation are very intertwined. Now that digital photography is used to record the decedent and scene, use the photos to assist you with your documentation. Your photos, scene notes, and the preliminary report of death should all support each other. Photograph what you need to write and write what you have photographed. Develop a report template to (1) shorten the time it takes to write your report and (2) maintain format consistency. This template is not a static document, and you will need to revise it from time to time, but the format should basically remain the same. Knowing what information is in your template will remind you of what you need to do on scene. You will need to photograph and visualize the scene surroundings. Do a 360-degree view. Take note of the items on and around the decedent's body, ask how the person was originally found, and by whom. The person is often moved for assessment and resuscitation purposes, but you need to consider the possibility of a staged scene. If anything was added, changed, moved, or removed from the decedent prior to your arrival, document that as well. Occasionally nurses or emergency medical services (EMS) personnel will remove medical devices prior to your arrival so that families can be with their loved ones. Of course, it is better that everything remains in place until you can take photos, but when it occurs, document that it was done. For example, if it isn't known that an airway tube, automatic chest compression device, or IV/IO had been used and were removed, it may be difficult for the pathologist to determine whether airway injuries and rib fractures were a result of trauma or resuscitation efforts or the origin of recent puncture marks. Another example is when a decedent is trapped in a vehicle following a motor vehicle crash or trapped under debris from a fire. Photographing from multiple perspectives and documenting the original location and position will be helpful for the pathologist. Also, if it is safe to do so, take pictures during the extrication process, occasionally asking the extrication team to stop so that you can take close-up photos. All of this will make your written report more detailed and complete.

Document the presence of odors such as chemicals, tobacco, decomposition, etc. Is there evidence of insect activity or animal predations? Was clothing cut by EMS or are there defects in the clothing consistent with the type of incident? (e.g., *gunpowder residue, soot, stippling, or hole defect?)* If law enforcement has removed the weapon or it has been found in another location, ask if you can take photos. Make sure to document the make, model, and serial number and look for any biological tissue present on the weapon. Document who owns it, where it was kept, was it kept loaded or unloaded, where were the bullets kept? Did the shooter have experience with this weapon? If it was a sharp-force injury, if it is available, photograph and document it. Describe the length and width of the blade, the handle, and the entire weapon. Is it intact or might there be a fragment embedded on or inside of the decedent? You will need to describe injuries and marks on the body in a factual manner. (e.g., *"Healing 10-inch vertical scar on the left lateral thigh that is consistent with the decedent's recent hip repair."*) Remember to describe and not diagnose.

Occasionally a death that was originally reported and investigated to be a suicide may later be investigated as a homicide. The thoroughness of your report and photographs may turn out to be especially useful to support the (now) homicide investigation and with changing the manner of death.

Your office may use a supplemental form or have a place to add case notes so that you can add additional information received after you've submitted your report. Be sure to notify the pathologist so that he/she is aware and can review the latest information.

Review your report for spelling, grammar, and punctuation errors and make corrections as needed. Take advantage of AI, spell check, and the editing options that are included in the document program you use.

Submit your report, photos, and any other documentation in a timely manner. Your agency most likely has a set time to have them in by, for example, within 3 days from the date of death.

Lastly, as previously stated, many agencies may see your report and should the case go to court whether criminal or civil, it will reflect your professionalism. Write all reports as if they will be used in court (See Appendix E—Witness Court Testimony).

Appendix B
Preliminary Report of Death

LAURAMAE WILLIAMS

Most medical examiner/coroner's offices use a preliminary report of death form (PROD) that is to be used when you respond to a scene. The form is useful in many ways. First, it can quickly and easily be filled out on scene. Second, the information boxes remind you to ask the decedent's demographics, basic reporting information, who identified the decedent and how, next of kin information, and allows you to write a brief summary of the field circumstances, medical history, scene and decedent. Third, the notes you jot down on the form can then be used to write your narrative report that you will submit and the pathologist will review to assist him/her in determining cause and manner of death. A copy of the form used by the New Mexico Office of the Medical Investigator is included in this appendix for review (Figures B.1a and b).

Once a case number has been assigned, document it on the form. Additional information in the *Demographic* section includes the Social Security number, passport or driver's license number, whether the decedent was a veteran, and the branch of the military they served in, and if applicable, the Tribal affiliation. In the *Reporting Information* section make sure to document the name and agency of the person (usually a dispatcher) who contacted you. The name of the officer and/or detective handling the case, their agency, contact information, and their case number is information that will be useful if your office needs to request the law enforcement case report and/or any of their scene photos. Because you may not have been the person who pronounced the decedent, document the name and agency of the person who made pronouncement and the time of death. Law enforcement may provide you with the next of kin (NOK) information but always confirm the information with family or neighbors on scene or when you speak to family at a later time. Remember that the power of attorney may not and oftentimes is not the legal NOK.

As you interview law enforcement, family, neighbors, and witnesses as to the timeline of events prior to being found deceased, put your notes in the *Field Circumstances* section. Try to write your notes in the order from last known alive to the time discovered. That is easier said than done, because as information is coming in, it is often provided in a disorganized fashion. Plus, each person you interview may give the information in a slightly different

PRELIMINARY REPORT OF DEATH

OMI Office of the Medical Investigator New Mexico

Date: ______ OMI Case#: ______ Case Type: ______ EXPECTED | DCD | BRAIN DEATH

Central Office Investigator: ______ Field Deputy Investigator: ______

Demographics

Name (*Last, First, Middle*): ______ / ______ / ______ Date of Birth: ______ Time: ______
Residential Address: ______ SSN: ______
City: ______ State: ______ Zip Code: ______ Passport/OLN: ______
Age: ___ Sex: ______ Race: ______ Hispanic Flag: Veteran: VA Contacted:
Tribal Affiliation: ______ Full Sew: Military Branch: ______

Reporting Info

Reported Date: ______ Reporting Agency : ______
Reported Time: ______ Reported By: ______
Primary Outside Investigator: ______ Contact Information: ______
Primary Investigating Agency: ______ Investigating Agency Case Number: ______

Identification

Identified By: ______
Relation: ______
Method: ______
Identification Date: ______ Time: ______

Pronouncement

Pronounced By: ______
Agency: ______
Pronouncement Date: ______ Time: ______
Address: ______
City: ______ State: ______ Zip Code: ______

Next of Kin

Name: ______ Relation: ______
Address: ______ Telephone: ______
Notified: Date Notified: ______ Method: ______
Additional Relative/Friend Contact Information:
______ Telephone: ______

Field Circumstances

Past Medical / Social History

MRN: ______ Hospital Name: ______ AMs: MRs:

Transportation

Scene Transporter: ______ Funeral Home: ______ Body Bag Seal#: ______
Long Distance Transporter: ______ Notified Date: ______ Time: ______ Method: ______
Comments: ______

Signature

Field Deputy / Central Office Investigator Signature | Deputy Number Date

WORKSHEET

Figure B.1a and b The New Mexico office of the medical investigator preliminary report of death form.

timeframe. It is best to transcribe your scene notes as soon as possible into an organized narrative while the information you were given is fresh in your mind.

Getting a medical and social history is important and may provide clues as to the cause and manner of death (COD/MOD). If the decedent has recently been hospitalized, make sure to document the facility name and the medical

PRELIMINARY REPORT OF DEATH

OFFICE OF THE MEDICAL INVESTIGATOR OMI New Mexico

Consult Agency: ____________ **FBI | BIA | NPD | FAMILY** Representative Requesting Consult: ____________
Jurisdiction Transferred to Agency: ____________ Jurisdiction Transferred Date: ____________
Jurisdiction Transferred to Contact: ____________ Contact Number: ____________

Report / Injury

Removed from scene: Injury:
Injury Date: Injury Date Estimated: Injury Date Unknown:
Injury Time: ____________ Injury Time Estimated: Injury Time Unknown: No
Location Injury Occurred: ____________
Investigator at Scene: Scene Secured:
Drug Use Suspected: If so, type: ____________
Alcohol Use Suspected: Tobacco Use Suspected:
If female, pregnant: If yes, how many weeks: ____________
Prenatal Care: If yes, where and how long: ____________
SUIDI Form Complete:
Doll Re-enactment:

Scene Description

Decedent Description

Clothing / Valuables

Comments

Initials: ________

WORKSHEET

Figure B.1a and b (Continued)

record number. Both make it easier for the Records Department to request records when necessary. For chain of custody purposes, you will need to document the funeral home, scene, or long-distance transport agency. Making note of the body bag seal number is also important in maintaining chain of custody. To assist the pathologist in determining COD & MOD it is important to ask and document positive findings as well as pertinent negatives when interviewing witnesses and family. Ask about any recent falls resulting in trauma and whether the decedent was seen by a healthcare provider. Follow-up as necessary to include what injury was found, how it was treated, and whether the decedent was improving. Case-dependent additional questions may need to be asked. Asked whether the decedent had a history of alcohol, illicit substances, electronic cigarettes, or tobacco use. Even if they were no longer using any of these, it may still provide a clue as to underlying health status. For females ask if they were pregnant prior to death, the gestational length, whether they delivered early, on-time, or late, and if they had received pre-natal care. Follow-up as needed, for example: "*When did she begin pre-natal care, and did she have regular visits?*" Of course, you'll want to ask about any pregnancy-related health concerns.

If the decedent was an infant (less than 1 year of age) and your office uses the CDC Sudden Unexplained Infant Death Investigative Form (SUIDIRF), have that available so that you can interview the parents and caregivers. It is a lengthy document, but it is well worth the time you put in to gather the information. A fillable SUIDIRF form can be found on the CDC website at: https://www.cdc.gov/sudden-infant-death/media/pdfs/2024/04/SUID-Investigation_Fillable_2021-printer-friendly_508_1.pdf

The *Scene Description* section is where you will jot down notes about the scene. Remember to document important aspects of the scene but also things that aren't seen. As an example, writing down that no suicide notes, text messages, or social media posts were located on a suicide scene. When describing the decedent, use an orderly system. Consider starting with the head, torso (anterior and posterior), and extremities. Avoid diagnosing and describe what you find (use your senses). Medical terminology here is acceptable but be sure that it is correctly used. Examples: "*A well-healed 8-inch vertical scar was seen over the sternum consistent with the decedent's history of a CABG.*" "*There was a soft bulge near the navel suggestive of a possible hernia.*" "*Multiple purple discolorations with a closed deformity were noted on the left forearm.*"

When you are doing your palpated exam of the body, be sure to check the clothing for any personal belongings, then write down the items found. Oftentimes people who cross the southern border are found to have identification, photos, and money sewn into or hidden in their clothing. Check the inside of the shoes and socks if you are allowed to remove them on a scene. Then place the items inside of the body bag, and document that you removed them to check for identification and valuables.

Make sure to sign and date your PROD when it is complete, and you are ready to scan it into the electronic file. The best advice is to become familiar with the PROD and electronic reporting system your office uses so that you come across as prepared, professional, and organized. Knowing what you need to document really does help you know what you need to do on any type of scene.

Appendix C
Scene Supply List

LAURAMAE WILLIAMS

Your supply needs may vary by region. Here is a list of the common supplies needed to respond to a scene. Also added is a list of miscellaneous items to get you thinking about other supplies you may need to have in your vehicle.

Supply List

PPE:

- Multiple pairs of gloves, keep one box in your response vehicle; cotton glove liners (helps when changing gloves)
- Two Tyvek suits, plastic disposable apron, sleeve covers, shoe or boot covers
- Protective eyewear or goggles
- N-95 or face mask

Scene Tools:

- Paper bags to place over the hands, small skeletal remains of bones, or miscellaneous items that will be placed in the body bag.
- Two rolls of tape
- ID armbands and body bag seals
- Body bags
- "L" and straight ruler, tape measure
- Reflective vest
- Flashlights
- Packing tape in case the body bag gets torn
- Biohazard bag, trash bag

Administrative:

- Pens and permanent markers
- Preliminary report of death, evidence receipts, subpoena, toxicology, & SUID (Sudden Unexpected Infant Death) forms, medication log
- SUID placard
- Camera with spare SD card and battery
- Scissors

Disinfecting wipes and hand sanitizer
Pill counter (use phone app to count the meds)
Business cards

Environmental supplies:

Hat, water, sturdy boots, moist cooling necktie, sunglasses, sunscreen, mittens, warm coat

Miscellaneous:

Cooler with extra fluids and snacks, change of shoes

Appendix D
Vicarious Trauma

LAUREN E. DVORSCAK

Often dubbed "the last of the first responders", medicolegal death investigators are exposed to death and other's grief on a near-daily basis which may result in second-hand or vicarious trauma. Continuous workplace exposure to victims of violence, along with their grieving families, can take an often-unseen toll on the mental and physical health of death investigators. Mitigation of workplace stressors that are inherent to death investigation by the very nature of the job is a major challenge faced by medical examiner and coroner offices in efforts to recruit and retain medicolegal death investigators.

Individuals can respond to trauma as well as vicarious trauma in a number of ways, based on their own internal resilience, coping strategies, past experiences, or support systems in place. However, a common denominator in responses is that a change in the individual's world view is inevitable. Those exposed to the trauma of others can react negatively or positively, and this varies between individuals, especially with repeated or prolonged exposure to the traumatizing events of others.

Terminology related to vicarious trauma defined, as per the Department of Justice's Office for Victims of Crime, is as follows:

Vicarious trauma is a negative reaction to trauma exposure and encompasses a variety of reactions including secondary traumatic stress, compassion fatigue, and critical incident stress. Common reactions include emotional fragility, numbness, physical aches, distractibility, irritability, avoiding work, and may include symptoms of post-traumatic stress disorder, among others.

Neutral reactions to indirect trauma do not mean there isn't an underlying effect, but simply that an individual's own resilience, coping strategies, past experiences, or support manages the traumatic material without a negative or positive reaction.

Vicarious resilience reflects a positive reaction to the work, including a strengthening of one's mental resilience and renewed appreciation or sense of meaning that the work has fundamentally in helping others through a difficult period in their lives. Drawing inspiration from positive ways families react to a death can strengthen an investigator's own sense of meaning and resilience.

The Department of Justice's Office for Victims of Crime recommends a number of intervention strategies to mitigate vicarious trauma, for managers, coworkers, and family members. They also offer a toolkit (US Department of Justice, 2025) that includes a model for organizational responses to workplace-related secondhand traumatic experiences. Medicolegal death investigators are encouraged to be self-aware in recognizing the signs of vicarious trauma in both themselves and coworkers and be informed of strategies to mitigate negative responses to trauma.

Reference

The Vicarious Trauma Toolkit. Office for victims of crime, US department of Justice. https://ovc.ojp.gov/program/vtt/introduction. Accessed July 2025.

Appendix E
Witness Testimony

MARY H. DUDLEY

Pretrial Interview

In any jurisdiction in the United States, a majority of the criminal and civil cases come to a resolution before trial. Although you may be on the witness list of one side or another, you are not necessarily "their witness." The lawyers need to talk to the witnesses to find out information and facts of the case. In the initial stages of the case, the lawyer's goal is to obtain information to present to the judge and jury, or resolve the case without a trial.

Subpoena

A subpoena is an official order from the court that you must comply with, otherwise a fine or imprisonment may be issued. A subpoena tells you to appear at a certain date, time, and place to testify. Also, it may tell you to bring certain documents, notes, reports, and photographs related to the case.

Reports and Records

Reports are important in your work to document your actions and findings related to the case. Write your reports according to the policies and procedures of your job description and do not leave out or add things that you think may influence the outcome of the trial. For additional information regarding report writing in general, please refer to Appendix A. Bring all your reports as well as any photographs, and review them before you are asked questions, regardless of whether you are interviewed in a lawyer's office or testify at a deposition, grand jury, or trial.

Lay Witness and Expert Witness

According to most rules of evidence including the Federal Rules of Evidence, "Every person is competent to be a witness, except as otherwise provided in these rules" (Federal Rule of Evidence 601). Thus, unless you are somehow "incompetent," there is nothing to bar you from being a witness. Incompetent witnesses are generally people such as very small children or those with significant mental health/psychological diagnoses.

The question then is whether you are going to testify as a lay witness or an expert witness. Generally speaking, a lay witness testifies only about something that he or she perceived with any of the five senses—what he or she saw, heard, touched, felt, or smelled. The only time a lay witness is supposed to give an opinion is when it is based on perception from the senses. (See Federal Rule of Evidence 701. [A lay witness can testify as to his opinion "rationally based on the perception of the witness, be helpful to a clear understanding of the witness's testimony or determination of a fact or issue, and not based on scientific, technical, or other specialized knowledge…"].)

Conversely, an expert witness can offer opinions based on his or her "specialized knowledge" or a specialized skill, experience, training, or education. Specialized knowledge does not necessarily mean advanced degrees. Expert's testimony is supposed to help the jury better understand the evidence (See Federal Rule of Evidence 702.) Thus, even experts are not allowed to give an opinion on the "ultimate issue" as to, for example, whether or not the defendant is guilty. An expert could testify as to cause of death, but not, for example, who caused the death.

Court Testimony

Dress appropriately and arrive early or on time for court. Wait to be called into the courtroom, where you will be directed to the witness box. Stand until directed to be seated by the judge, typically after your testimony is sworn in. The judge will typically say something similar to "Do you agree to tell the truth under penalty of perjury?" To which you respond "I do."

Lawyers will then ask you questions. Be prepared first to describe your title, and job description, or duties. You then may be asked to general processes, prior to getting into specific findings regarding the case. For example, have a good recollection of what you did at the scene, who you interviewed, and to include knowledge of photographs taken and/or evidence collected. Do not refer to your reports or any other notes, unless you ask to do so and are granted permission. When answering questions, wait for the lawyers to finish completely before responding and only answer the question asked. It is the attorney's job to ask you for more clarification if needed. Remember to speak clearly and slowly as a court reporter is documenting every word spoken for the record.

Occasionally, objections from either attorney may arise during a question asked or immediately after. A judge may rule on objection to determine what information a jury is legally permitted to consider. During a trial, "sustained" and "overruled" are rulings made by a judge in response to an attorney's objection. A sustained objection means the judge agrees with the lawyer's challenge to a question or piece of evidence. An overruled objection signifies the judge disagrees, allowing the question or evidence to proceed. Do not answer the question until the judge has made a ruling on the objection.

Bibliography

McWhiter, R. 2017. In Dudley, M. ed., *Chapter 7: Forensic Legal Issues and Expert Witness Testimony. Forensic Medicolegal Injury and Death Investigation*, 1st ed., CRC Press. pp. 69–76.

United States Courts Federal Rules of Evidence. 2024. https://www.uscourts.gov/file/78325/download

Appendix F

Checklist and Summary of the Sexual Assault Evidence Collection and Exam Procedures

Examiner: The evidence you collect will be examined by either the New Mexico State Crime Lab or the Albuquerque Police Dept. Crime Lab.

Accurate and legible documentation provided in this checklist increases the value of the evidence collected should patient consent to investigation.

Link to SAEK instructions and Medical History Forms: (https://Unmcsap.org/resources/documents-and-downloadsD:

Patient Name: ______________________________

Check each item below to verify action was performed or evidence was collected. If not performed or collected, leave blank.

☐ 1. **RAPE CRISIS/MENTAL HEALTH ADVOCATE CONTACTED**

☐ 2. **PATIENT CONSENT** obtained.

☐ 3. The **SEAL** to the Sexual Assault Evidence Collection Kit (SAEK) was intact prior to examiner opening it.

☐ 4. **CLOTHING**—collected, air dried if necessary, and placed loosely in labeled large brown bag.

☐ 5. **UNDERGARMENTS**—collected, air-dried, and placed in a labeled paper bag.

☐ 6. **AIR-DRIED MONS PUBIS/OUTER LABIA MAJORA SWABS**—collected, air-dried, and two swabs placed in labeled envelope.

☐ 7. **AIR-DRIED ORAL SWABS**—collected, air-dried, and two swabs placed in labeled envelope.

☐ 8. **AIR-DRIED VAGINAL SWABS**—collected, air-dried, and two swabs placed in labeled envelope.

☐ 9. **AIR-DRIED CERVICAL SWABS**—collected, air-dried, and two swabs placed in labeled envelope.

☐ 10. **AIR-DRIED ANAL SWABS**—collected, air-dried, and two swabs placed in labeled envelope.

☐ 11. **AIR-DRIED MALE GENITALIA SWABS**—collected, air-dried, and two swabs placed in labeled envelope.

☐ 12. **MISCELLANEOUS EVIDENCE**—envelope(s) and/or small brown bags labeled as to contents and location collected. List all miscellaneous items collected: ______________________________

____

☐ 13. **PATIENT STANDARD/BUCCAL SWABS**—collected, air-dried, and two swabs placed in labeled envelope.

☐ 14. **PREGNANCY TEST**

☐ 15. **PREGNANCY PREVENTION**—if patient's pregnancy test was negative, emergency contraception provided.

☐ 16. **STI PREVENTION**—prescribed doses provided to the patient. STI testing is not recommended for adults. Medications are given as a preventative, prophylactic measure. For pediatric patients, refer to separate protocol.

☐ 17. **DOCUMENTATION**:

HOSPITALS—complete and place Sexual Assault History Form and this Checklist in SAEK large white envelope.

SANE PROGRAMS—complete and include copies of relevant pages (post-assault hygiene, narrative, summary of acts, clothing) from SANE Medical Record and this Checklist in SAEK large white envelope.

☐ 18. **OTHER EVIDENCE COLLECTED BUT NOT INCLUDED IN SAEK PACKAGING** (photographic images and/or blood/urine for suspected drug facilitated sexual assault)—need coordination with law enforcement.

☐ 19. **SEXUAL ASSAULT EVIDENCE KIT PACKAGING**—All small white envelopes sealed, taped, initialed, dated, and placed in the large white envelope along with undergarments small brown bag, also stapled, taped, with integrity seal. Large white envelope sealed, taped, initialed, and dated with integrity seal. Small brown bags folded, stapled, taped with integrity seal, and placed in large brown bag which is stapled, taped, with integrity seal. The information on the front labels of both the SAEK white envelope and the large brown bag is completed and signed by examiner. Chain of custody is maintained throughout.

☐ 20. **PATIENT DISCHARGE INFORMATION, REFERRALS, and RESOURCES PROVIDED** to patient with encouragement to seek counseling. Brochure "From victim to survivor" given to patient, highlighting referrals on back page.

Please print clearly:

Examiner's Name/Title:__________

Signature of Examiner:__________

Exam Assistant
{Name and Position):____________

Medical Facility: ________________

Date of Assault:__________________

Date of Exam: __________________

<u>Place this completed form INTO the large 10" x 15" envelope of the Sexual Assault Evidence Kit ISAEK.</u>

SAEK Checklist

Index

Pages in *italics* refer to figures and pages in **bold** refer to tables.

G

H

I

J

K

L

M

Q

R

S

For Product Safety Concerns and Information please contact our EU representative GPSR@taylorandfrancis.com Taylor & Francis Verlag GmbH, Kaufingerstraße 24, 80331 München, Germany

Batch number: 10810156

Printed by Printforce, the Netherlands